FALL: DUCK MIGRATION CORRIDORS

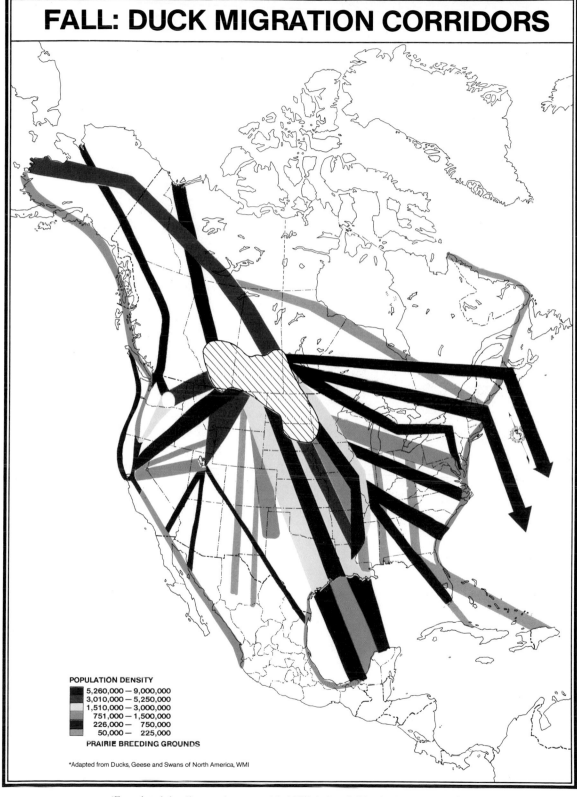

POPULATION DENSITY

- 5,260,000 — 9,000,000
- 3,010,000 — 5,250,000
- 1,510,000 — 3,000,000
- 751,000 — 1,500,000
- 226,000 — 750,000
- 50,000 — 225,000

PRAIRIE BREEDING GROUNDS

*Adapted from Ducks, Geese and Swans of North America, WMI

(For related details, see chapter entitled "Flight South," beginning on page 136).

FALL: GOOSE MIGRATION CORRIDORS

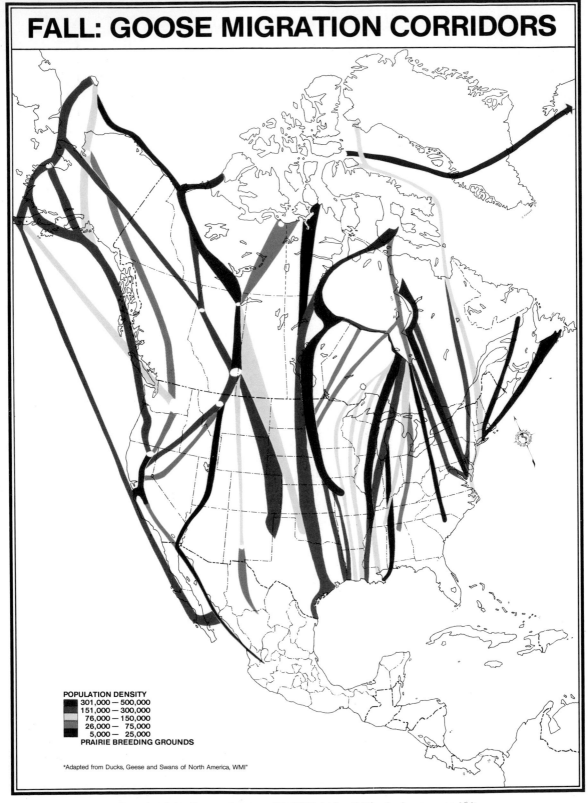

POPULATION DENSITY

301,000 — 500,000
151,000 — 300,000
76,000 — 150,000
26,000 — 75,000
5,000 — 25,000
PRAIRIE BREEDING GROUNDS

Adapted from Ducks, Geese and Swans of North America, WMI

(For related details, see chapter entitled "Flight South," beginning on page 136).

Fireside Waterfowler

How Satellite and Computer Cooperate to Map the Wetlands Quickly, Accurately

(For related details, see chapter entitled "The Future," starting on page 337.)

Restricting the bag and shortening the seasons are the ineffective tools of today's waterfowl-management programs. But the waterfowl manager's tools for the future will include accurate computerized inventories of the remaining wetlands. From these inventories, habitats — which are critical for waterfowl — and realistic population goals can be determined.

Recent advances in satellite technology are making available computerized wetland inventories for the most critical waterfowl-production areas in North America. Ducks Unlimited, using the advanced technology of Landsat's satellite sensor — called the Thematic Mapper (TM) — will complete the first computerized inventory of wetlands in the Primary Waterfowl Production Area (PWPA) prior to 1990.

The PWPA is a 350,000-square-mile area containing the plains and parklands in Canada and the United States. It is on this area, which makes up only 10 percent of the waterfowl breeding habitat, that more than 50 percent of all North America's waterfowl breed.

Currently, DU is using the Thematic Mapper on the Landsat-5 satellite to acquire a computerized wetland inventory of the PWPA. The TM sensor was the first satellite sensor with the capabilities to accurately map wetlands. The Landsat-5

Key Map: The perimeter of the Primary Waterfowl Production Area (PWPA) is shown by the dashed line (A). The perimeter of one full scene of Landsat's Thematic Mapper (TM) data in North Dakota is shown by the solid line (B) near the center of that state. Location of the Goodrich East map sheet is shown as the black area (C) within the full scene of TM data.

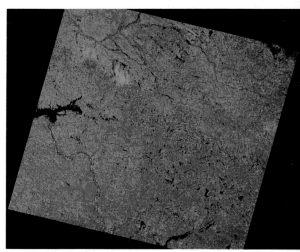

This view shows a nearly full scene of data from the Landsat-5 satellite's sensor — called the Thematic Mapper (abbreviated TM). The white area represents clouds, black and blue represent water, pale grays and greens represent agricultural fields, and the orange-to-red areas represent various types of green vegetation, including trees, winter wheat, and tamed hay. The tan colors represent rangeland. This scene, acquired May 20, 1986, covers nearly eight million acres in North Dakota, corresponding generally to area B on the accompanying map.

This is TM data for the Goodrich East map sheet (area C on key map, previous page) of North Dakota. This image covers nearly 33,000 acres, or approximately 0.4 percent of an entire TM scene (area B on key map).

This is a computer-enhanced TM image of the same Goodrich East map sheet. Open water is depicted by blue, deep marsh (wetland vegetation growing in more than one foot of water) is shown by magenta, and shallow marsh (wetland vegetation growing in less than a foot of water) is shown as yellow. On this map, TM data detected 839 separate wetland basins totalling 5,018 acres. The total shoreline length for these wetlands is 267 miles. The majority of the wetlands (484, or 58 percent of the 839 wetlands) cover less than one acre apiece. Nine of the wetlands on this map are greater than 100 acres each. Similar wetland information for the entire TM scene covering eight million acres was derived in less than two weeks.

satellite orbits, from north to south, 438 miles above the earth. The satellite completely covers the world in 233 orbits and provides coverage of a specific area every 16 days.

Throughout the orbit, the TM scans a 115-mile-wide path. Each Landsat scene covers an area 115 miles from east to west by 107 miles from north to south. Approximately 30,000 scenes are required to cover the entire world. It takes 60 scenes to completely cover the PWPA. Within a scene, the sensor can detect features as small as 0.22 acres.

The satellite records the intensity of visible light, infrared energy, and heat being reflected by or emitted from earth features. Computers at DU facilities then convert these energy values to wetland information.

For each wetland, the location, size, number of acres of various types of wetland habitat, shoreline miles, and other information, which can be used to evaluate the importance of a particular wetland to waterfowl, are extracted from the satellite

data and stored in computer data files for access by field biologists.

By utilizing the technology of the Thematic Mapper, DU, prior to 1990, will complete the first computerized inventory of wetlands on the PWPA. By the mid-1990's, the satellite and computer technologies probably will have advanced far enough for a computerized inventory of all wetlands on the PWPA to be completed in one year.

With these tools — accurate and current inventories of the wetlands and surrounding uplands — management of the waterfowl resource will switch from managing hunting regulations (an ineffective management tool) to managing habitat. — Gregory T. Koeln.

Fireside Waterfowler

*Fundamentals of
Duck and Goose Ecology*

A Ducks Unlimited Book

Edited by

David E. Wesley and William G. Leitch

Illustrated by

Glenn D. Chambers

Published by STACKPOLE BOOKS

Published by
STACKPOLE BOOKS
Cameron and Kelker Streets
P.O. Box 1831
Harrisburg, PA 17105

Printed in the U.S.A.

Library of Congress Cataloging-in-Publication Data

Fireside waterfowler.

  Includes index.
    1. Waterfowl management — North America.
2. Waterfowl — North America.   3. Waterfowl shooting —
North America.   4. Birds — North America.   I. Wesley,
David E.   II. Leitch, William G.
SK331.F57   1987   799.2′44′097   86-14568
ISBN 0-8117-0617-6

Contents

Part III   Fall and Migration

Part IV   The Hunter's Moon

Part V   Winter Homes

Part VI
Managing an International Resource

Part VII   The Future

Foreword

These authoritative chapters form a comprehensive and informative treatise intended for everybody who is concerned about our dwindling continental waterfowl populations and desires to help perpetuate that extremely valuable resource. *Fireside Waterfowler* is an interesting and fascinating compilation, designed for leisure reading and armchair contemplation. The book is an excellent composite of concise summarizations by some of North America's foremost waterfowl authorities and technicians. Yet everything here is written in simple and clear terminology, and in a most readable manner. At your discretion, you may read the book straight through or select topics at random for more careful review.

You hold in your hands an all-inclusive volume, covering nearly every phase of waterfowl management, research, and conditions on the North American continent. The diverse and varied subjects offer appealing and inspiring interludes for relaxed perusal between enjoyable trips afield. This delightful book is difficult to lay aside. The contents embrace several generations of research, investigation, experimentation, and management activities in many parts of the United States, Canada, and Mexico. Little is overlooked in the book's thorough coverage of waterfowl's far-reaching problems. Nothing quite like it has been written before. It is of classic proportions.

This splendid volume on "duckology" comes at a most propitious time. With the recent signing of the long-awaited North American Waterfowl Management Plan by the United States Secretary of the Interior and the Canadian Environment Minister, we now have the framework for international cooperation needed to set mutual goals for waterfowl populations and wetland protection. The plan's aim is to restore the continental populations to the levels common in the 1970s — approximately 62 million breeding ducks, with a fall population of more than 100 million birds.

Fireside Waterfowler will do much toward stimulating the complete understanding that is necessary if serious hunters are to gain the widespread public support and assistance that is so urgently needed to implement the provisions of this international cooperative program. Every serious waterfowler and waterfowl enthusiast, amateur and professional alike, will find much of interest and benefit in this truly outstanding and useful book.

C. R. Gutermuth, President
Wildfowl Foundation, Inc.
Washington, D.C.

Preface

While it touches on most aspects of waterfowl biology and associated problems, this book is by no means a waterfowl encyclopedia. Nor was it ever intended to be. Rather, it is meant for quiet reading by duck hunters with a continuing interest in waterfowl beyond the duck blind.

The scientific community may regret the lack of references, but the book was not compiled for them, and the data, other than those of obviously personal experience, are available in the scientific literature or other published sources.

This book is for duck hunters!

Acknowledgments

The editors would like to thank the staff members of Ducks Unlimited, Inc., Ducks Unlimited Canada, Ducks Unlimited Mexico, and numerous individuals outside of Ducks Unlimited who participated in the initiation and development of this book. By dedicating time, energy, and intellect, they contributed to a project that we hope will benefit the waterfowl resource by educating and entertaining many waterfowl enthusiasts seated quietly by the fire.

Peter Coors, President of Ducks Unlimited, Inc., from 1984 to 1986, deserves special acknowledgment for his support of this effort and for approving the funds to initiate, develop, and print *Fireside Waterfowler*. Hazard K. Campbell, current Ducks Unlimited President, has been instrumental in bringing the effort to fruition and also deserves special recognition.

Ducks Unlimited Canada in Winnipeg deserves a note of appreciation for supplying office space and facilities so that the book could be compiled. Thanks are also due to the Head Office biological staff for their tolerance of repeated probing into their areas of expertise.

The editors are particularly grateful to the DU provincial biologists in Ontario, Quebec, and the Maritimes: Ted Richard Gadawski, Patrick Plante, and R. Keith McAloney.

Scott Smallwood of Ducks Unlimited Canada was particularly helpful with the finer (and frequently controversial) aspects of editing. Rich Grozik of the public-relations department of Ducks Unlimited, Inc., provided helpful hints and shortcuts during the editing process.

And finally, very special thanks to Pat Alvestad of Ducks Unlimited Canada, without whose cheerful. cooperation and patient tolerance of endless revisions this book could never have been completed; and to Angie Cevallos of Ducks Unlimited, Inc., who spent countless hours assembling papers from numerous individuals and pulling together the loose ends.

Part I

Spring

Spring is a beginning, not only for waterfowl but for people as well. The longer the winter and the firmer the grip of cold, ice, and snow, the greater the sense of release and surge of optimism from the first trickling water and cries of returning geese.

People on the street, farmers and native hunters, housewives in their back yards — all raise their eyes skyward, feeling uplifted and confident of a new beginning and good things to come.

Where better to begin our waterfowl year?

1

Up from the South

F. C. Bellrose and R. A. Wishart

Early in February on the more southerly wintering grounds, waterfowl begin to show a restlessness that foretells the start of their flight north, which will eventually cover 3,000 miles or more for those bound for the Arctic. Although the vanguard starts in February, it may be late April before southern marshes are emptied of winter residents.

The timing of waterfowl departures depends upon their physiological drive. The farther south, the more protracted the spread in departures. Not all species, nor all individuals of the same species, respond alike. Spring migration is spread over a period of weeks, the time frame depending on geography, weather, and the programmed chronology of species and individuals.

Considering the vagaries of spring weather, the degree of chronology water-fowl display on their "seasonal clock" is more precise than the weather. This desire to migrate at a certain time is largely governed by the increasing day length, modified by the age of the bird and the surplus fat needed for flight energy.

Increasing daylight stimulates release of hormones that results in gonad development and creates restlessness; older birds react earlier to this stimulus than do young of the year. Individuals that first amass sufficient fat are likely to migrate first.

Probably the female plays an important role in departure; if pairing has occurred, she leads the male back to her natal wetland. The homing of the female to her natal site or previous breeding area determines the destination of a pair departing from their winter grounds.

As the breeding grounds are approached, momentum accelerates; the birds stay for briefer periods at each stop before advancing northward. For most species, the spring flight is compressed into a shorter time frame than the fall migration. There are also greater chronological differences among species in the fall. As a result, in the spring several species move north in unison.

Over much of the United States, spring flights are distributed more widely than those in the fall. Spring floods make new food resources available in fields and bottomlands. Free of the threat of hunters, ducks find farm ponds and highway dugouts acceptable resting and feeding sites. Over many millennia, ducks seem to have become aware that food resources in the spring may be at different places than they are in the fall, and that adequate food may not be at the same places each spring. Radar surveillance of nocturnal spring migration suggests substantial lateral weaving back and forth in a general northward flight, as ducks search for wetlands holding promise of food. Wetland use in the spring is therefore often more fortuitous than planned; fall migrants, in contrast, are programmed to fly to traditional sites that older birds have used in previous years.

Spring migrants are more flexible; they search for new, temporary overflows and drop out of the sky to appraise the food supply. Spotting a bonanza, they loudly announce their find, attracting other passing waterfowl; soon multitudes share in the treasure.

But no matter how good the food resource, the urge northward is so strong that, with a south wind, flocks depart even as new ones arrive. A turnover results; new individuals and new species continually occupy a wetland as long as food is readily available and the seasonal time frame for departure has not been exceeded.

The first bird north is invariably the Canada goose, which appears to follow the receding ice and snow line, the 32°F isotherm that Frederick Lincoln noted years ago. Nearing their breeding areas, they often move ahead of the 32°F isotherm, to wait, amid snow and ice, for the spring thaw to catch up and permit feeding and nesting.

Pintail and mallard follow only a few days behind. Then an avalanche of species appears: green-winged teal, wigeon, gadwall, canvasback, redhead, and scaup. Bringing up the rear of the spring parade are the shoveler, blue-winged teal, and ruddy duck. On some migration corridors, bad weather may delay the orderly seasonal passage; on other corridors, ducks forge ahead on schedule. When abnormally cold weather and snow halt spring migrants, others may continue to arrive from farther south, so that a melange of early, middle, and late migrants appears on the same wetland — all awaiting the signal, which a warm front will bring, to move northward again.

First arrival dates in Canada for early spring migrants — pintail, mallard, black duck, and Canada geese — are masked by wintering birds on both coasts, and to a lesser extent in the Great Lakes area. Since few waterfowl winter successfully on the prairies, arrival dates are clear-cut; and their return is an occasion for rejoicing that the long, cold winter is over.

Earliest migrants are usually mated pairs, anxious to begin housekeeping. This builds quickly to a flood, if warm weather continues. Flocks of later arrivals usually contain many unpaired birds, and the mad frenzy of courtship brings exciting new life

Snow geese — a noisy and dramatic part of a Manitoba spring. *Ed Bry photo.*

to marshes frozen and silent for many months.

In British Columbia, migrating waterfowl follow the corridors between mountain ranges and along the coast. The coastal area and the southern parts of the inland corridors winter significant numbers of waterfowl. It is thus difficult to establish first arrival dates, and migration is indicated only by increases in the local population.

On the coast, the earliest pintail may appear in numbers in January, to remain or move northward if good weather persists, or even retreat if conditions deteriorate, returning again with improvement. However, by mid-February, migration is usually underway along the coastal route. Canada geese and mallard arrive at the southern interior corridors by late February. From this point the birds move northward as weather conditions permit, usually during mid-March. But it is usually early April before the early nesting species move to the central plateau and northern lakes to breed.

Canada geese, pintail, and mallard are the first to return to the prairies, the date determined by the first open water. Sudden return of winter is a frequent occurrence; it brings spectacular concentrations on remaining open water, or even a temporary retreat southward. The later-arriving species — shoveler, wigeon, blue-winged teal, and others — arrive by the calendar, about the same date each year, when surface water is abundant.

Spring comes first to southern Alberta; by the middle of March the first birds will be present. But occasionally and exceptionally, this is delayed until early April. Southern Saskatchewan is at least a week later.

In Manitoba, winter tends to linger. While in some years first arrivals may be almost as early as southern Saskatchewan, frequently a cold polar high becomes entrenched over Manitoba, and first arrivals may be delayed until early April.

Lesser snow geese play a noisy, dramatic role in spring waterfowl migration in Manitoba. In late April, snows and blues congregate on the sheet water of flooded fields, feeding on waste grain. The flight north from Manitoba in early May is awesome. A seemingly endless string of rolling flocks wing their way all day on a front that may stretch fifty miles wide. By the time they're gone, over half a million birds will have passed noisily on their way to the shores of Hudson and James bays.

Wintering mallard, black duck, and Canada geese in the Great Lakes area of Ontario obscure the first arrival dates of true migrants. But the main surge of these species comes the last week of March and early April.

Mississippi Valley Canada geese breeding on the James Bay and Hudson Bay lowlands arrive north of Moosonee about the same time: when the ground is still snow-covered and will remain so for at least another two weeks. Good body fat from southern cornfields is essential to survive and then nest under such harsh conditions. Mallard, pintail, and black duck, dependent on open water, rarely arrive in this area before the end of the third week in April.

In Quebec, arrival dates for the early migrants coincide with Ontario: late March to early April. Lac St. Pierre and lac St. Francois, along the St. Lawrence River, are major staging areas. In eastern Quebec, greater snow geese in spectacular numbers stage at Cap-Tourmente en route from their wintering ground on the U.S. East Coast to their breeding grounds on Baffin Island in the Canadian Arctic.

Black duck and Canada geese winter in the salt water along the southern coast of Nova Scotia, so it is difficult to establish first arrival dates for these migrants.

However, pintail are usually present on inland marshes by April 1. The arrival of migrants at Yarmouth, in extreme southern Nova Scotia, is usually two weeks ahead of that in Cape Breton and on the great marshes of the St. John River in adjacent New Brunswick. Arrival dates for sea ducks vary little from year to year and from region to region. Most saltwater bays are open by late March or early April.

After a hard winter, the moist scent of spring is a godsend to the Canadian landscape. Even urbanites impatiently await the arrival of the first robin. Spring is a time of hope, romance, and new beginnings. It is also a time of expectation for the waterfowler, who looks up and wonders if this will be a kind year to his returning birds.

2

Habitat Conditions and Waterfowl Overflights

R. A. Wishart

Vagaries of weather and man have the greatest impact on wetland habitat. Waterfowl respond quickly to these changes. If they find an area to their liking, they'll stay. If something important like food, cover, or space is missing, they'll push on to more favorable places. Only when they have no alternatives will they remain in suboptimal habitats.

People often meet their stiffest competition from those most like themselves, and ducks are no different. Members of the same species are frequently at odds with one another simply because they need similar food and habitat resources. The greatest competition occurs during nesting when the demand for resources peaks. Pairs able to return quickly to a proven breeding location can immediately set up shop. Then, once established, they can guard their chosen area from latecomers and stake their claim to these vital resources.

The naive young of the previous year often arrive last, and either are forced to delay nesting until suitable habitat becomes vacant or are relegated to less favorable areas. In most cases, late nesters produce fewer offspring.

Female ducks call the shots when selecting a breeding area, since they have the most to lose if the nesting attempt fails. Although the male is important in defending the territory, he's a follower and a henpecked mate from the time the pair is formed in winter until incubation is underway. Should he fail to perform, he will be thrown over for another willing suitor. Competition for females is intense because duck populations characteristically have a preponderance of males.

Not a risk taker, the hen will usually return year after year to her natal area to nest. This seems to be an appropriate strategy. If she successfully nested there one year, she should be able to again. This rationalization, of course, depends on suitable nesting habitat. Obviously, water is a vital constituent in the make-up of such habitat.

Usually, the indications of severe drought show up the year before. If the soil is dry at the fall freeze, runoff into potholes and sloughs may be minimal the following spring. Most of the water will percolate into the soil. Obviously, poor snow accumulation, a slow thaw, or an extremely dry spring will lead to the same thing — reduced surface water.

Drought is often widespread, but in some years, due to freak weather patterns, it may be confined to a restricted area. This occurred in 1976 when the Dakotas were extremely dry, while on the Canadian prairies, near-optimal water conditions prevailed.

What happens to waterfowl during drought periods?

If drought is widespread, waterfowl will meet with adversity during migration and may be in poor condition to begin nesting. Lack of adequate food, both qualitatively and quantitatively, in their nesting areas, will aggravate the situation.

Ducks have several alternatives when they encounter poor habitat. If surface water is limited, not all will be able to breed. And while they'll crowd into existing permanent wetlands, few will nest successfully because of social conflict and scarcity of food. Many will opt to continue their northern migration until they encounter more favorable conditions.

Such overflights have been well documented by biologists over the past 30 years. It has been shown that, when pothole numbers decline due to drought, prairie duck populations decrease correspondingly. Under these conditions, however, duck populations in more northern boreal and taiga areas increase, demonstrating that waterfowl bypass drought areas and continue on to regions where habitat is more secure.

Unfortunately, many make no attempt to breed once they arrive in the north. This may be a result of unfamiliarity with the area, inability to compete with local residents, or low productivity of this habitat. It also may be because extended migration leaves them without sufficient energy to make a nesting effort.

When breeding habitat is degraded by drainage, cultivation, and so on, even on a small scale, the effect is similar to drought but permanent. In short-term droughts, although annual production may suffer, adult birds survive. When conditions improve in subsequent years, they are willing and able to respond if the potential of the prairie habitat has been maintained.

This underlines the importance of all breeding habitats. Seemingly unproductive areas in the northern Pre-Cambrian Shield play a vital role in preserving basic breeding stock through prairie droughts. Unfortunately, even now, thousands of these deceivingly picturesque wetlands in eastern Canada are being pushed to the brink of sterility. Acid rain, windblown north from the coal-fired heartland of the continent, is the invisible culprit.

Clearly we must continue to emphasize the preservation of priority waterfowl production areas. However, in concert with this, an appreciation for the holistic needs of waterfowl is vital. It is paramount that we protect the most valuable resource of all — the breeding stock — if we are to pass on healthy waterfowl populations for future generations.

During prairie droughts when potholes and sloughs are most vulnerable to encroachment, our dedication to this conviction is put to the greatest challenge.

3

Major Canadian Production Areas

W. G. Leitch
with
T. R. Gadawski, Ducks Unlimited provincial biologist, Ontario
P. Plante, Ducks Unlimited provincial biologist, Quebec
R. K. McAloney, Ducks Unlimited provincial biologist, Maritime Provinces

Canada is a big country. With an area of 3,852,000 square miles (some 237,000 square miles more than the United States including Alaska and Hawaii), it's the second largest country in the world.

Canada also has more than its share of the world's fresh water — 291,000 square miles of it. And that's just the permanent water. The uninitiated looking at a large-scale map of Canada might understandably wonder why, with all that water, ducks could have habitat problems.

But just as all that glitters isn't gold, all those water bodies that glisten and gleam in the sunlight aren't necessarily duck habitat either. For successful reproduction, waterfowl need water. But they need the right kind, in the right place, at the right time.

These conditions are most completely met on the Great Northern Plain, which comprises some 250,000 square miles of prairie and parkland in southwestern Manitoba, southcentral Saskatchewan, the eastern half of southcentral Alberta, and parts of western Minnesota and North and South Dakota.

Although this is less than 10 percent of the continent's total waterfowl breeding area, it produces at least 70 percent of the total duck crop in an average year. Smaller areas of equally high quality habitat exist in British Columbia's Cariboo and Chilcotin regions, Ontario's southern glacial moraines, and the Slave River parklands in the Northwest Territories. But the prairies and parklands are North America's prime waterfowl breeding areas.

The undulating glacial till and great moraines (the stony ridges, abundant depressions, and soil debris left as part of the legacy of the last Ice Age) provide the

Typical marshes of the Peace-Athabasca Delta. *Canadian Wildlife Service photo.*

topographical opportunity for the abundant ponds of great physical and ecological diversity that characterize the Northern Plains in wet years. Within the Canadian prairies and parklands, ponds per square mile average about 30 in a normal year and may reach 100 in the typical "knob and kettle" areas of glacial moraines. Temporary rivers, formed as the glacial ice melted, carved deep channels across the landscape, which now host chains of shallow lakes and marshes important to waterfowl.

Prairie ponds and marshes are characteristically temporary and unreliable. Their stability depends on shoreline and bottom configurations, porosity, and the size of the watershed supplying them.

Spring snow melt is by far the most important water source for these wetlands.

This varies greatly with soil moisture at freezeup, snowfall amounts, and speed of the spring thaw. The effect of these variables is dramatically illustrated by the fluctuation in the number of spring ponds in the Canadian section of the Northern Plains: from approximately 6,760,000 in 1954 (a wet year) to 1,443,000 in the dry spring of 1981.

The number of spring ponds by itself is not necessarily an indication of high potential productivity in a particular year. Many may be unsuitable breeding habitat because of low water, exposed mudflats, and other related deficiencies. Annual reproductive success reflects these varying habitat conditions.

While exceptionally heavy rains can affect water levels on prairie wetlands, rainfall is usually a minor and local factor.

The overall success of a breeding season is usually dictated by the spring runoff. Normally, pond levels decline and pond numbers decrease by more than 50 percent during the summer.

Because of improved precipitation levels, temperature, and evaporation rates, which result in a better moisture regime in more northerly areas, the open shores of prairie ponds give way to increasing amounts of shoreline willow and aspen north and east across the Great Plains.

Aspen groves are also found on the uplands in situations with better soil moisture; this area is known physiographically as the Aspen Parklands. Here wetlands are more reliable; when drought has eliminated southern prairie production, the parkland breeding population is usually significantly augmented by displaced prairie ducks. There is evidence that, because of repeated fires and heavy grazing pressure from buffalo herds, areas now aspen forest were once open prairie and parkland. Thus parkland marshes often exhibit fertility levels equal to prairie ponds.

Waterfowl are gregarious creatures except during the early part of the nesting season, when territorial demands for space distribute pairs over wide areas. The myriad prairie and parkland ponds provide the optimum opportunity for dispersal. In addition, they are highly fertile, producing the profusion of protein-rich aquatic invertebrates essential to laying females and developing broods, as well as abundant emergents and aquatic food plants.

A wet year can see average breeding populations of 30 pairs per square mile and as many as 250 pairs in particularly favorable prairie habitat. During droughts, these figures are dramatically reduced, as the ducks abandon the prairies for the more stable water of the north.

The great physical and ecological diversity of prairie and parkland ponds not only accommodates species with differing habitat requirements, but provides other essential annual waterfowl habitat needs. These include spring staging and dispersal areas, moulting areas, and staging areas for fall migration.

The prairies and parklands support not only the greatest concentration of breeding ducks on the continent but also the greatest number of species, several of which — redhead and canvasback, for example — are uncommon elsewhere. Despite the impact of man, the variety, number, and high fertility of these ponds, coupled with the long prairie summer, still provide waterfowl with the continent's best opportunity for successful reproduction.

Under pristine conditions, the productivity of these ponds in wet years must have resulted in almost incredible waterfowl numbers, giving credence to the stories of early pioneers. Witness an 1881 report by the renowned pioneer prairie botanist John Macoun, which probably refers to the later half of the 1870s:

> About the middle of September, the sea ducks [sic] began to arrive and it is no figure of speech to say that the ponds and lakelets were alive with them. For the following six weeks feathered game of every kind were so abundant that any person in a week could have shot enough ducks and geese to have lasted a family all winter. . . . Within a day's journey of the Cree Reserve on the north side of the Cypress Hills, is a large lake, named by me Gull Lake, that during the last days of August was literally alive with birds, and when one shot was enough to supply six of us with a dinner. . . . Geese, ducks and prairie chickens are taking to the stubble fields in the fall so that no difficulty will be found by incoming settlers to lay up a supply of fat fowl for the winter. . . . None but those who

reside in the interior or have been there in the autumn can realize the number of birds living or passing through it at that season.

Not every year was a bonanza, of course. There were periods of drought when few waterfowl were produced. But the potential always remained for a great upsurge once water returned.

This opportunity is now much reduced by the impact of agriculture. Drainage has eliminated innumerable ponds; heavy grazing and cultivation have rendered others mere depressions in cultivated fields. And, while some of these still attract waterfowl, their production levels are low.

Only in moraines too rugged to cultivate, and where cattle have replaced the native bison, do waterfowl retain the opportunity to reproduce under near-pristine conditions. These areas demonstrate how it once could have been. One such area produced an average of 60 broods per square mile during the wet years of 1950–1957 and an astounding 110 broods in 1971.

One of the more gratifying prairie and parkland developments since the great drought of the 1930s is the phenomenal increase in nesting Canada geese. A rarity immediately after World War II, these birds are now common nesters and continue to increase. Some races were native to the prairies but were almost extirpated by hungry pioneers and drought. Their resurgence is the result of a prolonged drought-free period as well as the tolerance and affection landowners now show toward them.

Although the prairies and parklands of western Canada hold the key to continental waterfowl populations, a thin breeding population spread over the rest of the country produces a significant number of waterfowl.

Northward from the prairies and parklands, through northern Alberta, Saskatchewan, and the Northwest Territories, the aspens are replaced by closed coniferous forest and the muskegs and shallow lakes of the lowlands between the fringe of agriculture and the deep, rock-bound lakes and forests of the Pre-Cambrian Shield. To a geologist, this shield area refers to a region of hard rock formed prior to the Paleozoic era. Beyond the shield, the forests first dwindle into the open barren grounds, and then to the coastal tundra of the Arctic Ocean. This area, plus the forested sections of northern British Columbia, Ontario, and Quebec, comprises some 2,568,000 square miles of almost pristine habitat—almost two-thirds the total area of Canada.

These areas produce waterfowl, too. But, in contrast to the prairies, they average only about five pairs per square mile through the forested sections, and much less in the open barrens and tundra.

In this northern habitat, water is no problem—except there is sometimes too much! But when prairie ducks, displaced by drought, migrate to it, their productivity is much lower than on the prairies.

Perhaps psychological factors such as unfamiliar surroundings inhibit the urge to nest. Or, since the fertility of northern lakes and ponds is generally low, food, both quantity and quality, may be a factor. Certainly weather and a short season offering little time for renesting are limitations. Nevertheless, production is sufficient to provide a reservoir of birds to repopulate the prairies after a drought.

Some of these factors obviously must limit productivity of the indigenous breed-

MAJOR CANADIAN PRODUCTION AREAS

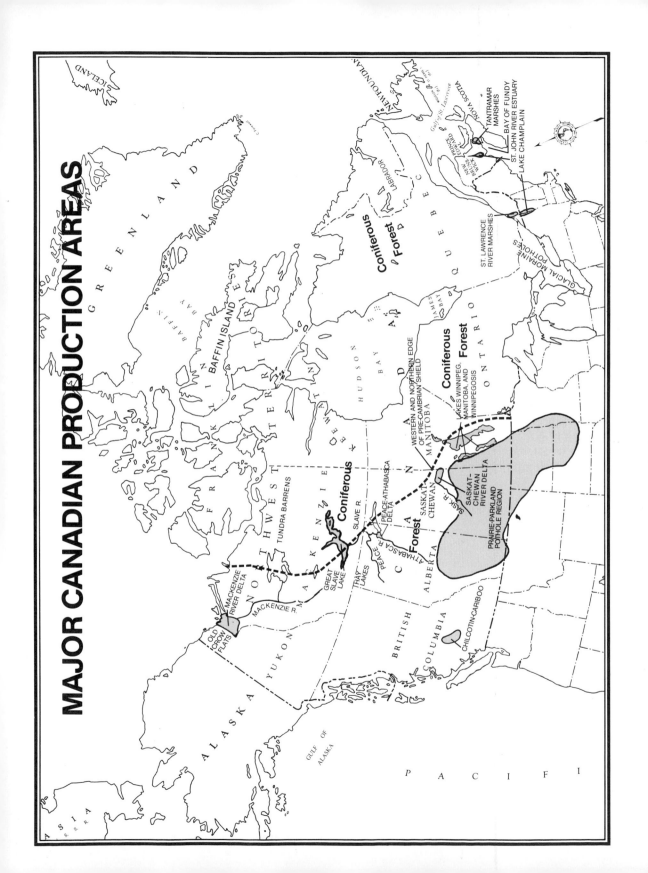

ing population. This perhaps explains why this huge area has never developed breeding populations equal to those of the prairies. If water were the only important factor in waterfowl production, the northern area would far outstrip the south on the basis of size alone. Obviously, it is only one of many factors.

Within this area of muskeg, forests, and lakes are the deltas of the great northern rivers, whose shallow, fertile lakes support waterfowl populations approaching those of the prairies. Here the major limiting factor to production is widely fluctuating water levels.

In northern Manitoba, despite agricultural encroachment and hydroelectric developments, the Saskatchewan River Delta still has some 2,500 square miles of high-quality habitat, and the Peace-Athabasca Delta in northern Alberta, although affected by upstream developments, has 1,625 square miles.

In the extreme northwest corner of Alberta, the Hay Lakes lie in the floodplain of the Hay River. Farther north still is the biggest delta of them all—5,000 square miles of lakes and ponds where the mighty Mackenzie River enters the Arctic Ocean.

Species composition of the waterfowl breeding population changes northward. The Athabasca Delta seems the northern limit for most prairie ducks, blue-winged teal, shoveler, gadwall, canvasback, and redhead. Canvasback, however, are found in small numbers in the Mackenzie Delta, and on the Yukon's Old Crow Flats just across the Richardson Mountains to the west.

Mallard and pintail are thinly and almost equally represented in the southern part of the coniferous forest but decline steadily northward, becoming locally abundant in the northern river deltas.

However, in the Mackenzie Delta, the pintail is still found in numbers, and also on the adjacent tundra, but the mallard is much less numerous.

Lesser scaup, or bluebill, are the most abundant sporting ducks in the coniferous forest ponds; greater scaup hold this distinction through to the Arctic coast. Common goldeneye and bufflehead are also found in the coniferous forest.

Green-winged teal occur regularly from the prairies to the Arctic coast. But wigeon are more numerous, or perhaps more easily observed, and, after the scaup, are frequently the most plentiful breeding species in the forested region. Ring-necked duck occupy the low boggy wetlands and shallow lakes between the fringe of northern agriculture and the Pre-Cambrian Shield.

Surf and white-winged scoter and red-breasted and common mergansers are also common in northern areas. Oldsquaw become more numerous on the treeless barrens and tundra.

The Mackenzie Delta, the Arctic islands, and the tundra to the east, particularly where rivers empty into the Arctic Ocean, support nesting Canada geese, colonies of nesting snow and blue geese, white-fronted geese, and magnificent tundra swans.

Northern Manitoba, dominated by the deep, rock-bound lakes of the Pre-Cambrian Shield, hosts low duck breeding populations. But Canada geese are surprisingly numerous, both in the interior and on the coastal flats of Hudson Bay, where there are also extensive colonies of nesting snow and blue geese. In the southern part of the province, the extensive marshes bordering Lake Manitoba and Lake Winnipeg are internationally known for staging and waterfowl production.

Most of northern Ontario is dominated

by the Pre-Cambrian Shield, and water-fowl production is low. However, inland coastal flats along Hudson Bay and James Bay produce large numbers of Canada geese and some ducks. South of the Shield, duck populations increase. Black duck and wood duck are common breeders in the beaver ponds of the southern hard-wood forests. The old glacial moraines north of Toronto and around London have been mentioned. The Kitchener and Kingston areas also contain important ponds and marshes. Marshes along the shores of the Great Lakes also have some production capability but are more impor-tant for spring and fall staging.

Except for the extreme south along the Ottawa and St. Lawrence rivers, Quebec is dominated by forest. The northern conif-erous areas contain numerous lakes that support modest waterfowl numbers, mostly black duck, common goldeneye, bufflehead, surf scoter, common and red-breasted mergansers, and scattered pairs of Canada geese.

Beaver ponds in southern hardwood for-ests provide excellent habitat for black duck and wood duck. There are also small but important marshes along the flood-plains of the Ottawa River. The floodplain and islands of the St. Lawrence River and the Abitibi region have extensive marshes.

Baffin Island, a hugh Arctic island off

Quebec's north coast, supports a large nesting colony of lesser snow and blue geese, and the only nesting colony of greater snow geese in the world.

The Atlantic provinces — New Bruns-wick, Nova Scotia, Prince Edward Island, and Newfoundland — are also dominated by coniferous forest where forest ponds, marshy streams, and beaver ponds support nesting populations of wood duck, ring-necked duck, green-winged teal, black duck, and goldeneye. The floodplain of the St. John River in New Brunswick and the Bay of Fundy marshes between New Brunswick and Nova Scotia are also im-portant waterfowl marshes.

An overview of Canadian waterfowl production areas shows clearly that future continental waterfowl population levels, both annually and long-term, will be de-termined by what happens on a very small part of the total waterfowl breeding range — the Great Northern Plains. An-nual water conditions here dictate relative yearly abundance. But in the long term, waterfowl populations can rebound from drought levels, as they have in the past, only so long as the opportunity to do so exists. This opportunity can be provided only by preserving the prairie and park-land habitat from further human en-croachment.

4

Production in the Tri-State and Nebraska

T. L. Kuck and J. M. Hyland

When Mother Nature sent her last glacier across the North American continent, there were no state boundaries or borders between countries. As the glacier receded, it left as its aftermath a great area with abundant water basins of all sizes, shapes and depths, now known to waterfowl biologists as the Prairie Pothole Region. This area originally included parts of what are now Iowa, Minnesota, North Dakota, South Dakota, and Montana, and the Canadian provinces of Manitoba, Saskatchewan, and Alberta. It is the most important block of waterfowl breeding habitat in North America.

The Prairie Pothole Region comprises more than 250,000 square miles, not including small amounts in Iowa and Montana. Of this, 169,000 square miles are in Canada and 83,000 in the tri-state area of North and South Dakota and Minnesota.

In the United States, a higher percentage of the original wetlands have been lost because of drainage than in Canada. But Canada is closing the gap, as large farming equipment facilitates drainage by individual farmers.

As soon as white settlers moved into Iowa, southern Minnesota, and South Dakota, wetlands began to disappear. Farmers found the fertile prairie soils produced bumper crops, and the wetlands were soon drained when they proved to be a nuisance. Crops were more important than ducks. Similar practices soon extended to North Dakota and eastern Montana. Later, government subsidies encouraged drainage by farmers to make these "wastelands" productive.

Following the end of World War II, a period that was very wet throughout the prairies, drainage was in full swing. This

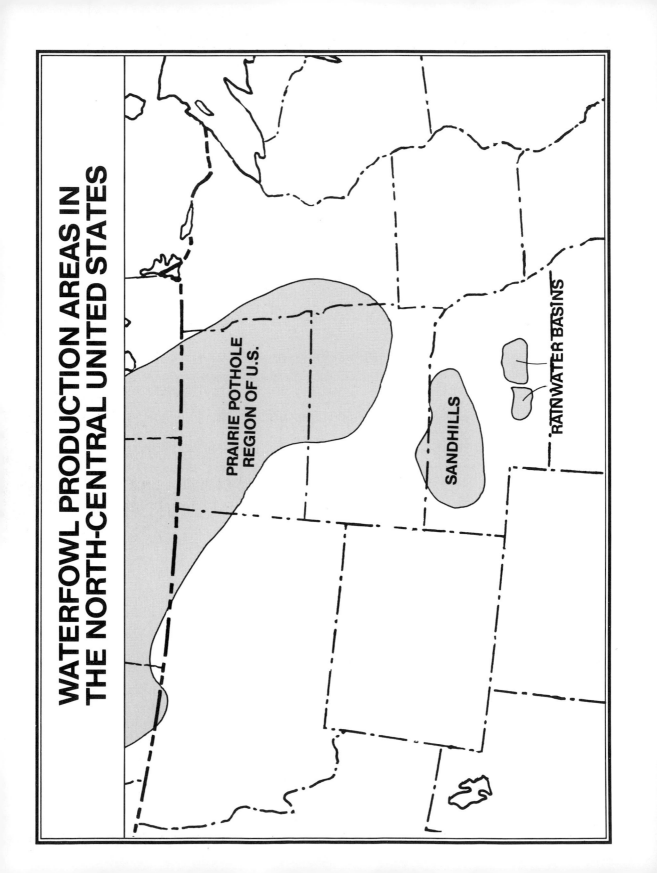

WATERFOWL PRODUCTION AREAS IN THE NORTH-CENTRAL UNITED STATES

PRAIRIE POTHOLE REGION OF U.S.

SANDHILLS

RAINWATER BASINS

persisted well into the 1950s, when sportsmen's groups were successful in removing the federal drainage subsidy, making it much less attractive for the farmer to drain his wetlands when Uncle Sam wasn't helping to pay the bill.

By the early 1960s, sportsmen were beginning to see the impact intensive agriculture was having on the waterfowl resource. The ducks were still attracted to the prairie potholes, but farmers had found other ways to continue drainage. Although federal dollars were no longer available, larger farm machinery allowed the landowner to accomplish this task on his own.

In 1961 the U.S. Congress passed the Wetlands Loan Act. This allowed duck-stamp dollars to be used for purchasing perpetual easements on private wetlands to prevent destruction by draining, filling, or burning. It also empowered the federal government, through the U.S. Fish and Wildlife Service, to purchase lands in fee title. These wetlands would be protected and managed to provide nesting, brood rearing, concentration, and migration habitat for ducks, geese, and other wildlife. They would also provide public hunting for the duck-stamp buyer who, after all, was paying the bill.

Over the past twenty years, under the U.S. Fish and Wildlife Service Small Wetlands Program, 1.1 million acres of wetlands, with adjacent uplands, have been preserved by easement on private lands; 400,000 additional acres are held in fee title. Approximately $71 million has been spent to acquire these Waterfowl Production Areas (WPAs).

State conservation agencies have also been involved in similar land acquisition programs. North and South Dakota, for example, have 70,000 and 151,000 acres respectively under their ownership, most of them located in the prairie pothole area of their state. Minnesota has 520,000 acres and Montana 32,000. These lands are managed for a multitude of wildlife species, but primarily for waterfowl. However, in spite of state and federal programs, wetland losses still continue.

What does this all mean? Remember, while the North American waterfowl resource is primarily dependent on the prairie wetlands in Canada (figures show that annually about 70 percent of the ducks produced in the Prairie Pothole Region come from Canada), the remaining 30 percent come from the United States. This contribution may seem pretty meager but it's very important, for a number of reasons.

First of all, no one should look down their nose at the ten to twenty million ducks that Montana, the Dakotas, and western Minnesota contribute each year to the fall flight. In 1982, for example, North and South Dakota were wet, and combined to produce as many ducks as came from the dry Canadian prairies. The U.S. production, although originating almost entirely in the Central Flyway, supplies ducks to all flyways. Broken down, it looks like this: 5 percent of the production from the two Dakotas goes into the Pacific Flyway; 51 percent to the Central Flyway; 32 percent to the Mississippi Flyway; and 2 percent to the Atlantic Flyway. Ten percent of waterfowl from the Dakotas end up outside the United States; some are taken in Canada, and many teal and pintail in Mexico and Central America.

The annual distribution of waterfowl breeding in the Prairie Pothole Region in both the United States and Canada is partially determined by the fact that the U.S. potholes are the first breeding areas the spring migrants encounter each year. If

Hatching canvasbacks—more ducks from the prairies. *Mike Anderson photo.*

wetlands in Minnesota, Montana, and the Dakotas are well watered, they will entice large numbers of ducks, of a wide variety of species, to nest without going farther north. This could be called "short stopping" on the northern migration.

This doesn't mean all northbound ducks will stop short of Canada. Homing is too strong for that. However, survey data do show that in years of good water on the U.S. prairies, breeding pair counts decrease in Canada. On the other hand, in drought years in the U.S. section, "overflights" occur, and the survey data usually reveal an influx from the U.S. prairies into Canada.

The success of ducks nesting in the U.S.

section will of course determine the contribution this segment of the breeding range makes to the overall fall flight. Good nesting success should achieve a 1:1 adult-juvenile ratio in the fall flight, or better. Then everyone will be happy—including the ducks—if they think about such things. Hunters will have good hunting and spend more money on that activity and the things that complement it, including Ducks Unlimited dinners.

But most important, a successful breeding season in the United States adds birds to the continental waterfowl population. These birds will return to nest in their natal areas if conditions there are suitable; if not, they continue north to areas more to their liking. In either case the United States breeding grounds will have made a significant contribution to the continental breeding population, a contribution that should not be understated.

Changes in the U.S. segment of the Prairie Pothole Region have reduced the potential for successful waterfowl nesting and caused great concern for waterfowl managers. During the past 100 years, most of the native prairie was converted to fertile cropland. In 1860 (only 120 years ago), the prairie sod was still unbroken. Now, less than 20 percent of original grasslands in the U.S. Prairie Pothole Region remain, and most are heavily grazed. Farming has become more efficient. This has resulted in continued wetland drainage, elimination of grassy field strips and fencerows, and tillage of road ditches.

Modern farming practices also include increased use of herbicides and insecticides. From a predator standpoint, this has reduced the animal foods available during the duck nesting season and concentrated predators in remaining untilled areas—the same restricted habitat that upland nesting ducks depend on for nesting and where they are thus increasingly vulnerable to predation.

Most native gamebird species have not withstood the change, but ducks still find the region irresistible and will continue to attempt to nest as long as fertile wetlands remain.

Waterfowl in the U.S. Prairie Pothole

Prairie pothole drainage—a critical loss. *B. J. Rose photo.*

Region, until recently, have been produced primarily on unmanaged habitat. However, a major part of this production habitat is now reduced in both quality and quantity, resulting in low recruitment from some areas. As the total wetland base becomes more restricted, it puts more emphasis on producing large numbers of ducks on public lands.

The basic information for effective management of wetlands is available. High waterfowl production can be obtained. Environmental factors must be manipulated so that more birds are produced from lands controlled by state and federal conservation agencies and private organizations.

While the potholes of the tri-state are well known for waterfowl production, the Nebraska Sandhills are also an important waterfowl production area, contributing many birds to the fall flights of the Central and Mississippi Flyways. Lying on the southern edge of the Prairie Pothole Region, this area comprises some 19,000 square miles of native mixed-grass prairie, interspersed with more than 1,600 lakes and 2,000 temporary wetlands.

Unlike the "harder" soils of the prairie pothole country, Sandhill soils are young and fragile. Although the sandy soils readily absorb even heavy rainfalls, allowing virtually no runoff, they are particularly susceptible to wind erosion. Most of the permanent wetlands occur in deeper valleys that cut through the water table. The level of these wetlands thus fluctuates with the groundwater, a situation markedly different from northern prairie wetlands, which depend almost entirely on surface runoff.

During years when weather and habitat combine to create ideal waterfowl production conditions, hundreds of Canada geese and tens of thousands of ducks are produced in the region. During the late 1950s and early 1960s, the estimated number of breeding ducks in the Sandhills ranged from 99,000 to 176,000 annually. Recent changes in land-use practices have been primarily responsible for a reduction in breeding populations. Since 1972, annual estimates have ranged from 62,000 to 91,000.

Puddle ducks are the majority of the Sandhill breeding population, with blue-winged teal, mallard, shoveler, and gadwall accounting for nearly 90 percent of the broods produced. Divers such as redhead, canvasback, and ruddy duck, are found on some of the larger lakes and marshes, but account for less than 5 percent of annual waterfowl production. Canada geese have recently been reestablished in parts of the Sandhills through the cooperation of ranchers, sportsmen, the Nebraska Game and Parks Commission, and the U.S. Fish and Wildlife Service. As natural production increased, these geese have pioneered into new areas.

Though there are important differences, the Sandhills share many similarities with the prairie potholes. The Sandhills area has a long history of high waterfowl productivity and hunting. The economy is principally agricultural and, until recently, almost totally based on cattle production. Grazing and native hay production were long considered the only acceptable land use for the vast majority of the region.

Over the last fifteen years, as with the prairie potholes, there have been drastic changes in the traditional agricultural pattern of the Sandhills. Development and spread of center-pivot irrigation and the availability of chemical fertilizers have encouraged the conversion of thousands of acres of rangeland to cropland. This change may be a relatively short-lived boom, or the beginning of a long-term trend.

This issue is the center of a hot debate, which more than likely will be resolved only by time. There can be little doubt, however, that the loss of nesting cover and the draining and filling of wetlands are having a negative impact on annual duck production, one that waterfowl can ill afford.

As rangeland and hay meadows are converted to row crop and alfalfa production, secure nesting cover is destroyed. As irrigation increases, the supply of underground water is depleted and the water table falls, reducing the size and number of permanent wetlands available to carry waterfowl through dry years.

Maintaining the ideal combination of permanent and temporary wetlands, plus an adequate supply of secure nesting cover on adjacent upland areas, will be a continuing challenge, requiring the best efforts of wildlife managers and waterfowlers alike.

Once the Nebraska Sandhills breeding habitat is gone, it would take many years to restore it to its former importance as a waterfowl production area, and even longer to rebuild a breeding population to match the production of today.

The rainwater basin area of Nebraska also represents an important part of the habitat required by waterfowl during their annual migrations.

No longer a significant production area, because of the loss of over 80 percent of the once-numerous small wetlands within the area to drainage, filling and encroachment by agriculture and development, the area remains important as a spring staging area to hundreds of thousands of ducks, geese, and other migratory birds. This spring period extends from early or mid-February to mid-April or later, depending upon weather and water conditions.

The importance of this area may be best appreciated by recognizing that for nearly two months of the year it is home for over 80 percent of the midcontinent population of white-fronted geese, over a quarter of a million Canada geese, and more than a million ducks, including mallard, pintail, and virtually all species of North American puddle ducks, except the black duck.

5

Alaska

D. E. Timm

Going to Extremes, the title of a recent book about Alaska, aptly describes the state's people, history, geography, climate, and most things Alaskan. Alaska has the highest mountains; is our farthest north and largest state; is the most easterly (remember the date line!) *and* most westerly part of North America; has the smallest and youngest human population; experiences tidal fluctuations of forty feet; has over half the U.S. coastline and two-thirds of its continental shelf; experiences temperatures from $-80°F$ to $+100°F$; has the world's largest floatplane base and greatest per capita number of pilots; boasts the largest oilfield in North America; and has many, many more "going to extremes." Waterfowl and their habitat are no exception.

Alaska has 586,400 square miles of real estate, and over 20 percent is waterfowl production habitat. For comparison, nesting habitat exceeds in size the combined states of Iowa and Illinois. Thousands of additional miles of coastal marshes and intertidal flats are used mostly for feeding and resting; and about a half-million square miles of continental shelf and near-shore marine waters support tens of millions of sea birds and several million sea ducks, eider, harlequin, scoter, and old-squaw. Waterfowl from Alaska migrate to nearly every state and province and many foreign countries.

The average annual fall flight of ducks exceeds ten million, and another two million use Alaskan habitat on their way to and from Canadian and Russian nesting grounds. Alaska, and other far north regions, provide secure habitat for ducks that overfly prairie pothole country in drought years. Sixteen species of dabblers have been recorded, and they constitute about 15 percent of the North American fall flight. Alaska hosts twenty-one species of divers, sea ducks, and mergansers, including such North American rarities as the smew, common pochard, tufted duck, and king, spectacled, and Steller's eiders.

The fall flight of geese and brant from Alaska now numbers about 850,000 (down from over 1.25 million a decade ago), plus some 300,000 snow geese and brant that "refuel" and rest in Alaska on their migration to and from Russia and Canada. Six of the world's eleven subspecies of Canada geese nest in Alaska, including the endangered Aleutian Canada goose and now relatively rare cackling and dusky Canada goose, which nest here exclusively. The greater part of the populations of the other three subspecies are also found here, Vancouver, lesser, and Taverner's Canada geese. Other nesting geese are two subspecies of white-fronted, including the large tule goose, which nests solely in Alaska; Pacific brant; emperor and lesser snow geese. Pacific brant is a collective term for both dark and light color phases; both are found in the Pacific Flyway. Although rare in Alaska, Ross' and bean geese have also been recorded.

The fall exodus of tundra (whistling) swan exceeds 70,000 birds; they travel to every flyway, although most go to the Pacific (western Alaska nesters) and Atlantic (North Slope birds). Trumpeter swan are the world's largest waterfowl and nest in the interior and southcentral boreal forest habitat. They now number about 8,000, or over 90 percent of the world's wild population. Not twenty years ago the trumpeter was considered endangered, but a 1968 count in Alaska revealed thousands of "unknown" birds. A nearly threefold increase in the Alaskan population is one of

waterfowl management's great successes. The whooper swan, Asia's ecological equivalent of the trumpeter, has nested at least once in northwest Alaska, and perhaps a few hundred winter in the Aleutian Islands.

Although several million ducks, emperor geese, and Vancouver Canada geese do not leave the state (wintering along southern coasts or in rich pelagic ocean waters), most migrate south, contributing immensely to the enjoyment of people from Canada to Mexico. The following birds from Alaska contribute significantly to the fall flight along the major flyways:

Pacific. Pintail, American wigeon, green-winged teal, lesser and greater scaups, canvasback, common and Barrow's goldeneyes, spectacled and common eiders, dusky, cackling, Vancouver, Aleutian, and most "medium" sized Canada geese, white-fronted, tule, and emperor geese, brant, tundra, and trumpeter swans.

Central. White-fronted geese.

Mississippi. Greater and lesser scaups.

Atlantic. Tundra swan, greater and lesser scaups.

The next time you "squeeze on," or otherwise enjoy one of these birds, think of Alaska!

Alaska lies at the top of the Pacific Rim and demonstrates the wildlife and vegetative transition between North America and Asia. Tempered by eons of time, many major factors have shaped the quantity and quality of Alaska's waterfowl habitat: glacial action; volcanos and earthquakes; meandering and periodic flooding in the great river valleys of the interior; tidal action and fresh and salt water mixing

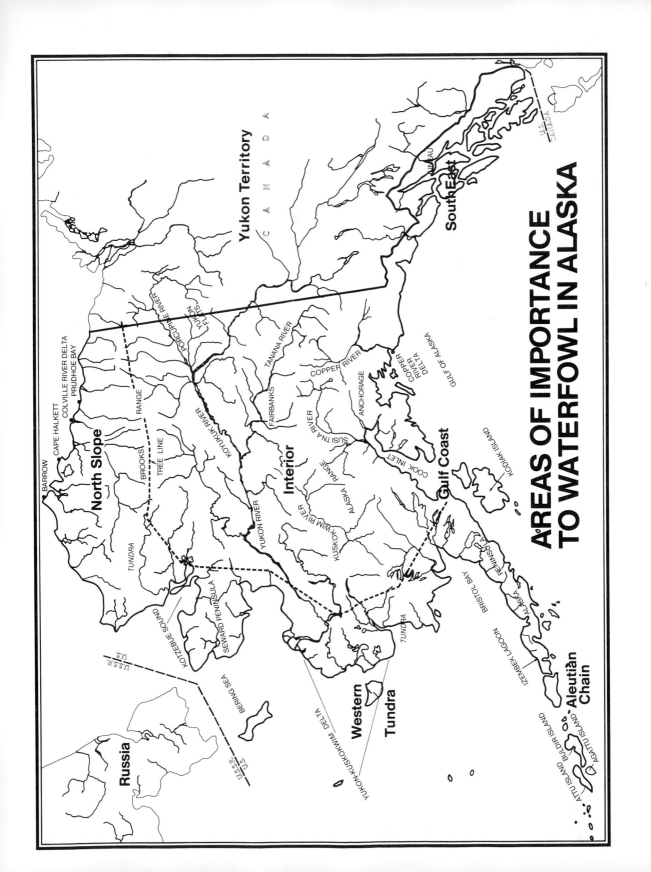

AREAS OF IMPORTANCE TO WATERFOWL IN ALASKA

Russia

North Slope

BARROW
CAPE HALKETT
COLVILLE RIVER DELTA
PRUDHOE BAY

TUNDRA

BROOKS RANGE
TREE LINE

KOYUKUK RIVER

Yukon Territory

C A N A D A

PORCUPINE RIVER

NOATAK FLATS

Interior

TANANA RIVER

FAIRBANKS

COPPER RIVER

COPPER RIVER DELTA

GULF OF ALASKA

Juneau

SouthEast

U.S.
CANADA

ANCHORAGE

SUSITNA RIVER

ALASKA RANGE

KUSKOKWIM RIVER

YUKON RIVER

COOK INLET

Gulf Coast

KODIAK ISLAND

KOTZEBUE SOUND

SEWARD PENINSULA

BERING SEA

YUKON-KUSKOKWIM DELTA

Western Tundra

TUNDRA

BRISTOL BAY

ALASKA PENINSULA

IZEMBEK LAGOON

Aleutian Chain

ATTU ISLAND
BULDIR ISLAND
AGATTU ISLAND

U.S.S.R.
U.S.

Emperor goose—another Alaska product. *Bird Photographs, Inc., Arthur and David Allen photo.*

along the coast; silt deposition at river mouths, forming large fertile deltas and salt marshes; high mountain ranges that create their own microclimates; cold winters, but surprisingly warm summers; and long daylight hours.

From the tip of southeastern Alaska north and west over 2,300 miles to Attu in the Aleutian Islands, and north to Barrow, over 350 miles above the Arctic Circle, waterfowl are found virtually everywhere there is water—and water is virtually everywhere! While Alaska may be divided into six regions for a discussion of habitat, the vast and richly fertile outer continental shelf, wintering grounds for many species, constitutes a seventh.

Southeastern Alaska, known as the Panhandle, is a rugged region of spruce-hem-lock rain forest, with tundra above the 3,000 foot elevation, and snow-capped mountains. Waterfowl habitat is composed of a myriad of bays, fjords, and islands; salt marshes fringed with broad and rich intertidal flats; thousands of streams and rivers; and various-sized lakes and mountain ponds.

The ocean not only moderates temperatures; it's the "breadbasket" of southeastern Alaska. Plants and invertebrate animals in intertidal flats and salt marshes provide a major food source for resident and migrant birds, and support many thousands of wintering mallard and Canada geese. Small fish, such as herring, hooligan (smelt), needlefish, and stickleback, are a primary food for divers, sea ducks, and mergansers, which winter by the hun-

The Susitna Flats dotted with duck shacks. *Alaska Fish and Game photo.*

dreds of thousands, if not millions. Millions of spawning salmon attract a variety of waterfowl that gobble the eggs; mallard and Canada geese even eat the flesh of spawned-out salmon.

Although actual numbers are undetermined, probably several hundred thousand ducks nest in and around the larger river valleys and deltas, ponds, streams, and beach fringes in this region. Vancouver Canada geese nest on small islands in bays and ponds, on the forest floor, in trees, in subalpine bogs, and near salt marshes.

The Gulf Coast region has the most varied habitat of all. It extends west and north from the Panhandle, around the Gulf of Alaska, through the Bristol Bay lowlands and Alaska Peninsula, including Kodiak and adjacent islands. The eastern part of the region is bounded on the north by towering mountains and glaciers, and heavily forested at lower elevations by spruce, birch, and aspen. Much of the land has been scoured by glaciers, which left thousands of lakes and ponds. River and stream valleys, such as those associated with the Copper and Susitna, abound with marshes and beaver ponds. Huge coastal river deltas, salt marshes, and intertidal flats maintain high productivity through tidal action; the mixing of fresh and salt water ensures constant nutrient interchange. Earthquakes have abruptly changed land forms, both creating and destroying waterfowl habitat.

Kodiak and nearby islands demonstrate an interesting transition within a few hundred miles, from rain forest in the north to low brush and tundra in the south. As in southeastern Alaska, waterfowl depend primarily on the estuarine and intertidal flats of the numerous bays and fjords. Here they feed throughout the year on various grasses and sedges and on invertebrates such as mollusks, crustaceans, insects, small fish, and fish eggs. Dabblers, divers, and sea ducks all nest, but geese are rare, except for high overhead migrants and a few thousand wintering emperors.

The Alaska Peninsula and Bristol Bay lowlands are mostly treeless sub-Arctic tundra, with heath-type vegetation of sedges, grasses, and shrubs and with lichens in the northern lowlands. The tundra is rippled with low tussocks formed by frost heave. Broad outwash plains have abundant potholes and lakes, which attract several hundred thousand nesting ducks and tundra swan. Like most of Alaska, mountains are seldom out of sight, and the Aleutian range is an active volcanic spine running the length of the peninsula. Eight large lagoons and estuaries on the north side are feeding-resting-migration staging areas for over a million ducks and geese and countless millions of shorebirds.

The 1964 Good Friday earthquake dramatically changed waterfowl habitat in parts of the Gulf Coast. The Copper River Delta uplifted about six feet; other areas lowered. Habitat on the delta changed from a brackish to a fresh-water environment. For example, prior to the earthquake, most nest loss of dusky Canada

geese was from flooding by high storm tides. Now, most loss is from brown bears, coyotes, and gulls.

The delta was formerly sedge flats dissected by numerous streams, paralleled by slightly raised berms vegetated by grasses and forbs. Those same stream banks are now tree- and brush-covered, and the sedge flats are patched with alder and sweet gale. Low offshore islands also uplifted, enabling gull colonies to proliferate.

Perhaps as nature's way of compensating, beaver have flourished, and their action has created habitat favored by other wildlife such as trumpeter swan and mink. Northwest of the Copper River Delta about 250 miles, around Cook Inlet, the land was lowered, creating more brackish marsh and wet inland bogs. Poorly drained areas created secure nest sites for Canada geese, and an expanding population of lesser Canadas, now several thousand, has developed since the earthquake.

Although the Gulf Coast region contributes perhaps a million ducks to the fall flight, over one-third of the trumpeter swan in Alaska, some 11,000 tundra swan, and about 30,000 geese, its most important waterfowl value is as coastal habitat, much of which both produces and overwinters waterfowl. Most of the Alaskan ducks, geese, and swans in the Pacific Flyway use the coastal migration routes. Coastal marshes and intertidal flats provide essential food and resting sites, to sustain long flights to and from nesting and wintering areas.

In the spring, coastal habitat enables birds to "push the thaw line," making an earlier arrival on more northerly nesting grounds possible and with ample energy reserves (fat and protein) to complete a clutch of eggs before adequate local food becomes available. Conversely, during early fall, most waterfowl are low in energy reserves after the rigors of nesting and molt, and require abundant food to complete their leisurely migration south. This the coastal habitat supplies. Izembek Lagoon is the outstanding example of coastal Alaskan habitat.

Izembek lies at the western tip of the Alaska Peninsula; its eelgrass bed is the world's largest. Here each fall all Pacific brant, about 75,000 Taverner's Canada geese; most emperor geese; hundreds of thousands of divers, sea ducks, dabblers, and countless other birds "refuel" before making their transoceanic flight to West Coast and Mexican wintering areas. Some go west to the Aleutian Islands, others continue on to Japan. Eelgrass and other food items in the lagoon, along with tundra berries in surrounding uplands, provide the high-energy food necessary for long nonstop migration flights. If you think a corn-fed mallard is fat, you've never seen an October pintail or Canada goose from Izembek.

Although small in land area, the Aleutian Islands are an important region to waterfowl. Over seventy named and unnamed islands extend in a great 1,100-mile arc westward from the Alaska peninsula. The Aleutians have been called the birthplace of storms and North American weather and are well described by the title of Corey Ford's book, *Where the Sea Breaks Its Back*. Trees are nonexistent, except for those planted since World War II

Lagoon of the Izembek National Wildlife Refuge. *Paul D. Arneson photo.*

by homesick GIs. A more inhospitable climate is hard to imagine.

The islands, mostly ruggedly mountainous, are volcanic in origin. However, the small estuaries, saltwater bays and marshes, and surrounding ocean waters fed by the Japanese current are rich in nutrients, and host many hundreds of thousands of waterfowl, some of them nesting, but mostly wintering. Inland waters provide aquatic animal life for food, and emergent plants for food and cover. Beach ridges and riparian meadows bordering streams serve as nesting cover for dabblers, divers, and sea ducks, while intertidal flats and beaches provide food for emperor geese and other waterfowl.

Many a birder dreams of a trip to the Aleutian chain because of its proximity to Asia and the rare — for North America — waterfowl and other birds seen there. Smew, Chinese spot-billed duck, common pochard, whooper swan, tufted duck, and falcated and Baikal teal are a few of the once-in-a-lifetime birding treats.

The Aleutian Canada goose, small in size and endangered in status, once nested by the tens of thousands throughout much of the chain, but the introduction of fox farming led to their demise on all islands but tiny Buldir. Here they nest and molt on steep mountain slopes, but winter in central California. During the past ten years, foxes have been eradicated from several islands, and in 1983 the first nesting on one such island, Agattu, was documented. U.S. Fish and Wildlife Service biologists capture flightless geese on Buldir and release them on fox-free islands such as Agattu. Barring the unforeseen, Aleutian Canada geese will cease to be an endangered species in the not too distant future.

Foxes, and also rats from shipwrecks, have taken their toll on other nesting waterfowl and other birds, particularly sea birds such as murres, kittiwakes and auklets, which still number in the millions. The relationship of sea birds in the food chain of the Aleutians and other areas is important. Their excrement, rich in potash, is the base for the invertebrate food chain, the larger members of which are important food items for waterfowl. It has been said that sea bird colonies are the fertilizing factories of the northern seas, and sea birds certainly contribute to the welfare of many Alaskan waterfowl, as well as man.

The western tundra region is the subArctic tundra of western Alaska, extending from northwestern Bristol Bay to the Brooks Range. Land along the Bering Sea is barely above sea level, particularly on the great Yukon-Kuskokwim (Y-K) Delta, and waterfowl habitat is especially influenced by tidal erosion and alluvial deposition. For example, the land is only a few feet above sea level a hundred miles inland. The tundra is dotted by countless thaw lakes on underlying permafrost. Inland, fragments of boreal forest form a discontinuous edge (ecotone) between tundra and interior forest habitat. Winters are cold and windy and summers cool. Onshore winds, fog, and overcast skies are common. Although annual precipitation rarely exceeds fifteen inches, permafrost and flat terrain retard runoff.

Waterfowl habitats of the western tundra are generally less fertile than those of more productive interior areas, in part because annual "heat budgets" on the tundra are lower. However, the great profusion of ponds, lakes, and associated wetland habitat partially offsets lower productivity. A relatively narrow coastal fringe of tideland on the Y-K Delta, acre for acre, far overshadows other waterfowl production habi-

Yukon-Kuskokwin Delta. *Alaska Fish and Game photo.*

tat in Alaska, and is one of the world's most important waterfowl areas.

From this area of a few thousand square miles come all cackling Canada geese, about 90 percent of all emperor geese, about half of all Pacific brant, nearly all spectacled eider, and hundreds of thousands of divers, dabblers, tundra swan, white-fronted geese and cranes, and millions of shore and other waterbirds. The remaining inland portions of the 26,000-square-mile Y-K Delta support additional hundreds of thousands of ducks, Canada and white-fronted geese, crane and swan, and millions more other birds.

The flat land and low vegetation of the outer delta are susceptible to high wind-driven storm tides. Late May and June storms sometimes cause widespread nest loss, while even fiercer fall storm tides destroy traditional goose nesting habitat and affect production until the birds reestablish elsewhere.

Geese, nesting in colonies of sometimes 200 or more nests per square mile, are predictably susceptible to predators, but compensate by having many angry ganders to harass the numerous glaucous gulls and sometimes common Arctic foxes. When small mammal populations are low, a hungry fox can overcome defending geese and take a significant toll of nests and goslings.

Dispersed nesters, such as white-fronts, depend primarily on concealment for protection.

Most Arctic and sub-Arctic nesting geese are characterized by "boom or bust" production. In years of late snow and ice melt, nesting is delayed, clutch sizes and nest densities are smaller, and hatching success may be reduced. Although the geese arrive on their nesting grounds very fat, delays in nesting require energy reserves for survival, which would otherwise go into egg production. In a really late spring, eggs will be resorbed, and they may not nest at all. White-fronts use more elevated nest sites, such as stream banks, where the snow clears more quickly. This trait helps account for their generally better and more consistent annual production than other geese.

Like other coastal-bounded regions of Alaska, the western tundra region has immense areas of intertidal flats and salt marsh. Migrating waterfowl use these for feeding and resting, and particularly for molting during midsummer.

The Seward Peninsula and lowlands of Kotzebue Sound have important areas of breeding and molting habitat, although temperatures average slightly cooler than on the Y-K Delta. However, inland areas on the Seward Peninsula have average breeding duck densities of sixty per square mile. White-fronted geese, which winter in the Central Flyway, and Taverner's Canada geese, which stay in the Pacific Flyway, both nest throughout the northern part of the western tundra region, but particularly in river and stream valleys. Small colonies of brant and a few emperor geese nest in isolated coastal areas.

The Arctic North Slope of Alaska is a vast region north of the continental divide of the Brooks range. Altogether, it is 82,000 square miles, about 26,000 of which is waterfowl habitat.

A coastal plain rises gradually from the Arctic Ocean to an elevation of 600 feet between 50 and 200 miles inland. Much of the plain is poorly drained, with many thousand elongated "thaw" lakes oriented to the northwest-southeast prevailing summer winds. These range from a few feet to nine miles long, from two to twenty feet in depth, and most have ice bottoms even in summer. Plant communities of tussock-heath tundra, sedge-grass marsh, and dwarf shrubs compose the upland nesting habitat.

The Arctic Ocean shoreline varies from a few inches to ten feet above tidal waters, and offshore is a series of sand and gravel barrier islands formed by wave action. The lagoon between islands and shore is used by millions of molting and migrating ducks; the barrier islands support thousands of nesting eider, other ducks, and a few geese. Alaska's only snow goose colony is located on one such island. Lakes on the coastal plain are constantly undergoing formation and drainage; partially drained basins contain stands of emergent vegetation and receive heavy waterfowl use.

The Colville River Delta is the single largest production area on the coastal plain, and is best noted for Central Flyway–bound white-fronts, Atlantic Flyway tundra swans, Pacific and a few Central Flyway Canada geese, and ducks that winter in all four flyways. The Cape Halkett area, located between Point Barrow and the Colville Delta, is a well-known goose "molting resort" for some 60,000 or more Canadas, brants, white-fronts, and snows. These are mostly failed or nonbreeders from local nesting areas or from elsewhere in Alaska, Canada, and Russia. Several hundred thousand snow geese use eastern coastal plain habitat during the early fall for feeding and resting while in migration to staging areas in Saskatchewan and Alberta, and eventually to California wintering grounds.

An estimated two-thirds of the birds of the Canadian Arctic islands use the coastal migration route along the North Slope, including a million king eider, several tens of thousands of brant, several hundred thousand oldsquaw, and countless other birds. Although the Arctic Ocean is a surprisingly good source of food, particularly for eider and oldsquaw, mean tides of only six inches are insufficient to create the extensive intertidal flats found in other parts of Alaska.

While the North Slope supports many summer resident and migrating waterfowl, the mere presence of a great abundance of water does not necessarily indicate highly fertile and productive habitat. The slope is truly high Arctic in climate, but its great size and continuous summer daylight combine to afford a region of unique and vital waterfowl habitat.

Last, but by no means least, is Alaska's vast area of sub-Arctic boreal forest or taiga, extending from the Canadian border westward to tundra, and bounded on the north and south by mountains of the Brooks and Alaska ranges, respectively. The broad floodplains of the Yukon, Kuskokwim, Tanana and lesser rivers are, in total, the most productive of all Alaska's waterfowl habitats. Through eons of time, these great rivers have carved wide valleys through many mountain systems, leaving fertile floodplains liberally endowed with lakes, ponds, sloughs, and oxbows.

Only six to fifteen inches of precipitation fall annually, but a low mean annual temperature causes permanent ground frost, which prevents percolation. Wet and marshy habitat is therefore common. Evapotranspiration dries some ponds, but periodic river flooding refills them. Continental temperature extremes of $+100°F$ to $-60°F$ and even $-80°F$ are common. River valleys and plains become warm "solar basins" during summer, and "cold sinks" during winter. Continuous summer sunlight and short winter days contribute to the extremes, and habitat productivity owes much to the long summer days.

Floating vegetative mats, formed by sedges, buckbean, and marsh fivefinger, gradually cover and eventually fill lake, slough, and pond basins. These mats are frequently the most available nesting habitat, and waterfowl nesting on such sites are often the only successful nesters during severe spring floods. Scrub spruce and mixed forest provide habitat for tree nesters such as bufflehead and goldeneye and ground-nesting scoters.

Shallow ponds with lush stands of emergent horsetail, sedges, and grasses are popular feeding areas for duck broods. River oxbows and larger lakes are rearing and molting areas for white-fronted and Canada geese. Natural drawdown from evaporation and intricate drainage systems stimulate lush stands of spike rush, smartweed, burreed and fleabane, all preferred waterfowl food and escape cover. Periodic forest fires retard vegetational succession, and contribute to overall productivity by causing quick nutrient release.

Nearly 35,000 square miles of interior habitat produce an estimated fall flight of six million ducks, a quarter-million geese and about 5,000 trumpeter swan. Among the most important areas are the Innoko, Koyukuk and Tanana River drainages, the Kanuti, Minto and Tetlin Flats, the Nelchina Basin, and, above all, the Yukon

Flats of central Alaska.

The Yukon Flats first gained prominence as a waterfowl area about twenty years ago, when the proposed Rampart Dam would have inundated an area the size of Maryland. Although the Yukon Flats is transected by the Arctic Circle, it's probably the world's single most productive Arctic solar basin. Its 10,800 square miles of waterfowl habitat supports 100 breeding ducks per square mile which, after production, constitute a fall flight of over two million birds annually. White-fronted geese nest along tributary streams of the Yukon and Porcupine rivers, and Canada geese on islands in the great Yukon River. Waterfowl migrate to and from the flats via interior routes through large river valleys, and via the coastal route and then up the Copper and Susitna River valleys.

The peak of hatch usually coincides, as it does over much of Alaska, with the longest day of the year, the warmest temperatures, the peak of insect abundance, and vegetative growth. It was long thought that ducklings fledged more quickly in the far north than in the south. However, a study showed that, although ducks developed from downy to fully feathered stages more quickly, it takes just as long for a duckling to fly in Alaska as it does elsewhere.

In recognition of Alaska's outstanding wildlife, scenic, and wilderness values, the Alaska National Interest Lands Conservation Act (ANILCA) was passed by Congress in 1980 on a tide of national sentiment. In the single biggest land and resource preservation initiative ever, over 100 million acres of land were *added* to the federal refuge, park, forest, and wild and scenic river systems in Alaska. National refuges, parks, and forests now total over 76 million, 50 million, and 20 million acres respectively, and comprise almost 40 per-

cent of Alaska. The Bureau of Land Management, the state of Alaska, and various native entities control most remaining lands. Comparatively, private individuals own very little.

Waterfowl were a major beneficiary of ANILCA. In combination with established protected areas and new ones created by ANILCA, nearly every important migratory bird upland habitat is now federally managed, with wildlife as the primary objective. These areas include much of the Yukon-Kuskokwim River Delta, the Copper River Delta, Yukon flats, Innoko and Koyukuk Rivers, Kanuti, Selawik and Tetlin Flats, and offshore islands of the Alaska Maritime Refuge. Other refuges, parks, and forests also have significant waterfowl values.

The state of Alaska owns coastal waters and lands below mean high tide as well as 105 million acres of uplands after all lands are conveyed under the Statehood Act. Under the state's refuge, critical habitat, and sanctuary classification system, nearly 1.8 million acres have been reserved with waterfowl primarily in mind. The state emphasized prime coastal migration-feeding areas for protection, which are also among the most important waterfowl hunting areas. These include coastal marshes of Cook Inlet, Izembek Lagoon and other estuaries along the Alaska Peninsula, and tidelands of the Copper River Delta.

Besides formal land classification, waterfowl and their habitat receive major consideration through a host of federal, state, and local laws, regulations, and policies. The Clean Water Act requires an Army Corps of Engineers "404" permit for any development on wetlands to ensure minimum habitat loss. While perhaps not directly stopping or modifying potentially damaging habitat destruction, the National Environmental Protection Act (NEPA) requires an environmental impact statement or environmental assessment for major federal, state, or private actions where federal money is involved. NEPA ensures that alternative actions are considered and that the public is aware of what's happening.

While very little federal duck-stamp money has been spent in Alaska, the first Alaska state duck stamp was initiated in 1985 and will provide hundreds of thousands of dollars for waterfowl conservation. The federal Endangered Species Act was followed by a comparable Alaskan state law, and the Aleutian Canada goose has staged a dramatic comeback because of action in Alaska and California. The Coastal Zone Management Act requires local planning and zoning to ensure coastal wetland protection.

The Pittman-Robertson Act (known as PR) established an excise tax on arms, ammunition, and components to provide federal funds for cost sharing with states for wildlife management programs and habitat purchase. "PR" provides the monetary backbone of state wildlife and waterfowl management programs. Treaties with Canada, Mexico, Japan, and other countries provide the basis for federal waterfowl management; and some as yet unratified portions of a recent treaty with Russia provide for significant—and controversial—federal jurisdiction on state and privately owned wetlands.

As in much of Canada's far north, Alaskan habitat is in relatively pristine condition and productivity has not, except in local areas, been greatly affected by man's influence. But the future of Alaska was dramatically altered with the discovery of Prudhoe Bay oil. Oil, the pipeline, and a tremendous amount of money brought predictable results: new jobs and a doubling of the state's population, urban expansion and rural "bush" development, and new international recognition for Alaska.

The infusion of oil money has been compared to drug addiction; the more one gets the more one wants, and when the supply runs low, almost anything will be done to get more. Former Alaska governor Jay Hammond said, "Never underestimate the ability of a politician to spend money." The fear of many concerned with waterfowl and other wildlife is that when the state's honeymoon with oil money is over, politicians may pull all environmental safeguards they possibly can to replenish state (and federal) coffers. The affluent probably make the best conservationists.

Predictions of disastrous pipeline breaks and tanker accidents in Prince William Sound have not materialized, nor has there been even one major oil spill from offshore drilling rigs in Cook Inlet during twenty years of operation. However, future outer continental shelf oil development could have devastating effects if spills reached critical waterfowl areas such as Izembek Lagoon and the Y-K and Copper River deltas. If the worst happens, Alaska's weather, size, and logistic problems would preclude meaningful oil containment efforts.

Hydroelectric projects, such as the once-proposed Rampart Dam, could inundate thousands of miles of productive wetlands. However, small "upstream" dams for water control may be just as harmful to waterfowl if spring floods—vital to river valley wetland productivity—are controlled. Future water level control may be desirable to protect rapidly growing interior villages that are mostly located on rivers, or to enhance potential agricultural projects in fertile river valleys.

An active state land disposal program has affected the trumpeter swan. There is an inverse correlation between increased human disturbance, associated with a mushrooming number of remote cabins in parts of Alaska, and the use of wetlands by swan after cabins appear.

Other forms of increasing human disturbance are a growing concern to waterfowl managers in Alaska. Low-flying aircraft disturb spring and fall staging geese. With enough harassment, some species could decline as a result of their inability to store sufficient energy reserves for migration. While clouds of seabirds frantically cascading off nesting cliffs at the approach of an aircraft is a spectacular sight, also spectacular are the eggs and flightless young dashed on the rocks below.

The advent of all-terrain vehicles, particularly the popular three-wheeler, has created a means of access to formerly difficult country. Three-wheelers, criss-crossing vital waterfowl habitat during nesting, make nests easy prey for foxes, gulls, and other predators, and may induce nest desertion.

Reindeer grazing and herding reportedly caused the demise of snow goose colonies on the Seward Peninsula. Reindeer herding is under active consideration in other parts of Alaska, including the Y-K Delta.

Waterfowl subsistence hunting is being scrutinized, and blamed by some, for the alarming declines of cackling Canada, white-fronted, and emperor geese, and Pacific brant. While natives have been hunting, egging, and catching flightless molters for thousands of years, there are now major differences from the past. The population of rural Alaska is growing rapidly, and waterfowl, particularly geese, cannot withstand unlimited harvest, if

they are to sustain their numbers. The timing of harvest also appears critical. For example, early spring hunting with modern arms concentrates pressure on adult mated pairs, which are proportionately more abundant then.

The first key to addressing subsistence hunting is mutual understanding among many people. Native Alaskans have no less concern for the future of waterfowl than people elsewhere. They react predictably to news of wetland drainage on wintering grounds and reports of selenium, lead, and mercury poisoning, and some still have doubts about the origin of the down in their parkas.

Political interference, hidden agendas, prejudices and mutual misunderstanding have all prevented waterfowl managers from doing their job. Only imminent disaster for some Alaskan goose species has forced the reality upon Washington and Juneau that, in combination with all other forms of mortality, uncontrolled waterfowl subsistence hunting will result in waterfowl populations reduced below huntable levels—or even worse.

It would appear that the politicians' responsibility is to develop a legal means to provide for a regulated harvest; the biologists' to determine the allowable extent and relative biological effects of that harvest; and the public's to determine how that harvest will be divided.

Perhaps as a surprise to some, the growth in number and influence of quasi-conservation groups carrying antihunting as their banner is a serious threat to the future abundance of waterfowl and other wildlife populations. Sportsmen have a long history of providing "bucks for ducks" and applying pressure on politicians to protect habitat. Besides producing waterfowl for hunters, wetlands have many other values. However, every time antihunting groups succeed in stopping a hunt, giving hunting a bad name, or otherwise discouraging hunters from actively defending their sport, wildlife's major ally weakens a bit more. Consider for a moment the far smaller bird populations and wetland areas it takes to satisfy viewers than hunters, should the hunter's voice be silenced.

Wildlife managers in Alaska, and elsewhere, must now spend increasing amounts of money—and time—defending agency programs, and even their profession, from antihunters. Some "antis" have the federal Pittman-Robertson Act, the very backbone of state wildlife conservation programs, in their sights. When biologists must spend time and money justifying hunting programs, sometimes in minute detail, less is available to provide optimum hunting seasons and to address the *real* threats to waterfowl.

Threats to waterfowl can best be curbed by an aware and active public. For example, a biologist's request to modify a wetland fill can fall on deaf administrative ears; fifty telegrams from the public will be heard. Ducks Unlimited not only enhances wetlands, but in Alaska and elsewhere it arouses public concern for waterfowl. Industry responds to public concern, and the incorporation of conservation safeguards frequently is the most profitable course of development.

Other than a continually growing human population, the antihunting sentiment may be the most difficult threat to overcome. Antihunters thrive on emotionalism, sometimes generated by actions of "slob" hunters; on management agency errors seen in retrospect; on a biased press; and many other things. Apathy toward these groups, however, is *not* in the best interest of wildlife.

6

The Pairing Process and Social Behavior of Waterfowl in Spring

R. A. Wishart

Northern marshes locked in March ice are stark and quiet, the silence broken only by the rustling of frozen cattail. One cannot imagine how they will support the continent's millions of breeding waterfowl, soon to return.

But quickly the scene changes. As field snow melts into sheet water, small flocks of early migrants return. And as the marshes thaw, the air is filled with the musty scent of last year's decaying vegetation. Teeming invertebrates provide an important food source for the new arrivals; each day another species appears, and numbers build steadily. The marsh is vibrant with change.

A close look at the newly arrived flocks swimming and feeding on the open water reveals that distribution is not random. Everywhere groups of two can be picked out, a female followed by her mate. Clearly many of the birds have paired on their wintering grounds.

Study has shown this bonding process is a complex affair; female ducks choose new mates annually, unlike geese and swans, which pair for life. The sex ratio is unbalanced, and males, with less severe mortality (females are in jeopardy while nesting), are generally in excess, so competition for the limited number of hens is keen.

Despite the appearance that most females are paired when they arrive in spring, courtship is far from over. The bursts of activity seen in April demonstrate what has gone on all winter. Likely many of the females embroiled in late courtship are yearlings, only now showing interest in the activity. While most pairs at this time have more solid bonds, formed months earlier, even among them, some mate swapping goes on.

Pair formation in ducks makes for fascinating observation, but things usually happen quickly in a blur of wings and water. Groups of from three to twenty un-attached males mill about a receptive fe-male, vying for position close to her. The objective of each seems to be to catch her eye, while at the same time intimidating the other competitors. The drakes, in bursts of activity, "display," highlighting particular areas of their striking plumage. A series of displays often follow in chain reaction, adding to the effect.

At just the right distance from the hen, and with his best side forward, each male goes through his routine. Often a display initiated by one male will trigger others to perform, so that the female is surrounded by a knot of gyrating suitors. This activity draws attention to the group, and other males fly over to take part.

Most of the displays in the courtship repertoire are exaggerated forms of normal body maintenance activities. Preening, tail wagging, bill dipping, scratching, stretch-ing, and even feeding and drinking move-ments have been ritualized to convey new meaning at this time of year.

Preening behind the wing results in the flash of the brilliant speculum. A wing flap adds attention-grabbing sound to the color; this, followed by a splashing move-ment by the bill or a tailwag, draws the eye over the entire body. A wing stretch with ruffled feathers, like muscle flexing in the

Early arrivals: a mallard drake follows his mate. *DU Canada photo.*

Mallard courtship flight. *Ed Bry photo.*

human world, makes bodies appear larger than life and more impressive.

Vocalizations are intermingled with the movements, again for greater impact, each bird shouting for attention. Individual calls are slightly different, and eventually the female can pinpoint a preferred suitor, even if he is hidden from view.

For ease of description and comparison among species, scientists have named the various displays. The "head-up-tail-up," "wing-flap," and "preen-behind-the-wing," common to several species, are easy to visualize. Others, such as the "triumph ceremony" of geese, the "head-throw" of the canvasback, and the "grunt-whistle" of

the mallard, leave much more to the imagination. Study has shown that, similar to other physical characteristics, displays are useful in tracing the lineage and evolution of waterfowl species.

Despite the similarities, each species has its unique set of ritualized pair formation displays. This functions to reduce inter-species mating, which could lead to nonviable offspring. Occasionally, however, one sees a misplaced European wigeon in the middle of a group of courting American wigeon. To him, with none of his own kind around, the courtship antics of his American relatives are appealing. In most cases his attempts go unrewarded; the slight differences in his appearance and movements are detected by the female.

Black duck and mallard displays are quite similar, and where the two species range together mistakes are made, hybridization is common, and progeny fertile. Black duck females actually seem more attracted to the colorful male mallard. As a result, genetic swapping may soon lead to the demise of the black in areas where the mallard has recently expanded its range.

As courtship continues, competition heightens. Wing-beating, pecking fights may break out among the drakes. In an effort to gain position, some flip up into the air in a "jump-flight," attracting attention with their wing noise and landing in front of the female. Others attempt to lead the female away from the group with the "turn-back-of-head" display. If she follows, she is interested. But just as suddenly she may change her mind and coquettishly swim back through the group of followers.

At such times displaying reaches a fever pitch, and some males may nip at the female in an effort to herd her away. Often this leads to splashing chases over the water and the female may flush, with most

of the males in hot pursuit. The ensuing flight is a cacophony of sight and sound as it weaves up and down, back and forth over the marsh landscape. Some may lose interest and drop out, others fly up belatedly to join in. Again these flights seem to be a process of evaluation for the female, and likely also for the males, each testing the others' vigor and flying ability. It is also hazardous! Males are often killed or maimed when their attention is focused on the female; she avoids obstacles such as power lines and fences that, in their eagerness, they fail to see.

While courtship displays are less complex among diving species, courtship flights on the other hand are conducted at breakneck, hair-raising speeds that are a wonder to behold.

Eventually the flight ends with a splashing return to the water, sometimes after more than fifteen minutes on the wing. Once down, courtship usually resumes, but many more flights may ensue before the female selects a mate whom she follows away from the group. This is not to say the bond is yet solid. Attentiveness by either partner may wane, and several mate

Blue-wing competition as mating pairs form. *Ed Bry photo.*

changes can occur before a final lasting selection is made.

Close study indicates that the older, experienced, fully plumaged males in the best physical condition succeed in acquiring mates first. Dominance, attentiveness, and flying ability are all important male characteristics needed to win and keep a mate. Logically, these same characteristics are important later on during nesting, to ensure that a pair will successfully produce a brood.

Soon, the sociality among pairs within the migrant flocks diminishes. Tolerance wanes, and the pairs begin to disperse to separate isolated patches of marsh. These territories, as they are called, are defended by the male against other pairs of the same species. They provide a protected place for feeding, preening, and nuptial activities.

The resident male is alert to intruders; he rises and directs his attack at the female of a trespassing pair, while her mate, particularly in pintail and mallard, follows languidly behind the dispute. In wigeon and some other species, the intruding male is much more aggressive; contacts with the territorial male are common.

These "three-bird-flights" are a common sight among dabbling ducks in May. They are usually brief, ending abruptly when the resident male breaks off his attack to return to his mate, who has remained behind on the territory. If she is in hiding among the reeds, a few familiar calls from the male will bring her back into view.

Because of the unbalanced sex ratio, some males are unsuccessful in winning a mate. These bachelors move widely about the area trying to break existing bonds. Skirmishes with territorial males result in "two-bird-flights" in which the bachelors are chased away. The flights are short, but may be repeated over and over again, de-

pending on the persistence of the interloper.

The significance of territorial defense, and the need for the female to be selective during courtship, become apparent when the male she chooses is incapable of evicting intruders.

If her mate is inattentive, or is not sufficiently aggressive to keep others of their species away, the female will be forced to flee or hide. Harassment and waste of her precious time and energy will occur, and may lead to lower egg production or nest success.

Males, finding a female unattended during the nesting season, may attempt rape. Mass aerial chases, composed of the single female and many males, similar in appearance to chases in pair formation seen in May and June, may result. One difference, however, is that when the flights end back on the water, forced copulation rather than courtship is the result.

Some observers believe that in some species, females that have apparently lost their mates may, in fact, incite "rape." In such cases a distinctive vocalization is given, which alerts males of that species in the vicinity. In the instances involving pintails in which this was observed, a spectacular flight occurred, almost vertical and nearly to the limit of vision. Upon return to land, several of the pursuing males copulated with the hen. Both mallard and pintail drakes will join in these flights in pursuit of females of either species. Mallard/pintail hybrids, found occasionally in natural waterfowl populations, may result from these flights.

As nesting by successful pairs proceeds, the attentiveness of the paired male gradually wanes. He no longer follows the female as closely; he may be off attempting to rape other females, or in company with other males. Eventually, when the female returns to the water on one of her short breaks from incubation, she will find him permanently gone. She is alone to complete nesting and raise her offspring until they fledge.

Male "buddy" groups gradually increase in numbers and become flocks, which depart for larger lakes and marshes for the summer moult. These flocks usually contain some hens that have been unsuccessful in nesting and are no longer sexually active.

Not until late fall and winter will photoperiod conditions again be right to rekindle the pairing process. With the intervening events of moult and fall migration, it is unlikely that the same mates will meet again. Indeed the male may pair with a female who will lead him to her nesting grounds in a different flyway altogether.

The casual birdwatcher or hunter usually recalls his waterfowl experiences only in terms of the species he encountered. All shovelers, for example, look alike, beyond the distinction of male from female. Observations are fleeting, permitting only a flip to the appropriate page in the bird guide in one instance, or a decision to pull or not pull the trigger in the other.

It is only through close observation that one realizes the individuality of ducks. Size, shape, color, voice, age, and temperament are all highly variable. The birds learn to recognize one another; it is in their interest to do so if they are to select the best possible mate and nest successfully. It is even apparent that mothers can recognize their daughters the next spring when both return to their traditional nesting areas, each accompanied by a new mate.

The intricate process of pair formation and social behavior in waterfowl is geared to individual recognition, and it provides fantastic watching for those fortunate enough to be afoot in the marsh come spring.

Part II
Summer

Settled down at last, waterfowl struggle to produce a brood. With everything apparently against them—drought, agriculture, and predation—they can be surprisingly successful if given even half a chance.

Man's role is to enhance that chance. How well waterfowl prosper in the long run will, in large part, depend on him.

7

Problems and Potentials for Prairie Ducks

L. M. Cowardin, A. B. Sargeant, and H. F. Duebbert

The Prairie Pothole Region is the primary production area for ducks in the Central and Mississippi flyways. Recent studies by us and our co-workers at the Northern Prairie Wildlife Research Center, Jamestown, North Dakota, reveal that in much of the region, mallards and other ducks face a particular problem. Recruitment, the rate at which breeding hens produce young for the fall population, is alarmingly low in many areas. The purpose of this chapter is to identify the magnitude of that problem, the major reasons for its occurrence, and the challenge it poses to waterfowl management. Much of the information highlighted by this chapter is from technical papers that have been or soon will be published.

Increases or decreases in duck populations are determined by the delicate balance between births and deaths. For popu-lation size to remain constant, numbers of young recruited must equal numbers of adults that die. Waterfowl raise at most only one brood per year. Biologists refer to hen success as the percentage of hens that hatch a clutch of eggs. If the hen's initial nest is destroyed, she may nest repeatedly. The proportion of initiated nests that are successful is called nest success. Nest success is one of the most important factors affecting recruitment; if it is low, few young are added to the fall population.

Recent studies show that, in most areas of central and eastern North Dakota, less than 15 percent of the duck nests are successful. Results for western Minnesota and eastern South Dakota reveal that nest success is very low in those areas also. In contrast, limited information from northwest-ern North Dakota and Montana indicates that nest success in those areas is relatively

Nesting ducks, such as this blue-winged teal and its eggs, are extremely vulnerable to predators. *Arnold Kruse photo.*

good, about 40 percent in two recent studies. Other studies are currently underway to determine nest success in the Canadian pothole region.

Awareness of low nest success and growing concern over the welfare of the mallard prompted initiation of a detailed study to determine mallard recruitment rates in central North Dakota and to identify the importance of factors affecting recruitment. That study began in 1977 and was completed in 1980.

Recruitment is difficult to measure. During four years of the North Dakota study, radio telemetry was used to study 338 mal-

lard hens from shortly after they arrived on the breeding grounds until we knew if they succeeded in rearing young. Radio-equipped hens provided information on nest site selection, nest fate, rate of renesting, and survival of ducklings. The hens were captured throughout a large area to provide results that would reflect general rather than local conditions. This study gave us insight into the relation between prairie duck habitat, predation, and mallard populations.

Prairie wetlands are dynamic. Weather has a major impact because during drought years the number of ponds is reduced. This not only affects the number of pairs attracted to an area but also reduces the nesting effort. The telemetry study revealed that in dry years, on the average, hens attempted only one nest, whereas in wet years they averaged 2.6 attempts. Water conditions, therefore, have a powerful impact on recruitment.

Ironically, the very droughts that periodically devastate waterfowl production are also responsible for cycles of drying and reflooding that contribute to the fertility of wetland basins and allow high duck production in wet years. Prairie ducks have evolved in this boom or bust environment and are capable of maintaining their num-

bers if nest success is good when water conditions are good. Unfortunately, the telemetry study showed that nest success and therefore recruitment was not good during any year.

The Prairie Pothole Region is one of North America's most intensively manipulated environments. Waterfowl biologists have known for years that drainage of wetlands and the less obvious agricultural impacts on wetland quality have gradually decreased the region's ability to produce large numbers of ducks. Even more drastic changes have occurred on uplands, where most dabbling ducks nest. During the past 100 years most of the native grasslands in

Radio-marked mallards in central North Dakota showed a preference for road right-of-ways, odd areas of cover, and hayland as nesting sites, and almost complete rejection of annually tilled cropland. *Jan Eldridge photo.*

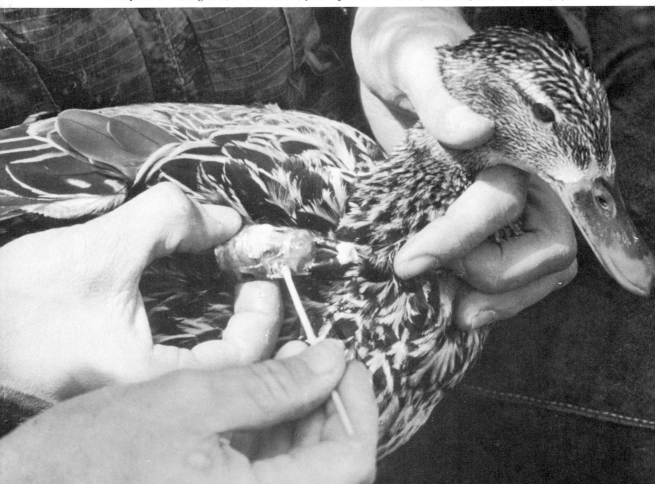

the Dakotas and western Minnesota have been converted to croplands that are tilled annually. In North Dakota less than 20 percent of the original grasslands remain, and most are heavily grazed. The croplands, under current agricultural practices, are of little value to nesting ducks. On our central North Dakota study area, 38 percent of the area was cropland, but it contained only 2 percent of the mallard nests. In addition, nest success was lower in cropland than in any other habitat. Native grassland and hayland furnished much of the remaining nesting habitat. Much of the grassland was heavily grazed, which decreased its attractiveness to nesting mallards. The hayland attracted many hens, but most clutches were destroyed by haying operations. Hens often chose nest sites in odd areas such as fencerows, shelterbelts, and rock piles, but they were generally unsuccessful in these habitats.

An average of only 8 percent of the nests initiated were successful during the four years of the telemetry study. These results are similar to those of numerous other studies where nests were found by different methods. At this low rate of nest success only 15 percent of the mallard hens were successful in hatching a clutch, even with persistent renesting.

The principal reason for the low rate of nest success was predation. Seventy percent of the nest failures were known to have resulted from predation, and predators were implicated in many of the others. In addition, predators killed a minimum of 20 percent of the nesting hens. Predators also were strongly implicated in duckling mortality: 26 percent of the broods failed to survive the initial move to water, and continuing loss of ducklings resulted in an average brood size of five at fledging. The reasons for mortality of ducklings

were largely unknown, but predation was the known cause in some deaths.

The important question for waterfowl management is "what impact does the high rate of nest failure and loss of hens and ducklings have on population size?" It is possible to combine an estimate of recruitment and survival to predict population trends. Based on the available data, we conclude that the mallard population in central North Dakota should be declining. If it is not, it must be maintained by birds pioneering to the area from other regions. To obtain population stability, about 30 percent of the hens would have to be successful in one of their nesting attempts. For this to occur, nest success would have to be about 15 percent, as compared with 8 percent observed in the telemetry study.

Predation ranks high as an important factor in the evolution of prairie ducks. The effects of predation are evident in many characteristics of ducks, such as agile flight, keen eyesight, and cryptic coloration of hens and molting drakes, as well as distractive behaviors to lure predators from young and feigning death to escape from predators. The antipredator behaviors of each duck species vary to complement other aspects of their biology, but all are aimed at perpetuating the species.

The most important strategy ducks have for coping with predation, and with other environmental stresses, is to produce maximum numbers of young—to overproduce. This strategy increases chances for survival of at least some young. The existence of an annual surplus of ducks is the cornerstone of modern-day waterfowling.

Nowhere in the annual cycle of ducks is the risk of predation greater than on the breeding grounds. Returning hens space themselves out across the pothole region in

The red fox, abundant throughout the eastern Dakotas and western Minnesota, is an effective predator of upland nesting ducks and their eggs. *Alan B. Sargeant photo.*

the spring, where hens on nests expose themselves to predators for the thirty-five days needed for egg-laying and incubation. The risk associated with nesting is a chance that must be taken.

Although prairie ducks have always been subjected to considerable predation, the impact has probably increased in recent decades. In pristine times, ducks lived in habitats largely untouched by man. The impact of predators on duck populations represented a balance that evolved over a long period of time. However, as settlement of the prairie by Europeans progressed, the region and its predator populations were subjected to considerable change. We are still in the midst of this change; man has not yet completed his transformation of the prairie. The consequences of man's impact on prairie duck

populations are becoming increasingly clear, and increased predation is one present-day result of that change.

As farming has become less diversified, field size has increased to efficiently utilize modern equipment. Economics has discouraged leaving land idle. These changes are clearly evident from drainage of wetlands, elimination of fencerows, tillage of road ditches, burying of rock piles, increased use of herbicides and insecticides, and new cropping practices. Intensive farming has reduced the amount of prey available to predators during the duck nesting season and has concentrated prey and predator activity in remaining untilled habitats—the same habitat that most ducks use for nesting.

Results from a recent study of striped skunks in eastern North Dakota revealed this influence. During spring and summer the skunks foraged primarily for insects and spent about 85 percent of their foraging time in grassland habitats (including road ditches, tree rows, and waterfowl production areas) that represented about 20 percent of the area. The foraging skunks destroyed many duck nests; nest success on the area was about 10 percent.

Another major change affecting prairie ducks has been alteration of the composition and abundance of predator species. Although this change is related to habitat modifications, it also reflects direct human-inflicted mortality of predators. At present, predators with the greatest impact on ducks in the Dakotas and western Minnesota include the red fox, striped skunk, raccoon, mink, and Franklin's ground squirrel. Species with lesser impact, but which may be important locally, include the badger, coyote, long-tailed weasel, crow, and possibly some gulls and raptors. During pristine times, many of these predator species were uncommon or scarce, but other species such as the wolf and kit fox that had an unknown impact on ducks were common.

Settlement of the prairie has benefited most present-day predators. For example, raccoons now have grain to eat and buildings in which to spend the winter and rear young, red foxes have diverse foods including sunflower seeds and livestock carrion during winter, crows and great horned owls have trees for nesting, and mink have impoundments to help them withstand drought. Together, these factors have favored the maintenance of a rather stable, diverse community of mid-size predators that are highly adapted to prey on ducks, their eggs, and their young.

Direct human impacts have been a major influence on certain predator species; information is best for canids. Wolves suppress coyote populations and coyotes suppress red fox populations. Hence, it is no surprise that after wolves were largely eliminated by man from the pothole region during the mid to late 1800s, the coyote population expanded greatly. Kit foxes disappeared at that time, for reasons not fully understood, and red foxes became very scarce. Because coyotes preyed on livestock, efforts were undertaken to reduce their numbers.

As control became more effective during the 1930s and 1940s, the number of coyotes in farmland areas was reduced substantially and the red fox population began to expand. After 1940 the red fox became far more numerous than ever before in recorded history of the region, and during most years occupied almost every square mile of prairie pothole habitat in the eastern Dakotas and western Minnesota. Recently, the coyote population has begun to reoccupy areas where it has been absent for many years, and red foxes are becoming less numerous.

The increase in red foxes after 1940 was detrimental to duck production. Information collected from 1969 to 1973 indicated that about 18 percent of the breeding hen mallards in North Dakota were taken annually by foxes. Most hens were believed killed on nests, but some were scavenged. Other information showed that individual fox families often take forty or more adult ducks in spring (mostly dabbling hens) and that foxes have a particularly strong attraction to duck eggs. Information about the impact of coyotes on ducks is scant, but it appears that coyote predation on ducks and duck eggs is much less severe than red fox predation. The relatively high nesting success reported for northwestern North Dakota and Montana was in areas where

CANID POPULATION CHANGES

(EASTERN PRAIRIE POTHOLE REGION)

	1860	1890	1920	1950	1980
WOLF					
COYOTE					
RED FOX					
KIT FOX					

Since the mid-1800s canid populations in the eastern portion of the Prairie Pothole Region have undergone considerable change that resulted in an abundance of red foxes during recent decades. *Alan B. Sargeant photo.*

coyotes were numerous.

The environmental changes that have occurred in the prairie pothole region create special problems for prairie ducks. The loss of wetland habitat poses the greatest threat. Although wetland habitat guarantees a place for breeding ducks, it does not guarantee that hens will fledge young. The problem of high predation on adult ducks, eggs, and young, and its underlying cause, an environment that has been drastically altered, pose a challenge to waterfowl management.

Reprinted with permission from *Naturalist*, the Journal of the Natural History Society of Minnesota. Volume 34, No. 4, "Managing Prairie Ducks." Winter, 1983.

8

Drought, Floods, Predation

T. G. Neraasen

Waterfowl live and breed in highly change-able environments. Glacial history and climate affect soils, land form, and vegetation, all of which ultimately determine the fertility and attraction of an area for waterfowl. But the most important component of a waterfowl area is the water regime — the most changeable of all.

The amount and condition of wetland habitat varies annually from spring to fall. Waterfowl ponds and lakes in prairie regions are subject to extreme fluctuations because flood-drought cycles are pronounced. More northerly park land, forest, and Arctic regions have more stable, though more severe, climatic regimes. Their wetlands are more stable. But the extreme variability of prairie habitats is what makes them productive, and partially explains why at least 70 percent of all North American ducks are produced there.

Annual waterfowl production is directly related to spring water conditions, both qualitatively and quantitatively.

When spring pond numbers and breeding populations are high, brood production and fall flights have been correspondingly high. Unfortunately, the converse is also true. When drought strikes the prairies, the effect on waterfowl can be devastating.

An obvious effect of drought on the prairies is a reduction in numbers of breeding waterfowl and an overflight to more northerly but better-watered habitat. Although ducks breed less successfully in these northern regions, they maintain a reservoir of birds that return to the prairies when water conditions improve. In good water years, there were 600 breeding pairs on a study area near Redvers, Saskatchewan; in poor water years, as few as 52.

Drought can be devastating to duck production. *Duck Unlimited Canada photo.*

Similar observations were recorded in Manitoba and South Dakota when good water and drought years were compared.

What happens to breeding pairs in areas that are going dry?

In many cases they fail to breed at all, or, if attempts are made, they are desultory. For instance, in 1959 — a dry year — only 8 percent of lesser scaup breeding pairs resident on a study area attempted to nest, compared to between 60 and 64 percent of pairs in normal years. Most sat around in apparent confusion and then abruptly left the area.

Obviously, lack of breeding pairs, and poor or nonexistent breeding effort of those that do attempt to nest, result in very poor brood production during droughts. The effects on lesser scaup brood production in the above study were dramatic. Production decreased 93 percent between 1957 and the first drought year of 1958 and remained very low through 1960, when the study terminated.

Divers — lesser scaup, redhead, and canvasback — are more susceptible to drought than dabblers. This is because they nest relatively late, and their young don't fly until late August or early September. Drought can leave a large proportion of young, flightless divers on dry or drying ponds, where they are prone to starvation, exposure, and increased predation. Although they involved a dabbler species, studies have shown that mallard brood sizes, and percentage of broods surviving to fledging, were greater in both prairie and parkland for early nesters who escape the effects of late summer drought. A greater proportion of early nests hatched as well.

Although drought affects breeding success of different species of waterfowl in different ways, the end result is the same — a significant loss in production and even breeding stock. The overall result is a reduction in the fall flight and a concomitant reduction in the number of breeding pairs that return to breed the next year.

Ducks adapt, however, and thus all is not doom and gloom. Pintail, at least, are particularly well adapted to the arid prairie grasslands in which they breed. By flying on north in large numbers during drought years, they waste no breeding effort, and avoid the increased stresses and predation to which they would be subjected had they attempted to breed on the prairies. They thus live longer and are able to reproduce abundantly, when favorable prairie habitat conditions return. The same is true of other waterfowl species, although perhaps not to the same degree.

Periodic droughts, which rejuvenate vegetation and recycle nutrients, are natural and necessary in maintaining the bursts of productivity that so characterize prairie wetlands. All that is needed, following dry years, is for a basin to hold water when the moisture regime swings again to the wetter end of the scale.

But as each drought passes into history, so do more such basins — a chilling thought.

Wetland modification, by cultivation, brushing, filling, and draining, accelerates during drought years. The end result will be to reduce wetland numbers permanently to drought levels. Even more chilling is the realization that modern man and his machinery need no assistance from nature to produce this effect.

Waterfowl have evolved strategies to cope with natural droughts, but it is unlikely that many can evolve quickly enough to adapt to the rapid changes in the environment caused by human activities.

One could get the erroneous impression from this discussion of drought that all waterfowl need is water. Although there is much truth in this, too much water, at the wrong place and time, is tough on waterfowl. Long-term water level fluctuations benefit waterfowl by improving habitat. But short-term flooding at the wrong time can wipe out much of the local nesting effort.

Diving ducks nesting over water in emergent vegetation, such as cattails and bulrush, are able to accommodate and adjust to increases in water level of three to six inches over a twenty-four-hour period. There are even reports of canvasback hens building up nests as much as fourteen inches in attempts to keep ahead of rapidly rising water. Flooding can completely eliminate a nesting attempt, either directly or indirectly through desertion. At the very least, flooding causes loss of some eggs, which are covered as the hen attempts to build up her nest.

The degree to which waterfowl nesting is disrupted depends not only on the maximum rise in water level but also the rate at which it occurs, the quality of the emergent stands, and the anchorage for nests they provide.

Dabbling ducks, which typically nest in dry upland sites, are particularly prone to nest destruction and desertion even from shallow floods. Nests situated at the edges of large marshes can almost all be destroyed when even relatively minor wind tides push water into the peripheral areas.

As with other environmental variables, waterfowl can adapt to natural floods, either through renesting or avoiding flood-prone habitat. Flooding caused by human activities, however, such as the regime that accompanies hydroelectric reservoir development and management, renders habitat almost completely useless to most waterfowl.

Waterfowl are subject to predation throughout life, either directly on adults and ducklings, or indirectly on unhatched eggs.

Band recoveries of fledged North American waterfowl indicate that predation on flying birds is relatively insignificant: 0.1 percent of more than two million reported observations. This is less than collisions with utility wires, automobiles, and the like.

It is difficult to estimate fully the overall impact of predation on continental waterfowl populations, since it is so rarely observed. We can, however, get some idea of its importance from studies of waterfowl breeding biology and specific studies on predation and predator control.

Most of our information about predation on waterfowl involves nest predation,

Skunks are among the most destructive of nest predators. *U.S. Fish and Wildlife Service photo.*

The destructive work of a skunk. *Ducks Unlimited Canada photo.*

or nesting hens, because nest predators often leave identifiable signs at the scene of the crime. One need not catch the culprit in the act. There is less information on predation on ducklings or adult birds. Most is indirect. Direct observations of predators in the act of taking waterfowl are relatively rare.

Many mammals and birds, and some reptiles and fish, prey on waterfowl, their nests, and their young. Of the mammals, the most important are skunks, raccoons, red foxes, badgers, ground squirrels (particularly Franklin's), coyotes, mink, and weasels. Dogs, cats, humans, bears, and woodchucks are sometimes involved,

though infrequently.

Among avian predators, crows, magpies, various gulls, and jaegers are most often implicated in predation on nests and young. Hawks and eagles are important predators on both ducklings and adults.

Snakes commonly prey on avian nests but seldom on those of waterfowl. Snapping turtles are known to partake of raw duckling. Pike and muskellunge in northern waters are said to eat ducklings much as you or I would popcorn, and with as much crunching and smacking of lips.

Crows and magpies are particularly important predators in parkland situations with abundant nesting and roosting sites.

Foxes and coyotes are prominent in prairie situations and in highly man-modified habitats. Skunks and raccoons are universally important because of their close association with wetlands in other ways.

The nub of all this is that many factors, such as drought, habitat condition, land use, and predation, control waterfowl productivity, and all are closely interrelated.

There is much we can do to improve waterfowl production that does not demand such drastic and undesirable measures as eliminating local predator populations. We can encourage rest-rotational grazing systems, zero tillage, and stubble mulching to improve upland nesting cover. We can also preserve both wetlands and grasslands, and manage designated areas for intensive waterfowl production. All these measures can have significant beneficial effects for the waterfowl resource, and significant spinoff effects for wildlife in general.

9

Essential Ingredients of Breeding Habitat

R. M. Kaminski

Without adequate space, food, and shelter, ducks, like any other living organisms, simply cannot survive to reproduce. And when we consider the transient nature of waterfowl and the dynamic nature of wetland habitats, we have to acknowledge the problems ducks face in their constant search for suitable habitat. They must be "sampling specialists," forever evaluating habitat quality.

Spring surface water determines the availability of wetland space for breeding ducks. During wet years on the prairies, water inundates the numerous depressions of the landscape and ducks can spread out. Drought forces them to crowd into remaining wetlands or move on to areas (usually more northerly) with better water conditions.

Breeding ducks space themselves because of their need for isolation during the breeding season. The less they're interrupted, the better their chances of success. Ducks in breeding condition are especially intolerant of intrusions by other members of the same species. Drakes zealously defend their mates, and some species even guard critical resources such as food. Male northern shovelers not only defend their mates, but also exhibit classical territorial behavior in defending an exclusive area against other shovelers, thereby enhancing their female's chance for maximum undisturbed feeding within the territory. Clearly, opportunities for securing isolated breeding space are greatly improved for all species in wet years, when many wetlands are available.

Abundant surface water creates a variety of wetland types, ranging from shallow temporarily flooded meadows and ponds to deep permanent marshes. This increased diversity correspondingly broadens the range of food items available to breeding pairs, and the opportunity to secure a balanced and nutrient-rich diet. For example, mallard and pintail can feed on unharvested grain in flooded stubble, as well as forage in shallow flooded meadows that typically harbor abundant aquatic invertebrates.

Although abundant surface water offers real waterfowl benefits, long-term flooding can have negative effects on marshes. Prairie marshes are productive largely because the prairie climate is erratic. Wetlands dry and refill, and periodic drying maintains high levels of productivity.

When a marsh dries out, organic matter decomposes, releasing nutrients previously tied up in dead plants and sediments. This natural fertilizer, coupled with adequate moisture, enables the seeds contained in the wetland sods to germinate. The end product is lush vegetation.

When water returns to a revegetated basin, ducks and other marsh birds resume use. This increases as the impacts of standing water, ice action, and muskrat activity combine to create small natural openings interspersed throughout the vegetation.

However, continued deep flooding and increased muskrat numbers greatly diminish the coverage of emergents like cattail and bulrush. Eventually, the marsh becomes lakelike, with emergent vegetation restricted primarily to the shoreline, and the number and species of breeding ducks decline.

One possible reason for the decline is that lake marshes provide less privacy for breeding pairs than marshes with patchy distribution of vegetation and water. Open lake marshes allow territory-defending drakes to detect intrusions by the same species easier and at greater distances. Unable to secure real estate elsewhere in the marsh, the evicted trespassers move on. The marsh hotel increases occupancy level when it offers plenty of interspersed water and vegetation.

If a lake marsh represents less than ideal habitat, what kind of marsh is ideal? The answer is a hemi-marsh, one with a 50:50 interspersion of emergent vegetation and open water. This provides breeding ducks not only with isolation, but with a situation where aquatic invertebrate food organisms tend to be abundant.

Did you ever enter a living room that lacked chairs or a sofa? Plenty of available space but no place to loaf. Waterfowl also relish an opportunity to "put their feet up" and out of the water. A drake mallard, for example, may keep vigil atop a protruding rock, a short stretch of mud bar, or a muskrat house, while patiently awaiting the return of his mate from the nest. When she returns, they often share the loafing site. Good loafing sites greatly add to the attractiveness of breeding habitat.

The second essential element of habitat is food. Without adequate and readily available food, habitat space is of little use to breeding ducks. For example, despite abundant wetland space in the northern Canadian Shield, breeding duck densities are much lower than in the prairie or parkland because, among other things, adequate food resources are lacking. The erratic climate and the resulting fertility of prairie and parkland wetlands enable these biomes to produce abundant food and thus support much larger breeding populations.

Specialized nutrient requirements during breeding must also be satisfied. Although most ducks feed on vegetation for a substantial part of the year, aquatic invertebrates, specifically aquatic insects

A good example of a hemi-marsh. *Ed Bry photo.*

both larval and adult, snails, and crustaceans, dominate breeding-season diets. These foods, rich in protein and other essential nutrients necessary for egg production, are an essential part of females' diets. Without them, production of eggs, and ultimately ducklings, decreases.

Poor duck production during drought is believed to be linked not only to a basic lack of water but also to invertebrate availability. Wet meadow habitats harboring an abundance of snails and insect larvae are scarce in drought years. A duck attempting to breed in drought-stricken habitat must spend increased time and energy foraging for invertebrates to maintain a balanced, nutritious diet.

Availability of invertebrates is even more important for renesting hens. If a nesting attempt fails late in egg laying or, even worse, during incubation, a hen will have expended a significant portion of her body fat. An abundant invertebrate supply must be available for her to produce another clutch of eggs without excessively drawing on her already depleted energy stores.

When renesting females are confronted with suboptimal water conditions, reduced invertebrate availability, and a shortened brood rearing period, it is not surprising that their production decreases markedly.

The need for a diet rich in invertebrates doesn't end with the nesting season. Ducklings need a high-protein diet to grow

Blue-winged teal on a loafing site. *Ed Bry photo.*

quickly and develop feathers. Similarly, feather replacement in molting adults is aided by a protein-rich diet.

As summer draws to a close in northern latitudes, juvenile and adult ducks switch to vegetative foods to build fat reserves for the southward migration. The number of young recruited into the southward movement will have been largely determined by wetland conditions and food resources on the breeding grounds during the current year.

Cover provided by emergents like cattail, bulrush, sedges, and aquatic grasses is also important. It gives protection to ducks, and particularly ducklings, during inclement weather. It also provides an escape for females pursued by male rape parties, and for flightless young and adults pursued by predators.

Quality and availability of both upland and emergent cover profoundly influence duck nesting density and success. Upland nesting ducks reach highest densities and success in large areas of undisturbed dense cover, because interaction with predators is reduced.

Over-water nesters such as canvasback and redhead also experience increased nesting success in dense emergent cover, especially if it is flooded deep enough to deter predators like raccoons and skunks.

The importance of safe nesting habitat is further underscored by the widespread use of natural and man-made islands by waterfowl. Ducks nest at higher densities on islands than in uplands, particularly when upland cover is limited. Nesting success is also better on islands, apparently because the surrounding water acts as a moat against mammalian predators. And where quality upland cover is limited and predators a threat, traditional upland nesters like the adaptable mallard may even nest over water in dense emergent vegetation for protection.

Wetland habitats in North America are declining at an alarming rate because of competing demands for space from agriculture, industry, and urbanization. Preservation, restoration, development, and maintenance of our wetland resources are urgently needed if productive waterfowl populations are to be sustained. Just as fire requires three integral elements—fuel, oxygen, and ignition—so must habitat provide adequate space, food, and shelter to be of any value to wild ducks.

Man's destructive impact on North American wetland habitats must be restrained if waterfowl breeding, staging, and wintering habitats are to provide these fundamentals in sufficient quantity to ensure the future of the resource. As users of this planet, we must remember the truth of Lester R. Brown's proverb, "We have not inherited the earth from our fathers; we are borrowing it from our children."

10

Nesting, Renesting, Hatching, Brooding

E. G. Hennan

Waterfowl are often treated as one group with certain common characteristics. In many respects this is true, but the capacity for survival of each species depends on the fact that each has evolved to utilize a slightly different portion, in time or in place, of the wetland ecosystem. Each species has its niche, which allows the entire group to successfully share a common habitat — wetlands.

Homing is basic to waterfowl reproductive success. If a hen successfully rears a brood on a chosen pond one year, chances are relatively favorable that she, or her offspring, will be successful there in subsequent years. Wandering in search of new sites in new terrain each year is inefficient, and chances of success are reduced. But exceptions to this homing phenomenon do occur.

Species whose nest-habitat requirements are quite broad, such as the mallard, do tend to pioneer into new areas. Other species whose requirements are relatively specific (cavity-nesting goldeneyes, for instance) have a strong predisposition to home to their natal marshes.

Since most ducks pair annually on their wintering areas, drakes, following their current mate back to her natal marsh, range extensively during their lifetime. This enhances genetic mixing. Canada geese, on the other hand, mate for life, and the population gene pools are relatively closed.

To breeding waterfowl, a wetland must be more than just a body of water. All waterfowl have certain basic requirements: water, space, resting areas, food, protective cover, and seclusion from predators.

Each species has preferences in these components. Pintail prefer open-prairie wetlands; bufflehead like deep boreal ponds; canvasback and ruddy must have marshes with substantial beds of emergent cover; common merganser seek out clear-water rivers with large riparian trees; harlequin return to turbulent mountain streams; and common eider look for tundra lakes with small islands.

Having found appropriate breeding habitat, the hen, usually accompanied by her mate, begins the search for a suitable nest site. She will scrutinize numerous possible sites before she makes her selection. She's looking for just the right tuft of matted grasses, that overhanging rose bush, the muskrat lodge with adjacent patches of cattail, or, in the case of tree nesters, a cavity at just the right height with an opening of traditional dimensions.

Choice of nest sites classifies ducks as upland (or ground) nesters, overwater nesters, or cavity (tree) nesters. Mallard, black duck, pintail, gadwall, wigeon, shoveler, teal, and scaup are typical ground nesters. Redhead, canvasback, and ruddy most commonly nest over water in bulrush or cattail. Ring-neck strike a compromise, typically nesting on floating sedge mats of deepwater ponds. Cavity nesters include wood duck, goldeneye, bufflehead, and common and hooded mergansers.

Further site-selection preferences are exhibited within each of the three categories. Mallard and pintail will nest farther from water than other upland nesters, but mallard select denser nest cover. Gadwall, oldsquaw, eider, and geese prefer islands, so much so that they will nest virtually in colonies. Again, these are the preferences. Very often preferred sites are already taken or are otherwise unavailable, and suboptimal sites must be accepted. Mallard will nest in crows' nests, pintail over water, and goldeneye on cliffs or in holes in the ground.

Some species are more adaptable than others. While adaptability can, in some instances, increase the likelihood of success, generally there is a reproductive advantage in selecting nesting sites typical for the species. Ducks relegated to less than ideal sites stand greater risk of failure during both nesting and brood-rearing phases of reproduction. That loss, in fact, is substantial. Depending on species and environmental factors, continental waterfowl nesting success in a given year may range from 25 to 70 percent.

Two interesting phenomena are associated with nesting activity: nest parasitism and egg "dumping." Parasitism consists of laying eggs in another duck's nest, be it of the same or another species. Such a tactic, from a reproductive standpoint, can be successful only when synchronized with the laying-incubation period of the host duck. Nest parasitism is most commonly associated with redhead, but normal, semiparasitic, and fully parasitic nesting all occur within this species.

Dumping is a loose, careless form of parasitism. Hens of some species will lay eggs in the nearest nest available. Such nests are soon abandoned by the originator, and may receive eggs from several hens—eggs that are wasted. The evolutionary advantage of this behavior, if any, is unclear.

Niches and reproductive success involve time as well as place. The nesting period (including renesting) for all waterfowl species in a single locale may extend from the ice-edged days of mid-March to the sultry days of late July, some 120 to 140 days. This is true of waterfowl breeding at southern latitudes where spring comes early and autumn is leisurely.

In the Arctic, however, no time is lost. Nests are initiated soon after arrival, and successful renesting is a rare event. For example, common eiders breeding along the Gulf of St. Lawrence initiate nests over a period of fifty to sixty days. Those breeding along Arctic Baffin Island begin most nests within a twenty-day period. Obviously, species that breed only in the Arctic are vulnerable to even brief delays in an already late spring.

For midcontinent latitudes, waterfowl biologists speak of early, midseason, and late nesters. The common species are grouped as follows:

Early	Midseason	Late
Pintail	Wigeon	Gadwall
Mallard	Shoveler	Blue-winged teal
Black duck	Green-winged teal	Lesser scaup
Canvasback	Wood duck	Ruddy duck
Goldeneye	Ring-necked duck	White-winged scoter
Hooded merganser	Redhead	
Common merganser	Bufflehead	
Canada goose	Harlequin	

The period during which most clutches of a particular species hatch is approximately in harmony with the appearance of substantial quantities of the preferred foods of the young of that species. This is ecological efficiency.

Differences in nesting chronology among species also help reduce pressure on limited food resources. A brood hatched sooner or later than the optimum period has reduced chances of survival.

Average clutch sizes of North American ducks fall within a remarkably narrow range, roughly seven to ten eggs. Occasional departures from this average, particularly on the plus side, can be quite dramatic. Arctic breeding species have somewhat smaller clutches. Geese and swans average four to five eggs.

Average clutch size has been determined through evolutionary processes. But variations from the mean are induced by environmental factors and individual characteristics. A late spring, or lack of suitable food on traditional spring migration areas, may result in smaller clutches. The hen's diet has a very significant impact on clutch size, hatchability, and duckling survival. The evolutionary determinant of clutch size is thought to be, at least partially, the hen's ability to protect and provide food for the young.

Physiological mechanisms are triggered to terminate egg laying when the clutch is complete. We could almost believe that ducks can count! If eggs are removed during the laying period (eggs are laid at a rate of one to one and a half days per egg), the hen will continue to lay until the physiological drain causes cessation or until other factors, such as the disturbance of the nest, intervene.

Waterfowl biologists differentiate between hatching success, which is the ratio of the number of eggs hatched to the number of eggs laid in successful nests, and nesting success, which is the ratio of successful nests (those hatching at least one egg) to the number of nests initiated.

Some egg loss is inevitable. Again, hereditary factors may be involved, as well as such proximate causes as predation or the accidental dislodging of an egg from the nest. A few eggs are infertile. Hatching success is usually above 90 percent. However, in species that practice nest parasitism, the rates are lower because of asynchrony of egg laying.

Nesting success has been of much greater interest to waterfowl managers because of the greater potential for modifying the factors that reduce it. The potential lies in increasing, in appropriate locations, the amount of preferred nesting habitat secure from predation, flooding, drought, or other dangers. If the success rate were raised by just 1 percent, one million breeding pairs would produce 10,000 more broods, or 50,000 to 60,000 more ducks!

Nesting success varies among species. Those that exhibit rather flexible nesting requirements, or that nest in upland habitat vulnerable to human disturbance, may suffer relatively large losses. These losses are compensated for by a strong renesting propensity. Acceptance of a wide variety of nesting sites is beneficial to a species when traditional sites are scarce. Species with specific nest-habitat requirements, which are not subject to severe impact by man, achieve greater initial success; examples are goldeneye and bufflehead. Species such as canvasback, with specific nest-site requirements that are vulnerable to both natural and human degradation, are in greatest danger.

Waterfowl, with rare exceptions, are single-brood species, but they will renest as many as four times if the clutches are lost in the laying or early incubation stages.

Renesting is critical to the survival of waterfowl in general, but obviously more so for species that typically suffer heavy nest losses. Renesting is more prevalent at southern latitudes than northern, and the tendency is stronger among early-nesting species than late. A strong renesting effort requires that an abundance of good habitat be maintained well into the summer. Thus, in drought years renesting is reduced, partly because of displacement of pairs and partly because of reduced food availability for hens.

As previously mentioned, there are optimum periods for each species to nest and hatch their young, and nesting outside those periods tends to be less successful. It follows that renesting efforts are usually less successful than initial nests. Second and subsequent clutches are usually smaller than the first, possibly a consequence of the deteriorating physiological condition of the hen, or perhaps a matter of evolutionary constraint based on the ability of all young to survive.

But what if both initial clutches and renests could be successful? Waterfowl managers have eagerly applied this concept to enhance duck and goose production. If nests are robbed at an appropriate point during laying, the hen is induced to renest. The eggs of the first clutch are incubated artificially and, just prior to fledging, are released in areas where breeding populations have been depleted or where new wetland habitat has been established. The renest proceeds normally; if it is successful, production from the hen can be almost doubled.

Young ducks and geese leave the nest within twenty-four to forty hours of hatching. The first step into the world by young tree cavity-nesting ducks is breathtaking, sometimes a thirty-foot drop to the ground. But the downy young of all species, imprinted to follow instinctively the voice and form of their mother, undertake remarkable expeditions over rocks and hills, through jungles of weeds and reeds, and across death-dealing highways and railways, in order to reach the brood pond selected by the hen.

Newly hatched mallard ducklings en route to water. *Ducks Unlimited Canada photo.*

Considering the length of a duckling's leg, a kilometer is a very long journey, but they are known to travel much farther. And since the hen does not feed them, they must rely almost entirely on the contents of their yolk sac until they reach water. They must also evade the assiduous eye of the hawk and nose of the coyote throughout the journey.

Of course, not all broods undergo such traumatic journeys. The overall effect, however, is that productivity usually receives yet another blow, since the average brood often loses some of its members en route to water and whole broods are sometimes lost.

To grow and fledge, broods need water of suitable depths, a good distribution of escape cover, safe places to get out of the water to rest and preen, and an abundance of food, especially animal food such as mosquito larvae, freshwater shrimp, and aquatic insects. This high-protein diet is essential for rapid growth and feather development. Gradually this need declines, and a greater proportion of plant food is consumed.

And growth is indeed rapid. Young waterfowl are fully fledged and ready for initial test flights within as few as thirty-four days (green-winged teal) or sixty days (redhead, goldeneye). There is some (but not complete) correlation between the normal hatching peak of a species and the rate of development; late-hatched ducklings grow faster. There is also a relationship between latitude and rate of development. In harmony with shorter summers and longer days, Arctic nesting species tend to develop feathers faster than their southern relatives, although most evidence indicates that they don't take wing any sooner.

The strength of the hen-brood bond varies among species, but generally wanes as the young develop. Early-nesting hens tend to remain longer with their broods than late nesters of the same species, and dabblers longer than divers.

The formation of "gang broods" (sometimes called "creches") is a behavioral phenomenon peculiar to certain species, notably lesser scaup, Canada geese, Barrow's goldeneye, oldsquaw, white-winged scoter, eider, common and red-breasted mergansers, and snow geese. These amalgamated broods, consisting of perhaps ten to more than one hundred young, may be accompanied by one or several adults. Presumably, this behavior provides survival value for these species, but the mechanisms are not clearly understood. Perhaps they are less vulnerable to predation. Because food is of prime importance to developing waterfowl, it is appropriate to speculate that these gang broods may make more efficient use of available food resources.

Considering all the trials and tribulations imposed on waterfowl during the production season, it is a wonder that populations can maintain themselves, and not at all astonishing that many populations and species are in trouble.

To illustrate the effects of increment and attrition, let's mathematically consider a hypothetical "stable" population of one hundred autumn ducks over the course of

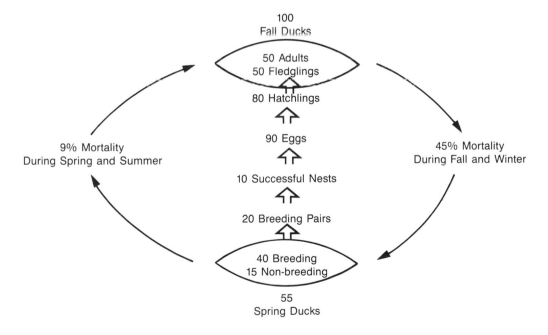

A typical one-year population chain.

a year. Fifty adults and fifty young compose our initial fall flock. During the fall and winter, forty-five are lost through hunting and other forms of mortality, leaving fifty-five to arrive on the breeding marshes next spring.

However, only forty are in breeding condition; assuming a 1:1 sex ratio, that makes just twenty breeding pairs. With a 50 percent nesting success, only ten of these pairs will produce broods (including renesting efforts).

While each of these ten nests may have an average clutch size of nine eggs, only eight are likely to hatch. Between hatching and fledging, a 38 percent loss of ducklings

occurs, leaving only five ducklings per brood, or a total of fifty young. Meanwhile, both the breeding and nonbreeding adults have been reduced from fifty-five to fifty birds by natural mortality. Hence, the fall ratio of young to adults has been reduced again to 1:1.

Of course this is a gross simplification of the biological facts, but it does represent the fundamentals of waterfowl population dynamics. Alteration of any component in this system can dramatically alter all other components, and the population will increase or decrease accordingly. The potential for preserving our waterfowl heritage lies in understanding these mechanisms.

11

Drought-Proofing the Prairies

W. G. Leitch

From a technical standpoint, we can't drought-proof the prairies — yet. Paradoxically, from a long-range waterfowl standpoint, maybe we shouldn't try, particularly when drought isn't, in the long term, the threat to waterfowl it appears to be. The insidious and permanent loss of habitat from human activities is the number one hazard.

But even if we can't control weather (and we must if we are to drought-proof the prairies), it's fun to imagine what might happen if we tried.

Mark Twain once said that everyone talks about the weather but no one does anything about it. To do anything about it, even on a local scale, would take more courage than most of us have. Imagine the controversies: Farmer Brown desperately needs a heavy rain for his sugar beets, but Farmer Smith has a hundred acres of al-

falfa hay in swath and the last thing he wants is rain. Besides, today is the church picnic.

And these are just local problems. Drought-proofing the prairies means climate control, and that, in turn, means interference in natural air mass phenomena, with worldwide implications.

For centuries man has stoically tolerated the natural vagaries of weather and blamed various gods, demons, and space science for his woes. How wonderful it would be to be able to blame a particular individual or nation for our weather miseries. But imagine nations trying to reach an accord on mutually acceptable weather when they can't even agree on simple things. Fooling around with weather might easily bring us more problems than solutions.

Ducks have an innate ability to thrive on

the prairies, and they always have, regardless of periodic drought. Most species mature at one year, lay a large number of eggs, and persistently renest if their first nest is destroyed. They are relatively long-lived, capable of surviving most droughts and then quickly rebuilding to predrought population levels by releasing all that wonderful productivity when water returns to the prairies. Even if a drought is abnormally prolonged, there still remains a basic population scattered thinly across the well-watered north, which repopulates the prairies when water returns.

Continental waterfowl populations have always fluctuated with prairie water conditions. This has been well demonstrated in recent times. The Great Drought of the 1930s brought fears that waterfowling was finished, but by the early 1940s, when good prairie water conditions returned, duck populations bounced back.

This was attributed in some quarters to reduced wartime hunting pressure. However, after relatively poor production years in the late 1940s, populations again rebounded during the wet years of the 1950s, despite greater hunting pressure. Similarly, the poor to mediocre years of the late 1950s and 1960s were followed by greatly increased waterfowl numbers in the early 1970s. In each instance, populations declined in drought years and increased dramatically when water returned.

Strangely enough, waterfowl populations recover rapidly after dry years *because* of drought, rather than in spite of it.

The prairie environment develops and persists in a climate that, by definition, approaches semiaridity and is characteristically drought-prone. The rich prairie soils result from this moisture regime.

Where precipitation is low, little water moves through the soil, and nutrients remain within the plant root zone. Prairie vegetation thus develops a deep humus with abundant nitrogen and phosphorus. Runoff water, flowing over and through these soils, brings a rich load of nutrients to prairie ponds.

Periodic droughts, in the long term, actually preserve ponds by maintaining their basins. Ponds with constant water levels accumulate decaying organic matter at a relatively rapid rate. Under these conditions, fertility declines and the ponds become dominated by plant species of little value to waterfowl. Finally, these basins fill with plant debris. What was once a pond becomes dry land.

But prairie pond bottoms are periodically exposed to the air, and then accumulated organic residues decay rapidly. The result is that about as much organic matter is consumed during dry years as is produced during wet. Because of this, the pond retains its identity.

Drying also converts nutrients bound up in raw organic residues to forms usable by plants. Thus, when prairie ponds refill after a drought, they are highly fertile.

While waterfowl populations will inevitably rise and fall with prairie water conditions, these fluctuations can be made less extreme by building drought-resistant projects such as those developed by Ducks Unlimited across Canada.

In the most recent drought, Ducks Unlimited projects were found to be in much better condition than natural unmanaged wetlands. The U.S. Fish and Wildlife Service reported that 70 percent of the natural ponds present in 1979 were dry by the spring of 1981. Of the 1,100 Ducks Unlimited projects in the affected area, 78 percent had sufficient water to carry broods through to the end of this second drought year. In the spring 53 percent were at the

Periodic drying of wetlands helps maintain long-term productivity. *Ed Bry photo.*

normal full supply level, and 42 percent were still full in July.

The greatest opportunities for drought-resistant project development lie where an assured water supply from irrigation, stream diversions, or large reservoirs can be used to duplicate the natural prairie water regime. Where these water sources exist, quality breeding habitat can be maintained even during long droughts. But these areas must be properly managed to be productive. When the prairies are wet, Ducks Unlimited projects must be revitalized by subjecting them to drawdowns that simulate droughts; when dry, reflooding is carried out to simulate the wet cycles.

Projects built immediately north of the prairie drought zone, where water is more dependable and can be managed specifically for waterfowl, are particularly valuable for drought-displaced prairie ducks. These marshes carry greatly increased waterfowl breeding populations in drought years.

If climate can't be controlled and the opportunities for developing drought-proof habitat are limited, what other opportunities exist to maintain waterfowl populations?

First, we must take a long-range view of the waterfowl resource.

Drought will never eliminate waterfowl or waterfowling. In some years hunters may have disappointing seasons, but other years will be very satisfying. We must learn to accept these natural fluctuations.

Given the vagaries of weather on the prairies, where upward of 70 percent of all ducks are produced, there's no way the same number of birds will zip past hunters' blinds each season. What should concern us is evidence of a continuing long-term decline in waterfowl numbers despite good

water years on the prairies. This will confirm that vital habitat is being permanently destroyed by factors other than drought. If this continues, waterfowl populations will permanently decline to drought levels, with no hope of a comeback — something no one wants to see.

Since man destroys prairie waterfowl habitat by drainage, land leveling, and intensive cultivation, we must look to him for the solution. Difficult as the task may sometimes be, it is still far more important to change public attitudes toward wetlands than to control the weather. Drought is only a temporary loss, but a drained wetland is gone forever.

Preservation of prairie habitat holds the key to future waterfowl populations. Every dam Ducks Unlimited builds establishes a waterfowl right to that piece of habitat. Not all these developments will remain productive through a prolonged drought. But that's not the point. When water returns to the prairies, they will still be there for the birds to use.

Unfortunately, there are relatively few situations where man can create sufficient habitat through construction. The huge numbers of waterfowl produced in wet prairie years come from innumerable privately owned ponds where no development possibilities exist. To preserve these areas, we must convince landowners that it's in their best interest to leave them undisturbed.

Let's learn to live with nature, and accept drought and the lean waterfowl years that go with it as natural events. But let us, on the other hand, use every resource at our command to maintain the potential waterfowl bounty the prairies can provide in wet years.

12

Of Ducks and Dikes

R. W. Coley and J. D. Giles

Bulldozers, hard hats, and concrete seem a world apart from a hen mallard and her ducklings swimming serenely in a quiet marsh. Yet man, through his increasing awareness of the environment and his many efforts to protect and enhance it, is drawing these two alien worlds closer together. That's what Ducks Unlimited is all about.

After standing at the edge of a Ducks Unlimited marsh, people usually retain a lasting impression of marsh vegetation and water. Not so obvious are the engineering works, the dams, channels, and control structures that created the marsh. Half of the funds expended by Ducks Unlimited Canada go toward construction of these works, plus the essential engineering investigations and surveys.

Why spend so much time and money to control water? Why not simply leave the existing marshes in their natural state, and concentrate on securing them by obtaining agreements from landowners?

Dams, dikes, and controls are needed for many reasons; all have a sound biological basis for waterfowl production. Some are needed to keep water in — others to keep it out!

Many marshes on the Canadian prairies have sufficient water in the spring from snow melt and early spring rains. Waterfowl migrate, breed, and nest successfully on these natural marshes. However, as summer progresses and the water evaporates, many become dry, leaving newly hatched ducklings with little chance of survival. Ducks Unlimited constructs dams to store additional spring water, to minimize the effects of evaporation and better assure waterfowl survival.

Ducks Unlimited structures are also

TYPICAL SMALL EARTH DAM

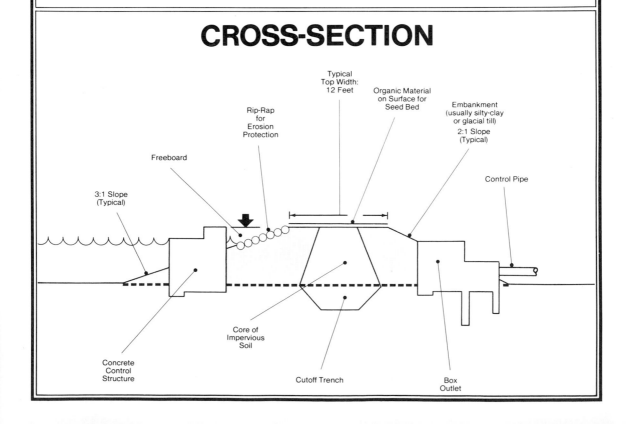

Embankment

Control
Pipe

Natural
Drainage

Box Outlet
With Control Pipe

Emergency
Spillway

CROSS-SECTION

Typical
Top Width:
12 Feet

Rip-Rap
for
Erosion
Protection

Organic Material
on Surface for
Seed Bed

Embankment
(usually silty-clay
or glacial till)
2:1 Slope
(Typical)

Freeboard

Control Pipe

3:1 Slope
(Typical)

Concrete
Control
Structure

Core of
Impervious
Soil

Cutoff Trench

Box
Outlet

Dike construction for the ducks. *Ducks Unlimited Canada photo.*

used to keep water out. Many valuable marshes in Canada are located adjacent to major river or lake systems, which are subject to summer flooding from rains and snow melt, sometimes in distant mountains. Waterfowl arrive at the marsh to breed and nest when water levels are optimum, but before hatching can take place, nearby rivers may swell over their levees into the marshes, submerging nests and destroying the eggs. Dikes built along the levees protect waterfowl nests from flooding.

Usually, working conditions on Ducks Unlimited projects are very wet. Dikes and other structures are built in areas normally avoided by highway or railway engineers. Often soggy soils have to be piled into a dike while the crew is working in water a foot deep. Sometimes the water is too deep, and the work has to be done on the ice. To allow for settling and sloughing, soil often has to be piled 30 or 40 percent

higher than the final elevations.

Control structures are an integral part of a Ducks Unlimited project. These are usually culverts, or steel or concrete overflow structures, with stop-logged controls, which can be used to pass floods through the marsh without raising the water levels significantly, or to manipulate water levels for management of marsh vegetation.

Water-level fluctuation is essential to marsh management. Periodic drawdown and reflooding are important tools, particularly on marshes where natural flood/dry cycles have been disrupted, usually by man-made works, either upstream or downstream. The short dry spell during a drawdown gives the seeds of valuable emergent plants a chance to germinate in the marsh bed. When reflooded, the marsh is benefited by an improved interspersion of open water and vegetation.

Control structures are also used to raise the water level to control excessive cattail growth and the entrenchment of willows or other woody vegetation along the marsh edge.

The type of control structure installed depends on flow conditions. Usually the most economical design is a drop inlet culvert with a stop-log control. An emergency spillway is usually added to take care of extreme flood conditions. In areas where the design flood is relatively high, a steel sheet pile or concrete overflow weir with a section for stop-log controls is used. Where fish migration is significant, fishways are incorporated into the design of the control. Often foundation conditions are so poor that controls must be placed on piles driven to a solid foundation to prevent excessive settlement.

Construction proceeds only after a long series of investigations into the technical viability of a proposed project and negotiations with the landowner, municipality, and provincial authorities.

About three years prior to construction, engineering feasibility studies are made to determine if the project can economically meet biological requirements. These requirements are provided by Ducks Unlimited biologists who recommend the water levels and management techniques needed to maintain and improve waterfowl production on the area. If a prospective project passes these tests, detailed engineering studies then determine the magnitude and frequency of flood and drought, and topographic surveys delineate the marsh basin and locate potential control structures. Soils investigations establish the quality of the foundation and the availability of embankment materials.

These are relatively simple projects. Many are much more complex. Controlling water levels and distribution on complex northern projects calls for a high degree of engineering and construction skills. Extensive projects associated with irrigation water in the south demand a corresponding high level of planning and execution.

At the outset, in response to a current drought, all efforts to preserve breeding grounds were focused on the Canadian prairies where over 70 percent of the ducks are hatched in good years. Soon project planners began eyeing the forest and marshland fringe lying in a broad ribbon above the prairie region. Here were huge marshes in the deltas of very large rivers. While the fertile prairie potholes were the first choice of most discriminating ducks, the extensive marshes to the north were a good second choice, particularly in years of low runoff and rainfall on the prairies.

Wide-angle vision took over in the late 1960s, when British Columbia was added to the Ducks Unlimited territory, followed in quick succession by the Maritime Provinces of New Brunswick, Nova Scotia, and Prince Edward Island, then Ontario and later by "la belle province," Quebec. In January 1985, Yukon, the vast territory next door to Alaska, signed an agreement to join forces with Ducks Unlimited to preserve threatened wetlands in that northern latitude.

Early in 1984, Ducks Unlimited, Inc. introduced a habitat development program in the U.S.A. by expanding into the primary waterfowl production states of Alaska, North Dakota, South Dakota, Minnesota, and Montana. In January 1985, Ducks Unlimited, Inc. also introduced a cost-sharing program with all fifty states for waterfowl habitat enhancement. This program is known as MARSH, which is an acronym for Matching Aid To Restore States Habitat.

Over the years something else has

Stop-log control structure on a Ducks Unlimited project. *Ducks Unlimited Canada photo.*

evolved in waterfowl management. A lot
has been learned about ducks and their
environmental needs. The ecology of
marshes has become a matter of intense
study, and a good deal of information has
been produced.

This new knowledge is now being incorporated into the design of wetland improvement projects, and the projects are
becoming much more sophisticated. The
best vegetation/open water mix will be
carefully maintained for optimum waterfowl production by water-level manipulation. We're no longer satisfied to get water
into a depression and simply hold it there.

Skillful control of marsh water levels
means more food, just the right amount of
cover, and better protection for a greater
variety of waterfowl and wetland wildlife.
It also opens the door to more multiple-use
projects and greater cooperation by groups
of people who are not persuaded that

ducks are the only thing to get enthusiastic
about.

Taking the new management ideas to
large delta marshes, such as Cumberland
in Saskatchewan and the Carrot River
Triangle in northern Manitoba, requires
a coordinating complex of structures to
control water levels in individual segments
of the marshes. The end result is better
production capability for the wetlands, because man is helping nature along, rather
than passively waiting for natural events to
occur at random.

Since 1938, when Ducks Unlimited
Canada received $100,000 for marsh
rebuilding, the organization has spent
approximately $275 million in wetland im-
provement projects. In its 1986 annual report, Ducks Unlimited Canada could
claim 1.9 million acres of habitat developed, including 16,000 shoreline miles.
This necessitated a range of functional

water-holding, water-directing, and water-level control works on approximately 2,900 projects across the country. While much can be said for the contributions made by sportsmen, the success of the vast program must also be credited to 5,000 private landowners and provincial governments who permitted construction to occur simply by concurring to an agreement that allows Ducks Unlimited Canada to use a portion of their lands for a certain number of years. Land sales are not part of the enterprise.

The habitat program in the United States, under the direction of Ducks Unlimited, Inc., has completed 80,000 acres of wetland enhancement after only three years of operation. The MARSH effort boasted of an additional 60,000 acres.

And what about duck numbers? They are still up and down, as Mother Nature demonstrates her fickleness. The U.S. Fish and Wildlife Service estimated the fall flight index to be slightly over 70,000,000 in 1986, which is a pretty good number, considering man's alteration of the landscape through his agriculture, recreation, commercial, industrial, and residential practices.

Man the destroyer is also man the builder, and Ducks Unlimited is building as quickly as it can.

13

Agriculture and Waterfowl

W. F. Cowan

The prairies of Canada and the northcentral United States, some 250,000 square miles, produce more than 70 percent of North America's ducks. Millions of wetlands vary annually in number and quality, depending on precipitation, and breeding duck populations fluctuate accordingly.

Drought is the cyclical generator of waterfowl productivity. Low water levels that restrict nesting effort and reduce production also promote oxidation of pond soils. Subsequent years of abundant water bring vigorous growth of nesting and brood cover and food. Ducks respond readily by increasing breeding effort and producing large numbers of ducklings.

This has always been so. In the wet 1950s, fall flights of adult ducks and their offspring sometimes darkened the prairie skies around large staging marshes such as Delta on the south shore of Lake Manitoba. Then, during the drought of the early 1960s, Canadian and U.S. federal waterfowl surveys showed drastic population reductions. More than a decade of improved, often very wet, conditions followed. Numbers again increased but not to the levels predicted. The continental duck population has never attained predrought numbers. What happened?

Part of the duck problem can be traced to the phenomenal growth of the agricultural industry and intensified land use. Mechanization began in earnest following World War II. Horsepower replaced "horse" power, then big tractors replaced little ones. Present-day giants attain more than 300 horsepower. A burgeoning world population provided markets for western grain; this stimulated research and development, improved crop yields, and promoted extension into less productive

Intensified agriculture is destroying upland nesting cover. *Ducks Unlimited Canada photo.*

lands. The objective: maximize yields from every possible acre.

On southern Canadian farms, where all the high-capability land has long been under cultivation, grain farming is replacing mixed farming. Farmers are draining wetlands, removing vestiges of native cover, and putting pasture and marginal lands into grain and forage production. Meanwhile, the livestock industry is pushing northward into the less productive boreal fringe, where woodlands are cleared

and new frontiers conquered with huge inputs of machinery, chemicals, and fossil fuels.

To grain farmers, wetlands cost money. They provide no income, keep land out of production, and hinder farming operations. Taxes on them must be paid and the extra costs of "farming around" them absorbed.

Attempting to farm wetlands is expensive, and often initiates soil processes that reduce crop growth. Farmers cultivate as close to the water's edge as possible, bringing to the surface water that often contains salt. Without vegetation to consume it, the water spreads like a blotter, forming salt rings that sour the soil. Intensive upland cultivation causes soil and water to fill wetlands and puddle in low spots, spoiling waterfowl habitat and reducing crop production.

The normal reaction to a wetland problem is to get rid of the wetland. Tax deductions and government grants provide incentives; powerful tractors, scrapers, bulldozers, and backhoes provide the muscle. Farmers level the fields, fill the small potholes, and drain the larger sloughs as much as possible. Some consolidate the water on their own land but most run it off to artificial drains.

Intensive grain production impacts severely on waterfowl production. Each spring millions of breeding ducks descend on the pothole-studded agricultural lands of the Canadian prairies and search for nest sites in the previous year's residual vegetation. Dense, erect grasses and herbs with a thatch of older, deteriorating plants give protection against weather and predators.

Early breeders, like mallard and pintail, begin nesting in April and early May. In intensively farmed areas, the only available native cover is in narrow bands around wetlands, along fencelines, roadsides, and rights of way, and in small wooded bluffs and scraps of unused land. In some areas, spring fires eradicate many of these coverts and their complement of duck nests.

Between 25 and 50 percent of upland duck nests are set in cropland stubble. These become traps. In the past, spring

Cultivating to the edge of the pond leaves little cover for nesting ducks. *Ducks Unlimited Canada photo.*

seeding was a prolonged task often delayed by rain. Today's modern machinery can till an entire quarter section in a day. Tillage destroys virtually all the nests; only very early nests hatch, unless extremely wet conditions delay field work. Overall, only about 5 percent produce broods on croplands.

As stubble is plowed down, ducks shift their nesting effort into the remaining native cover. Nests concentrated into these smaller areas are easy for predators to find, and the majority are destroyed. During the 1930s, nest success rates in farmland native cover were consistently above 60 percent. It has since dropped to below 40 percent, and is often only 10 or 20 percent.

As the season progresses, new green growth provides improved cover for late nesters in native vegetation and croplands. However, broods from these nests are generally smaller, and fewer survive because of decreased brood habitat late in the season.

Harvested haylands provide poor cover in early spring, and the success rate is usually very low. But blue-winged teal, mallard, pintail, shoveler, and gadwall will utilize them heavily by late May or early June when growth is well underway.

Native and tame forage plants have different growth characteristics and are managed accordingly. Tame forages may be harvested more than once; in mid-June or early July, and again in August or early September. Native grasses are cut once, just after growth ceases (usually no earlier than mid-July), giving waterfowl nests a better chance of success.

Tame forage fields potentially could produce as many ducks as native hayland. But late nesters (late May or early June) have little chance of bringing off a brood. The majority of ducks require until early July for their eggs to hatch, but mowing is usu-

ally done earlier. Mowing operations and predators destroy practically all nests and some hens as well.

Conversely, farmers mow native hay for the second time later than the first week of July, well after the peak hatch. As a result, more broods survive from late nesters, renesters, or the few successful early nesters in these areas.

Mixed farming is on the wane in much of the parkland. But the total area of pasture is still quite large in some areas of high wetland density. Improved pasture operation would result in better duck production, but economic conditions discourage this potential. The need to produce maximum amounts of beef promotes continuous heavy grazing. Large acreages of pasture, if properly managed, could provide good nesting cover.

Proper management of pastures can be accomplished by adapting a few basic rules to local conditions. The farmer divides his pasture into several smaller paddocks and moves his cattle from one to another over the grazing season. Stocking rate is high, but the grazing period in each paddock is short. Intensive grazing, trampling, and manuring, followed by long rest periods, stimulate vegetative regrowth, similar to the effects of free-ranging bison a century ago. Environmental damage is reduced, and beef production increases. With no grazing on most paddocks during the nesting season, ducks find improved nesting cover over large acreages, reduced predation rates because the nests are dispersed, and improved shoreline cover.

But this is an ideal situation; in reality it is rare. Pastures are managed for beef production, not waterfowl, and nesting ducks must face the consequences. The farmers' objective is to harvest every pound of available forage from every square inch of

Cattle and ducks can coexist at recommended grazing rates. *Ducks Unlimited Canada photo.*

land. Few feel they can afford to leave ungrazed cover as nesting habitat.

Many farmers fail to realize the long-term economic advantage of managing vegetation to sustain high forage yields. Instead, short-term financial benefits of maximum beef production guide them. Overstocking and continuous grazing from early spring to late fall cause deterioration of the better forage plants and add to downstream flooding, sedimentation, and pollution.

Cattle are often released onto pastures much too early in the spring. In the Canadian prairies, new growth of native grass requires until mid-June to replace diminished root reserves. Yet, by early May, cat-

tle are "chasing snowbanks," to nibble off the young shoots as they are uncovered by the melt. All vegetation may be grazed down to a height of only a few inches, leaving little for waterfowl cover.

Severe depletion of upland range forces ducks to concentrate their nesting efforts in lowland cover. Up to 80 percent of nests may be located within 100 feet of the water's edge. Hungry cattle also congregate here for food and shelter, trampling cover and nests. Predators then scrounge with ease. Cattle may also reduce or eliminate aquatic plant and invertebrate communities. Duck production under these conditions is minimal.

Understocking can also reduce duck

production where cattle are left on a pasture over an extended period and at a low stocking rate. They graze preferred plants repeatedly, leaving less palatable species in islandlike patches. Predators search these efficiently and destroy virtually all nests.

Mechanically efficient modern agricultural production is making it more and more difficult for waterfowl to thrive and replenish their number. Population rebounds that historically follow natural drought-inflicted reductions are now less extensive and impressive than in the past. Farm production priorities have caused great reductions in native cover, mechanical destruction of cropland nests, and increased predator effectiveness.

The industrial mentality that demands all-out production at any cost is placing stresses on our resources and threatening the quality of the human environment. Western farmers are facing a worsening economic situation caused, in part, by massive increases in the energy demands of their own technology. It now requires two units of fuel energy to produce one unit of food energy. Agricultural efficiency, rather than bringing prosperity, is becoming North America's greatest problem. The associated duck problem is an early indicator of the growing imbalances that affect the environment, society, and the farming industry itself.

A change in land use objectives is required, indeed necessary. Technology should be applied in ways that utilize soil and water for production without depleting renewable resources and causing economic stresses on farmers and society in general. Conservation-minded government policies, encouraged by an enlightened public, could bring agriculture back toward a balance with nature, and sustain healthy populations of waterfowl for North Americans to enjoy.

14

More Ducks per Acre Through Habitat Management

R. M. Kaminski

Acquisition and preservation of wetland habitat are the most basic management tactics of any natural resources steward. On protected wetlands that are naturally productive, man need intervene no further.

But what about those producing far below their potential? Fortunately, habitat management techniques are available to improve such wetlands for wildlife.

Wetland management techniques fall under two broad categories: natural and artificial. Natural methods are controlled manipulations that mimic natural environmental forces. Examples include water-level regulation, fire, and muskrat population management. Artificial methods are techniques like level ditching, vegetation cutting, and man-made nesting islands.

Whenever possible, wetland managers should take the natural approach. It makes sense to let Mother Nature do the job if she's able. Besides, natural methods are generally more esthetically pleasing and generally produce multi-species benefits.

Let's examine natural and artificial methods in more detail, and consider which works best under various conditions.

Water-level manipulation is a valuable natural technique. Marshes are highly productive systems, especially in the North American prairies where water levels fluctuate through natural wet-dry cycles. While it was once believed that stable water levels were best for marshes and waterfowl, there is now abundant evidence that periodic drying of marsh basins improves the habitat for wildlife.

Consider, for example, Duck Marsh, a hypothetical 300-acre wetland more like a lake than a marsh. If one runs a number of imaginary lines across Duck Marsh, the lines rarely intersect a bulrush or cattail stand; most often these are located along the shoreline.

Because of its lake marsh nature, Duck Marsh supports far less than its potential of marsh wildlife. Research indicates that hemi-marshes, those with a 50:50 interspersion of vegetation and water, are more productive.

With water-level control through a drawdown (dewatering of the marsh), Duck Marsh can be transformed into a productive hemi-marsh.

The procedure involves building a water-level control structure where Duck Marsh drains into a creek. After spring breakup, the control structure will be opened and water will flow out of the marsh. Soon after, Duck Marsh will be completely drawn down as if a natural drought had occurred.

A vast expanse of seemingly ugly mud is exposed. However, by summer's end, with adequate rainfall, the marsh floor will be carpeted by lush green vegetation, with bulrush and cattail predominating. Where did this vegetation come from?

Buried in the marsh bottom, like a hidden treasure, were millions of seeds of bulrush, cattail, and other aquatic plants, the legacy of plants that once thrived in Duck Marsh. When the marsh bottom was exposed to sun and rain, the buried "seed bank" germinated. A successful drawdown was expected, because biologists confirmed beforehand the presence of a rich seed bank.

Following revegetation, which usually takes one to two growing seasons, the control gates are closed and Duck Marsh is allowed to refill, either naturally with runoff water or with water pumped from nearby sources, and soon becomes a "closed marsh."

Responding to this increased food supply, muskrat populations increase, and their feeding and house-building activities create natural openings in the dense vegetation. Increased muskrat populations and higher water levels function in concert to eventually transform Duck Marsh into a hemi-marsh, capable of supporting high marsh-bird densities.

Waterfowl and muskrat benefits from this simulated natural drought will continue for several years. But eventually, the muskrats and increased water levels will take their toll on the marsh vegetation. Duck Marsh will become a lake/marsh again, and it will be time for another drawdown.

Just as water-level regulation can revegetate marshes, it can also be employed to thin out dense emergent vegetation. For example, cattail flourishes in less than one foot of water. Under these conditions, densities often exceed thirty stems per square yard. However, when water levels and muskrat populations are allowed to increase, the marsh will open naturally for marsh-bird use.

When used in conjunction with water-level management, fire is an effective natural tool for opening up vegetation-choked marshes. However, burning should not be permitted during the nesting season, for obvious reasons. The use of fire in northern marshes is in its infancy, but the technique holds promise once careful evaluations are completed.

If, for logistic, economic, or other reasons, natural methods cannot be used to correct habitat deficiencies, artificial techniques like level ditching and over-ice mowing are available to enhance vegetation-water interspersion.

Level ditching involves excavating ditches in overgrown marshes to create

In overgrown marshes, level ditches provide open water for ducks. *Ducks Unlimited Canada photo.*

open-water areas (territorial space) for breeding ducks. Nesting ducks also benefit. The excavated soil, when vegetated, provides suitable nesting habitat. In addition, muskrat populations frequently increase. Instead of building houses, however, "ditch rats" commonly use bank burrows.

A recent Ducks Unlimited Canada evaluation of breeding duck use of level-ditches across the prairie provinces indicates:

- Dabblers, like mallard, blue-winged teal, and northern shoveler, are the principal species using level ditches.

- Breeding pair densities are usually greater on ditches that meander like natural creeks than on straight channels.
- More hens nest on spoil banks that are completely surrounded by the ditches. The ditches seem to function as "moats" to deter nest predators like raccoons and coyotes.

Another artificial technique useful for opening up marshes in northern latitudes is dubbed "over-ice mowing." A tractor-drawn rotary mower is used to cut cattail, for example, after freezeup. The technique is most effective in marshes where adequate water is available in spring to flood the cut stems, suffocating the plants.

Besides enhancing cover-water interspersion, over-ice mowing promotes production of aquatic invertebrates, providing a protein source essential for egg-laying females.

Duck production may still be low in a healthy marsh if suitable nesting habitat is not available nearby. On the breeding grounds, nesting cover preservation and development are valuable management techniques. Extensive research by the U.S. Fish and Wildlife Service shows ducks nest more successfully in dense, undisturbed cover. The studies also indicate that agricultural land can be restored for duck nesting by establishing cover plots of domestic grasses and legumes.

If upland acreages are unavailable, one alternative is artificial nesting structures. Wildlife managers have long been creative architects of nesting structures, using everything from metal rocket-shaped units designed to accommodate one female, to earthen islands (one quarter-acre or more in size) on which many ducks of many species can nest.

Nest boxes are widely used for cavity nesters like wood duck and goldeneye. Pole-top, grass-lined baskets have been erected along shorelines of prairie wetlands to attract nesting mallard. These structures can be very effective if placed in productive wetlands and if measures are taken to ward off egg-robbing predators.

Man-made islands are also a proven means of increasing waterfowl production when nesting cover is limited. Ducks and geese nest more densely and successfully on islands than on mainlands, largely because predators such as coyotes, foxes, skunks, and raccoons are less likely to be threats.

Ducks Unlimited Canada has recently completed a lengthy evaluation of island use by nesting waterfowl in several regions of western Canada. The study revealed that mallard, blue-winged teal, gadwall, and lesser scaup were common nesting species. Canada geese nested on islands primarily in the prairie and the intermountain valleys of British Columbia.

In addition, duck use of Ducks Unlimited earthen islands was greater in prairie and parkland biomes than in the northern forested region, where populations are less dense. Moreover, well-vegetated islands in the prairie and parkland were especially effective when other upland cover was limited or of poor quality, and when islands were located more than 100 yards offshore.

It's specific results like these that help waterfowl biologists to become more skillful habitat managers.

This has been but a glimpse at some techniques used to improve waterfowl breeding habitat. Habitat improvements, whether natural or artificial, must be products of careful planning. Thorough evaluations must precede habitat improvement work to identify major limiting factors, and to quantitatively demonstrate justifiable amounts of proposed improvements. Only through a process like this will habitat improvements prove to be more beneficial than simply preserving the habitat.

15

Interspersed Breeding Marshes: Generators of High-Protein Food

J. W. Nelson

As all who have lived on the prairies know, weather is anything but predictable. Depending on the year, waterfowl arrive each spring to a landscape dominated by seemingly endless water, or to one consisting of a few remnant water pockets and countless acres of parched fields and sloughs.

In this highly variable regime, individual marshes can be dry or flood hundreds of acres. During drier years, cattail and bulrush expand across mudflats and open marshes can become overrun with rank vegetation. When wet conditions return, muskrats move into these newly attractive marshes and begin to open up the vegetation by feeding and building lodges. Their activity, along with continued flooding, creates openings in the overgrowth, allowing the establishment of pondweeds.

But if high water levels persist, the marsh soon again resembles a lake, as it did prior to the onset of dry weather, with only a thin, narrow emergent fringe. Muskrat and breeding duck populations decline, and the remaining pondweeds struggle against the forces of wind and wave.

As might be expected, waterfowl use of marshes is strongly affected by such marked water and plant changes. Marsh managers have long known that both open, windswept lakelike marshes and marshes overgrown with rank vegetation are undesirable for breeding waterfowl. The best situation lies somewhere between.

The preference shown by breeding pairs for habitat of mixed openings and vegetation patches, termed interspersion, has been largely attributed to pair spacing requirements. Evidence now indicates that invertebrates, an essential food source for breeding hens and broods, are most abundant in interspersed habitat, and thus are also an important determinant in breeding habitat selection.

Upon spring arrival on the breeding grounds, pairs go about selecting marshes that combine suitable habitat for nesting, feeding, and brood rearing. The hens, many of whom were raised in the same area during previous years, take the active role in selecting a breeding marsh. Once an area is selected, it is defended from other pairs of the same species by the pair drake.

It is important that breeding habitat rich in invertebrates is selected, because hens must feed heavily on pond invertebrates to obtain the protein required for egg production. Equally important, an abundance of invertebrates must be assured throughout spring and into summer. Because of high nest predation, hens may need a continued source of invertebrates in order to produce an additional clutch of eggs; later on, young ducklings will rely heavily on high-protein diets provided by invertebrates to sustain rapid growth. Apparently, in breeding habitat selection, the pattern of vegetation and flooded openings in a marsh may help hens instinctively predict potential invertebrate food production in the upcoming nesting and brood-rearing season.

Just how the pattern of openings in a marsh relates to invertebrate production is now beginning to be better understood. With further knowledge of the interactions of openings, adjacent stands of marsh vegetation, and invertebrate production, we can gain much insight into how breeding marshes should best be managed. Additionally, the effects on invertebrate populations of removing emergent vegetation such as cattail, through burning, grazing, or other agricultural practices, will also be better known.

What we do know is that stands of rank emergent vegetation such as cattail and bulrush produce enormous quantities of plant debris each year. When these slowly decomposing accumulations are flooded by spring meltwater, they create a diverse underwater complex of substrates ideal for colonization by algae and other micro-organisms. Invertebrates feed on these tiny algal plants, fungi, and bacteria; and at the same time are better protected from wave action and predators in interspersed habitats than in adjacent barren openings. Thus, during wet years when fallen cattail litter surrounding marsh openings is flooded, invertebrate production is high, compared to years of drought, when water levels are low and cattails remain stranded.

Although large amounts of litter might be flooded within an overgrown marsh during wet years, deficient underwater oxygen may limit invertebrate populations in large densely vegetated areas not subject to wave action. As summer approaches, shading by new vegetation reduces the production of oxygen by algae growing on the flooded understory of litter. At the same time, once decomposition of the litter begins, decomposers compete vigorously for any remaining oxygen. Unless the invertebrates involved can tolerate low oxygen supplies, little production will be associated with the interiors of overgrown marshes. Most are probably found near the edges of openings among the flooded complex of substrates provided by plant debris.

However, some invertebrates can withstand low-oxygen conditions, and they are abundant even in shallow ponds choked with plant litter. Many of these, some very important in the diet of waterfowl during spring, breathe oxygen from the pond surface through air tubes. Mosquito larvae are an example of this adaptation to low oxygen levels.

Breeding hens often forage for inverte-

A brood in a marsh that supplies the needs of young, growing ducklings. The aquatic vegetation houses numerous invertebrates that provide a high-protein diet. *Ed Bry photo.*

brates in these small shallow wetlands. However, most are dry early in the summer, and there is little use of them by re-nesting hens and broods except during exceptionally wet years.

Breeding hens, in search of protein-rich invertebrates, concentrate their feeding efforts in areas of flooded litter and along edges of openings during the spring egg-laying period. Invertebrates are very abundant in these areas, and sufficient protein is easily consumed over a short time for egg laying. Pair drakes are especially protective of these areas, chasing other hens and their drakes out of the vicinity.

As summer progresses, water levels decline, and even conditions near the edges of flooded openings may become unsuitable for some invertebrates. However, pondweeds begin to grow during early summer in the openings adjacent to the cattail and bulrush stands. Pondweeds typically have fine-textured leaves and offer algae, microorganisms, and invertebrates a complex of surfaces for colonization, much the same as did the more coarsely textured emergent litter accumulations earlier in the season. Invertebrates find similar protection from predators and abundant food resources among submersed pondweeds in the summer. Production increases as formerly barren openings are transformed into lush beds of pondweeds.

At the same time, summer wave action washes at the edges of shallowly flooded cattail and bulrush stands. This washing carries tiny suspended particles and nutrients from decaying vegetation toward the flooded openings. Filter-feeding invertebrates are able to strain out these fine particles from among the pondweeds. Similarly, the combination of nutrients and ample sunshine provides an abundance of rich algal pastures within the pondweed beds for grazing invertebrates.

Broods begin hatching as pondweed beds are becoming established in the flooded openings. Emerging aquatic insects provide an abundant source of food for the young ducklings feeding within pondweed beds. The adjacent emergent vegetation, formerly important hen feeding areas, now provides broods with dense escape cover close to the productive pondweed areas. Hens commonly guide their broods quietly along the edges of openings, keeping a sharp eye for potential danger.

Large openings are less productive brood-rearing areas than smaller openings interspersed among stands of emergent vegetation. Wave action, associated with large openings on prairie marshes, often prevents pondweeds from becoming well established. Young broods generally use only the peripheral emergent vegetation along edges of large openings. The combination of limited escape cover and few productive feeding areas makes large openings low-quality, brood-rearing habitat for many species of ducks.

Marshes with abundant cattail or other emergent vegetation bordering on numerous small flooded openings that support dense pondweed beds are very productive of invertebrates. If spring melt waters flood the emergent vegetation edges of these openings, the resulting pattern of small openings within the overall emergent vegetation of the marsh may indicate the potential for an abundance of invertebrate foods throughout the season, to pairs selecting breeding areas during early spring. Invertebrates are productive in interspersed marshes because an abundance of emergent–open water edge provides extensive high-quality invertebrate habitat. The many protected openings, common in interspersed marshes, also allow establishment of rich pondweed beds, with their abundant invertebrate communities.

By providing this interspersion of flooded openings and emergent vegetation, marsh managers should be able to maintain productive feeding areas for breeding waterfowl. Water-level control, by simulating natural drought and flooding cycles common to the prairie climate, is commonly used to develop and maintain such interspersion.

Interspersion thus not only provides for pair isolation, nesting, loafing, and brood escape cover, but also an enhanced invertebrate food source. And it encourages increased use not only by breeding waterfowl, but also by a diverse array of other water birds and muskrats.

16

Rehabilitating Northern Marshes

E. E. Mowbray

Some 350 miles north of the Canada–United States border, a series of large wetland complexes stretch 100 miles east and west and 20 miles wide, across the provincial boundary between Saskatchewan and Manitoba. Wooded levees of numerous rivers, creeks, and streams crisscross this 2,000 square miles of bush, shallow lakes, meadows, and fens. (A fen is a low, flat area partially or totally covered with water, and supporting little or no true emergent vegetation. By contrast, a productive marsh is characterized by significant amounts of grasses, bulrush, cattails, and other plants.)

The rivers and creeks through these wetlands play a major role in the region's ecology by frequently overflowing their natural levees during spring runoff and spreading a sheet of water over the huge lowland complex. When river levels drop, water is trapped behind the levees. It recedes slowly

in succeeding months and years because of low evaporation rates, local runoff from rain and melt water, and poor drainage characteristics. Water levels continue to drop slowly until the creeks and rivers overtop their levees once more, and again cause widespread flooding.

This cycle continually repeats itself over the centuries. Flooding is so regular and drainage so poor that the region is always wet—and therein lies the problem. Constant saturation over thousands of years has resulted in peat accumulations of up to ten feet deep in some of Canada's northern marshes.

Peat has a major impact on productivity. It limits fertility by tying up nutrients needed for plant growth. Such areas are widespread in northern Canada, particularly between the northern edge of agriculture and Pre-Cambrian Shield.

Unlike southern marshes, which are re-

Open northern lake surrounded by encroaching fen. *Ducks Unlimited Canada photo.*

juvenated by periodic drying and reflooding, many large northern wetlands seldom dry out enough to complete the life-giving cycle. The open, windswept northern lakes often associated with them can average five feet in depth—too deep for ducks and too shallow for fish. The characteristic lake bed is flat, with water depths nearly as great at the shoreline as in the center. A deep layer of soft organic muck covers the bottom and a steep peat ridge, three to six feet thick, often surrounds the shoreline.

The accumulation of peat in poorly drained northern lowland complexes results in the formation of large floating fens often enclosing numerous shallow lakes of varying size and shape. Most of

the lakes are little used by waterfowl, other than some ring-neck and scaup, because they lack both food and cover.

These large fens develop on floating mats of tangled roots and vegetation up to two feet thick. The constantly saturated mat moves up and down with changing water levels. Plants that can tolerate these conditions—willow, bog birch, sweet gale, sedge, bog bean, and tamarack—offer little to nesting waterfowl.

If a peat ridge has not formed around a lake, the floating fen gradually extends over the water. The lake becomes smaller and eventually, over hundreds of years, becomes covered by the floating mat. It is ultimately transformed into a quaking fen, which may have ten feet of water and organic muck below. The resulting lack of interspersion of land and water, and the lack of diversification of habitat required for nesting and brood rearing, are major obstacles to waterfowl production.

Shorelines are important to ducks, which require both land and water. Land provides nesting habitat and dry places to rest, while water provides food and safety from predators. Physical characteristics of the shoreline, species of plants, presence of nesting sites, depth of water, and availability of food all have a major impact on waterfowl production.

The inadequacies of many of the shallow lakes and the marshes spread across northern Canada can be summed up by their overriding characteristics. They are generally shallow, infertile, and flat-bottomed, with poor shoreline properties and vegetative growth. Constantly saturated fens, unattractive and generally unsuitable for waterfowl use, often surround them. They are in no way similar to productive prairie marshes with gently sloping contours, contiguous dry uplands, lush vegetation, and an abundance of waterfowl food.

Fortunately, northern wetlands have several redeeming qualities that make their development worthwhile. Although they are incapable of producing as many ducks per acre as fertile prairie marshes, they are important for their sheer size and number. In addition, they can be improved by management. If dikes, canals, and control structures are built, the closed systems that resist drainage and perpetuate their saturated unproductive characteristics can be corrected.

Facilities that allow floodwaters to pass quickly through the wetland complex, retaining only enough water to satisfy the requirements of desirable aquatic plants and to create optimum conditions for waterfowl, are the key. They also provide the valuable capability to drain lakes completely, exposing the deep organic muck on the lake beds. When allowed to dry, the soft muck becomes a solid substrate, providing anchorage for rooted aquatic vegetation upon reflooding.

Drainage also promotes decomposition of the bottom organic muck and creates conditions conducive to germination of emergent vegetation. Seeds, which have lain dormant for many years, suddenly sprout, transforming the lake bed into a lush green sea of bulrush, cattail, sweet flag, and burreed. When the seedlings attain sufficient height and density (usually in one or two years), the lake can be refilled to create an inviting environment where ducks will nest and rear their broods.

After draining, establishing emergent vegetation, and refilling, water depths will vary from one to three feet depending upon lake contours, species of plants that have become established, and requirements of waterfowl. Careful management of water levels after a lake is refilled provides optimum conditions for ducks to feed and emergent vegetation to flourish. Submergent vegetation also establishes rapidly in the post-drawdown period, providing food and abundant habitat for invertebrates, an essential protein source for laying hens and developing broods.

Drawdown and refilling provide benefits in addition to re-establishing aquatic vegetation. Drying the organic sediments that have accumulated over many years permits bacterial and fungal decomposition and releases nutrients into the lake for plants established during drawdown. Increased nutrients also provide a lusher environment for invertebrates. Freshwater shrimp, water boatmen, water fleas, clam shrimp, snails, and aquatic insect larvae all provide food for waterfowl.

The techniques described here successfully transform unproductive northern marshes into good waterfowl habitat. Dams, dikes, and control structures help provide the rejuvenating cycle of wet and dry that maintains productivity in southern marshes. Northern habitat can also be further enhanced by the construction of nesting islands. These provide dry nesting habitat, pair sites, and dry places to which hens can take their broods.

But the greatest challenge in managing northern wetlands is transforming the large, floating fens into lush, dry nesting habitat. The accumulation of peat in fens and its tenacious water-holding capacity poses the greatest obstacle to management. Drawdown and water-level management readily transform shallow lakes into productive marshes. Large fens, on the other hand, resist drainage and peat decomposition, making it more difficult to establish dry nesting sites and desirable vegetation for upland nesting.

A strange machine called a cookie cutter, originally used to clear water hyacinth from canals in Florida, has found a place in the management of such northern fens. The cookie cutter chews a ditch six feet wide and three feet deep, and can be used to create a network of creeklike channels throughout the huge expanses of fen. These canals are connected to the lakes, and ducks can thus penetrate deep into fens for breeding activities and nesting.

Drier conditions caused by drawdowns and reduced water levels in the lakes, coupled with many miles of cookie cutter canals, improve plant composition and vigor and also land and water interspersion. Improved nesting habitat increases waterfowl use, and the narrow fen canals allow hens to move their broods easily to the food and shelter developed in the lake.

As agricultural pressure continues to increase on southern wetlands, it is imperative that the northern habitat be developed to its fullest potential.

17

A New Look at
U.S. Duck Production

J. M. Hyland

For many years waterfowl hunters in the United States relied on their Canadian neighbors to provide the greater share of the annual duck production needed to maintain North American populations. Since 1975 the annual breeding waterfowl survey has indicated that 70 percent of the duck breeding population, and 75 percent of the mallard breeding population, is in Canadian production areas. Until recently, this disparity was acceptable, even though not entirely satisfactory, to our Canadian friends.

It was acceptable because the human population and demands on land and waterfowl resources in Canada were much less than in the United States. During the past twenty to thirty years these conditions have changed. Accelerated development of industrial and agricultural technology and an increase in the population of both Can-

ada and the United States have created new demands on land and waterfowl.

Rapid growth in the United States after World War II was accompanied by a tremendous loss of wetlands and associated upland cover needed to produce ducks. This placed additional pressure on Canadian production areas to offset U.S. losses.

Until recently, Canadian production during wet years was able to compensate for the loss of U.S. production, and major or long-term declines in the number of ducks coming south each year were postponed. This make-up production was possible because of land-use practices in Canada. A wetland in the Canadian prairie or parkland regions more than likely was surrounded, or at least accompanied, by adequate upland nesting cover, which provided security for nesting hens and ensured good nesting success. In years when enough water remained to provide brood habitat, a relatively high proportion of young survived to migrate south in the fall.

As early as the drought years of the 1930s the dependence of waterfowl on wetland habitat, and the need to preserve it, were recognized. It resulted in the federal duck stamp and the organization of a private fund-raising group, Ducks Unlimited. These public and private programs to save waterfowl habitat actually began before many people realized or accepted that a need existed. Funds generated by the sale of duck stamps were used to acquire, preserve, and manage waterfowl habitat in the United States. Early duck-stamp dollars were used primarily to establish refuges in the United States. Ducks Unlimited took on the job of raising funds to preserve and develop wetland habitat in Canada.

This two-pronged approach was reasonable and commendable under the circumstances. Though slightly different in approach, both efforts addressed the problem of dwindling wetland habitat.

Accompanying these moves to preserve habitat, hunting regulations were designed to reflect changes in the supply of ducks as established by annual surveys. Fewer ducks resulted in shorter seasons or reduced bag limits, or both; more ducks permitted the converse.

This system worked well for a period of years. The number of ducks produced continued to vary with wet and dry conditions. Losses suffered in dry years were regained when wet years restored the Canadian production areas to their full potential, with ponds, potholes, and nesting cover in abundance.

During this period wetlands continued to be lost at an increasing rate, and by the mid 1960s exceeded the capacity of waterfowl habitat programs to maintain duck

populations at desired levels. Existing programs were expanded and new ones initiated. Congress established the Small Wetlands Acquisition Program by advancing a loan to the U.S. Fish and Wildlife Service. This money was to acquire, in fee title or by easement, those small wetlands important to duck production. Legislation was enacted to protect wetlands from destruction and degradation. The price of duck stamps was increased. Ducks Unlimited raised more money for waterfowl habitat in Canadian production areas, and increased its efforts to protect essential habitat there.

During this same time, Canadian and U.S. waterfowl research and surveys were intensified, hoping for answers and programs that would help maintain duck populations. But all this extra effort on behalf of North American waterfowl and waterfowlers was nullified by changes in agriculture, which would have been difficult, if not impossible, to foresee back in 1945 or even 1950.

The 1950s approach toward managing North American waterfowl would probably still be adequate were it not for this dramatic change in agriculture brought about by a swelling human population, changing economic conditions, and more sophisticated technology.

These changes occurred earlier, and probably more gradually, in the U.S. production areas. In recent years the same changes have come to the prairie and parkland of Canada. Now, even during wet years, there are fewer ponds to hold water. Equally important is the decline in secure nesting cover essential for hens to nest successfully. It is the size and number of broods that determine the magnitude of the fall flight and next spring's breeding population. They are the replacements for

A good marsh with good cover for hens and broods. *Ed Bry photo.*

ducks lost each year to a variety of causes.

This loss of nesting cover in Canada creates the need to take a second look at U.S. production areas. Preservation and development of wetlands to carry duck populations through years of drought is still a critical need, but is no longer enough. Now when wet years return to the prairie and the remaining ponds fill with water, they are not only fewer in numbers but are surrounded by cultivated cropland instead of the secure nesting cover pro-

vided by native plants. The high quantity and quality of nesting cover, once synonymous with Canadian wetlands, has been reduced to a mere fringe around the ponds. Though ponds may remain and attract breeding ducks, any attempt by a hen to nest in the remnant cover is likely to fail and, in some cases, even result in her death.

Agricultural operations, such as cultivation or mowing, account directly for part of the toll. Indirectly, predators are able to concentrate on the few remaining areas of suitable cover with increased efficiency. Hen mallards seldom come out the winner in a confrontation with a fox, raccoon or skunk. Eggs never do.

All the adversities breeding ducks have faced for several decades in the United States are now facing them in Canada. This has narrowed the advantage Canadian production areas had over those in the United States, and caused waterfowl managers to consider intensive nesting cover management as an alternative to the extensive practices that were successful in the past.

Increasingly we are seeing the benefit of providing secure nesting conditions in areas attractive to breeding ducks, or attracting breeding ducks to areas with secure nesting conditions. Techniques for doing this are already available to waterfowl managers, and new methods are being developed to keep pace with the need. Construction of islands and artificial nesting structures has proven to be highly beneficial in some areas. Predator-resistant barriers, such as woven wire or electric fences, also show promise for improving nest success. Manipulating cover vegetation by seeding, burning, or deferred rotation grazing can be helpful in some cases.

Implementing some of these practices will require further acquisition or special easements, and thus be more expensive than others. Some areas remain where nesting success is relatively good. These areas must be maintained or enhanced through wetland preservation and development. Many occur within the U.S. portion of the North American duck production area, the prairie pothole country of the Dakotas, eastern Montana, and western Minnesota. These U.S. production areas have regained a prominent role as poten-

tially significant contributors to the annual supply of ducks. There are two underlying reasons for this return to prominence; one relates to the ducks themselves, the other is primarily economic.

With agricultural intensification in Canada during the last thirty years, the cost of preserving or restoring wetlands there has risen sharply. A hypothetical example will illustrate this point.

It is 1950 and we have two areas with equally good duck production potential. One is in the Prairie Provinces of Canada and the other in North Dakota. The U.S. wetland can be saved from further deterioration by acquisition and constructing a dike and a water-level control structure. But the waterfowl production potential will be realized only if construction is complemented by acquisition of enough surrounding land to establish the quantity and quality of nesting cover required for safe nesting by hens attracted to the wetland.

The 1950 version of the Canadian wetland requires only those actions needed to protect the wetland as it exists. Nesting cover is already present, and no further acquisition is necessary for the area to realize its full duck production potential. It's obvious that if we want the most ducks for our dollars, we should spend the money on wetland areas requiring the least expenditure to produce an equal number of ducks.

The second half of the example takes place in 1987. We again have the choice of two wetlands. They are located as before and have equal potential for producing ducks. The U.S. area will still require all the inputs described for the 1950 example to realize its duck production potential. Because of intensification of agricultural practices, the Canadian wetland will also now require nearly the same inputs as the

U.S. area to attain its potential. Furthermore, this development may cost more in Canada than it does in the United States because alternatives for construction and cover establishment, in this instance, may be more limited than they are in the States. In contrast to 1950, it is entirely possible that we may get more ducks for our 1987 dollars by choosing to spend the dollars on the U.S. area.

The second reason for renewed interest in U.S. waterfowl production areas is not quite as simple to demonstrate. Ducks are more complex than dollars, a virtue that probably accounts for the lifelong interest waterfowlers tend to maintain in these unique birds.

Research has provided us with at least a limited understanding of ducks and how they might be expected to respond to certain conditions. We now have some tools that will be useful in maintaining populations. For instance, most ducks, at least the females, demonstrate a strong homing tendency. They usually return to the area in which they were hatched or were last successful in hatching young of their own.

This homing instinct, however, is tempered by opportunism. When poor water conditions in the Dakotas, Montana, and southern Canada provide little attraction to breeding ducks, they continue north to breeding grounds many have not used before. On the other hand, there have been good water years in the United States when ducks, which normally would have continued on to Canadian production areas, apparently could not resist the opportunity to take advantage of the excellent water conditions available to them en route.

It is believed that breeding ducks coming north in the spring will tend to fill available breeding habitat from south to north. This may be particularly true of yearling females nesting for the first time. This belief is supported by the results of breeding populations surveys over the years, which included both wet and dry periods in the various production areas.

Present waterfowl habitat programs must be continued and expanded to include new production areas. We must move into the intensive management required to maintain duck populations in our high-tech world of today.

The agricultural and industrial technology, which has made increased crop production possible, has created a hostile environment for breeding ducks in both Canada and the United States. Ducks will be able to maintain their present numbers in this environment only with our help. This help is needed throughout the breeding range. But the areas that can produce the best return on our investment may very well include many right here in this country. The ponds, potholes, and marshes of the Dakotas, Montana, and Minnesota have the potential to produce significant numbers of ducks under intensive management.

This intensive management requirement is no longer exclusive to Ducks Unlimited projects. It is required for many Canadian areas if they are to produce ducks at desired levels. This approach has a high probability of success, but it will not be easy or cheap. It will require a coordinated effort by all the people, organizations, and agencies involved with waterfowl management.

Glenn D. Chambers
1986

Part III
Fall and Migration

Late summer and early fall are pleasant times for waterfowl. The problems and perils of the breeding season are past; the days are warm and food abundant. Birds of the year strengthen their wings for migration; flocks begin to build on traditional staging areas, sorting into flocks of their own species in preparation for migration—when triggered by tradition or weather.

18

Spring, Fall, and Migration Staging

W. G. Leitch
with
T. R. Gadawski, Ducks Unlimited provincial biologist, Ontario
P. Plante, Ducks Unlimited provincial biologist, Quebec
R. K. McAloney, Ducks Unlimited provincial biologist, Maritime Provinces

Ducks are fond of their kinfolk. So, except for a short period in spring and early summer when they seek solitude for family affairs, gatherings of kith and kin are the normal thing.

But they don't flock simply because they like one another's company. Rather, natural selection has determined that there is safety in numbers and they'll live longer if they stick together, so they do so instinctively. After all, a hundred pairs of eyes are more likely to see danger than one. And flocks react to the wariest bird.

Although flocking is effective survival behavior, it has its negative aspects, too. When a hunter puts out decoys, he's taking advantage of this instinct. Fortunately for the ducks, the old birds know a thing or two about decoys and blinds. After a poor breeding year on the prairies, southern hunters complain the birds fly high and won't decoy.

Darn right, they won't!

There are a lot of old birds in those flocks, and they've been that route before. Young birds, by themselves, are suckers, but if they survive, they learn the lesson well.

The flocking instinct also works against waterfowl when a hostile environment produces crowding and stress, making them susceptible to disease epidemics. Large numbers of dead and dying ducks in a botulism outbreak only attract other ducks to a similar fate. One of the problems in controlling these outbreaks is to devise ways to keep healthy birds away from affected areas.

Since nature, by the selection process, demonstrates that togetherness is beneficial for ducks, suitable areas for them to congregate for spring dispersal, molting, and fall staging are essential parts of total annual waterfowl habitat requirements. In reality, however, few areas provide suitable habitat for all functions. Some may provide only fall staging while other marshes are used for nesting and molting as well.

Spring concentrations are usually more dispersed than those of autumn. This is because, in part, spring sexual tensions are beginning to demand isolation, but also because there is usually much more water on the prairies in the spring. Also, when the early migrants—the mallard, Canada goose, and pintail—return in the spring, the previous fall's staging areas are often still ice-bound. The only open water is often shallow sheet water on cultivated fields from local snow melt. This is sometimes abundant and covers large areas, providing the opportunity for wide dispersal.

Spectacular spring concentrations do occur if a late freeze closes most water areas, or if drought limits water availability to permanent areas offering open water along the ice edge.

Later migrants—blue-winged teal, shoveler, wigeon, gadwall, and the divers, such as canvasback, redhead and scaup—usually find sufficient open water in larger permanent marshes before dispersing to smaller water areas to nest.

During spring and early summer, waterfowl populations on staging areas are reduced to the breeding pairs nesting there, and the overall population will be at its lowest seasonal level. This wide dispersal of waterfowl during the nesting season is an aspect of waterfowl biology that often perplexes those seeing the prairie nesting ground for the first time. Accustomed to the concentrations characteristic of the southern wintering grounds, they often find the apparent lack of ducks disappointing and confusing.

But this is short-lived. By mid-June, these large marshes will begin to fill once more with drakes and unsuccessful hens returning to molt.

The molt is a stressful period for waterfowl, which are unique in that they molt their flight feathers all at one time. For a period of three to four weeks, they are flightless. Successful hens, which raised broods, molt after the brood reaches flight and often in the same area where the brood was raised.

Most surface-feeding ducks seek the security of large marshes with abundant food and cover for the molt. Flocks of molting drakes of many species are a common sight on many prairie marshes, and may be presumed to be of relatively local origin.

Diving ducks, on the other hand, make a distinct molt migration to large, shallow, fertile lakes between the northern fringe of agriculture and the Pre-Cambrian Shield. Here large numbers of molting canvasback and redhead are found, far north of their breeding range, along with great populations of scaup.

Prairie-breeding Canada geese make an even longer molt migration. While successful breeding pairs molt where they nest and raise their young, immatures and unsuccessful pairs migrate to the rivers and lakes of the Arctic barrens, where they gather in large flocks to molt.

Molting concentrations regain flight and gradually become premigration or staging flocks as the season progresses and the young of the year and successful females, once more on the wing, join them.

Summer flocks are often composed of many species, but on the staging areas the birds begin to sort themselves into flocks by species, in preparation for migration. During this time, they accumulate fat for migration—almost analagous to gassing up for a long trip — so a staging area must supply sufficient food, not only for the resident population but for successive waves of southbound migrants.

Mallard, some pintail and wigeon, and geese, have learned to field feed, and are not so completely dependant on marshes for food. Consequently, staging flocks of these species are found in a wide variety of habitats, including large, open, saline lakes, reservoirs, and river sandbars — in fact, wherever they find safe open shorelines for midday and night roosting. Many of these wetlands, because of their size, depth, or high salinity, remain open after natural marshes freeze. Waterfowl continue to use them until snow covers the fields, forcing them to migrate.

Western Canada's prairies and parklands provide abundant staging habitat of all types, but there is a great difference in the annual use. Some are traditional and used year after year; others develop to exploit a local food source, and others emerge in response to current migration patterns.

The deltas of the great northern rivers — Saskatchewan, Peace-Athabasca, Hay, and Mackenzie — provide local staging areas and stepping stones southward for Arctic-breeding ducks, geese, and swans. In 1971 the Peace-Athabasca Delta was estimated to provide spring staging for over 400,000 ducks and 145,000 geese and swans northbound to nest. The fall population was estimated at 1,200,000 ducks and 166,000 geese and swans.

Each province has its traditional staging areas. These are usually well known because they also provide good hunting.

In British Columbia, important staging marshes are found in the Chilcotin and Cariboo regions of the intermountain Fraser Plateau, and in the north-south river

valley corridors. The 50,000-acre Columbia River floodplain provides extensive migration habitat, and the Creston Valley, at the mouth of the Kootenay River, is a major stopover for ducks, geese, and swans.

Along the coast, the main staging areas are the estuaries at the heads of northern fjords and the coastal plains of northern Queen Charlotte Islands. But the Fraser River Delta opposite Vancouver Island is by far the most important and provides both staging and wintering for ducks and geese.

In addition to such well-known northern staging areas as the Hay Lakes and Peace-Athabasca Delta in northern Alberta and the Saskatchewan River Delta in Saskatchewan, both provinces have a plethora of large marshes and open-shored alkaline lakes, providing abundant staging habitat the length of the provinces. The extent to which each area is used in any year depends on water conditions and local feeding opportunity.

New water impounds built for purposes other than waterfowl use often have a profound effect on waterfowl distribution. Lake Diefenbaker on the South Saskatchewan River in westcentral Saskatchewan is an interesting example.

Prior to construction, sandbars on this section of the river staged large numbers of "short grass prairie" Canada geese, and the small lakes and grainfields lying to the north in the Kindersley-Kerrobert area had an international reputation as the "white-front capital." Immediately to the west, in the Hanna-Alberta district, large numbers of snow geese dominated fall staging populations.

With the formation of Lake Diefenbaker in 1968 these staging patterns began a change. The small Canadas moved up-

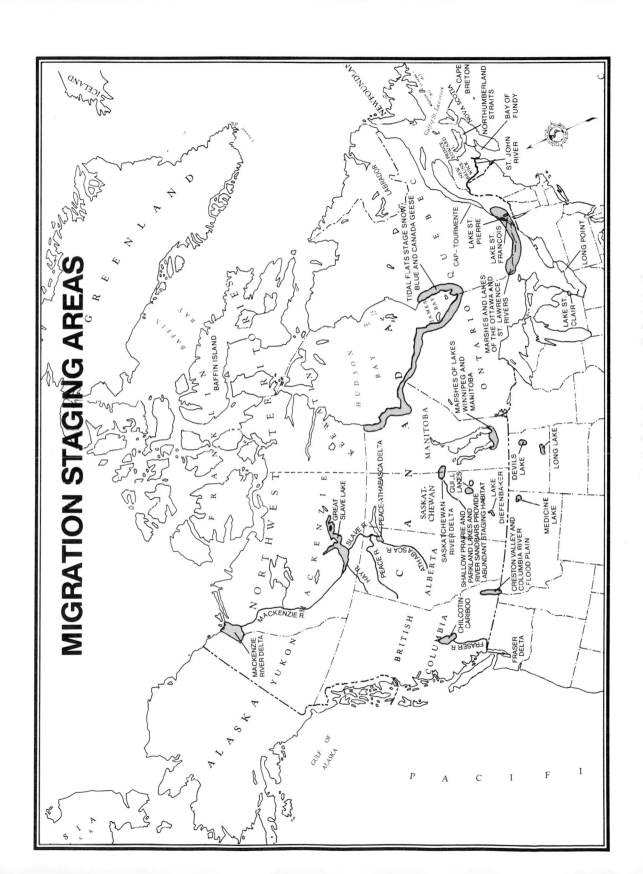

MIGRATION STAGING AREAS

ICELAND

GREENLAND

BAFFIN ISLAND

FRANKLIN DISTRICT

NORTHWEST TERRITORIES

KEEWATIN

HUDSON BAY

JAMES BAY

LABRADOR

NEWFOUNDLAND

Gulf of St. Lawrence

CAPE BRETON
NOVA SCOTIA
PRINCE EDWARD ISLAND
NEW BRUNSWICK
NORTHUMBERLAND STRAITS
BAY OF FUNDY
ST. JOHN RIVER

QUEBEC

ONTARIO

CAP-TOURMENTE
LAKE ST. PIERRE
LAKE ST. FRANCOIS
MARSHES AND LAKES OF THE OTTAWA AND ST. LAWRENCE RIVERS
LONG POINT
LAKE ST. CLAIR

TIDAL FLATS STAGE SNOW, BLUE AND CANADA GEESE

MARSHES OF LAKES WINNIPEG AND MANITOBA

MANITOBA

PEACE-ATHABASCA DELTA

GREAT SLAVE LAKE
SLAVE R.
MACKENZIE R.
MACKENZIE RIVER DELTA

ALASKA
YUKON

BAFFIN BAY

C A N A D A

SASKAT-CHEWAN
SASKATCHEWAN RIVER DELTA

QUILL LAKES

DEVILS LAKE
LAKE DIEFENBAKER
LONG LAKE
MEDICINE LAKE

SHALLOW PRAIRIE AND PARKLAND LAKES AND RIVER SANDBARS PROVIDE ABUNDANT STAGING HABITAT

CRESTON VALLEY AND COLUMBIA RIVER FLOOD PLAIN

ALBERTA
ATHABASCA R.
PEACE R.
HAY R.

BRITISH COLUMBIA

CHILCOTIN-CARIBOO

FRASER R.
FRASER DELTA

GULF OF ALASKA

PACIFI

SIBERIA
U.S.S.R.

stream in search of sandbars, and the white-front almost totally moved south from the small lakes to the forebay of the new reservoir. This was followed by an eastward movement of snow geese into the lakes vacated by the white-front; unlike two decades ago, snow geese are now also a common sight to goose hunters along the Saskatchewan River, where the blue component of the population continues to increase.

Large alkaline lakes, which are the last to freeze, frequently hold spectacular numbers of waterfowl for a few days after the freshwater marshes are frozen. The Quill Lakes in central Saskatchewan are a prime example.

The sandbars of the Red Deer River in Alberta and the South Saskatchewan in Saskatchewan hold large numbers of staging Canada geese.

As in Canada, ducks produced in the prairie breeding habitat of the central United States must congregate somewhere before the whisper of north wind sends them southward. Well-known staging areas in this pothole country of the United States include Devil's Lake and Long Lake National Wildlife Refuge in North Dakota and Medicine Lake National Wildlife Refuge in Montana.

Although staging occurs on many lakes scattered throughout this region, the larger ones draw more attention by virtue of

Large alkaline lakes, the last to freeze, sometimes hold spectacular numbers of ducks. *Ducks Unlimited Canada photo.*

sheer numbers of waterfowl congregated. As in Canada, most ducks prefer a lake with a sloping shoreline and one that is usually open along some portion of that shoreline.

Manitoba's major staging areas include Lakes Winnipegosis, Manitoba, and Winnipeg; their marshes, many thousands of acres in extent, are internationally renowned. The 2,500 square miles of the Saskatchewan River Delta supports large numbers of staging waterfowl, probably more than the Peace-Athabasca Delta.

Manitoba's share of the Hudson Bay shoreline also stages large numbers of snow, blue, and Canada geese, as they move slowly southward along the coast. Geese moving along both coasts of Hudson Bay and from the Arctic islands congregate in spectacular numbers at the south end of James Bay, the southern extension of Hudson Bay, from whence some snow and blue geese begin a nonstop flight to the marshes of Louisiana.

In Ontario, in addition to the James Bay concentration, the shorelines of the Great Lakes are vital to staging continental waterfowl populations. The long tradition of migratory use of these areas is most pronounced during the fall, as tens of thousands of Mississippi and Atlantic Flyway birds linger on their way south.

The marshes and shallow bays associated with Long Point on Lake Erie and the upper shore of Lake St. Clair are of particular importance. These two areas play host to the majority of waterfowl species indigenous to North America, including most dabbling, diving, and sea ducks and large numbers of geese and swans. Long Point and Lake St. Clair are among the most important continental staging areas for canvasback, redhead, and scaup, which are attracted by the lush submergent beds of plants such as wild celery and sago pondweed. The arrival of the "cans and reds" is a highlight of the migration.

The marshes associated with the floodplains of the St. Lawrence and Ottawa rivers provide Quebec's best staging habitat. The large, shallow lakes along the St. Lawrence — lac St. Pierre, lac St. Francois, lac St. Louis, and lac des Deux Montagnes — are important, lac St. Pierre particularly for Canada geese and scaup.

The tidal flats at Cap-Tourmente on the St. Lawrence River host virtually the continent's entire population of greater snow geese both spring and fall as they migrate between their U.S. East Coast wintering grounds and their Baffin Island nesting grounds.

Many of the tidal salt marshes of the Maritimes, particularly those on the Bay of Fundy, Northumberland Straits, and in the Yarmouth area, provide staging and wintering habitat for Canada geese, black duck, and goldeneye. The extensive floodplains of the St. John River in New Brunswick are important staging areas for blacks and wood duck.

Staging areas are important for waterfowl but also for people. Ducks and geese are exciting because they can so often be seen in such great numbers. On staging areas, hunters, naturalists, and even casual observers thrill to the sight and sounds of great masses of birds as they gather for migration. For a short period, rare in our time, one can be caught up in the pulse of nature and overwhelmed by a great natural drama in which man has no part.

It humbles us when our vanity lets us believe nature is our plaything.

19

Fall Migration: Moving Out

R. T. Sterling
with
T. R. Gadawski, Ducks Unlimited provincial biologist, Ontario
P. Plante, Ducks Unlimited provincial biologist, Quebec
R. K. McAloney, Ducks Unlimited biologist, Maritime Provinces

Waterfowl migration is a fascinating and gratifying reminder of our inherent bond with nature. The resonant calls of geese in flight or a silent wedge of ducks cleaving the sky arouse, at the very least, a fleeting moment of satisfaction and wonder at their passage. They may thrill us with promise of spring, the nostalgia of a season's ending, or simply the comforting thought that the natural world is still with us in all its intriguing wonder.

The mystery of waterfowl migration stimulates man's historical curiosity about the life of birds. It poses perplexing questions of how migration evolved and how the birds time their departures, know where to go, and find their way. Modern science has only partial answers. Some of the mystery will likely always remain.

Simply defined, waterfowl migration is the annual spring and fall movement of a population between its breeding and wintering ranges. Generally, a specific population will use the same routes and be found in the same locality at approximately the same time each year. The consistency and orderliness with which waterfowl accomplish this feat, involving nearly a hundred million ducks and geese in any fall, is inherent within them.

Migration has obvious survival values. Anyone who has experienced the ruthless cold of a prairie winter, where most of the common species breed, will agree to the wisdom, if not the necessity, of an autumn move to a less hostile climate.

One migration theory suggests that wintering areas were once the ancestral home, but because of competition for space and food during the breeding season, the annual rhythm of spring dispersal to unoccupied habitat in the north evolved. A more commonly held theory is that migration is triggered by an innate desire to return to a northern ancestral home. This theory assumes that the northern breeding grounds, once the home of nonmigratory species, were made uninhabitable during the Pleistocene Ice Age. They now return because present climatic conditions permit.

Support for either theory can be found in waterfowl migration patterns. But in either case, by exploiting their mobility, waterfowl can more efficiently utilize the total habitat available to them. For the breeding season, they return to the northern latitudes where myriad fertile marshes, long daylight hours, and high temperatures produce an abundance of foods essential to egg laying and brood development. In addition to maximizing reproductive potential, the rotational use of the habitat relieves pressure on southern food supplies and allows higher populations to be supported throughout all seasons.

We know cold weather triggers fall migration in some species, but the stimulus for early migrating species is not so certain. Most puzzling is the late summer departure of blue-winged teal, which leave the breeding grounds in balmy weather while food is still abundant. Similarly, pintail, which challenge winter's icy grip without hesitation in the spring, usually leave for the Deep South well before the first hard autumn frosts.

These early migrants also winter farther south than other species that share their breeding marshes. Most blue-winged teal winter in Central and South America as far south as Brazil. Pintail winter mainly in California, along the Gulf Coast, and from Mexico to Colombia.

Mid-fall migrants—the Arctic nesting geese, prairie-breeding wigeon, gadwall, shoveler, canvasback, and redheads—also

seem to have an internal clock that prompts them to leave at about the same time each year.

Physiological condition and shortening days are apparently the principal stimuli inducing these species to migrate. In contrast, late season migrants—major segments of the mallard and scaup populations and large races of Canada geese—are more inclined to be weather migrants, lingering in the north until freezeup. Even then, some hardy flocks will move only far enough south to find tolerable conditions. If the cold spell is early in the season and short-lived, they may shift north again until cold or snow once more forces them out.

Faced with a lifetime of travel, how then does each bird find its way? Mostly by learning from adult companions, but the ability is also innate and inexperienced young can find their way unaided.

Ducks and geese recognize familiar landmarks in their local flight patterns and in homing to breeding and wintering habitat sites. Major landscape features such as coastlines, lakeshores, river valleys, and mountain ranges provide clues to general flight direction. For example, some migration landmarks, such as the confluence of major rivers, are prominent divisional points where flock members will part company and continue on different courses.

However, experiments have shown that migratory orientation is also instinctive. Ducks and geese are capable of crossing vast expanses of featureless terrain and trackless water to reach their destinations. Blue-winged teal cross the 1,000-kilometer Gulf of Mexico. Pintail unerringly travel thousands of ocean kilometers between Alaskan and Hawaiian Island breeding and wintering areas. Celestial cues, it is believed, are used in accomplishing this feat. It is also believed they are responsive to the earth's magnetic field and perhaps to the Coriolis force caused by the earth's rotation. These may serve as guidance mechanisms when skies are overcast.

Flight routes of ducks and geese in North America have been determined through extensive band recovery records. Four major flyways — Pacific, Central, Mississippi and Atlantic — have been identified by government regulatory agencies for management purposes.

Recently, more definitive flight corridors have been mapped for the more common ducks and geese. These corridors are a composite of the network of routes determined from band recoveries, visual observations, and radar surveillance. Routes are usually less than sixteen kilometers wide and follow landscape features such as coastlines and river valleys. Corridors can be wide, some more than eighty kilometers, and although corridors do take an east-west direction for considerable distances, especially with sea and diving ducks, the general direction is north-south.

Although the urge to migrate is instinctive in both ducks and geese, the process by which apprentice migrants learn their individual routes differs because of their very different social organizations.

Ducks seek new mates each year on the wintering grounds or en route to the nesting area. The female leads her mate to her natal marsh. In many cases, this is distant from his own natal marsh or previous breeding site. There is much evidence to indicate, however, that once his familial duties are completed with the laying of the clutch, he tends to return to familiar territory of the previous year.

The bond between female and brood, and between broodmates, is not retained beyond the brood maturing period. The young must learn the environmental migration cues from the adults they associate with on their maiden journey.

Once joined in flock, ducks have a tendency to remain together. But this is only a temporary association of individuals with various experiences. At each landmark or resting place on migration, there may be an exchange between flocks as routes meet or diverge. Broodmates, simply through such chance encounters, may winter as far apart as the Atlantic and Pacific coasts.

Young geese, on the other hand, do not pioneer their migration paths. Theirs is a different social order. Pair, family, and flock bonds are maintained throughout life. The young travel with their parents and close relatives, learning the stopping places and wintering sites from them.

The landmarks are learned well. Unless there are significant changes in the habitat, or disturbances that force the bird to relocate, the resting and feeding stops along the route are adhered to consistently. This assures that immature geese, sometimes separated from the breeding segment by a thousand kilometers during the summer period, will rejoin their family flocks by early autumn, thus maintaining the genetic integrity of the subspecies or race.

The typical annual chronology of migration begins well before we normally see signs of the season's end. On the far northern breeding grounds, where spring comes late and summers are short, the stage is set for migration by the time the last egg is laid. By late June, post-breeding males of the tundra-nesting ducks are already on the move, foreshadowing the hastened departure of the females and young. The inland Arctic climate allows only enough time for the essentials of the breeding cycle.

In the prairie region, midsummer is a

Late summer flocks are a mixture of many species. *Ed Bry photo.*

quiescent time for ducks. Females are tending broods, while molting adults enjoy the seclusion of the larger marshes until the signs of autumn begin to appear.

Soon Arctic breeding shorebirds are noisily en route south, and early fledged juvenile ducks practice their new-found flight, their airmanship still awkward, unlike the skillful aerobatic displays of adult courting parties only weeks earlier. But skill and strength improve, and they soon leave the small mixed flocks of the brood ponds for the larger marshes, where they join larger flocks of their own species prior to migration.

September is the hinge month for migration, opening the floodgates to October when most migration occurs. By mid-month, most of the blue-winged teal and pintail have gone, the adult females and young following in the wake of the adult males, which left a month earlier.

Although they overlap, the departure sequence for the various species is quite consistent. Wigeon and shoveler leave mainly in late September; gadwall, redhead, and ringneck in early October; canvasback, scaup, and mallard from mid to late October. Green-winged teal are less specific; their migration peaks anytime from late

September through October. Some mallard, scaup, goldeneye, and bufflehead tough it out until even the largest marshes are frozen over.

Arctic-breeding small races of Canada geese, white-front, Ross' and lesser snows move to prairie staging areas beginning in mid-September. Here they rest and feed before moving on in mid-October. The large, locally breeding Canada geese leave later, about mid-November, in company with the mallard.

Mallards are the last ducks to leave. Although they have trickled south all through October, the final mass exodus comes at the month end or at least by mid-November. They have been in the northern part of their range for eight months, longer than any other waterfowl except prairie-breeding Canada geese.

When they finally depart for good, some have already been three months in migration, beginning with a northward post-breeding dispersal, mainly of juvenile and adult drakes, in early September.

This northward migration may take them some 800 kilometers beyond their breeding marshes, to the Athabasca Delta at the northern boundary of Alberta and to marshy bordered northern lakes and eastward to the Saskatchewan and Churchill River systems. The northern lakes, ice-bound when the shallow prairie marshes were abundant in animal protein necessary for the nesting and brood season, have by this time warmed. They are at their most productive stage and many produce abundant seed-bearing aquatics in their shallower waters. The birds meet little disturbance on these remote marshes and rapidly improve body condition.

The stay-at-home juvenile females are apparently less adventurous than the males, or perhaps have a stronger attach-ment to their natal areas, for they remain with the adult females and the younger broods, migrating south directly, usually before the northern wanderers return.

By early October, mallard are distributed the full length of their annual range, with a predominance of males in the north and females in the south.

Northern vagabond mallard drakes return to the south in October, when the first persistent freezing weather has settled over the prairie region. These are the "big northerns" waterfowlers look for down the flyways.

A dramatic change occurs in the local scene when they arrive, with 50,000 birds or more added to the population of a staging marsh overnight. Most are in bright nuptial plumage and their behavior is robust and wary. As long as open water remains or can be kept open, and the grainfields are free of heavy snow, the flocks remain. Occasionally some mallards attempt to over-winter on the ice of frozen marshes, feeding in adjacent stubble fields. Few survive; frozen feet, then ultimately death, are their usual fate.

Migration patterns vary, of course, from year to year. Typically, early fall migration is a leisurely affair, the birds reveling in "bluebird" weather. For weeks, small flocks of a species may linger on a marsh, feeding and loafing before moving south as habitat or inclination influences them.

Premigration behavior can be recognized by midday feeding, restlessness, and frequent seemingly purposeless flights. Departures are usually near dusk, in clear weather with favorable winds.

As the season progresses, the tempo increases, but migration is still more often demonstrated by decreasing bird numbers than by anything else. Suddenly we realize that a species is no longer present. Occasionally, though, on a clear, chilly day in late October, we may witness a mass migration of waterfowl precipitated by impending deterioration in the weather. This usually happens at the end of an extended period of Indian Summer, which entices more than the usual number of birds to remain past their normal migration period, until collectively they sense it is time to move out. We may then be treated to the rare and unforgettable experience of strings of waterfowl in purposeful flight woven against a transparent sky.

Flocks of mallard, scaup, Canadas, white-front, snow and blue geese, tundra swan, and sometimes a straggling flock of late-staying sandhill crane can be seen, interspersed at elevations from 500 to 1,500 meters, riding on favorable winds.

These flights, with all members locked into an unveering direction, are easily distinguishable from local low-level feeding excursions. Cruising at air speeds of eighty kilometers per hour, they pass quickly. As soon as a flock is overhead, others come into view on the horizon. As quickly as the volume builds, it abruptly ceases, with only the occasional reluctant flock of mallard or local Canada geese seen afterward.

The climax of most prairie waterfowl seasons comes with the biting edge of a deep Arctic front. In a day or two, the last of the mallard, scaup, goldeneye, and bufflehead, along with several thousand large Canada geese, are forced out on a broad front extending from the foothills of the Rocky Mountains to the marshes of eastern Manitoba. They may migrate only as far south as necessary to find suitable weather and habitat again. However, once on the move, some mallards continue nonstop to their winter terminus, traveling over 3,000 kilometers in less than fifty hours.

While migration is predominately southward from the prairies, many waterfowl take a more southeasterly course to the Great Lakes and the large shallow lakes of the St. Lawrence River lowlands en route to their Atlantic coast wintering grounds.

The fall movement of waterfowl to these traditional lakeshore areas begins relatively early with the arrival of blue-winged teal in late August. They usually peak in mid-September, and quite often most are gone before the hunting season begins. But migration doesn't really hit its stride until late September, with the arrival of pintail and wigeon, and doesn't shift into high gear until the middle of October. Some mallard and blacks also arrive early but do not peak until November, with the hardier black peaking closer to month's end.

As October winds down, waterfowl numbers rise dramatically as waves of scaup move in, followed by redhead, which marginally precede the "king of ducks," the lordly canvasback. Attracted by lush beds of wild celery and sago pond weed, the "cans and reds" arrive in a highlight of the migration. Females and immatures form the vanguard of the "can" migration, with the percentage of "bulls" rising steadily to a point where late season flocks are virtually all male. Accompanying the late season surge in ducks is a similar increase in Canada geese. Waterfowl numbers start to decline in December, but a hard freeze, several days in duration, is normally required to drive migrating flocks from the province.

In Quebec, pintail and blue- and green-winged teal are abundant from mid-August through mid-September on the Ottawa, St. Lawrence, and Richelieu rivers. At the first real cold, they leave the St. Lawrence valley for the south. The opening of the hunting season also has an effect on migration, pushing the birds south.

The highlight of the migration is the arrival of the greater snow goose in the St. Lawrence estuary. First flocks appear in the early days of October, and have left by the end of the month. Peaks are attained between October 10 and 15. They congregate mainly at the Cap-Tourmente National Wildlife Area and the Ile aux Grues–Ile aux Oies complex.

Mallard and blacks are present from early October. Migration seems to be regular, with a few peaks during the season. Blacks from northern breeding grounds congregate on the St. Lawrence River in November where they feed on large invertebrates and small fish; some over-winter.

Early November brings mixed flocks of greater and lesser scaup en route to the eastern seaboard. At the peak in the first week of November, 100,000 birds are present on lac des Deux Montagnes, lac St. Louis, and lac St. Francois. Some 20,000 canvasback were counted in 1983 on these areas. On lac St. Pierre, there were 20,000 scaup in mixed flocks and 15,000 goldeneye; 10,000 mixed blacks and mallard are also there at their peak.

Canada geese stage on the numerous lakes of the Pre-Cambrian Shield and Appalachians, but few stop in the St. Lawrence lowlands.

In the Maritimes, blue-winged teal begin staging in late August and most have left by October 1 except in frost-free falls. Green-winged teal migrate into the area in early October and move through during the month. Some hardy drakes remain until early December.

The first migrant Canada geese often appear in Prince Edward Island by mid-August, but are not common in the rest of the Maritimes until late September. Stag-

ing on tidal bays and feeding on grain stubble, they remain until cold weather drives them south, often well into December. Some over-winter in southern Nova Scotia.

The major movement of black duck into the area occurs about October 20 in most years, evidenced by the appearance of large numbers of adult males, known as redlegs. These birds spend November and part of December on salt water before moving south. Some over-winter in all provinces.

Scaup and goldeneye stage in the estuarine marshes of the St. John River and are still present in southern Nova Scotia in late December. Some goldeneye over-winter.

The coastal areas also stage large numbers of sea ducks. Locally produced eiders leave the region by early October to winter in Maine and Massachusetts. Northern eider, oldsquaw, and scoters arrive in November and persist through January.

Back across the continent, British Columbia and the Pacific Northwest have a migration pattern all their own, which is oriented to the coast and the Pacific Flyway, and little influenced by the prairies.

Fall migration is first evident in late August by the subtle movement of blue-winged teal and pintail from the inter-mountain plateau breeding marshes to riverine lakes and deltas of the south-trending valley corridors.

However, sea ducks breeding in remote areas of the far Northwest have already been on the move, as adult males leave their mates even before incubation is far advanced. The low fertility of the tundra ponds isn't conducive to supporting birds that, for survival of the species, are better off elsewhere. Snow and Canada geese from northern breeding grounds move inland to river deltas, as soon as their broods reach flight stage, to feed and prepare for the long flight south.

Brant follow the coastal route, and along with most snow and some Canada geese, take the nonstop outside passage to wintering areas south of British Columbia. By early September, pintails from Alaska, also following the coastal route, are joined on favored estuaries by other inland nesting species, including wigeon and green-winged teal.

The inland corridors in the far north are less well defined; some birds use mountain passes to enter the Great Plains region, while others funnel into the confining valleys of the south.

By mid-September, pintail and blue-winged teal have mainly moved on, but their numbers have been more than replaced by other species as smaller ponds freeze and hunting pressure forces them into the larger staging areas. The coastal corridor and the internal corridors of the Okanagan and Columbia valleys usually witness a leisurely movement from mid-September to mid-October. By late October, depending on weather fronts and northern freezeup, there are sometimes impressive concentrations of mallard, wigeon, goldeneye, and scaup.

In very late falls, the passage from the north is usually nonstop, and southern interior lakes are left with only small wintering populations of large Canada geese and tundra and trumpeter swan. But the lower coast is never without a substantial wintering population of geese, swan, and most species of ducks.

In the aftermath of the settling cold, especially if followed by heavy snow, the northern marshes are eerily silent. There are no bird calls, no sound of waves on shorelines. Even the frozen reeds make no rustle in the persistent wind. So ends the drama of the waterfowl migration from the north country.

20

Flight South

F. C. Bellrose

Ducks depart prairie breeding grounds along myriads of lines that, as they progress southward, tend to converge into corridors. Corridors are a recent concept in understanding the distribution of waterfowl in migration. Although waterfowl may follow paths or routes during the daytime and perhaps for part of a journey, these terms are too restrictive in defining the actual passage of populations or their elements.

Radar observations of waterfowl migration at night show consistent directional passage over areas from 50 to 200 miles in width, suggesting that departures after sunset are directionally oriented rather than cued to landscape. There is evidence that migrating ducks flow in a particular direction at specific times and places, much like a stream, rather than proceeding like a convoy passing down a road.

Most waterfowl depart in migration after sunset; ducks migrate almost exclusively at night but extend their flights into the daylight when necessary to reach a wetland site that was in their flight plan prior to departure.

Geese are more prone to continue their migratory flights into and even through the day. Perhaps such prolonged migration occurs in geese because of their greater fuel reserves in the form of body fat. Or perhaps it is because geese are more exacting in habitat requirements, necessitating longer diurnal flights to reach their scheduled destinations.

Flyways encompass corridors coming from various directions. Flyways are more political than biological in makeup, for they separate the United States into four east-west regions that are aligned north-south. It is obvious, from the location

A harbinger of coming winter — blues and snows moving south. *Ed Bry photo.*

and limited area of the prairie breeding grounds, that to reach the far corners of the United States prairie ducks need to radiate out over many different directions other than along the north-south axis of the flyways.

To better understand the distribution of migrating waterfowl between breeding and wintering areas, let us examine the more prominent migration corridors (see also color maps preceding book's title page).

The Atlantic Coast is served by corridors that extend east from prairie breeding grounds to the New England states; by others that stretch east-southeastward to the middle Atlantic states; and still others that reach South Carolina, Georgia, and Florida on a south-southeast bearing. Blue-winged teal dominate on the most

northerly corridors; lesser scaup, canvasback, and redheads on the middle ones; and mallards, wigeons, pintails, and green-winged teal on the far south corridors. Black ducks, from their breeding grounds in eastern Canada, pass along north-south aligned corridors to the Atlantic Coast.

Several corridors funnel ducks southeastward from the prairies into the Midwest. The largest one arrives at the Mississippi River between Davenport, Iowa, and St. Louis, Missouri. In this area, mallards outnumber all other ducks by a wide margin; in mid-November, a million of them may amass along the Mississippi and Illinois rivers. Upon departure, most alter direction about forty-five degrees to the south or southwest to arrive at their principal winter grounds in eastern Arkansas and northeastern Louisiana.

Migration corridors extend across the Great Plains on tracks that vary between south-southeast and south. Although the mallard is again the most abundant species, it shares these corridors with large numbers of pintails, wigeons, gadwalls, green-winged teal, and redheads. Indeed, over a third of all redheads follow a corridor that extends due south from western Manitoba to the lower Texas coast.

Migration corridors into the Pacific Flyway are the most complex of all. No doubt their pattern stems from the dispersed location of wetlands in valleys and basins amid the mountain ranges. Several corridors emanate from Alaska, but the vast majority of ducks follow corridors southwest from Alberta and Saskatchewan to reach such diverse regions as the Columbia Basin in Washington, the Klamath Basin in California, and the Bear River marshes in Utah. Large numbers move from these migration areas into the Central Valley of California.

Mallards predominate on the corridors to the Columbia Basin. Pintails, wigeons, green-winged teal, and shovelers are all heavy users of the other corridors. More than half of all the pintails that breed north of the United States pursue corridors to the Central Valley of California. A corridor followed by pintails and green-winged teal stretches down the west coast of Mexico as far as Panama.

Geese follow different migration corridors than ducks because of their different breeding and wintering areas and migration behavior. Most geese nest in the Arctic or sub-Arctic and migrate more or less south all across Canada and the northern United States. There are several migration corridors in each flyway, and they conform

to the north-south alignment of the flyways much better than corridors used by ducks. Corridors followed by geese tend to be narrower (thirty to fifty miles) and more segregated than corridors followed by ducks, because geese have more localized and exacting breeding, migration, and wintering requirements. Geese, more than ducks, utilize specific areas more precisely in each phase of their seasonal activity.

Migration corridors for lesser snow geese and certain races of small Canada geese extend from Baffin Island, north of Hudson Bay, to the gulf marshes of Texas and Louisiana. Others originate from the Queen Maud Gulf area, the Mackenzie River Delta, and from a number of areas in coastal Alaska. Hudson and James bays not only supply several hundred thousand geese from nearby breeding colonies that depart along numerous corridors, but these bays are also important staging areas for geese nesting farther north.

One of the most impressive migration corridors extends from Izembek Bay, near the tip of the Alaska peninsula, to San Quentin and other bays on Baja California. This corridor is followed nonstop by a large proportion of the black brant population. These birds have been known to make this protracted flight of 3,300 miles in sixty hours, most of it over the Pacific Ocean. This feat is the most noteworthy among waterfowl, demonstrating phenomenal navigation and endurance capabilities.

Tundra swans (formerly called whistling) also follow a remarkable migration corridor, extending up the Mackenzie River to the Athabasca Delta and on south-southeastward to central North Dakota. There the corridor turns east-southeastward to reach Chesapeake Bay, principal wintering grounds of tundra swans in

With the last migrants come the tundra (whistling) swans. *Ducks Unlimited Canada photo.*

eastern United States. Comparable numbers of these swans migrate along several corridors—the most important via the Bear River marshes of Utah—to winter in the San Francisco Bay area. Swans, like geese, make long nonstop flights that embrace both nocturnal and diurnal hours.

Diurnally, swans may fly highly specific routes in migration. Arthur S. Hawkins, retired flyway representative of the U.S. Fish and Wildlife Service, has observed the migration of swans for most of the forty years he has lived north of Twin Cities, Minnesota. Hawkins has noted that tundra swans in both spring and fall adhere to the same course over his home, a remarkable feat of exacting navigation. A spectacular passage occurred on November 23, 1983, when Hawkins saw several thousand pass. There were other lines of flight that day over the Twin Cities. When observers tallied their sightings, almost 10,000 swans

had been seen, a large part of the total eastern population.

Canada geese have also been observed migrating along specific lines of flight, pinpointing particular landscape features. How well waterfowl maintain a particular line of flight in darkness is unknown. Available evidence suggests that a flanking wind at night may drift them off course. During the day, landscape in relation to wind direction provides a means of correcting for wind drift. The correction for wind drift is easy to discern in swans and geese because of their long necks; sometimes their heads are pointed in one direction but they are moving in another!

What makes the delimitation of waterfowl migration corridors feasible is the propensity of these birds to home to specific sites, whether they are breeding, winter, or migration areas. Some species adhere to the use of traditional sites and lines of migration more precisely than others. Geese and swans follow traditional routes more than ducks. Both geese and swans migrate in family units and undertake a significant part of their migratory flights during daylight. Both young geese and swans, making their first migratory flights, have enhanced opportunities to become imprinted with landscape cues as they follow their parents to traditional migration areas in the fall, then on to winter grounds, and finally on a return trip to their natal areas.

Although strong traditionalists, geese are sufficiently flexible to alter their migration habits to adjust for changing food resources. A few examples illustrate their ability to exploit new conditions. Four decades ago, Canada geese bypassed the Horicon Marsh National Wildlife Refuge northwest of Milwaukee, Wisconsin, winging overhead on their way from James Bay to refuges in southern Illinois. Then small numbers stopped at Horicon, crop programs were initiated to provide food, and, over the years, numbers soared to about 250,000. Crop depredation and other programs developed, so dispersal programs were inaugurated to reduce the concentrations that at first appeared to be a bonanza. In the early 1950s, most of the Canada geese on the Atlantic Coast wintered at Mattamuskeet National Wildlife Refuge, North Carolina. By the mid-1960s, large numbers began stopping in eastern Maryland, and this number steadily increased to 500,000 by the 1980s.

The traditional return to particular breeding, migration, and winter areas also plays an important role in the life of ducks. For survival, however, ducks need to be more flexible than swans and geese in resorting to specific places and habitats. Ducks have more options built in to their selection of seasonal habitats; therefore, their homing is more fluid. This characteristic is particularly evident in first-year birds. Young and adult ducks do not migrate in family flocks but in a heterogeneous mixture of young and old. Individuals probably shift flocks numerous times between breeding and wintering areas.

Yearling ducks are more prone than adults to pioneer into different breeding habitats or to return less precisely than their parents to natal areas. Species differ in their propensity to exploit new wetlands; pintails, blue-winged teal, and ruddy ducks are among the most noted in this respect.

To better understand how homing functions in waterfowl, we made several studies involving the displacement of waterfowl in time and space. One experiment was conducted over a period of years with migrating blue-winged teal. We captured several hundred birds during August and September and held the juvenile birds in pens until late in November or early December. At the time of their release, the species had migrated farther south so that there were no adults in the area. Band recoveries, the same fall-winter season, revealed that most of the juveniles flew southeast and south along customary courses of flight even though there were no adults available for guidance.

In a second experiment, we transported drake mallards from central Illinois to marshes adjacent to Great Salt Lake, Utah; 470 adults were released at Ogden Bay State Refuge and 425 juveniles twenty-five miles to the north at the Bear River National Wildlife Refuge. Band recoveries the same season were all within the region. However, in the following two autumns, two-thirds of the band recoveries of the adults and one-third of the former juveniles occurred back in the Mississippi Flyway.

A third experiment concerned the release of 215 hand-reared wood ducks three to six weeks old at three sites 175 to 200 miles distant. At the time there were no known breeding wood ducks at the release sites: Madison, Wisconsin; Medaryville, Indiana; and Wheaton, Illinois.

The following summer, banded wood ducks were found nesting at their respective release sites; none of the transported wood ducks nested at Havana, Illinois, where they had been reared.

These experiments point to the development of homing cues after hatching and either prior to or during the first migration. We and many others have conducted experiments in an effort to determine the cues that birds use in navigation.

We were the first to discover that at least four species of waterfowl—mallard, pintail, blue-winged teal, and Canada goose—use the sun during the day and the stars at night for directional information. We were able to demonstrate the use of the sun and stars by moving wild waterfowl various distances from the trap sites and releasing them one at a time. Release sites were intersecting farm land roads, one to ninety-five miles from the trap sites. The course of each bird was charted for a mile or more. We attached a small pen light to one leg of each bird released at night so its flight pattern was visible.

On clear days and nights the flight courses were direct and grouped in a particular direction that differed among the species. Under overcast skies, the flight paths were torturous, almost random, in direction. No matter the time of release on clear days and nights, these experimental birds maintained the same flight directions, pointing to an internal clock that enabled them to adjust headings fifteen degrees per hour as a compensation for the earth's rotation.

G. V. T. Matthews, experimenting with mallards in England, found that when birds were exposed to differently timed light regimens, their initial flight direction could be altered according to the time shift; six hours resulted in a 90-degree change and twelve hours in a 180-degree change in direction. The evidence of an internal clock in mallards and other birds has been so well documented that it is now an accepted fact.

Soon after these findings, radar surveillance of waterfowl migration under overcast skies indicated that migrating birds must use other cues besides the sun and stars. This conclusion was reached from the orderly and oriented migration tracks on photographs of radar scopes at times when cloud cover prevented the migrants from viewing either the sun, stars, or landscape.

Subsequent experiments with homing pigeons demonstrated that these birds can derive directional cues from the earth's magnetic field, weak as it is. Experiments with other birds—gulls and indigo bunting in North America and European robin, pied flycatcher, and blackcaps in Europe—provide evidence that they too use the earth's magnetic field for directional guidance.

Scientists recently were excited by the discovery that homing pigeons had concentrations of magnetite (Fe_3O_4) in their heads and necks. This magnetic material provides the first plausible explanation as to how birds detect and use the earth's magnetic field in their navigational system. A later study revealed that magnetite is present in several species of wild birds, including the pintail. Thus all migratory birds may have this material as a receptor of magnetic intensity.

Other sources of navigational cues have not been neglected by scientists. Evidence that the flights of homing pigeons are sensitive to barometric pressure, infrasound, polarized light, and gravity variation have been recognized, but not well documented.

Researchers in this field generally agree that most migratory birds have a redundancy of navigational aids at their command. They use the easiest cue first; if that is impossible, they shift to a second, third, and perhaps a fourth cue as the situation necessitates. The cues used and their order of facility probably vary by species, depending upon the degree of difficulty each species has experienced over its migrational history.

Some species, such as wood ducks, black ducks, and mallards, make comparatively short migratory flights. Other species—black brant, pintail, and blue-winged teal—make long flights, often 1,000 or more miles over the open sea. The short-distance migrants probably have much less sophisticated redundancy of navigational cues than the long-distance migrants. Eventually researchers will understand the navigational capabilities of the different types of migrants.

The hundreds of experiments performed with homing pigeons, and the scores of experiments conducted with other birds, have established no satisfactory "map" that birds might use with their sun, star, or magnetic compass. A bird obviously needs more information than the points of a compass to compensate for displacement or to reach a distant goal. Whatever provides the map, it has not been identified in spite of diligent search for three decades in both Europe and North America.

A great mystery remains: What do migrating birds use, along with directional cues, to find their way? It has been speculated that the earth's magnetic field provides the map, the missing link in true bicoordinate navigation. Researchers are now evaluating this hypothesis more thoroughly than ever before. We may have an answer before the decade is out.

21

Crop Depredation: The Problem and the Politics

C. A. Radimer

While waterfowlers may wax eloquent over the majesty and splendor of the annual waterfowl migration, that same prospect elicits far less enthusiasm—and, in some instances, outright hostility—from western Canadian farmers.

To North America's sportsmen, the annual phenomenon heralds an opportunity to refresh the spirit and replenish the freezer. To prairie farmers, the arrival of waterfowl flocks in their fields is simply one more way nature conspires to deprive grain growers of their rightful dues.

When farmers feel their livelihoods threatened by uninvited guests, they react predictably: they withdraw the welcome mat and demand better protection from the government agencies pledged to protect their interests.

The indisputable fact is that some species of waterfowl relish a good feed of grain, and that their table habits and appetites can cost grain growers money in terms of grain consumed, trampled, or fouled. Total depredation losses vary from year to year. While they represent less than 1 percent of the total crop value, they can mean losses of several hundred to tens of thousands of dollars to individual producers.

For government and private wildlife agencies dedicated to improving waterfowl production, the depredation issue is a serious public relations problem. Farmers who have lost income to marauding waterfowl are understandably reluctant to endorse land use programs designed to increase this perceived threat.

The wildlife argument to counter farm criticism centers on the fact that research into the depredation issue has proved no relationship between depredation losses and waterfowl populations. The key element in the formula is the weather. If the weather turns bad during harvest and grain is left for extended periods in swath on the field, losses will be high regardless of duck populations. If the weather cooperates and the harvest progresses quickly, losses are minimal.

This approach, though backed by solid research, does little to pacify negative farmer attitudes, particularly since those attitudes are often the result of frustrations caused by poor harvesting weather. Farmers watching waterfowl feed on grain that can't be harvested because of the weather tend to have negative attitudes toward the interlopers.

Research also shows barley is twice as likely to be affected by depredation as wheat, the mainstay of the prairie grain industry. Durum is next in terms of waterfowl preference.

While this suggests an obvious solution would be a swing in crops to cereals and oilseeds less attractive to waterfowl, barley is popular, easy to grow, and versatile, offering marketing flexibility or on-farm feeding potential. In 1981, for example, Canadian farmers produced over 565 million bushels of barley worth more than $1.5 billion. Suggestions that farmers abandon this important crop to accommodate waterfowl are not seriously considered in farm communities!

Nor are grain growers comforted by the fact that of the twenty-two duck species found on the Canadian prairies, only two — mallard and pintail — are responsible for most crop damage. Farmers realize that these two species represent a substantial part of the annual duck migration.

Although depredation has been a sporadic source of conflict between farmers and waterfowlers ever since pioneer grain growers first invaded the natural wetlands

of prairie Canada, the problem increased significantly in the late 1940s, when farmers adopted swathing — a technique involving cutting the crop and laying it in rows to ripen prior to combining — as a standard harvesting practice.

Prior to the development of swathing, grain crops were cut and bundled into sheaves, stacked into "stooks" to ripen, then hauled off the fields for threshing. Tight, well-placed stooks designed to keep the grain heads off the ground protected the crop from feeding waterfowl and minimized depredation losses.

Introduction of the combine harvester brought greater efficiency into the grain business by allowing farmers to reap and thresh their crops in one operation. And as long as crops could be "straight combined," or cut and threshed directly, waterfowl had little opportunity or inclination to feed off the standing crops.

But straight combining wasn't practical in the short growing seasons common in western Canada. Crops didn't always ripen uniformly and farmers faced yield and quality losses because of uneven crop ripening. The solution was swathing, which involves cutting and laying the crop in rows on the stubble to dry prior to picking it up with a combine harvester.

Swathing is now the universally accepted harvesting method in western Canada. But swaths are inviting cafeterias for feeding waterfowl. Since in many areas of western Canada the harvest and the fall migration coincide, the situation is tailormade for major depredation problems.

Despite the fact that waterfowl depredation is a real and complex economic threat to many grain producers, few western Canadian farmers consider extermination programs an acceptable solution. However, many are convinced that existing dep-

When grain was stooked, depredation was minimized. *Ducks Unlimited Canada photo.*

redation policies are inadequate. They feel they neither effectively reduce losses nor adequately compensate those who suffer them.

The size of the depredation problem can be appreciated by considering that between 1973 and 1977 depredation losses in Alberta, Saskatchewan, and Manitoba totaled over 10.3 million bushels ranging from a high of 3.2 million bushels in 1977 to a low of 1.5 million bushels in 1976.

Translated into dollar terms based on present barley prices, prairie grain growers lost more than $20 million during that four-year period because of waterfowl depredation. These losses, of course, rep-

resent only a very small part of the multi-billion-dollar Canadian grain industry, yet they have a devastating impact on individual farm incomes, where even a modest loss is a major concern to a cost-squeezed operator.

Depredation remains one of the major conflicts between waterfowl interests and agriculture. Farmers who have lost crops to ducks and geese are not likely to view with any sympathy the government or private conservation organization efforts to increase, or even maintain, waterfowl numbers. And, since agriculture is a powerful political force in Canada's prairie provinces, government officials are extremely

Swaths are an inviting cafeteria for hungry waterfowl. *Ducks Unlimited Canada photo.*

sensitive to depredation concerns when approving waterfowl habitat developments.

The political nature of the problem complicates the search for a mutually satisfactory solution. In 1972, the Canadian government implemented a joint federal-provincial depredation prevention and compensation program that was to run for five years. However, pressure from the provincial governments led to a series of annual extensions that have continued to present a solution most agree is merely a stopgap.

The federal-provincial program is cost-shared between the two levels of govern-

ment with somewhat less than half the funds allocated to prevention programs, including lure crops, bait station installations, and provision of scaring devices. The major portion of the funding is earmarked for compensation, which is administered by provincial crop insurance agencies.

Both agricultural spokesmen and wildlife managers agree the present policy leaves much to be desired. Wildlife officials, for example, are critical of the emphasis placed on compensation rather than prevention. Money expended on more extensive prevention efforts, they say, would be four times more cost-effective than paying compensation for damage already done.

At the same time, farmers cite the uncertainty of the present year-by-year program and the low levels of compensation it provides (a maximum of $50 per acre or $10,000 per farm) as serious weaknesses. Since little progress has been made to develop a satisfactory long-term federal-provincial program, some farm groups and government agencies have looked elsewhere for depredation relief.

Farmers generally prefer a "user pays" policy, under which those who benefit most from the waterfowl resource should contribute to the cost of producing it. And, the argument goes, since U.S. hunters take more than 80 percent of the annual fall harvest, U.S. sportsmen should be prepared to help out with the problem.

Taking the scenario one step further, proponents of the theory reason that since Ducks Unlimited, North America's foremost privately funded conservation organization, receives most of its funding from

Ducks in the swaths — they took the invitation! *Ed Bry photo.*

U.S. sportsmen, Ducks Unlimited should shoulder some of the costs.

Accepting the argument that those who utilize the resource should be prepared to contribute to producing it, Ducks Unlimited Canada spokesmen say the organization, over 90 percent of whose funding is contributed by U.S. sportsmen, has historically assisted the Canadian government fulfill its 1916 Migratory Bird Treaty responsibilities through a total investment of $254 million in project construction since 1938. Moreover, Ducks Unlimited is prepared to assist governments in their depredation prevention efforts, if governments will guarantee maintenance of waterfowl habitat.

These issues are central to large-scale cooperative habitat development agreements that Ducks Unlimited Canada recently negotiated with the governments of Saskatchewan and Alberta.

The organization has agreed, for example, to incorporate bait stations into traditional staging areas where depredation problems can be anticipated. The purpose of the stations is to encourage birds to feed in these relatively concentrated areas rather than ranging farther afield. In other instances Ducks Unlimited will assist governments and private conservation groups to negotiate lure cropland where necessary; and under the terms of the Saskatchewan agreement will supply propane-activated cannons to government agencies to use in depredation-prone fields.

Responsibility for establishing or contracting with local farmers for lure crops and for stocking bait stations with grain in depredation-prone areas lies with provincial government agencies who cost-share with the federal government.

Despite farmer criticism that existing prevention programs are often a case of "too little too late," government officials estimate that in 1979 depredation prevention programs on ninety-two individual sites across Manitoba, Saskatchewan, and Alberta involved expenditures of $1.8 million, for a per-site average of $20,000.

Both agriculture and wildlife interests recognize that prevention programs will not completely eliminate farm concerns over depredation losses. A compensation program, which adequately recognizes the real value of crop losses to farmers and apportions a share of the cost of producing the waterfowl resource to those who benefit from it, holds the only long-term solution to the problem.

But there's no consensus on an acceptable solution. Some farmers favor a straight compensation program funded entirely by government, on the premise that the cause of the problem is not only beyond their control but actually encouraged by other interests.

Other groups insist that a new compensation program should incorporate incentives to encourage farmers to minimize risks by growing crops unattractive to waterfowl and adopting field techniques to eliminate vulnerable swaths at harvest time. Some recommend a basic compensation payment with optional insurance coverage, but some farmers question why they should be forced to insure themselves for a risk that's encouraged and protected by government wildlife agencies.

While various compensation schemes are evaluated, debated, and found wanting, farmers continue to pressure their farm organizations and government representatives to find someone to foot the bill. And farm politicians confronted by these demands aren't interested in the subtle nuances of the problem.

As far as many are concerned, the presence of ducks implies a depredation threat. This simplistic, but highly visible and therefore politically expedient, view means that proposals designed to increase waterfowl production will be opposed.

Public education programs, the development and acceptance of less depredation-prone crops, and new harvesting techniques can provide large measures of depredation relief. Equally important is a strong, effective prevention program coupled with a compensation plan that recognizes the real losses farmers incur from depredating waterfowl.

As far as Canadian farm leaders and politicians are concerned, funding for these programs must be shared by all who benefit from the continental waterfowl resource. Until Canadian farmers see tangible evidence that those who value the waterfowl resource are prepared to pay their share of producing it, they will continue to oppose projects they see as increasing their depredation risks.

Part IV
The Hunter's Moon

Man evolved as a hunter-gatherer. And vicariously he still is, though this is masked by modern agricultural mechanization and animal husbandry, which keep a supply of food animals readily available and substitute the efficiency of the abattoir for the search and rigors of the hunt.

The atavistic urge to hunt, and to seek the companionship of those who do, is thus buried deep in the psyche of most men. It emerges most often in those who have, or have had, a continuing association with the land—or a parent who did.

It has been often said, and is offered here again as neither apology nor justification, for none is required, that the kill is a small part of the reason for hunting. If it were not, it would be infinitely cheaper and more convenient to buy a limit of ducks and take them to the chopping block. True, there is additional satisfaction in a successful hunt, as in any successful endeavor, but some of the most enjoyable hunts are not the most successful.

The significance of the kill decreases even further with maturity of the hunter. Companionship, and compounding the shared experiences with lifetime hunting friends, increasingly become the dominating motivations.

22

In the Old Days

W. Fuchs

The birds swung, a long, thin, wavering line just feet off the surface of the tule-studded swamp, driving ever closer to the rough judas birds, decoys woven of tule reeds, bobbing on the rippled water. Wings set, they drifted in, splashing to a halt only feet from where the well-concealed Indian waited, bow drawn. A twang of the bowstring and a big bull canvasback splashed helplessly in the water, an arrow embedded in his body.

Waterfowl had for centuries been a valuable addition to the food supply of the aboriginal natives of North America. When the white man first began to explore the North American continent, he saw a richness of wildlife that must have exceeded his wildest imagination. Waterfowl darkened the sky, and there were turkey, prairie chicken, and other birds in seemingly inexhaustible abundance. Bison roamed the prairies in numbers believed to exceed fifty million.

Even as late as 1804, the Lewis and Clark expedition was said to have noted enormous flocks of molting ducks and pelicans, whose shed feathers covered the surface of the Missouri River like a white blanket, for miles and miles.

Passenger pigeons, by the tens of millions, nested in the U.S. and eastern Canada until about 1860. In these early years, the birds had little to fear from man, save an occasional foray by Indian or frontiersman needing fare for the larder.

Great marshes covered much of the country. In the United States alone, there were approximately 127 million acres of wetlands exclusive of Alaska. Natural aquatic waterfowl foods flourished in abundance. Along the rivers and streams, the oaks, pecans, and hickories supplied abundant food for wildlife. Small wonder that to people of that day, waterfowl and other forms of wildlife were looked upon as a food source to last a thousand years.

As the white man began his westward settlement, wildlife was forced to retreat before his advance. Killing only for survival was replaced with complete exploitation. Decimation of the vast herds of bison is well known. The value of their hides and meat brought their demise in the span of a decade. But the birds, whose numbers were endless, would surely survive forever.

The story of the passenger pigeon shows only too well what wanton slaughter by market hunting can do to a wildlife popu-lation. The passenger pigeon, considered a real delicacy, was pursued relentlessly be-tween 1860 and 1880. Wisconsin, Illinois, Iowa, and Indiana were principal nesting areas. Through shooting and netting, com-bined with other possible factors not fully understood, the birds were eventually an-nihilated. By the turn of the century only a few scattered flocks, numbering in the hundreds, were returning to the nesting grounds. The last known passenger pigeon died in captivity in the Cincinnati Zoo in 1914.

Waterfowl fared a little better, although market hunting for these birds was a flour-ishing and reputable practice, primarily

Market hunters in the Bear River marshes of Utah in the late 1800s. *Utah Division of Wildlife Resources photo.*

in the Chesapeake Bay area, during the mid-1800s. It was a way of life for many residents of the area. A hard life, and not always as lucrative as painted. But it flourished for many years as a perfectly legitimate trade, requiring one to be a hardy and resourceful waterman.

It is debatable whether it was the market guns that led to the great reduction in the continental waterfowl population. Considering the relatively small number of sport hunters, market gunning may not have been out of place at that time. However, it could not last. As the resource dwindled, from the combined forces of gunning pressure and loss of habitat in the prairie states, restrictions were needed to reduce the take.

Chesapeake market gunners employed numerous devices for taking waterfowl. These included big bore guns, batteries or sinkboxes, duck traps, night lights, and bait. Bait! Corn and other feed were used to lure and hold more ducks and geese before the gun than any other previously known means. Many of these devices and methods evolved as a result of the commercial demand for more and more ducks.

The punt gun probably achieved the greatest reputation as a duck killer. These were little more than the present-day "scull" or "sneak" boat equipped with a single or multiple big bore (1½ to 2-inch) muzzleloader, designed to throw a tremendous shot charge into a group of sitting waterfowl. Their effectiveness was frequently increased by using a night light.

But they were not always as deadly as their reputation would have one believe. True, at times as many as a hundred ducks were killed with a single shot, but a couple of dozen was considered the norm. These guns varied from those with 2-inch bores

and weighing 200 pounds down to 2 and 4 gauge. The older flintlocks were gradually replaced with percussions, as that type of ignition became more popular.

The big guns were normally used after dark with a light. Usually an area was baited with grain, then once the birds were concentrated and feeding, a stalk was made. Gunning lights, mounted in the front of a scull boat, were made from a wooden box with one of its sides replaced by two panes of glass in a V-shape. A kerosene lantern with a reflector of some sort was placed inside the box. The dim, diffused light did not seem to alarm the birds as the skiff was sculled toward them.

Night lighting has always been recognized as a practice to be restricted, be it for deer, small game, or waterfowl. In fact, waterfowl gunning lights were legislated against as early as 1730 in Maryland, 1777 in North Carolina, and 1792 in Virginia.

The battery, or sinkbox, was another method utilized by gunners of that era. Used mainly on large expanses of open water, they were surrounded by as many as 500 decoys. Daily bags of up to 500 or 600 ducks for a single gunner were not too uncommon in bygone days. Sinkboxes came into general use after development of the modern breech-loading repeating shotgun.

Modern federal regulations define a sinkbox as a low, floating device that conceals the gunner's body beneath the surface of the water. The old-time "sit up" battery is long gone, but the modern-day layout boat is little different from the old lay-down sinkbox. The modern version sits higher in the water, to comply with the law, but it is still one of the most efficient hunting devices, especially for divers.

Market prices paid for birds during late

North Dakota waterfowl for market around 1903. *William H. Spencer and* **North Dakota Outdoors** *photo.*

1800s are interesting. They seem to reflect, even to this day, the edible values attached to different species.

Canvasback	$6.00 per pair
Blacks and mallards	1.25 per pair
Ruddy ducks	1.00 per pair
Sprig	.50 per pair
Geese	2.00 per pair
Blackheads (scaup)	.50 per pair
Redheads	2.50 per pair
Yellowlegs	1.00 per dozen
Curlews	3.00 per dozen
Blackbirds	.50 per dozen
Bobolinks	1.00 per dozen
Swan	2.00 each

As the frontier stage passed into history, a new awareness of the waning waterfowl resource developed. Legislation was demanded to restrict the consumption of wildlife.

Restrictions on taking game by prohibiting certain methods and designating special protection were initiated at an early date in this country, but often not until long after it was apparent such action was necessary. In 1730, a law was adopted in Maryland prohibiting hunting deer by firelight. To this day, all states prohibit shining or headlighting.

Conservation laws in the early days were enforced by local peace officers or other

Early 1900s near Devil's Lake, North Dakota. Such bags were neither illegal nor considered unsportsmanlike in these early days. *Devil's Lake Chamber of Commerce and North Dakota Game and Fish Department photo.*

officials. New York State, as late as 1820, assigned suing for penalties under the game laws to overseers of the poor. Later, it was found necessary to hire special officers, who became known as game protectors or wardens.

The earliest officers of this kind seem to have been the deer wardens of New Hampshire in 1741. They were known as deer reeves in Massachusetts in 1764, and as moose wardens in Maine in 1852. Fish commissions, whose duties were later extended to include game, were established in California and New Hampshire as early as 1878. The first salaried state game wardens were in Michigan, Minnesota, and Wisconsin in 1887.

Migratory birds received protection by individual states long before the Migratory Bird Treaty Act. One of the early waterfowl violations bringing national attention was appealed from the District Court of Jackson County, Minnesota, to the State Supreme Court, on the grounds of cruel and unusual punishment.

In this case, Robert Poole and William Kerr were charged on September 28, 1903, with having possession of wild ducks with intent to sell, contrary to the law. There were 2,000 ducks involved, all of them killed near Heron Lake, Minnesota. These five wagonloads of ducks were being smuggled to Montgomery, Iowa, for shipment to the eastern markets, when the game commissioner and the county sheriff seized them and arrested the defendants.

Poole and Kerr were subsequently tried and convicted in the district court. Fines of $20,000 each, and 200 and 300 days respectively, were assessed, the minimum allowable under the statute. Both defendants appealed the conviction. The state supreme court affirmed the sentence against Poole and reversed the decision against Kerr.

Penalties such as these certainly took the profit out of commercialization; they are a far cry from those customarily handed down in more recent times. This doctrine of state ownership of game and other wildlife was developed as early as 1842 in New Jersey and was eventually adopted by all states.

The federal government, finally, in direct response to the decimation of the passenger pigeon and the depletion of a number of other birds, took its first step in wildlife legislation with the passage of the Lacey Act in 1900. This act, still in force today, prohibited the interstate transportation of wild animals or birds taken in violation of state or other law. The source of this exercise of federal authority was the congressional power to regulate interstate and foreign commerce. Previously, commercial wildlife traffickers had a free hand, once they slipped by the boundaries of state authority.

North American waterfowl were recognized as an international resource by the Migratory Bird Treaty Act signed in 1916 with Great Britain (on behalf of Canada) for the protection of certain migratory birds. It was passed by Congress in 1918.

Its constitutionality was soon brought before the Supreme Court, however, when the state of Missouri filed a bill in equity to restrain one Ray P. Holland, a federal game warden, from enforcing the act within the state. The court upheld the validity of the Migratory Bird Treaty Act, thus dealing a stunning blow to those who felt that state ownership of wildlife was a bar to federal wildlife legislation.

Justice Oliver Wendell Holmes, in the decision for the seven-member majority, wrote: "But for the Treaty and the Statute, there might soon be no birds for any powers to deal with. We see nothing in the Constitution that compels the government to sit by while the food supply is cut off and the protectors of our forests and crops are destroyed."

23

Canvasbacks from North to South

V. C. Heilner

It was wonderful in the old days on the Chesapeake. You'd drive down to Havre de Grace in the afternoon from Philadelphia so's to be on hand for the Opening.

Everywhere you looked you'd see gunners. The air even felt "ducky."

The cans were there, too. Everybody said so. More than had been seen for years. They looked like plumes of smoke when they got up. And redheads! Man alive! They'd almost take the top of your head off if you stuck it out of the battery. There'd be some powder burnt on the Flats in the morning.

We'd get aboard our houseboat that night and go down to the "Line" and anchor so's we'd be on the grounds at daylight. Others had the same idea too, it seemed, and we could see the anchor lights of other boats twinkling in the dark across the water.

"Blowin' up, boys! Listen to that old nor'wester comin' down! They'll fly in the morning!"

Morning would come all too soon. Not much sleep. Too excited. And it was necessary to be up by three because by the time you had breakfast and then got the battery rig out, another two hours would have gone by.

We could only shoot Mondays, Wednesdays and Fridays in those days and then not before an hour before sunrise and until a half hour after sundown. It took three men to run the rig and we had about 400 decoys.

"Canvasbacks from North to South" is part of a chapter from *A Book on Duck Shooting* by Van Campen Heilner, copyright 1939 by Penn Publishing Co; renewed 1967 by Van Campen Heilner. Reprinted by permission of Alfred A. Knopf, Inc.

As a rule, if there were two of us, we would use a single battery and take turns, maybe two hours in and two out with a toss-up of course as to who went first. If, as occasionally happened, there were three of us, we would use a double battery and one fellow would change off every hour, which gave each man two hours in the sinkbox.

These were lie-down batteries, and I taught myself to shoot left-handed when I drew the right-hand side of a double-battery. In Currituck I've often shot out of sit-up batteries where the water was deeper, and this is far more comfortable. One of the worst cases of "battery back," or whatever you want to call it, I got from a lie-down battery, and I reached the point where I couldn't raise up when fowl came to us. My companion had to put one arm behind my back and raise me up, then grab his gun and shoot.

After you've lain for hours on your back in the bottom of a battery with maybe a little water slopping on you every once in a while, you get so you never complain at home anymore about whether your mattress has been turned recently or not. In later years, when I began to think about making duck shooting more comfortable, I had a kapok mattress made for our batteries in the Carolinas and from then on had many a delightful snooze when the fowl weren't flying!

But those days on the Chesapeake are the ones I will always remember. The Sassafras River, Kent Island Narrows, Spesutie, Carroll's Island, the Choptank and others were all places where you could load a boat with cans and redheads if you were so inclined.

I've seen the cans, and redheads too, strung out over the flats until it looked as if there never was an end to them. It was that way sometimes on Back Bay and Currituck before the saltwater came through from Norfolk and spoiled all the feed. But then they put the locks back in the Albemarle Sound and Chesapeake Canal, thanks to Messrs. Knapp and Corey, and the food's coming back. What with one thing and another the good old days are on the way back, let no one tell you to the contrary.

There were two big bodies of redheads that came every year to Pamlico Sound. There were about 5,000 in one raft and about half that number in the other. You couldn't get at them though because they always sat way out in the open and all got up together and settled together. It was only when a big blow came along and broke 'em up that you could get any shooting out of them.

There were quite a few cans with them too, and I remember one day in December, it was the day they dedicated the Wright Memorial at Kitty Hawk if I'm not mistaken, it stormed and blew a living gale. Hi and I were down in the ponds trying to get a shot at a black duck when the cans started to fly. Never expected to see cans way in there, you understand, lighting in potholes like black ducks, but I guess it was too rough for them outside because they sure piled in, in great style. In less time, almost, than it takes to write this, we had our limit and never expected it. Just one of those things that make duck shooting so fascinating.

And there was the day that the battery foundered on Linc and me. We were up on the Cape Reef and hadn't done much in the early morning when the wind shifted and started to get up and the ducks began to fly. First they were mostly redheads and then a lot of cans showed up and then nearly every other flock was cans, and we were banging away at them and never noticing

The canvasback, considered by many the king of ducks. *Ed Bry photo.*

that the water was coming in every time we jumped out to pick up game.

And then it got rougher and rougher. We turned the lead edging all the way up but it didn't do any good. We hated to wave for our boat because the shooting was so good, and yet the waves were breaking right into the battery now and it was one thing or the other.

At last we waved for the boat, but before it got halfway to us the battery sank, and we had to hop out and stand in water up to our waists until they could get to us. Even at that I killed a can that flew right over us just before the boat came.

The days of batteries are over for the moment and maybe they'll never come back. But who can tell? John J. Audubon, writing in 1845, states that in 1838 a law was passed in the state of New York pro-

hibiting batteries. For a short time it was respected, but the gunners who depended upon waterfowl shooting for a great part of their living considered it such an invasion of their rights that they defied it; at first shooting with masks, at the same time threatening to shoot the informer should one be found. They finally laid aside their masks, and the law became a dead letter and was later repealed. That was a hundred years ago, which gives some idea how long these contraptions have been used. Undoubtedly they are one of the most deceptive and most destructive devices used in fowling. But like so many other gadgets used in our sport, the mechanics of the thing are fascinating, and the mind that conceived it probably did so out of necessity.

24

Hunting the Atlantic Flyway

G. B. Will and O. E. Frye, Jr.

If hunting or watching waterfowl turns you on most of all, come to the upper half of the Atlantic Flyway. Opportunity abounds, with birds arriving in early September and others staying the entire winter in some states. And fortunately, hunting seasons are set, for the most part, to accommodate hunters with the influx of migrants.

Diversity is the name of the game, in species, habitat, techniques, and weather. The early-season hunter can begin with the fast and curious woodies and teal. Both blue- and green-winged are common. Beaver ponds and drainages lined with tag alder produce exciting jump shooting in the warm autumn weather.

With cooler nights these smaller birds head south and are almost unnoticeably replaced by larger flights of wigeon, gadwall, mallard, and black. With late

October now easing into November, it's increasingly colder in blinds made of cedar, cattail, reeds, and even brush. Decoys are quickly dusted, anchors attached, and splashed into the approaching dawn. Now most hunters are concentrating on larger, more open waters. Skim ice turns birds and hunters away from smaller ponds.

And what about geese—snow, brant, and Canada? Many have already arrived from the Canadian nesting grounds. Flock after endless flock quicken the spirit as they drop into freshly cut corn or newly planted winter rye. In recent years they have become almost overly abundant, and even a nuisance for a few landowners.

The Finger Lakes and southeastern New York are examples of areas where goose numbers are expanding. Private enterprise has caught up with this phenomena, with many a farmer guiding a party of goose

A morning in the Long Island Salt Marsh. *Steven J. Sanford and New York Department of Environmental Conservation photo.*

hunters to the fields. These birds are satisfied with acres of feed and the open water of deep lakes or rivers for resting. Only deep snow and long-lasting frigid temperatures will push them farther south or southeastward to the salt water and flatlands. The snow goose has also adapted, becoming plentiful in many areas of New Jersey and Delaware, and the population continues to grow.

December arrives, and so do the thousands of cans, redhead, and scaup. Diving-duck hunting on the Great Lakes, St. Lawrence River, Lake Champlain, and the seacoast can be an experience you will never forget. Snow, sleet, or rain driven by fierce winds make ducks fly and grown men shake.

And that's not all! The saltwater marshes and the shallow-water shorelines attract huge numbers of black duck and scaup; bufflehead, goldeneye, merganser, and oldsquaw offer some of the fastest shooting on the continent. Sea ducks such as eider and scoter add to the waterfowlers' delight. Pass shooting these birds while sitting on rocks or mussel flats, or "black flagging" them from boats, is a challenge for the best gunners.

Federal duck-stamp revenue and significant state funds have helped both hunters and watchers by developing areas of opportunity and access sites. State and federal wetland wildlife management areas abound in this portion of the nation, thanks to the lay of the land and abundance of water. To sum it up, waterfowling's great in the northern and central Atlantic states!

To a high percentage of south Atlantic waterfowlers, "duck" means wood duck. Federal records show the hands-down leader in ducks harvested in Georgia and North and South Carolina is the woodie.

This sporty little bird constitutes approximately half the total harvest in this three-state area.

This fact, plus its beauty, sporting qualities, and abundance, make it easy to understand why the wood duck is so highly regarded in the Deep South. In the other south Atlantic state, Florida, the ring-neck is number one, comprising about 30 percent of the total harvest.

Probably the most negative aspect of waterfowling in the south Atlantic states is the drastic decline in Canada goose hunting. Only North Carolina still supports some quality hunting, with about 10,000 birds harvested per year.

Thirty years ago Canada geese were common in all four states, principally in coastal areas. For example, in 1954 the Florida panhandle supported 60,000 birds. Today, thanks to northern reservoir developments now used for roosting, resting, and security; mechanical grain harvesting; and winter green forage crops, migratory Canada geese winter farther north and are practically nonexistent in the three southernmost states. All three have stocked nonmigratory strains, which are reproducing. Whether they will ever build up to a huntable population is questionable, but at least these magnificent birds can be seen and heard in several deep south localities.

A most welcome bonus to the south Atlantic waterfowl scene, especially to southern Florida, is the nonmigratory Florida duck, which occurs in the southern half of the Florida peninsula. It has counterparts in extreme southern Mississippi, Louisiana, Texas, New Mexico, Arizona, and Mexico. Introductions into South Carolina have shown no conclusive results

Florida-style Atlantic Coast hunting. *Florida Game and Freshwater Fish Commission photo.*

as yet. This fine mallard-type bird makes up about 10 percent of Florida's waterfowl harvest.

Surprisingly, Florida—noted primarily for its beaches, palm trees, winter vegetables, and oranges—is normally third in the nation in ducks harvested per duck stamp. Louisiana and California usually occupy the first two positions, and Florida occasionally loses its number three spot to Arkansas or Mississippi.

South Atlantic hunting techniques are as varied as its species and habitats: Open-water rigs for scoter and scaup, early-morning pass shooting for ring-neck at dawn, standing beside a tree in a wood duck swamp, shoot jumping puddle ducks from potholes in *Spartina* or black rush marshes, and so on.

But far the most common and generally most productive duck hunting arrangement is the conventional brush blind and decoy setup with—thank goodness—the customary disagreement about arrangement, numbers and kinds of decoys; neat blinds or scraggly blinds; concealing or not concealing the retriever. All this makes gabbing about duck hunting an international treasure. The motto is, everybody to his own thing!

A couple of special, or at least relatively uncommon, techniques are worth describing. In northern Florida, where mallard are scarce, a few hardy and dedicated mallard hunters wade the cypress swamps with half a dozen decoys. When they flush a small group of mallard they put out their decoys where the birds flushed, conceal themselves, and occasionally call. In a surprising number of instances the ducks—or some ducks—come back.

When bag limits on redhead were more attractive, a few southern Georgia and northern Florida hunters took advantage of the large flocks wintering in the Gulf south of St. Marks. Picking a day with a strong south wind of twenty knots or so, and preferably high tide, they set up a rough blind on the beach with a large stool of 100 or more decoys twenty or thirty yards out. Disturbed and pushed by the wind, redhead and scaup would swing in over those decoys like gangbusters!

In summary, the south Atlantic area has a tremendous variety of hunting opportunities for almost every kind of North American duck. High points are:

Wood duck. Beaver ponds and cypress swamps everywhere.

Mallard. Coastal marshes and rice fields of North and South Carolina; reservoirs, beaver ponds, and grain fields of northern Georgia.

Ring-neck. Florida's big shallow-water lakes and marshes, especially Lake Okeechobee.

Scoter. North Carolina coast.

Miscellaneous puddle ducks (wigeon, gadwall, teal, pintail). Salt and brackish marshes of all four states.

Scaup. Saltwater bays of all four states, especially Florida.

Geese. North Carolina only.

Before anyone starts throwing rocks, we'd like to point out that we are well aware that every duck hunter worth his salt has his own honey-hole—probably outside of the generalized areas we've mentioned. Just remember, we can't name them all— and you probably wouldn't want us to, anyway!

25

Dakota Waterfowling

T. L. Kuck

Although agriculture is the chief resource in both states, the outdoors person recognizes the Dakotas for their abundant natural resources. From border to border, east to west, north to south, the waterfowl hunter will find Dakota country a mecca for his or her sport.

The total human population of the two states is around 1,300,000 people; about 70,000 are waterfowl hunters. Spread them out over a total land area of slightly over 145,000 square miles, and hunting conditions aren't too crowded. To make it even more appealing, the state game and fish departments and the U.S. Fish and Wildlife Service together own and manage over 500,000 acres in the two states, most of it for waterfowl production.

These lands offer a tremendous assortment of public hunting areas, places where the hunter never has to ask permission to hunt or observe waterfowl and other spe-

cies of wildlife. It's on these same areas that Ducks Unlimited is now working under its U.S. Habitat Program to develop and improve waterfowl production and general use on many of these public hunting areas.

Both Dakotas are prominent waterfowl producers, ranking second and third overall behind Alaska in U.S. production. In 1985, an estimated 8.5 million ducks were added to the North American fall flight of waterfowl from these two states. In addition, both states have resident populations of giant Canada geese, around 20,000 in South Dakota and about 10,000 in North Dakota.

If duck hunting over decoys is the hunter's goal, the Dakotas have it. In early October, when the season opens, there may be eight to ten species of puddlers and divers working properly placed decoys. Pass shooting divers is also available. Redheads and canvasbacks, along with blue-bills, buffleheads, and ruddy ducks, often make a thrilling buzz over the not-quite-ready hunter en route to another lake or marsh. Ever hunt cornfield or stubble-field mallards late in the season? Lying face down or on your back, dressed in camo or white (if there's snow on the ground), your gun similarly camouflaged, you wait for that tornado of greenheads swirling out to the sky to give you that one good pass! You'll find all of this in Dakota country.

So you're into goose hunting, huh? What color and when? Snow geese by the hundreds of thousands abound in eastern Dakota from late September to mid-November. Add to this the resident giant Canadas scattered throughout eastern North and South Dakota counties, and it'll make for a quickened pulse and sweaty palms. A giant Canada goose at twelve to fifteen pounds rates as a real trophy in anybody's book!

Moving from eastern to the central Dakotas, you find the Missouri River, where as many as 750,000 to 1,000,000 geese (Canadas, white-fronts, and some snows) congregate beginning in early October and remain until late December. In South Dakota over 700,000 Canadas and white-fronts have been surveyed on the Missouri River in late October and early November. The large impoundments on the river offer refuge for the birds on their southern migration, and the irrigated corn and small grains, so abundant along the reservoir system, set up a banquet irresistible to geese and ducks passing through this portion of mid-America.

A variety of other hunting opportunities including pass shooting, field decoy set-ups, and pit hunting over decoys can be found in this area. The Missouri also offers some excellent mallard shooting over decoys. The hardy waterfowler, with the right equipment to traverse these big waters in all types of inclement weather, will find the finest mallard shooting to be had anywhere.

West of the Missouri River, the landscape is dotted with manmade water areas commonly called stock dams. These water

Dakota snow goose hunting with goose camouflage amid decoys. *Ed Bry photo.*

Appreciation of the beauty of the quarry should be of critical importance to every waterfowler. *Ed Bry photo.*

bodies range in size from as small as an acre to larger reservoirs of over 1,000 acres. The area, with a mixture of agriculture and prairie, is a prominent duck producer. Some fine early shooting can be found here.

Throughout a large portion of western Dakotas, the game and fish departments have reintroduced the giant Canada goose. Over 15,000 resident Canadas, along with migrants, offer a new hunting opportunity in this area. Late mallard shooting can be found along the approaches to the Black Hills and on the major tributaries and reservoirs, where mallards find the warm waters and irrigated crops to their liking.

South Dakota, "Land of Infinite Variety," and North Dakota "Roughrider Country"—these clichés certainly fit the waterfowl hunting available in this unique area once known as "Dakota Territory".

26

Duck Hunting, Louisiana Style

W. J. Lorio

Duck hunting in Louisiana's marshes, bayous, sloughs, and swamps is deeply rooted in Louisiana culture. Much has been written about the men, women, and children who hunt the marshes and swamps, from early market hunting days to the recreational hunting of our time.

Some make just one memorable duck hunt annually; others hunt eagerly every day of the season. But the casual hunter is no less enthusiastic than the addict. When you say "ducks" in Louisiana, everyone stops and listens. There is the story of the Cajun who went to the judge to ask for another month of duck season. The judge asked him, "What are you going to name this month, since you're already duck hunting twelve months of the year?"

There are two basic types of waterfowling in Louisiana: hunting coastal marsh habitat, or hunting the cypress-tupelo swamps, which are found in all parts of the state. The techniques are as different as day and night.

Duck hunting is a very social activity, and camp life is inherent in both types of hunting. Hunters gather at the camp, which is often isolated, the evening before the hunt. Old friends are greeted, new acquaintances made, and excitement and anticipation of the morning run high. Equipment is checked and boats test driven (mixed in with drinks and coffee) and then comes the cook's first call for supper, which is either gumbo or sauce piquante. During supper, decisions are made as to who will hunt what blind. This is followed by more stories, boo ray, poker, and then bed.

Before your head hits the pillow good, the 4:00 A.M. alarm sounds, and it's time to get up. It takes a good hot cup of black

A Louisiana ricefield blind . . . *Albert Stefanski photo.*

. . . filled with action! *Albert Stefanski photo.*

coffee to rejuvenate an enthusiasm dulled by drink, stories, cards, and little sleep. But soon, all senses are functioning properly, and it's off to the duck blind.

The cold, dark boat ride makes you wonder about your mental capacity. It has been suggested duck hunters are escapees from mental hospitals. Many normal Louisianans become insane during duck season!

There's special excitement in hunting Louisiana's coastal marshes. It begins with putting out dozens of decoys in small marsh ponds, or hundreds of decoys in large bays and open water. The placement and construction materials of the blind, and the decoy sets, are of prime importance in marsh hunting. Decoys are the key to attracting waterfowl, and a good blind is insurance for a successful hunt.

With the early morning boat ride over and the decoys out, one can then enjoy the sound of many whistling wings overhead in the dark, then the braking and setting of swift wings as the ducks turn for the decoys, followed by a gentle splash as they gracefully land. Straining eyes find it difficult to distinguish ducks from decoys. As dawn breaks and shooting hours begin, this scenario will be repeated many times before the hunters have their legal bag. And with several hunters in a blind, the retriever will be kept very busy.

Blue-winged and green-winged teal, gadwall, wigeon, pintail, mallard, shoveler, and coot (poule d'eau) are the common species inhabiting the coastal marshes. Teal are most numerous.

Coastal ducks become wary after the season starts, but continue to decoy if all other conditions seem natural. The duck call is not as important in the marsh as it is in swamp hunting, but good duck calling will ensure a greater degree of success.

The excitement of marsh or ricefield hunting lies in seeing thousands of waterfowl in flight to and from favorite resting or feeding areas. While actually shooting ducks varies in importance with each hunter, all enjoy seeing them in flight. Coastal marsh hunting is an exciting activity, matched only by hunting the cypress-tupelo swamps.

Hunting in cypress-tupelo swamps is duck hunting in its purest form. You don't need a blind and not many decoys; a dozen is plenty. Your blind is often a natural part of the swamp, such as a Spanish moss–draped cypress tree. The excitement of swamp hunting is that, while you can hear the whistling wings overhead, often you may not see the ducks because of the forest canopy. Prevalent species are mallard (locally called French duck) and wood duck. Occasionally other species are found, but not on a regular basis.

Shooting wood duck basically involves being in the right place at the right time; they don't decoy well, nor do they respond to a duck call. And shooting wood duck in a swamp challenges the most skillful hunter, requiring not only knowledge of feeding areas and flight paths but also the ability to hit a fast and elusive target through standing timber.

Hunting mallard in the swamps is discussed last because this is the favorite of many Louisiana duck hunters. Here expertise with a duck call is essential. Nothing in waterfowling is more exciting than seeing mallard brake in full flight and spin in midair, in response to a well-timed call. After the initial attraction, they must then be enticed within shooting range. This is accomplished by patience, concealment, and knowing when and when not to call. Mallard are very wary, and any error in calling or concealment will send them flying in the opposite direction. A bag limit of four drake mallard is indeed a prize to be proud of. Swamp hunters don't see the number of ducks or get the shots that marsh hunters do, but the excitement and enjoyment are unique. Only a swamp hunter can describe the thrill of hunting mallard and calling them in, for either shooting or pictures.

Duck hunting in Louisiana is like turkey hunting in Alabama, pheasant hunting in South Dakota, grouse hunting in Michigan, or elk hunting in Colorado—a fever. Most residents of the state have it, and it's contagious. There is no cure and no antidote once waterfowling gets into your blood. It fits the spirit of Louisiana: "Laissez les bons temps rouler"—Let the good times roll!

27

California Duck Hunting

L. F. Edgerton

We all have what I call crystal moments. While you're meditating or recalling the past, your insides suddenly warm up to a particular recollection—a crystal moment! It may relate to a sporting event in which you excelled, a beautiful sunset, or a specific fishing or hunting trip.

Perhaps we can recall a waterfowling crystal moment for you by mentioning a few examples of the varied hunts available in California's mountains and valleys.

Let's begin in the stark white snow at 7,000 feet around the edge of McGee Bay, Crowley Lake. You've arrived before the sun; and now you, your partner, and your favorite retriever are hidden under white camouflage, awaiting those wily honkers. Forget the cold you endured; the many times when no birds came within range; just remember the best of all days. A beautiful sunrise, dozens of those majestic birds in the air, decoying in, and then . . . a double to remember forever.

Maybe you don't like it that cold. Then let's head south to the Imperial Valley and the Salton Sea, 232 feet below sea level. In October, when the season opens, it's normally over 100°F, often over 110°! The flight through Utah and down the Colorado has produced sprig, mallard, teal, shoveler, wigeon, and others for the taking. State and federal areas provide hunting opportunities, and at the same time give the birds feed and refuge.

Your club is on the southeast side of the "Sea"; for the week preceding the opening, thousands of sprig have been using it and bypassing your neighbors. This particular crystal moment produces all the birds you can legally take; a sunrise over the Chocolate Mountains; and sprig so fat they take off like divers by paddling down the ponds.

One of those crystal moments that gets frozen in memory. *Glenn Chambers photo.*

These are extremes. But California *is* extreme, both topographically and in waterfowl habitat. A coastline of over 1,000 miles, as much as 12 eastern seaboard states; Mount Whitney is the highest point in the Lower 48 and Death Valley the lowest, at 280 feet below sea level.

Maybe a trip, starting in San Diego and culminating 800 miles north in the Tule Lake–Lower Klamath area, was your moment. Here many sportsmen utilize the fine guide services available. You are in the tules, the decoys are placed for you, and then, when the birds are there, could one want more?

Practically every species of ducks and geese come through this Pacific Flyway stopover. A little east, near Alturas and the Warner Mountains, is probably the best honker hunting in the west. Was your moment there? Or you can climb Sheepy Ridge, and pass shoot as the birds fly from Lower Klamath over the ridge to Tule Lake. Where else do you shoot *down* on birds from a blind?

If we haven't tickled your fancy yet, let's venture into the great Sacramento–San Joaquin Valley and Delta area. Places like the Butte Sink Suisun Marsh, the Grasslands, District 10, the Bypass, the Delta, and dozens of others have thrilled outdoorsmen since the days of the California Gold Rush. Here you can hunt in a rice-field with or without "dekes," a pothole, from a boat on one of the many waterways, on one of the many state or federal areas, or as a member or guest at one of the fabulous clubs.

Millions of waterfowl winter in this great expanse of water and food. The clubs regulate water and aquatics to attract them, and they come in abundance. Crossing on the ferry to this delta island, you are told there are 500,000 ducks and 200,000 geese awaiting you. That night before going to bed, after a wonderful meal with good wine and fine companionship, you venture onto the porch. Cupping your hands behind your ears, you listen. That might be your crystal moment right then. It doesn't take a gun or a full bag—those

thousands of talking waterfowl on this clear moonless night are something to remember.

You are to shoot the big pond tomorrow and sleep comes slowly. After an early breakfast, you and your partner are taken to the blind with an outboard, and are well settled before the sound of the motor dies away. Eight shooters can be accommodated. But the members have scattered, leaving the two of you a large pond, 2,000 decoys, and hopes for a wonderful sprig hunt. By the time the sun finds you from behind the Sierra Nevada mountains to the east, you have eight bull sprig on the water

A hunter's sunset in Butte County, California. *John Cowan photo.*

Pintails — a cherished tradition in California waterfowling. *Ed Bry photo.*

and a large flight is circling. When your partner says, "Now," you rise to over 1,000 pintail feet before your eyes. A double each, and ten minutes later limits are filled with fourteen cock pintail.

When was the crystal moment? Was it the birds in flight, the thrill of them re-sponding to your call, or later when you sat down and enjoyed the fruits of the hunt with the ducks prepared to your favorite recipe?

We all have our own. Sit back and think of yours.

28

Canadian Waterfowling Traditions

C. B. Forbes
with
T. R. Gadawski, Ducks Unlimited provincial biologist, Ontario
P. Plante, Ducks Unlimited provincial biologist, Quebec
R. K. McAloney, Ducks Unlimited provincial biologist, Maritime Provinces

About half a million Canadians and over one and a half million Americans hunt waterfowl each year. But Canadians seem even keener waterfowlers than Americans. One in every 44 Canadians hunts waterfowl, compared to one in 127 Americans. And the latter number may actually be somewhat inflated, since it is based on the number of duck stamps sold, and not everyone who buys a stamp (philatelists and other collectors) hunts. And as far as enthusiasm is concerned, this too, may be more demographic than real; a high percentage of the population lives in large cities, where the hunting tradition tends to disappear with the loss of easy opportunity.

The annual harvest reflects the difference in the total number of hunters. In recent years, Americans are estimated to harvest about 20.5 million ducks and 2.9 million geese annually; Canadians 6.1 million ducks and 1 million geese. These data include unretrieved birds and the native kill. Mexico is estimated to harvest about 1.38 million ducks.

The average annual kill per hunter in both Canada and the United States is about ten ducks. In the mid-1970s, Canadians annually killed about 50 percent more ducks per hunter than Americans, but by 1983 it was about equal. But individual Canadian hunters now kill more geese annually than Americans.

Canadian provinces establish waterfowl regulations within a federal framework similar to the system in the United States. Baiting and live decoys are prohibited and guns plugged to three shells. Canada, in cooperation with the United States, has been experimenting with a five-year program of stabilized regulations.

On the prairies and British Columbia, bag limits have been eight ducks daily, sixteen in possession, with special restrictions on mallard, canvasback, and redhead. For geese, the bag limit is eight with sixteen in possession, with special restrictions on Canada geese and white-fronted geese where they occur. In British Columbia, the goose limit is five, with special late-season restrictions to protect resident giant Canada geese.

In Ontario, Quebec, and the Maritime Provinces the basic daily bag limit has been six ducks with special protection for black duck, and bonus scaup at the end of the season. The daily limit for sea ducks, eiders, scoters, etc., is ten in the Maritimes; for geese five per day with no special provision for Canada geese. In Ontario part of the kill is lesser snow and blue geese, and in Quebec, greater snow geese.

In Canada, the season opens progressively from north to south; September 1 in the extreme north and about September 24 in the southern zone. Season length is legally about two months but practically, except in coastal areas, is seldom more than six weeks because of freezeup. In southern Manitoba, for instance, in 1984 the season opened September 24, but for all practical purposes was closed by freezeup on October 27.

Many Canadian hunting traditions and techniques originated in the United States; some are uniquely Canadian. Among these are the use of tolling dogs in the Maritime Provinces, stubble shooting in the prairie provinces, and hunting the greater snow goose on the tidal flats of the St. Lawrence River in Quebec.

The tolling dog is unique to Atlantic Canada. It takes advantage of the curiosity of ducks and geese and is said to have evolved from watching red foxes catch waterfowl. This is likely why a small reddish dog with a white flag was developed, and is now registered as a distinct breed by the Canadian Kennel Club. With the hunter always hidden, the tolling dog is sent out in front of the blind to retrieve small objects and play about. The curious waterfowl swim toward the dog, sometimes even walking up on the beach. The dog is trained to ignore them until after the shooting, and then to retrieve.

Saskatchewan and Alberta waterfowl hunting traditions have evolved from their grainfields rather than their marshes. Early settlers broke the prairie sod and seeded it to wheat around the turn of the century, and thereby unwittingly provided a banquet table for mallard and geese. A winter's supply of greenheads became part of the harvest when they were taken in late fall from stooked fields and grain butts. It was not uncommon to see braces of ducks hung on the north side of outbuildings, to be buried later in the grain piles to keep them frozen should a winter thaw occur. Because of their table qualities and the ease with which they were hunted in the grainfields, a mallard hunting tradition evolved, which continues to this present day with little change.

Despite an abundance of lakes, marshes, and potholes, relatively little hunting occurred on them, aside from jump shooting by the local town sports. "Slough ducks" was a generalized term used to describe any duck without a green head. A mixed bag definitely categorized the hunter as a "city type." Anyone hunting over water with decoys was considered a little weird.

Decoys were considered by local hunters to be expensive, cumbersome, and unnecessary. Stubble decoys, if used at all, were either tarpaper or metal profile goose de-

The tolling dog is unique to Atlantic Canada. *Ducks Unlimited Canada photo.*

coys. In other parts of the flyways, waterfowl decoy carvers were an important part of the industry, but Saskatchewan had none. For waterfowl decoy collectors, Saskatchewan and Alberta are virtually a wasteland. The collectible items have usually been left behind by visiting sportsmen.

This doesn't imply that waterfowl hunting wasn't a popular sport, but rather that it was unnecessary to acquire a large inventory of gear for a day's outing. Virtually unrestricted access and an abundance of game obviously didn't motivate local gunners to purchase much more than a full-choke shotgun and a supply of high base Imperial shot shells.

During the last three decades, the prairie goose hunter has emerged as the status waterfowl hunter. This trend has included pit diggers and field rigs numbering hundreds of decoys. With the exception of a few native guides in northern communities, goose calling is not generally practiced by the "pit dwellers." "Keep your head down and your mouth shut" is the advice usually given a novice, particularly if he has a new call hung about his neck! One must assume that geese fresh from the northern breeding grounds are not as hard to seduce as they may be farther south.

With extensive land use changes and fewer places to hunt, today's sportsman must be more opportunistic. Large staging populations of Arctic geese still dominate the prairie waterfowler's attention, but those wishing to harvest a few quackers have had to modify their standards. Boats, waders, dogs, and duck decoys are becoming more commonplace on prairie marshes. "Slough ducks," it seems, are becoming more fashionable, if not necessary, to complete a day's bag. Perhaps a new waterfowl tradition is about to emerge.

Manitoba combines the traditional boat and decoy waterfowling of eastern Canada and the United States with stubble shooting, which evolved with agriculture. In contrast to Saskatchewan and Alberta, stubble shooting evolved from marsh hunting as agriculture expanded. The great staging marshes associated with Lakes Winnipeg, Manitoba, and Winnipegosis were gunned from earliest times, and were famous not only for their mallard but for the concentrations of canvasback, redhead, and bluebill, which no one despised!

Prior to about 1960, few blue and snow geese staged in southern Manitoba in the fall, although they were abundant in the spring. Since that time, their fall numbers have steadily increased, particularly in recent years with the increase in the acreage planted to corn. There has also been a similar increase in small Canadas (Richardson's goose). Now hundreds of thousands of snow and blue geese add a new and thrilling dimension to the Manitoba fall.

Because of its rugged topography, gunning opportunities for waterfowl in British Columbia are largely confined to its river systems and estuaries. Unfortunately much waterfowl hunting opportunity has been severely restricted by expanding resi-

An early day bag of mallards for winter use. *Ducks Unlimited Canada photo.*

dential development and associated fire-arm regulations. Large flocks of wintering waterfowl wax fat on flooded market gardens, and literally go through the season unscathed.

Gunning along the mouth of the Fraser River and the lower mainland usually begins in early October, when pintail flights pass down the coastline, probably from Alaska en route to California. Mallard, wigeon, and green-winged teal increase in the bag as the fall advances.

One of the greatest waterfowl hunting traditions to suffer from the pressures of urbanization has been the brant hunt. Historically, wintering populations of Pacific black brant frequented the estuaries of Boundary Bay and the eel grass beds along Vancouver Island. Although no one knows the reason for certain, wintering brant appear to have shifted southward. Consequently, in Canada, these little sea geese can now be taken only on the northward migration in early March. Hunting on the tidal flats requires patience and dedication—plus an insensitivity to the elements! Brant decoy readily, but there are many days when the flocks either pass by out to sea, or don't come at all.

Brant hunting is now prohibited in all Vancouver Island coastal waters. On Boundary Bay, on the mainland, the preferred gunning sites are few, and heavy competition has forced additional regulations. Once restrictive regulations in the form of season closures have been invoked, they are seldom rescinded. So the younger generation of waterfowl hunters will never have the experience of hunting brant, and having never participated, will never know what they miss!

The rugged coastline of the Pacific and its tidal influence offer additional challenges to those who will brave the weather during the late fall and winter months, when fowling is at its best. Boats, dogs, raingear, and a tide book are standard equipment for those hunting the duskys and cacklers off Tofino or lying in ambush for a Russian snow off Westham Island.

Waterfowl hunting throughout the central interior of British Columbia is largely on an opportunistic basis by jump shooting small marshes. A mixed bag of divers and dabblers is only a part of the reward to those fortunate enough to enjoy the fall beauty of the Cariboo and Chilcotin.

Southbound waterfowl funneling down river systems through mountain valleys generally provide only passing opportunities, as they pause to rest and feed. One of the most important waterfowl staging areas to develop in recent years has been the Creston Valley Wildlife Management Area, located on the floodplain at the south end of Kootenay Lake. Developed by Ducks Unlimited Canada under federal-provincial agreement, these large marshes have become an important stopover for breeding and migrating waterfowl.

Some hunting methods are used countrywide and are opportunistic, requiring less technique and equipment than those used by serious waterfowlers. Not surprisingly, on a seasonal basis, they are also less successful. These include jump shooting or walking up birds, pond shooting without decoys, or jump shooting from a canoe. These are the most popular types of waterfowl hunting in Ontario and Quebec.

Traditional waterfowl hunting with blinds and decoys is practiced in the larger marshes. But for many waterfowlers in Ontario and Quebec, the big event is the arrival of the canvasback, redhead, and bluebill from the prairies, en route to wintering grounds on the U.S. East Coast. Arriving in the third week of October, the birds concentrate in the Lake St. Clair marshes, the northern shores of Lake Erie, near Long Point, and Lake Ontario, and in Quebec on lac St. Pierre, lac St. Louis, lac St. Francois, and lac des Deux Montagnes.

Diver shooting on these open waters means decoys and lots of them, as well as the fortitude to endure the cold and rough water of early winter. Here there are specialists among the specialists: the canvasback hunter, the bluebill hunter, and the goldeneye hunter.

Techniques boil down more to differences in concealment than differences in basic methodology. The decoy spread is the constant, concealment the variable. The permanent stake blind constructed in open water, the layout boat, the boat blind, the floating blind, and the point or shore blind are most commonly used techniques common to both sides of the international boundary.

Sculling or screen shooting is a holdover from the glory days of diver hunting on the Great Lakes. When birds are attracted into the decoys, a "drift" is initiated, the hunters moving down to their rig with the wind. When in range, the boat is jerked sideways, providing a clear shot at the departing birds. In Quebec and the Maritimes, sinkboxes with lots of decoys are also used in the open water.

Goose hunting in Ontario and Quebec was rather incidental until the opening of the James and Hudson Bay goose camps. Here snow and blue geese constitute the bulk of the kill. In the south, field shooting for Canada geese is now increasing in both provinces. A novel form of goose hunting, using the layout boat and lots of decoys on open-water goose resting areas, is increasing in popularity and is, surprisingly, very effective.

Hunting greater snow geese at Cap-Tourmente, on the tidal flats of the St. Lawrence River estuary in Quebec, is unique to that province. There are three sets of blinds, one for low tide, one for intermediate, and one for high tide. The blind is usually a wooden box sunk in the mud, with a waterproof cover closed when the blind is unused and covered with water. Travel to the blinds over the deep mud is traditionally by horse-drawn sleigh.

With two of the four Atlantic provinces islands, one a peninsula, and the fourth having a long irregular coastline, waterfowl hunting here, except for the great estuarine marshes of the St. John River and local beaver ponds, has traditionally been coastal and offshore-oriented. However, land use changes after the 1940s have greatly increased decoy shooting in agricultural fields and freshwater marshes. The unique hunting technique was the development of the Nova Scotia duck tolling retriever in southern Nova Scotia, as previously described.

Offshore shooting is common along the southeastern shore of Nova Scotia and the northeastern shore of New Brunswick. Large rigs of eider and scoter decoys are used; the hunters are in boats or gunning tubs, which are anchored, and float at water level with splash boards to reduce wave action.

In shallow coastal bays, sinkboxes are used; they can be raised and lowered with the tides, but shooting must stop at 1:00 P.M., a conservation measure. Another technique is the use of shoreline sand pits, which are bailed out following peak high tide and hunted until the high tide returns. Canada geese and black duck are commonly hunted in this manner.

Pass shooting is a common technique for several species. Oldsquaw and scoter are hunted this way at the mouth of bays,

At Cap-Tourmente, hunters are transported over the deep mud to the blinds by horse-drawn sleigh. *Canadian Wildlife Service photo.*

as they come in from the ocean in the morning and return in the evening; and black duck, merganser, and goldeneye in the early morning, as they fly upriver to feed. This is also a very effective method of hunting black ducks at dusk, as they come into a salt marsh from the ocean.

Stubble field shooting for black duck and Canada geese is common on Prince Edward Island and the Annapolis Valley of Nova Scotia. Commercial decoys with pit blinds or brush blinds in hedgerows are usually used.

Most decoys are now commercially made, although there are still a number of hand-carved sea duck decoys in use. Other regional adaptations for decoys include painted plastic jugs for scoters and bundles of seaweed for hunting black ducks in

grainfields and over-ice shooting. One still finds the occasional Maritime hunter using sea gull or heron decoys in his rig as confidence builders for the target ducks and geese.

Canadian waterfowling traditions vary little from American, and the reasons for waterfowling in the first place vary not at all. Distant flocks of waterfowl; the thrilling sight and sound as they approach the decoys, bobbing in the cold wind, or stark in the stubble against the early dawn; unseen wings rustling overhead before light; the outstanding shot and the unexplainable miss; the nearness and trust in a good friend; shared experiences—these speak to all waterfowlers, and with a common tongue.

29

Hunting the Black Brant

H. L. Thomas

Black brant, one of the most unique and least known of our waterfowl, provide some of the finest sport imaginable. Relatively unknown throughout the United States, owing to its marine migration pattern and coastal habitat, it provides a few knowledgeable hunters with outstanding sport and culinary qualities.

Pacific black brant are similar to the more popular Atlantic brant but larger and much darker. Over the Pacific and in the estuaries and bays along the coast, they are recognizable by their strong flight, with rapid wing beats about double those of their larger cousin, the Canada goose.

Primary nesting areas are Alaska's Kuskokwim Delta, and other bays and estuaries along the Bering Sea and the Alaskan peninsula. These nesting areas are particularly susceptible to so-called "sustenance or subsistence hunting" by natives.

Historically, the brant season in California started at the close of the regular waterfowl season in mid-January and continued for about thirty days. Most of the brant taken at this time were on their return migration from Mexico. In 1983, the regulations moved the season to the early part of migration, at the beginning of the waterfowl season. This was to help protect pair-bonded birds, which were normally harvested during the late season.

There are basically two ways of hunting black brant: the time-honored method of decoy shooting, and the method I prefer, sculling. Hunting with decoys is no different from most ocean bay duck shooting. A blind and a large number of decoys are set out on a sand spit or point projecting into a bay. Decoys may also be placed in a feeding area, usually an eel grass bed, offshore. With this setup, a layout boat or

Production from a western brant hunt. *Hugh Thomas photo.*

some type of floating blind is required. When "working" decoys, brant are quite vulnerable, and once committed to coming in, will do so. Calling is quite effective, and is usually by mouth and throat, plus a hunter's imagination. To my knowledge, there is no commercial call available and probably won't be, as the market is quite limited.

Sculling is truly a sporting method of taking brant. On ideal days, with a slight wind chop, minimal tide action, and available birds, it can be exceptional. However, with wary birds and a flat, calm day, you'll probably do as well playing golf.

Two types of scull boats can be used: the Humboldt Bay scull boat, about fourteen feet in length with a long, pointed bow and minimal freeboard, about two inches; or a "brush boat," a sneak type with a much higher profile, with brush and other material placed around it for camouflage, much like a mobile blind. Both are propelled by a single scull oar protruding through the transom, protected by a rubber "boot" to keep the water out.

Musts for brant hunting are a good pair of binoculars and a spotting scope if hunting a large body of water. They can save a lot of unnecessary sculling. Hunters use the glasses or scope to locate the birds from shore; then a scull is planned, using the tidal action and prevailing wind. This should be downwind, as brant take off upwind, and preferably with the current. Unfortunately, this doesn't work out most of the time! Once you decide your plan of approach, maneuver the boat upwind about 400 to 600 yards from the birds and start the scull. Then it is up to the strength of your arm, the tides, the winds—and your shooting ability!

It is difficult to put into words the enjoyment of working to get your birds. Sculling allows this. It's not the passive wait for birds of normal waterfowl hunting, but actually a pursuit, which to me is much more enjoyable.

30

Freezeout Swans

B. F. Brown

Tundra (whistling) swans are a highly prized trophy for those few sportsmen fortunate enough to draw a permit. Five hundred are customarily issued yearly for the area surrounding Freezeout Lake, Montana.

Fall swan migration begins in early October and peaks between the third week of October and the first week of November. It coincides closely with that of both Canada and lesser snow geese and many species of ducks. Thus, those who time their hunt with the arrival of a polar cold front have the opportunity for a mixed bag of waterfowl rivaled in few places.

Waterfowl in the truest sense of the term, swan seldom venture far on land. They don't graze like geese, preferring to feed by "tipping up" in shallow water like puddle ducks. Because of their feeding habits, most swan are taken as they trade between bodies of water. The more serious waterfowler, one willing to spend some time at his sport, can learn to imitate the resonant "who-who" and "wow-who" calls of these regal birds. Experience shows that these calls are best used when the hunter works the points of longer peninsulas.

Freezeout Lake is a public hunting area, and this means a respectable hike from the parking area to the better shooting spots. All gear is packed in on "shank's ponies."

The weather is less than balmy at this time of year. Therefore the wise hunter will burden himself with a good stash of warm clothing, food, coffee, wind-resistant camouflage material, and personal comfort items to tough out what can be a daylight to dusk event. This load, combined with the anticipation of an even bulkier and heavier load of wet feathers on the return trek, will tax the ingenuity of

A swan's song and beauty. *Glenn Chambers photo.*

any outdoorsman who believes in traveling light. Decoys, especially the giant Canadas, commonly painted white and set with the stool, are almost out of the question.

Enter the Man from Glad!

Tall white kitchen trash bags are compact, light, and as effective a decoy as anything. When at the selected site, simply blow up the bags, secure the opening with a heavy rubber band, and tie on a decoy line. Rig with a weight of at least six ounces, and set the bags in a loose pattern in the lee of the peninsula. As few as three bags have been used successfully, but "the more the merrier" rule probably prevails, as it does with geese.

Swans are likely to trade between feeding and resting spots at any time of day, so you can pass shoot ducks and geese while you wait for a swan flight.

Given the right weather conditions, you may also witness a noon-to-dark procession of geese, both snow and Canada, that come to rest at Freezeout. One such day provided a wave of honkers and snows that lasted from 11:00 A.M. to dusk, and numbered at least 30,000 birds.

Most swans are taken with the 12-gauge, simply because it's the most common shotgun, though the 10-gauge is occasionally seen. A three-inch magnum load of Number 2 copper-plated shot, or larger, is

needed. The ability of these birds to absorb a hammering is nothing short of
amazing. It is not uncommon to cripple a
swan with three or four pellets in the head
and neck area—a lethal dose for most
waterfowl. The birds' natatorial prowess
when crippled makes an experienced,
strong swimming dog, capable of retriev-
ing an angry eighteen-pounder, a necessity.

Few waterfowling experiences can equal
that of tagging one of these magnificent
birds.

Freezeout Lake is only one area offering
the one-bird permit for swan. In 1983 another permit season was initiated for the
Medicine Lake area of eastern Montana.
Both Utah and Nevada offer a limited swan
season as well. An inquiry to the game
departments of these states will provide the
procedures for applying for a permit.

31

Hunting Management

C. J. Barstow

Hunting management, "controlling the gun," boils down to the simple basics of when and how an area is hunted. Applying these basics to a specific unit of land becomes more complex, because it depends on the acreage involved, attractiveness of habitat, cover condition, success level desired, number of folks to satisfy, and perhaps number of birds in the general area.

Let's say that your dream has come true. Some way, somehow, you have acquired, or are responsible for, a beautiful piece of duck hunting property. You are either blessed with a natural wetland area, or have developed the necessary food and water requirements to make one attractive to the birds. Unless you are extremely fortunate you have probably put a lot of time and money into the project. Now, how do you manage the tract, peoplewise, to maintain waterfowl use and quality shooting; to

make your investment in time, interest, and money pay off?

There are many techniques available to help with your endeavor. Most were developed years ago by clubs in various parts of the country. They have been applied to assure optimum hunting; they wouldn't still be around if they weren't successful! The techniques have also been used extensively on a few public waterfowl areas, where quality hunting experience is a priority goal.

When to hunt and the number of guns allowed are the first points to be considered. Other techniques are secondary and only add polish to the chosen system. In the 1960s, managers of public areas in the Mississippi Flyway used two general rules of thumb to obtain "quality" hunting for public hunters. They allowed (1) either half-day or alternate-day shooting, and (2) one blind or about two hunters per minimum area of twenty-five acres. Together these two guidelines produced an average success rate of about one or one and a half birds per hunter per day. And that translates into quality hunting on public areas in the Mississippi Flyway!

At the opposite extreme are some of the finest clubs in the country that place only one blind per section (640 acres), and then gun the site only two or perhaps three half-days per week, or maintain an extensive "rest" area closed to all hunting. Under these circumstances bag limits for almost every shooter are a real potential. In real life this means that accomplished sportsmen are obtaining good bags and the novices practically nothing.

Experience and expertise in your local area should be used in determining your preliminary management guidelines. Such expertise, whether from a club or a professional waterfowl manager, can assure the success of your investment in time, money, or both.

Considering the two extremes above, and experience from many other management programs, shooting on your area should be initiated on a very conservative basis. Liberalizing can come later, if warranted. A conservative basis would probably mean shooting on alternate mornings only, with as few guns as practical. Decision on the number of hunters allowed would depend on the quality desired, the area (its size, shape, habitat, and so on), and experience on surrounding marshes.

Other "tools" that have had practical application and might be considered as further improvements are establishing rest areas or at least small undisturbed areas within the area; restricting access to and through the area; restricting time when hunters can enter the area; restricting very

early morning shooting; shell limits; refraining from shooting at (educating) large flocks of birds.

With the right conditions, even small rest areas of fifty to one hundred acres have successfully held good concentrations of mallard and other puddle ducks. Usually heavy cover and isolation are the key factors. Regardless of size, harassment or "pushing" the birds should be an absolute *no*!

Excellent gunning has been developed on habitat used by field-feeding birds for roosting or loafing. In such cases the birds are allowed to depart the site on their own; that is, not shot out! Then the birds are lightly hunted for only a couple of hours when they return.

Self-control can be the most effective management tool available for increasing average daily success. Shell limits have been used extensively and successfully, primarily on public goose hunting areas. They have had a positive impact on hunting success and hunting conditions wherever used. Poor sportsmanship, sky busting, and associated crippling are generally minimized. These factors alone make this technique worthwhile. It should be considered for duck areas as a means to provide better, more sporting hunting. Remember, each shot fired means more educated birds!

Most of you know of, or have experienced, the results of hunting under carefully controlled management. However, managed hunting has been hard to sell. So just in case you are still in doubt, consider this. Have you noticed:

- how many times you have really had top gunning in the same spot for more than two consecutive days?

- that it takes time — real time — for an area

or blind to recover after it has been "burned," that is, had the heck shot out of it?

• how many times you have shot a roost or loafing spot in the twilight and had the birds return in numbers? The old Reelfoot gumbooters used to say, "Damn ducks don't like da fire runnin' out of a gun barrel!"

• that large, nearby concentrations of even a quarter million birds have not offered good hunting opportunity in the best quality adjacent habitat (even flooded corn) when hunting management wasn't applied? The birds simply shifted to nighttime use of the area.

• that waterfowl use of an extremely attractive rest area or refuge will be minimized if it is periodically "pushed" or disturbed? This isn't a very good tradeoff for the possibility of a little extra gunning.

• how the Dakotas and Manitoba developed concentrations of hundreds of thousands of blue and snow geese and outstanding hunting opportunity with half-day hunting and the establishment of rest areas?

There is very little actual data on "with or without" hunting management on a given waterfowl area; however, tests were conducted for one year on two state units in the mid-South. Both units had blind spacing. One was traditionally shot half-days only, the other on alternate days. In the test year, hunting was opened up the last week of the season to all the law would allow, each day from dawn until dark.

Hunting success improved on the first day of change; then fell to almost nil in the last four days. The change was so evident, and so dramatic, that demands for reduced hunting controls ended on the spot.

In summary, a given tract of duck country can provide only so much really good hunting. This potential can only be reached by "controlling the gun" or applying good hunting management. Professional advice, good judgment, and local experience can provide the basics and background for developing the full potential of your area toward fulfilling your goals and needs.

Glenn
D. Chambers
1986

Part V
Winter Homes

The prairie breeding grounds, the waterfowl production from them, and their attrition by human activities and drought have been much publicized, but this emphasis may have been at the expense of the wintering habitat.

Production is dynamic, and the struggle of waterfowl to reproduce in spite of the heavy odds against them is easily dramatized. It is less easy with the equally essential wintering habitat. The impact of decreasing wintering habitat on waterfowl survival is not as easy to see and evaluate as a prairie drought.

Sportsmen tend to forget that although as much as 70 percent of waterfowl are produced in Canada, virtually 100 percent are wintered in the United States for a period of at least five months or pass through en route to Mexico and Central and South America. The birds are often crowded into dwindling habitat, posing difficult and expensive management problems.

The continuing prosperity of North American goose populations, particularly Canada geese, indicates that wintering-ground management, at least for these species, has been very successful. For ducks, whose habitat requirements are more diverse and more subject to encroachment and pollution, the situation is less clear—and less optimistic.

Before ducks can return to the prairies to nest, they must survive.

32

Wintering Grounds in Perspective

R. H. Chabreck

Winter habitat needs of waterfowl vary with the species, and, with almost fifty species present in North America during winter, a wide diversity of habitats is required. Some species display considerable flexibility in winter habitat and food requirements.

Mallards seem equally at home in the dry cornfields of Nebraska, wet ricefields in California, flooded pin oak flats of Arkansas, beaver ponds in Alabama, and coastal marshes in South Carolina. They'll feed on grass and weed seeds, leafy aquatic plants, acorns, and waste grain as well as aquatic insects, snails, and crustaceans.

But some species are more demanding. Gadwall, a close relative of the mallard, utilize shallow marshes, ponds, and wooded lakes, feeding on leafy aquatic plants and algae and, on rare occasions, venturing ashore to graze tender grasses.

The common merganser, a deepwater duck, remains on lakes, rivers, and reservoirs during winter with a diet composed almost entirely of small fish.

Wood ducks require forested wetlands; they feed on grass and weed seeds, nuts, leafy aquatic plants, and aquatic insects. Snow geese grub for roots and rhizomes and graze tender sprouts in harvested croplands, pastures, prairies, and coastal marshes, selecting areas with short vegetation that provides unobstructed view in all directions.

Other species of waterfowl also have special winter habitat requirements, frequently shifting about on the wintering grounds in search of them, often in response to changing habitat conditions and disturbance by man. Habitat changes may be gradual or very sudden. Gradual changes may be ecological, such as the invasion of a shallow lake by water hyacinth. An increase in turbidity may result in a gradual disappearance of submerged aquatics; or, conversely, decreasing turbidity may cause aquatic plants to increase.

Sudden changes, making a winter habitat unsuitable, are often associated with rainfall. Rapid flooding can make a marsh or pond too deep for feeding by dabblers. On the other hand, the altered conditions may meet the habitat requirements of diving ducks, and they may promptly occupy the area.

Waterfowl, because of their varying needs, use a wide diversity of winter habitats, and better distribution results. If they were confined to the sea, only coastal residents could enjoy them.

Waterfowl wintering areas must have climatic conditions that assure ample feeding sites throughout the winter. Those tied to water must have ponds, lakes, or rivers relatively free of ice. Upland feeders can contend only with minimum snow cover. Whenever these conditions are not met, waterfowl soon move southward in search of more desirable situations.

Warm-water wells, used to maintain some open water in frozen lakes, or grain spread over snow to provide food, may place the birds in unnecessary jeopardy. Under such conditions, large numbers of ducks and geese may concentrate on a small area for several weeks. In such crowded conditions, they are very vulnerable to diseases such as fowl cholera and duck plague, and heavy losses may occur. Permitting the birds to disperse naturally to more favorable habitat reduces the risk of disease outbreaks.

All geographical regions of North America with favorable weather serve as wintering grounds for waterfowl, the number of birds varying with the amount and quality of habitat available. Each region has special advantages and special problems, but all contribute to the welfare of the waterfowl resource. Waterfowl refuges, management areas, and private clubs are distributed throughout the wintering grounds, and they strive to improve habitat conditions locally. These areas will be discussed in greater detail by other authors writing on this aspect of waterfowl management.

The Pacific Coast provides a series of bays, inlets, and river valleys. While limited in number, these coastal areas afford essential wintering habitat for diving ducks and brant, although the quality has been greatly reduced by urbanization and industrial development. Major problems are dredging, siltation, and pollution.

The Columbia River basin of eastern Washington, Oregon, and southern Idaho encompasses a small but important wintering region. Dams and reservoirs constructed on many of the tributary streams provide rest areas for waterfowl that spread out to nearby cropland to feed. Although winters are severe, many birds, particularly mallard and Canada geese, remain throughout the season.

The Central Valley of California is relatively small but heavily used by waterfowl. Mild climate and abundance of wetland habitat provide ideal conditions for migrants. The Sacramento–San Joaquin river system, supplied with runoff water from the Sierra Nevadas, makes the valley a leader in habitat quality in the West.

The Great Basin, between the Rocky Mountains and the Sierra Nevada Range, is a large but arid region. The basin is actually mountain plateau terrain, with low rainfall and severe winters. Its numerous shallow lakes and potholes provide excellent winter habitat when rainfall is sufficient. While competition for available water is keen, reservoirs constructed for agricultural and municipal water supplies also provide waterfowl habitat.

Another large region, but among the lowest in habitat quality, is the Colorado basin. It encompasses much of the Southwest and is characterized by rugged terrain, low rainfall, and heavily silted rivers and streams. Here, reservoirs with nearby cropland provide the best waterfowl habitat available.

The vast area east of the Rockies to the 100° parallel comprises the short-grass prairies or Great Plains, the southern extent of which is wintering habitat although still greatly influenced by weather. Rainfall averages less than twenty inches annually; the amount received during the year determines the habitat available to waterfowl. The northern reaches include Montana, Wyoming, and the Dakotas and contain excellent breeding and migration habitat, but severe cold generally pushes the birds farther south during early winter. Reservoirs and farm ponds in the arid regions to the south are heavily used, and grainfields supply abundant food.

The playa lakes (shallow, flat-floored basins) of the Texas panhandle are good winter habitat when water is present. The Arkansas, Platte, and other river bottoms add another dimension and provide excellent habitat.

Ecologically and historically, tall-grass prairie extends from eastern Kansas and Nebraska eastward to Ohio and is often called the breadbasket of the United States. The region averages forty inches of rainfall, and the vast corn- and wheatfields make this a favorite wintering area for mallard and Canada geese.

The lower Mississippi River valley is a major waterfowl wintering area but has undergone drastic changes in recent decades. Much of the vast bottomland forest has been cleared and is now used for soybeans and pasture. The valley contains numerous abandoned river channels, sloughs, and lakes. Food is generally abundant. Many birds use the open water for resting, flying out to feed in harvested cropland. Wood duck, which require forested habitat, have suffered most from clearing the forests. Rainfall is usually adequate, but turbid water draining from cultivated land has greatly reduced aquatic plants in many water bodies.

Marshes and associated water bodies bordering the Gulf of Mexico from Florida westward around the Gulf's periphery to Yucatan provide winter habitat for many species of migratory waterfowl. A wide variety of habitat is available, ranging from freshwater marsh to hypersaline lagoons. The latter, with dense beds of wigeon grass and shoal grass, are attractive to pintail, wigeon, and shoveler. The region has ample water, mild temperature, minimal tidal fluctuation, and favorable food supplies. However, encroachment by man is rapidly degrading the quality. Canal dredging, diversion, urbanization, and pollution are pressing problems.

From the Atchafalaya River in Louisiana westward into Texas, coastal habitat is bordered by agricultural lands used for rice, soybeans, and pasture. Ducks and geese are abundant and fly between the two areas.

Eastward from the Atchafalaya River to central Florida, many large rivers empty into the Gulf of Mexico, providing widely diversified waterfowl habitat. Because this region is so flat, large swamps border the rivers and extend inland many miles. Wintering ducks frequently shift between coastal and inland habitat in response to

LOWER MISSISSIPPI
BOTTOMLANDS AND MARSHES

WHITE R.

ARKANSAS

MISSISSIPPI R.

ATCHAFALAYA
BASIN

changing seasonal conditions and disturbance.

Coastal marshes along the shorelines of rivers and bays provide the major waterfowl wintering grounds on the Atlantic Coast. Daily tides fluctuate over a much wider range than on the Gulf Coast, causing deeper flooding and higher salinity. The largest coastal marshes are in South Carolina. Much of this habitat was drained and put into agricultural crops a century ago. However, although the venture failed, the levee systems remained in place. Today, the same levees are used by marsh managers to form impoundments, providing ideal habitat for wintering waterfowl.

Bays, sounds, and lagoons along the Atlantic Coast attract a wide variety of diving ducks. Brant winter in bays along the middle Atlantic Coast where eelgrass is abundant.

The shallow continental shelf along the Gulf Coast also serves as winter habitat for diving ducks. Scaup, redhead, and other species may spend a large part of the winter several miles offshore and feed to depths of twenty feet.

The offshore waters of the Atlantic Coast provide important winter habitat for sea ducks. Scoters, eiders, and mergansers utilize offshore Atlantic waters from New England southward.

The Gulf and Atlantic coastal plain is a vast upland region paralleling the U.S. coast from Mexico to Canada. Topography ranges from flat to rolling hills. Where climatic conditions are favorable, the coastal plain is an important wintering area. Its importance lies not in the quality of winter habitat it provides but its extent. Outside of the many river bottoms, soils are generally marginal for agricultural crops; a major land use is timber production. Large river bottoms and sloughs provide the major winter habitat.

However, upland areas in the coastal plain offer excellent opportunity for waterfowl management projects. Land managers are able to attract winter migrants and locally produce wood duck by impounding water. Farm ponds and larger reservoirs have also greatly improved the region for waterfowl. Beaver populations have reached the point where the dam-building activities of these industrious animals are providing much additional waterfowl habitat in many areas.

All sections of the United States and Mexico that historically served as wintering grounds for waterfowl still do, but their dimension has been significantly reduced. Maintaining the quality of the habitat that remains will be a major challenge in the future.

The quality of winter habitat affects waterfowl survival and the condition of birds migrating northward in the spring. Breeders must arrive on the nesting grounds with high energy reserves for successful reproduction. Wintering grounds, therefore, play a key role in perpetuation of the waterfowl resource.

33

West Coast Wetlands

L. F. Edgerton and J. M. Parrish

There are several kinds of wetland habitat on the western coast of the United States: coastal bays and estuaries, rivers, lakes and adjacent riparian habitat, flooded agricultural lands, government-managed wetlands (state and federal refuges), and privately managed wetlands (duck clubs). Detailed discussion is necessary if their interrelationships and importance to waterfowl are to be understood.

West Coast bays and associated estuarine marshes vary greatly in size and importance to waterfowl. The larger, more notable ones such as Puget Sound (110,000 acres), Gray's Harbor (12,000 acres), Willapa Bay (16,000 acres), Columbia River estuary (59,000 acres), Coos Bay (6,600 acres), Humboldt Bay (16,000 acres), Tomales Bay (9,000 acres), and the San Francisco Bay area (94,000 acres) are well known to waterfowlers and wildlife administrators alike.

But numerous smaller and lesser known waterfowl havens along the coast, too numerous to list, are also cumulatively significant in making up this very important waterfowl habitat type. There are over 400 separate coastal areas identified variously as bays, estuaries, marshes, lagoons, sloughs, rivers, creeks, lakes, ponds, islands, spits, deltas, coves, inlets, passages, and so on, ranging in size from a few to several thousand acres—all important to waterfowl. All in all, there are nearly 400,000 acres of marsh, intertidal mud flats, and shallow open-water areas considered to be important habitat in Washington, Oregon, and California.

In most cases, these estuarine systems can no longer be described as natural unmanaged tidal marsh. Much of the former tidelands have been reclaimed for agricultural use or salt production ponds, but are still important to waterfowl. Many of the reclaimed pasture or haylands are seasonally flooded during the winter, and some of the saline salt production ponds are also attractive to waterfowl.

Many types of habitat are essential if all the requirements of the different waterfowl species are to be accommodated. Dabbling ducks feed in pasture and grainfields as well as salt, fresh, and brackish marshes. Brant feed on eelgrass beds in coastal bays and Puget Sound. Diving ducks use the deep water of the bays, the lagoons, nearby lakes, and reservoirs, as well as the shallow salt and brackish marshes. Scoters remain offshore or use the larger open bays and inlets of Puget Sound.

From the standpoint of relative numbers, impact on environment, economics, hunting, and birding, the most important waterfowl wintering on the Pacific Coast in Washington, Oregon, and California include tundra swan; dusky, Great Basin, and Aleutian Canada geese; white-fronted and snow geese; Pacific brant; pintail, American wigeon, mallard, green-winged teal, shoveler; canvasback, greater and lesser scaup; ruddy duck, bufflehead; common and Barrow's goldeneye; red-breasted and hooded mergansers; and white-winged, black, and surf scoters. These species contribute significantly to the hunting harvest, make up the large concentrations of interest to nonconsumptive users, or occur in high numbers relative to their flyway or continental population levels.

Other species present, but in smaller numbers, are trumpeter swan, other races of Canada geese, gadwall, cinnamon teal, ring-necked duck, redhead, oldsquaw, and harlequin. Virtually 100 percent of the Pacific Flyway canvasback, brant, and Aleutian geese use coastal wetlands at some time during the fall, winter, or spring migration.

Nearly the entire Pacific Flyway population of Aleutian geese can sometimes be found at their spring and fall staging grounds near Crescent City, California. Large numbers of canvasback congregate in the San Pablo Bay and nearby Napa marshes in California. Pacific brant, which formerly wintered in California bays, have moved farther south; most now winter in the coastal bays of Baja California, Mexico.

Thousands of miles of rivers and creeks, and thousands of reservoirs, lakes, and ponds contribute significantly to the waterfowl habitat of the West Coast states. Although waterfowl may not concentrate in such large numbers in these smaller and diverse habitats as they do in the flooded central valley of California or the larger bays and estuaries, they are nevertheless very important to some species, as well as some segments of the public.

Wood duck rely heavily on the smaller wooded creeks, and red-breasted merganser, although rarely seen in any great numbers, are fairly common along many of the smaller rivers. Mallard also readily adapt to tree-lined watercourses.

Many younger hunters get their start by jump shooting mallards along the river or pond just outside their town. Rivers, creeks, and small reservoirs on private land also provide shooting for rural residents.

Some of the larger rivers such as the Sacramento and lower Colorado were at one time major migration routes; they still serve this purpose, but to a much lesser degree. Water control and channelization have eliminated most of the associated sloughs, sandbars, and shallows that once provided both food and protection for a great many species.

Mountain and foothill lakes and ponds

serve as migration layovers, and are utilized by divers such as redhead and bufflehead, and also by Canada geese and the ever-present mallard. Larger lakes and reservoirs near duck concentrations are used as safe resting places on shoot days, much to the consternation of the hunter.

Flooded agricultural lands in California's Central Valley constitute an important segment of winter waterfowl habitat in the Pacific Flyway. Unfortunately, most are not consistently available from year to year, and probably cannot be expected to exist in the same magnitude in the future. The most striking examples of this type of habitat are the ricelands (average 580,000 acres), the Yolo and Sutter flood bypasses (70,400 acres and 20,160 acres respectively) in the Sacramento Valley, the purposely flooded islands in the San Joaquin Delta (up to 85,000 acres), and the floodwater retention basins and leach fields in the Tulare Lake Basin.

Much of this land has waste grain (corn, barley, and rice) available, and is attractive to waterfowl. The tremendous expanse and inaccessibility to human intrusion also provide the refuge needed by the more gregarious species of waterfowl such as geese, pintail, and wigeon.

Although some of the lands are purposely flooded to take advantage of soil moisture and waterfowl hunting, most California hunters are resigned to the fact that, in those years when the reservoirs throughout the Central Valley can no longer contain the runoff, hunting success on private clubs and state and federal shooting areas will drop off. But this seldom occurs before December, or about midway through the waterfowl hunting season.

A somewhat different situation exists with the purposely flooded islands of the San Joaquin Delta. Here nearby managed public areas and duck clubs must compete with these very attractive areas for the entire waterfowl season. Both have found that adequate refuge and waterfowl food are essential in this competition.

Waterfowl are generally discouraged from utilizing California Central Valley ricelands prior to harvest in October. Wet weather shortly thereafter often prevents immediate stubble burning and tillage, and these lands then become attractive to both ducks and geese. Although they are not generally available to the unattached shooter, considerable hunting by landowners and friends does take place.

Managed wetlands in the West, particularly those in California where water is a premium factor, differ from other wetlands in that most are not flooded the year around. Permanent marshland makes up only a small percentage of the total acreage. Available water is used to grow food plants attractive to waterfowl and to provide wetland habitat only during the fall and winter months, when waterfowl are present. Approximately 53,500 acres of federal refuges and 38,000 acres of state wildlife areas in central and southern California are, for the most part, managed in this manner. They extend from the Sacramento Refuge in the north to the Imperial Refuges near the Mexican border. Refuges and wildlife areas in California's Central Valley are particularly important since it is here, where it seldom freezes, that most of the migratory waterfowl of the Pacific Flyway spend the winter.

In northern California, Oregon, and Washington, where water is not quite as critical and winter weather more severe, government areas are managed somewhat differently. Water management still plays a vital role, but the emphasis is on water in the spring for waterfowl production and in early fall for accommodation of large numbers of migrants from Canada and Alaska. Prominent examples include Turnbull Refuge in Washington, Malheur and Summer Lake Refuges in Oregon, and Tule Lake Refuge in northern California.

Most of the privately managed wetlands are in central and southern California, where the majority of waterfowl spend the winter. While there may be a few small areas managed by such entities as the Audubon Society, the vast majority are private or commercial duck clubs. Many of these clubs are organized into groups such as the Grassland Water District in Merced County or the Suisun Resource Conservation District in Solano County. They are influential bodies, capable of protecting their interests. In 1976, there were over 1,000 clubs totaling 450,000 acres in California.

Like government-managed areas, these lands are primarily flooded for waterfowl food production and hunting in fall and winter. Management practices on most duck clubs emulate those of government areas. Some of the more progressive, well-to-do clubs excel in making their lands attractive to waterfowl. At the other end of the spectrum, some are haphazardly managed, with only the thought of a pond to shoot over foremost in mind. Nevertheless, these clubs, in aggregate, constitute an enormously important segment of the available wetlands of the Pacific Flyway. And while ducks and geese are the target of the investment and effort, all wetland wildlife benefits.

It would be impractical to describe all the changes that have taken place since the arrival of the white man. But a brief account of some of the more striking helps in understanding why so much concern and effort is devoted to protecting the remaining wetlands.

California's Central Valley, once a veritable paradise for wildlife, now bears no resemblance to the landscape known by the early settlers. In the early 1900s huge floating clamshell dredges, with booms exceeding 200 feet, built major levees along the Sacramento and San Joaquin rivers and in the delta, allowing farmers to convert thousands of square miles of sloughs and marshes into farmland. Twentieth-century dams and reservoirs in the upper reaches of the major rivers and tributaries also helped tame the wild rivers, whose annual flooding not only created marshlands but also prevented the encroachment of man.

Hoover Dam, built in the early 1900s, changed the lower Colorado River and virtually destroyed what was once an important waterfowl flyway through the intermountain region to the huge delta that once existed on the Gulf of California.

The coastal flyway has also undergone major degradation from increasing demands for land and water. Coastal wetlands and tidal flats have been lost by diking for pasture and other agricultural development, dredge fill operations, shellfishery operations, marina and port development, log storage and processing facilities, salt pond operations, and industrial and urban development. Remaining coastal wetlands have been degraded by pollution and human disturbances resulting from these activities.

Overall losses have not been quantified, but they are severe. Marsh loss has been estimated at 70 percent on eleven Puget Sound river deltas, 75 percent in San Francisco Bay, and 90 percent in San Diego Bay. More remote bays and estuaries are, of course, in much better condition, but pressures to destroy them still exist.

Obviously the number one problem

today is water. Ducks and water go together, and without it there will simply be no ducks. But most Westerners also know that there is keen competition for every drop. Neighboring states, even countries (United States and Mexico) squabble over water rights. Extensive aqueducts and canal systems transport vast quantities from areas of plenty to areas of need. Traditionally, domestic and agricultural needs take precedence over wildlife, and this has been disastrous for waterfowl.

Government waterfowl areas and private duck clubs alike are forced to pay exorbitant prices and to use wastewater where and when available. State and federal areas are thus limited in size and number by available funds. Many duck clubs are struggling to survive. If they acquire more members to increase capital, the quality of the hunting experience usually goes down. Then interest in maintaining the club wanes, and agriculture or some other land user steps in.

Property taxes are also forcing duck clubs out of business in some areas. Tax assessors have no responsibility to consider the public benefit of wildlife conservation afforded by duck clubs. Revenue is their bag, and the taxes on many clubs are influenced by nearby agricultural or otherwise developed lands. The ultimate consequence is that there are fewer and fewer acres of wetlands available for wintering waterfowl.

Unfortunately, one problem begets another. As waterfowl are forced to concentrate on fewer and fewer acres of wetlands, they become more and more susceptible to disease such as botulism, fowl cholera, and duck viral enteritis. Tremendous numbers of ducks, geese, and swans are lost every year on California wintering grounds.

The benefits of raising more ducks on the Canadian prairies can be significantly

reduced by major outbreaks of disease on the wintering grounds. Research and improved management practices will help minimize these losses, but the crowding factor cannot be overlooked. It is important to send healthy birds north in the spring, if we expect them to survive the rigors of migration and reproduction.

Putting it all together, the message is clear. There must be balance between breeding and wintering grounds. Pressures to reduce the quantity and quality of California's wintering grounds are immense, and it will take a major effort by waterfowl conservationists to preserve or expand what remains.

What has happened, and the problems we face, are depressing indeed. But there is a brighter side, so let's take a look at that. Hopefully, the foresight of some of our predecessors will inspire others to continue their all-important conservation efforts.

Early conservationists realized it would be wise to dedicate certain lands to migratory waterfowl, and a few marshlands, with very little value for anything else but ducks, were purchased. However, it was not until midcentury that an acquisition program by both state and federal governments gained momentum. Ironically, it received unexpected support from agricultural interests.

Farmers' cries of increasing crop depredation were heeded by legislators. Funds were made available for the purchase of lands to be managed for waterfowl, to which depredating ducks and geese could be herded. Federal duck stamp and California Wildlife Conservation Board monies were the two principal sources for land acquisition. Federal and state wildlife agency budgets, aided by federal Pittman-Robertson funds, provide for their operation.

More recently the U.S. Fish and Wildlife

Service has initiated a program of acquiring conservation easements. Under this program, wetlands remain in private ownership, but the easements are designed to preserve them in perpetuity. Landowners are allowed to continue existing uses such as grazing and to retain or replace buildings, but easement stipulations preclude altering the land in any way that would be detrimental to waterfowl use.

An era of ecological awareness, spawned in the 1960s, was responsible for a variety of legislative acts that provide the remaining wetlands considerable protection. Important federal legislation included the Fish and Wildlife Coordination Act, the National Environmental Policy Act, the Federal Water Pollution Control Act of 1972, and the Estuary Protection Act.

Both state and federal wildlife agencies have implemented environmental review functions to assess those activities and developments that may have an adverse impact on critical wildlife habitats. Mitigation, in the form of protection or enhancement of wetlands, has helped to compensate for losses. It is encouraging to see that California state legislators have recognized the importance of wetlands by enacting legislation (SCR 28) that requires the state wildlife agency to prepare and submit a plan for the protection, preservation, restoration, acquisition, and management of wetlands.

Another bright spot is that several prominent areas with significant wetland value have received the benefit of special protective legislation. The duck clubs, organized into the Grasslands Water District in California's San Joaquin Valley, have also received considerable legislative attention. A forty-year contract with the U.S. Bureau of Reclamation provides water to the clubs, and state legislation provides for stabilization of their tax assessments.

The 84,000 acres of bays, sloughs, duck clubs, and wildlife areas that compose the Suisun Marsh in California have also drawn the attention of legislators. The Suisun Marsh Preservation Act of 1977, a state mandate, precludes the encroachment of urban and industrial development in the marsh, and provides some upland buffer area to protect wildlife and recreational values. Pending federal legislation is also designed to protect water quality so that food plants attractive to waterfowl will continue to grow.

With the ever-increasing pressure on western lands and water, it becomes incumbent on those responsible for areas dedicated to waterfowl to see that they are managed to be most beneficial to them. State and federal wildlife agencies must take the lead in this effort with continuing research; but it is equally important that private entities, interested in waterfowl conservation, utilize the information.

All in all, the outlook for waterfowl is not hopeless. We trust that the foregoing facts on what we once had, what we have left, the problems we are facing, and what has been done thus far will inspire others to become active in helping preserve and enhance our waterfowl resources.

34

Interior Western Wetlands

J. E. Nagel

The area under discussion encompasses the western quarter of the United States from Canada to Mexico. Because of the tremendous range in habitat types in an area so vast, wetlands attractive to waterfowl are extremely diverse in terms of size, location, and variety, and the problems associated with them just as variable.

These wetlands can be categorized as: interior marshes (both alkaline and freshwater), high mountain lakes and beaver ponds, rivers, stock ponds and catch basins, irrigation reservoirs and associated areas. The role each of these habitat types plays in breeding, migration, wintering, and hunting opportunity also varies by size and location.

This diversity has created problems for professional wildlife managers in determining key areas (beyond the largest and most obvious), assessing their importance to waterfowl in the Pacific and Central Flyways, and in developing an integrated management plan for all wetlands in the interior of the West. However, development of additional data through continuing surveys and inventories, as well as constant refinement of older information, is providing a better data base for individuals and agencies involved in waterfowl management.

Western interior marshes can generally be categorized as either alkaline (saline) or fresh. Alkaline marshes usually occur in closed basins or sump areas and are characterized by brackish water, heavy clay soils, salt-tolerant emergent and submergent plants, and large stretches of sterile mudflats resulting from high concentrations of soil salts. Freshwater marshes are found in the upper portions of drainages, usually associated with lakes or river systems. Typically, they produce dense stands of emergent vegetation, with a low tolerance for dissolved salts, which tend to encroach rapidly on open-water areas. Soils are generally lighter and contain more organic matter than those of alkaline areas. Mudflats, characteristic of saline marshes, are generally lacking, because there are no high concentrations of dissolved salts to inhibit plant growth.

Examples of saline marshes include the Stillwater area in Nevada, Summer Lake (Oregon), Great Salt Lake marshes (Utah), and the Salton Sea area in California.

Freshwater marshes are illustrated by Dingell Marsh and Gray's Lake in Idaho, Ruby Lakes National Wildlife Refuge (Nevada), Red Rock Lakes (Montana), and the marshes associated with the upper reaches of major river systems throughout the West.

These interior marshes are critical for waterfowl and waterfowl hunters in the Pacific Flyway. At present they contain more than 500,000 acres. Most not only produce waterfowl and provide migration habitat but, depending on water conditions and the severity of the weather, serve as wintering grounds for both waterfowl and bald and golden eagles.

A wide variety of waterfowl are produced on these marshes, including trumpeter swan, Great Basin Canada geese, mallard, redhead, and gadwall. Pintail, green-winged teal, canvasback, and greater sandhill crane are also nesters. Nesting studies show Western interior marshes to be as productive as the best pothole country in Canada. It is estimated that between 5 and 10 percent of all North American waterfowl are produced here. During migration and wintering, all waterfowl species indigenous to the flyway use these marshes; most of the existing state, federal, and private waterfowl developments in the interior West are associated with them.

Because of the arid or semiarid climate of the interior Western U.S., natural lakes, other than those in coastal areas or in major mountain chains, are not numerous. Those that do exist vary in attractiveness and importance for waterfowl. However, all receive some use.

Most high mountain lakes in Utah and portions of the Rocky Mountains are relatively sterile. Food production is limited, and this factor, linked with a short ice-free period, reduces their value to waterfowl. Yet most are used during migration, particularly by lesser scaup. Production, however, is limited to an occasional brood of mallard, goldeneye, or merganser.

Beaver ponds generally produce more broods than mountain lakes. Nutrient levels are high, supporting fair amounts of aquatic vegetation and good populations of invertebrates. They are thus attractive to nesting waterfowl, and many are used for this purpose by mallard, goldeneye (both common and Barrow's), green-winged teal, and in some areas Canada geese. Mallard reared in beaver ponds at higher elevations in the intermountain area seem to undergo a distinct altitudinal migration. Banded as ducklings on beaver ponds, they were harvested later the same year on marshes or lakes at lower elevations.

Larger lakes at lower elevations (both freshwater and alkaline) receive heavy waterfowl use, both by breeding birds in the spring and by migrating waterfowl. Migration use is particularly heavy during the early fall immediately prior to the hunting season. In some areas, the east side of Great Salt Lake for instance, the peak of fall migration occurs no later than mid-September.

Stock ponds and catch basins provide small water areas for waterfowl. And while most often associated with western farming and ranching, they are also important

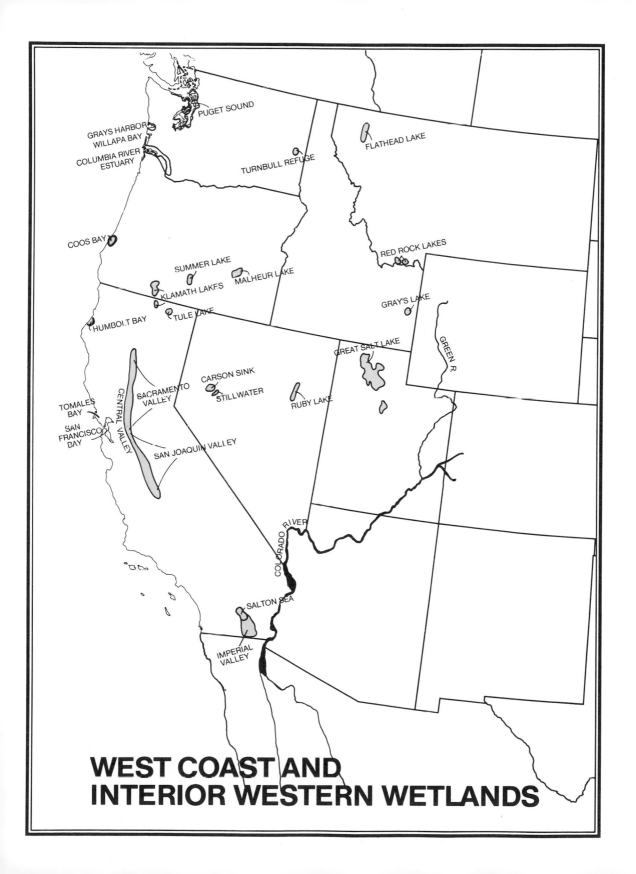

PUGET SOUND

GRAYS HARBOR
WILLAPA BAY

COLUMBIA RIVER
ESTUARY

FLATHEAD LAKE

TURNBULL REFUGE

COOS BAY

SUMMER LAKE

KLAMATH LAKES   MALHEUR LAKE

HUMBOLT BAY   TULE LAKE

RED ROCK LAKES

GRAY'S LAKE

GREAT SALT LAKE

GREEN R.

CARSON SINK
STILLWATER

CENTRAL VALLEY

SACRAMENTO
VALLEY

RUBY LAKE

TOMALES
BAY

SAN
FRANCISCO
BAY

SAN JOAQUIN VALLEY

COLORADO RIVER

SALTON SEA

IMPERIAL
VALLEY

WEST COAST AND
INTERIOR WESTERN WETLANDS

for local waterfowl production. Because most of the interior West at lower elevations is arid or semiarid, almost any water area is attractive to waterfowl. The attraction of stock ponds for nesting and migrating waterfowl is great throughout the West, as far south as northern Arizona and New Mexico.

Reliable data on the number of such ponds and basins is not readily available because new ponds are constantly being built, and older units become filled with sediment and eliminated. Also, no real effort to inventory these ponds is made.

River systems in the west have traditionally served as migration corridors for waterfowl. The importance of the Green, Colorado, and Columbia rivers to both local and migrant birds is well known. Their role in waterfowl management has been altered as the habitat associated with each has been modified, but all interior western rivers, streams, and watercourses are used by waterfowl some time during the year.

Irrigation development and diversion have greatly reduced stream flows and riparian vegetation on all major interior rivers. This resulted in habitat losses and reduced waterfowl numbers. In order to conserve water, runoff dams were built (usually in deep, narrow canyons to reduce evaporation losses) and channels between storage facilities straightened. This eliminated the natural marsh areas associated with oxbows and meandering turns, and because they were no longer attractive, waterfowl use declined dramatically.

Currently, the major role of rivers in the interior is that of migration corridors. Ducks and geese maintain tradition and still follow them up and down the flyway. However, the frequency and intensity have been reduced by destructive habitat changes. Only in the headwaters of the river systems does any significant production occur. Even this is jeopardized as water development and diversion projects continue to proliferate.

A hundred years ago irrigation storage reservoirs were virtually unknown in the West. As settlers moved into the arid interior, they found most valleys capable of producing some kind of crop—if water was available throughout the growing season. This need for water resulted in construction of irrigation storage reservoirs, and these man-made lakes presented both benefits and problems for waterfowl.

Because reservoirs are water-storage projects, levels vary widely during the irrigation season. Waterfowl production is therefore severely limited. In most cases, only early nesting species such as Canada geese and mallard can successfully bring off broods, before water level fluctuations begin to interfere with nesting. Later nesters, such as redhead and gadwall, are seldom successful.

But on the other side of the coin, water manipulations also result in severe drawdown by late summer. This exposes large areas of mudflats, which usually produce some type of annual plant growth prior to the first frosts. When these areas reflood in the fall, they are attractive to migrating waterfowl and support large numbers of both ducks and geese.

Storage reservoirs on private land also provide another benefit to waterfowl in the intermountain West. They are usually closed to public access, and thus are often used by nonbreeding Canada geese as molting areas. It is not unusual for more than 1,000 Western Canadas to molt on irrigation reservoirs throughout the Rocky Mountain states.

Reservoirs located in or adjacent to

large tracts of agricultural land often create problems by concentrating large numbers of waterfowl in areas that historically could sustain such use. Now these concentrations often result in crop depredation, changes in traditional migration patterns (short-stopping), enforcement problems, and a potential for such diseases as fowl cholera or botulism.

In addition to the problems waterfowl face on a day-to-day basis across the continent, there are two major additional problems dominant in the interior West today: diversion of water and increasing salinity and deterioration of water quality.

Since the interior of the West is largely semiarid, competition for existing water is keen. Experience demonstrates that wildlife requirements usually receive little consideration when allocations are made. The entire area is in a period of growth and general economic development, and it appears competition will become even more intense, not only for water currently available but for new supplies as they are developed.

Historically, water for wildlife was most abundant in lowland areas near the termination of natural drainages. This is where the most extensive marshes developed, and where early settlers saw the greatest waterfowl utilization. Unfortunately, such marshes are vulnerable to upstream diversions, and water, which normally helped sustain them, was suddenly being used for agriculture and no longer available for waterfowl.

Agricultural diversions for irrigated croplands were harmful enough, but the problem became even worse when urban populations began to grow. Cities placed additional demand for water on drainages and underground sources, and industry needed more for processes associated with their plants. Water rights were allocated and reallocated until they totaled four and five times the normal stream flow. All this resulted in severely reduced amounts reaching the marshes at lower elevations.

Today, energy development, particularly that associated with coalfields, and proposed transbasin transfers of water for industrial and domestic use, continue to put pressure on an overextended system. The potential impact on waterfowl in these areas is far from bright.

As diversions increase and water is used and reused, quality deteriorates. Dissolved salts and industrial residues reduce the quality of effluents from agricultural and industrial diversions to the point where such effluents truly become wastewater. Downstream users see crop yields drop off as salinity increases; industry must treat and re-treat water before it can be used. Much of the water now entering marshes is carrying enough dissolved solids and industrial residue to adversely affect plant growth and waterfowl use.

Marshes that were traditionally fresh or slightly brackish become more saline. Food plants such as pondweeds disappear, to be replaced by less desirable species. In some cases salinity and turbidity eliminate all submerged growth. Industrial residues including phenols, heavy metals, and petroleum also impact marshes, and ultimately waterfowl, adversely.

Because water is a severely limited natural resource over most of the West, demands on the limited supply become greater each day. Use and reuse of water compounds the problem in terms of quality. Without upstream commitments, downstream supplies will suffer in both quality and quantity, to the further detriment of waterfowl.

35

The Atlantic Coastal Area: How It Was

C. E. Addy

After looking at waterfowl habitat and waterfowl populations in the Atlantic coastal area today, one would be startled and overwhelmed by the contrast between the present and the past—were it possible to go back to the time of the white man's arrival.

Imagine being one of the first Europeans to explore and settle the new lands and waters of the Atlantic shore. You would experience extensive pristine tidal bays and marshes with lush vegetation, pure waters teeming with waterfowl and other wildlife, undisturbed meandering rivers and streams fed by myriad swamps and marshes, inland lakes and ponds stocked with a wide variety of pondweeds and other aquatic vegetation well used by waterfowl and other wildlife, and uplands largely wooded, with only a relatively few small natural open areas or fields maintained by native Indians.

Many of the areas that harbored large numbers of ducks, geese, swans, and shorebirds in the early days are still important today, though often on a much reduced scale. For example, the great Tantramar marsh on Canada's New Brunswick–Nova Scotia provincial border, an extensive natural tidal brackish marsh, was home to sizable nesting populations of black duck, pintail, and green-winged teal, and during the fall impressive numbers of many species congregated.

The great St. Lawrence River estuary was undoubtedly a prime nesting and spring and fall staging area, from Lake Ontario to Anticosti Island. And the concentrations of black duck, ring-necked duck, and teal in the St. John River estuary of New Brunswick must have been impressive.

Inland freshwater marshes and swamps, as well as many tidal estuaries in New Eng-

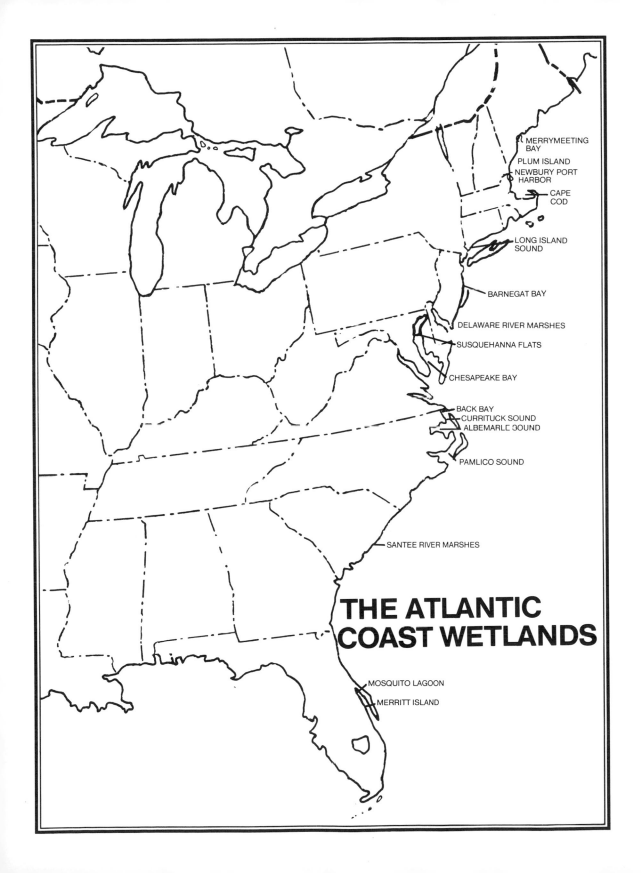

MERRYMEETING
BAY
PLUM ISLAND
NEWBURY PORT
HARBOR
CAPE
COD
LONG ISLAND
SOUND
BARNEGAT BAY
DELAWARE RIVER MARSHES
SUSQUEHANNA FLATS
CHESAPEAKE BAY
BACK BAY
CURRITUCK SOUND
ALBEMARLE SOUND
PAMLICO SOUND
SANTEE RIVER MARSHES

THE ATLANTIC
COAST WETLANDS

MOSQUITO LAGOON
MERRITT ISLAND

land, Pennsylvania, New York State, New Jersey, and Delaware, held many more waterfowl then. Spectacular fall concentrations could always be expected in the Lake Champlain marshes of Canada and the United States: Merrymeeting Bay in Maine; Back Bay and the coastal marshes of New Hampshire; Newburyport Harbor, Plum Island, and other Essex and Middlesex County marshes and the Cape Cod area in Massachusetts; the Long Island Sound area of New York State; New Jersey and southern New England; Barnegat Bay and the Delaware River marshes of southern New Jersey and Delaware; the great estuary known as Chesapeake Bay with its famous Susquehanna Flats, and its many marsh islands and river estuaries in Maryland and Virginia; the Back Bay area of Virginia; and Currituck Sound, Pamlico Sound, and Albemarle Sound of North Carolina. On to the south, the unbelievable extensive swamps and marshes of South Carolina, Georgia, and Florida very likely attracted large numbers of wintering ducks of almost every eastern freshwater species.

The original extent of tidal and freshwater wetlands of the Atlantic coastal area is unknown. Certainly less than half remains today, and, of the original high-quality habitat, it is doubtful if more than a fifth is still high-quality. The original size and distribution of the Atlantic coastal waterfowl population is also unknown. There are, of course, reports of birds "blackening the sky." But one has to be careful in interpreting such statements. Blackening the sky to one may only be a few thousand to another.

However, it is believable, and reasonable, that there were millions more waterfowl in the early 1500s than in recent decades. It is also justified to suppose that,

because of climatic and other natural phenomena, habitat conditions also changed from year to year. Changes in water levels and ice conditions would modify wintering distribution. And such variables as whether the prairies of the United States and Canada were wet or dry and in the eastern Arctic whether or not ice and snow prevented successful nesting would make or break the year's production for many species, just as they do today. But it is unlikely that waterfowl mortality from native Indian and Eskimo hunting had much effect on the species involved.

The aquatic habitats of the Atlantic coastal area provided an abundance of fish, shellfish, ducks, geese, swans, and fur animals, beyond the needs of the explorers and early settlers for food and clothing. Undoubtedly, they wouldn't have believed it possible to reduce the waterfowl population to what it is today. The same would apply to the passenger pigeon, shorebirds, and other species that also provided a seemingly endless supply of food.

In any case, early settlers couldn't afford the luxury of worrying about preserving and managing wildlife. Their urgency was to cut down trees, build homes, and clear and drain enough land for food crops and for hay and pasture for livestock.

Much of the most productive waterfowl and fur-bearer habitat was associated with river estuaries, including the lower meandering tidal reaches of the hundreds of streams and rivers. Some were prime locations for settlements, which soon became major cities, towns, and transportation terminals. Water was the highway for commercial transportation, which soon required the elimination of oxbows and meanders from rivers and navigable streams to facilitate the unimpeded flow of boat traffic.

So, in a few decades, much high-quality wetland wildlife habitat was summarily destroyed or made useless to its former inhabitants. Few folks today would even guess that some of our major coastal cities and towns were at one time a swamp or marsh, highly important to waterfowl, fur animals, and other wildlife.

These activities were a direct assault on a highly important segment of the aquatic environment at a time when no one even thought about perpetuating wetland environments. Three hundred years were to pass before a few people began to sound the alarm at the status of our declining wildlife and the loss of wetland habitat.

Equally important to the welfare of the resource were many other subtle, and some not so subtle, activities of man and nature, most of which were negative but very difficult to evaluate. For example, here are some of the items to consider:

Drainage. Expansion outward from the new population centers was soon necessary for more housing, roads, businesses, and agriculture. Huge acreages of swamp and marshland were drained. Many, such as the diking and draining of the Tantramar marshes by the early French settlers, were successful agricultural ventures. However, one such drainage project in eastern North Carolina was a financial disaster. This area was later included in what is now known as Mattamuskeet National Wildlife Refuge.

Dams and agriculture. The establishment of numerous large reservoirs during the last 150 years has not only modified major segments of habitat but has also caused shifts in duck and goose populations. Sometimes reservoirs help ducks. More often they don't. Impounding water

reduces downstream flows and sometimes causes detrimental increases in salinity in estuarine marshes. Diversion of the Santee River and the creation of two large reservoirs in South Carolina, for example, put an end to rice farming and eliminated thousands of acres of prime waterfowl habitat in the lower Santee and nearby coastal areas. Reservoirs in the East Coast area comprise well over a million acres.

In the early centuries, agriculture consisted of small plots operated as family farms. However, with the advent of mechanization and the invention of the corn picker, agriculture rapidly became big business. Small farms were combined and hedgerows eliminated, resulting in large fields plowed fence to fence. During the past fifty years this has had a major effect on the distribution and welfare of waterfowl and other wildlife.

Puddle ducks, particularly black duck and mallard, avidly utilize harvested grain fields. But the most startling effect has been with Canada geese. Grain production, mostly corn, in areas such as central New York State, Pennsylvania, and Maryland has become so attractive that it now holds the bulk of the Atlantic Flyway goose population. As a result only part of the birds move on south to traditional wintering areas in the Carolinas, and practically none to Georgia and Florida. With the advent of widespread corn production, Canada geese have also increased significantly. Management of the harvest, as well as improved food supplies, have played a role. There are probably more Canada geese today in the Atlantic Flyway than ever before.

Dredging. Dredging projects created deeper channels and opened up additional areas to boat traffic. Dredging destroyed some habitat directly, but often the resultant change in water quality and the increase in human activity were more important from a waterfowl standpoint. Dredging has been widespread in the rivers and estuaries of the Atlantic seaboard, often permanently destroying extensive beds of aquatics.

In 1925, for example, Manasquan Inlet and Bay Canal were opened as part of the Inland Waterway; and the once-famous Barnegat Bay and its marshes were changed from a predominantly brackish environment, where duck foods abounded, to a saline environment, where little food for ducks and geese could grow. Barnegat Bay no longer attracts thousands of canvasback, redhead, and other species.

Hunting. From the beginning the early settlers hunted waterfowl as well as all other game, not for sport but to provide food for the family or birds for the market. Powder and shot were much too scarce and expensive to permit the luxury of giving the birds a "sporting chance." Trapping, particularly from the Delmarva area to eastern North Carolina, was also widely used to obtain thousands of ducks for market.

The reported number of birds and poundage of down and feathers shipped to market annually is startling. Add to this the development of the swivel punt gun or boat cannon, which enabled the operator, under the right conditions, to kill or injure several hundred divers with one firing, and one wonders how the ducks and geese have survived as well as they have.

Supplying ducks and geese for the market was the dominant hunting activity until the latter part of the nineteenth century, when sport hunting, with improved guns and ammunition, gradually took over. For a while it was difficult to separate sport hunting from commercial gunning because there were no enforceable bag limits; and the sportsmen used many of the commercial gunners' techniques, such as baiting with corn and live decoys. Official bag limits were unheard of until shortly after the turn of the century.

In the early 1900s several drastic steps were taken by the government to help the declining waterfowl population. Commercial hunting was banned, and bag limits imposed in 1918. Live decoys and baiting were outlawed in 1935.

The duck hunter himself will remain a major participant in the success of waterfowl management in the future. Obviously, much more recreation per duck per hunter is being attained today compared to only a decade or so ago. Thirty-five years ago duck hunters said that if the bag limit dropped below ten ducks per day they might as well hang up their guns.

The facts are that every year a new group of younger hunters enter the ranks and older hunters retire; and we now have a group of hunters in the Atlantic Flyway who have never experienced ten- or twenty-bird bag limits. So it is expected that the modern hunter, who has known only four- or five-bird bag limits, will say he will hang up his gun when the limit drops below four.

Fortunately, while there are some preferred and scarcer species with one- and two-bird limits, he can still take a few more of less attractive species with larger limits. This calls for more sophisticated hunting, but is a way of spreading the resource among as many hunters as possible.

If duck hunters stop to think about it, they'll agree there can't be enough top-notch ducks to go around these days, if everybody gets his four- or five-bird limit.

Under conditions prevailing today if a fellow gets his limit, whether it be two, three, or four ducks, he will be happy and have a good day.

Eelgrass. The pondweed eelgrass, as far as is known, had always been the dominant aquatic of brackish tidal bays and estuaries from Virginia to Labrador and Hudson Bay. Growth was so luxuriant in many areas that boat travel was often difficult. The dense beds harbored a wealth of small crustaceans, mollusks, small fish, microscopic organisms, and various forms of algae, all of which, along with the eelgrass itself, provided abundant food for waterfowl, shorebirds, fish, and other wildlife. Eelgrass beds were a primary habitat for the growth and development of the bay scallop. Early food habit studies showed that over 80 percent of the winter food of the Atlantic brant was eelgrass.

Eelgrass covered such extensive areas, and was so fundamental to the welfare of so many aquatic wildlife species, that when, around 1930, it suddenly disappeared, virtual chaos resulted. Suddenly scallop, small fish, and other animal life had no cover; brant lost their primary food supply and other waterfowl an abundant food source. Serious erosion of tidal bottoms occurred, so severe in some areas that many years passed before any vegetation became established.

Within fifteen to twenty years eelgrass re-established itself on a limited scale, but almost nowhere along the Atlantic seaboard has it attained its former abundance. The eelgrass loss was perhaps the greatest natural ecological disaster known at that time, or since.

Pollution. This covers a wide variety of items ranging from chemical pollution to soil erosion and siltation. In the past, serious pollution was concerned mostly with domestic sewage and effluents from paper mills and other industries. For years, thousands of acres of productive bottoms have been closed to clamming because of seepage from septic systems and effluents from domestic and industrial sewers. Generally, all chemical and sewage pollution is highly detrimental, since, in a modern society, all sorts of poisons are involved.

Chemicals developed during the past few decades, pesticides, herbicides, agricultural and other new chemicals, have been applied to the land on such a large scale that the overall aquatic environment and the adjacent uplands have been adversely affected. Agricultural fertilizers are washed into aquatic environments in such large quantities that they have become serious pollutants too, affecting plant and algal growth and the chemical qualities of the water.

Add to this the millions of tons of soil washed by heavy rains into the bays and estuaries from upstream farms, new housing projects, and highway road cuts, and one wonders how much longer many of our productive tidal areas will continue to survive and produce marine life and ducks.

Chesapeake Bay, a truly national asset, continues to receive tremendous amounts of almost all these pollutants. In addition, the Susquehanna River, the main freshwater source at the head of the bay, still receives some highly acidic leaching from abandoned coal mines in eastern Pennsylvania. The health of the Susquehanna largely determines the health of the famous Susquehanna Flats at the head of the bay.

Another locally serious pollution is the introduction and spread of exotic aquatic plants. Many of these haven't the same restraints on them that natural ecological communities impose on native species. Often they are so aggressive that they crowd out desirable native species. Thus, some years ago Eurasian milfoil crowded out sago pondweed and other good duck foods on the Susquehanna Flats and in numerous other areas of Chesapeake Bay.

Several decades ago the lower Potomac River became blanketed with floating Chinese chestnut. When navigation became seriously affected, the government removed the plants over a twenty-year period at a cost of several hundred thousand dollars. This plant was also a serious pest in New York State, Massachusetts, and Vermont in the past. Alligatorweed, water hyacinth, and other exotic plants as well as native plants such as *Phragmites* are serious competitors locally, and require continual vigilance in order to control their spread.

Human interference. Many areas, potentially attractive for waterfowl, are devoid of ducks and geese during certain times of the year because of human interference. In the last three decades the increase in pleasure boating on tidal and inland waters has been tremendous. The Atlantic seaboard now has several million pleasure boats of all sorts, from small outboards to launches. There are now so many boaters that almost every navigable water is affected daily during the spring, summer, and fall in the middle and northern areas.

Population pressure in many places has reached a point where almost every walkable marsh or shoreline is visited frequently by people and their pets. There are relatively few high-quality duck areas that aren't subject to the uncertainty of the sudden appearance of people. Waterfowl often get used to daily crowds of people. It's the unexpected occasional appearance that makes ducks and geese uneasy. While many are driven out through direct harassment by boaters and others, just the sudden appearance of a person on foot is sometimes all that is needed to make them go elsewhere.

While the return of duck hunting and productive habitat to what they were in the "old days" is definitely not in the cards, all is not lost. Admittedly, after reading what has gone before, one would conclude that waterfowl and their habitat are definitely on a downhill roll to oblivion. But let's look at some of the things that are happening, and are likely to carry them through in the future.

An encouraging sign is that the American public is fed up with soiling its own nest and is on the warpath to clean up the environment, so that the air will eventually be clean enough that breathing isn't likely to cause premature death! The waters of Chesapeake Bay and other valuable coastal bays and rivers will some day be swimmable again, the waters clear and free of silt, heavy metals, pesticides, and other poisons so detrimental to fish and wildlife.

Of course, a lot of these things will take decades of diligence to accomplish, and money is no small requirement. State and federal wildlife and health agencies, and many universities, have contributed much so far, but many more factual data are needed. Continued public support for research and management is paramount if this dream of a clean environment is to come true.

The history of DDT gives encouragement that very complex environmental problems can be solved, or at least corrected. At first DDT appeared to be the compound that would solve all insect problems. But after a few years it was found that damage to fish and wildlife was becoming increasingly intolerable. Fish-eating birds, especially bald eagles, ospreys, and pelicans, declined drastically. Even the black duck, a heavy animal feeder, may have been affected.

It has now been almost two decades since DDT was banned, but it is only recently that noticeably more ospreys, eagles, and pelicans are being seen. Just the stroke of a pen thus often assures the survival — or loss — of our treasured wildlife.

Wildlife managers often say they aren't really managing wildlife, they're managing people. Regulations governing human activity often have more to do with the survival of wildlife than direct assistance to the wildlife itself.

Over the years, federal, state and provincial governments, private individuals, and associations such as the National Audubon Society, The Nature Conservancy, and Ducks Unlimited have built up an impressive record of preserving and managing habitat for production and other needs of waterfowl. More acquisitions and leases are planned.

In the Atlantic coastal area, most government-owned refuges and management areas provide hunting. Not only are about a million acres of publicly owned habitat being preserved and managed, but hunting space is also being provided for many ordinary duck hunters. The acreage and quality of private waterfowl management holdings probably surpasses public holdings, and in many instances provides top-quality shooting for those who can afford the cost of owning and managing the lands and waters.

36

Vanishing Hardwoods

M. J. Rogers

The most significant waterfowl habitat acquisition in this nation's history occurred in 1803, when the U.S. Congress, under the leadership of President Thomas Jefferson, concluded the Louisiana Purchase agreement with France.

At that time waterfowl were not a consideration in the minds of any of the parties involved. But today and for centuries past, the Mississippi River alluvial plain, and the alluvial plains of its many tributaries, has been the key wintering habitat for waterfowl in the interior of the continent. This once vast expanse of swamps and sloughs is dominated by flooded cypress, water tupelo, and ash, and the associated overflow lowland forests of gum, maple, and oak.

Today those once vast wilderness wetlands have diminished to scattered remnants. Although this region is still a vital

wintering ground for a large portion of this continent's waterfowl, land use changes over the last century have brought us to a critical crossroad. We must decide whether our waterfowl resource, as we know it today, will persist for another century in acceptable numbers, or diminish into oblivion.

To understand where we must go, and what we must do, we must look at the circumstances, forces, and attitudes that changed over 80 percent of this wetland wilderness into the intensively managed cropland it is today.

The Mississippi River lowlands covered over twenty-five million acres when it became a part of this nation in 1803. It mirrors the changes that have taken place in the lowland hardwood system nationwide. To early settlers and explorers it must have seemed a harsh, alien wasteland. Swamps

Cypress-tupelo gum swamp in the lower Mississippi valley. *Earl Norwood photo.*

hindered overland travel; severe flooding could destroy a lifetime of labor in a matter of days. Insects and disease sapped strength from those hardy enough to attempt to subdue even minute portions of the lowlands and swamps. The pioneer spirit detested "wasteland," and the attitude that the delta swamps and overflow lowlands are practically worthless persists even today.

The first significant step toward "reclaiming" these wetlands came with the passage of the Federal Lands Swamp Act of 1849. This gave the unwanted lowlands to the respective states to sell, and directed that proceeds from the sales be used for levees and drainage projects to reclaim the swamps and lowland forests for cropland.

Some states carried the Swamp Act a step further. In 1852 the Missouri legislature transferred most of Missouri's lowlands to the respective counties, then three years later permitted the counties to sell the lowlands so that they might "disencumber themselves of the burden these lands have proven to be."

An example of the value the public attached to swampland is the sale in 1868 of 80,000 acres of lowland in Stoddard County, Missouri, at public auction, for the total price of $668.95. The state of Arkansas received some 7.6 million acres of public domain land under the provisions of the Swamp Act. The bulk of this land sold at public auction for $0.50 to $1.25 per acre.

There was little done in the way of levee work, clearing, or draining during the next twenty years, for the Civil War and other pressing national issues of the time took precedence. The next major action to impact the Mississippi River Delta was the creation of the Mississippi River Commission (MRC) in 1870. This commission, composed of members from the U.S. Army Corps of Engineers, U.S. Coast Guard, Geodetic Survey, and civilians, was authorized by the President to study "reclamation and redemption of lands in the Alluvial basin of the Mississippi Valley."

In 1879 Congress gave the MRC broad authority, and it became a permanent force in the battle to "reclaim" the Mississippi lowlands. The primary impact of the MRC was that, for the first time, an agency high in the federal bureaucracy was coordinating efforts to reclaim Mississippi River wetlands.

Meanwhile, other forces were at work on the state level in many parts of the delta. State laws created drainage, levee, and other so-called improvement districts to battle the wetland wilderness on the local level. These improvement districts were given power to tax all lands within their district to finance wetland reclamation projects. As these districts implemented drainage and leveeing projects, a vicious circle emerged: the projects of one district caused flooding downstream, forcing the creation of additional districts to "solve" the problems created by the original district.

The first real concerted attack on the lowland forests came from lumber companies. They cleared the land for the virgin hardwood timber and then sold it to settlers for cropland. As communities sprang up around the lumber towns and more cleared lands became available, agriculture began to grow and soon surpassed lumbering as the prime use of the delta lowlands.

The influx of people into the delta for timber and agricultural activities, coupled with the development of large mechanized drainage and land-clearing equipment and unusually severe flooding in the early 1900s, initiated the final real push to subdue the lowlands. Heretofore, the overflow cycle that sustained the tremendously fertile delta and provided waterfowl wintering habitat had been only a temporary inconvenience to people living in the region. Their livelihood was based on trapping, fishing, small-scale lumbering, and subsistance farming, and overflow had caused little or no long-term losses.

Now, flooding was destroying entire communities, large-scale timber operations, and substantial acreages of increasingly valuable crops. Faced with mounting human suffering and ever-increasing economic losses, and with large mechanized equipment at hand, communities decided that the obvious solution was to control the river!

During the early 1900s most clearing and drainage had been on the perimeter of the lowlands, confined to the higher sites and lighter soils. Cotton was still king on the delta. Over half the delta wetlands were still present and undisturbed. Drainage and levee projects were not well organized, and were carried out primarily on private and state levels. So far the negative impacts of man's activities on waterfowl were not highly significant. Man had not yet controlled the Mississippi, as the flood of 1927 dramatically proved. However, the late 1920s saw the stage set for the final steps in that subjugation.

It was obvious by now that levees alone

Land clearing in a bottomland forest in the lower Mississippi valley. *Earl Norwood photo.*

would not contain the river. Therefore Congress enacted the Flood Control Act of 1928, calling for the construction of floodways on the Mississippi and flood-control reservoirs on the major tributaries. The Depression of the 1930s spawned numerous federally assisted flood control programs, and finally, in 1937, man controlled a major flood on the Mississippi.

The next twenty years saw numerous flood control acts passed by Congress, increased activity by the Corps of Engineers in both flood control and reservoir construction on tributaries, and drainage and channelization within the delta. The Soil Conservation Service also entered the scene during this period with various watershed projects involving stream channelization.

Cotton was slipping from the throne, as the introduction of synthetic fibers lowered demand and price. Soybeans and rice were rapidly gaining supremacy on the delta. Waterfowl use patterns were changing. Most feeding took place in croplands on waste grains. The remaining wetlands were used for resting, roosting, escape cover, and secondary feeding when the flooded fields froze over.

The 1960s saw soybeans soar in value and demand, because of the rapid growth of the plastics industry and an emphasis on vegetable oil and protein-rich soybean products. Since soybeans were highly suit-

1949 aerial photo of a section of the bottomland hardwoods and associated wetlands in lower Mississippi valley.
Army Map Service, Corps of Engineers and EROS Data Center photo.

1982 photo of the same area. *U.S. Department of Agriculture and EROS Data Center photo.*

able for the heavier clay soils in the interior of the delta, clearing of wetlands marginally suited for cultivation was greatly accelerated. Additionally, flood control projects on many tributaries of the Mississippi now controlled the spring and fall flood cycles, allowing cultivation of heretofore untillable wetlands.

As changes in land use continued in the delta, waterfowl continued to change use patterns, until waste grains supplied the majority of wintering foods. As the amounts of forested wetlands dwindled, sheet water standing on flooded cropland was used more and more for resting and roosting habitat.

The 1970s saw larger farm equipment, bigger farms, accelerated drainage projects, and pressure to convert the remnant of this once-vast lowland forest to cropland. Emphasis today is on alteration of the remaining natural stream channels to accelerate drainage from lands where upstream drainage has created downstream problems. An example is the St. Francis River basin downstream from the Wappapello Reservoir in Missouri and Arkansas where, according to the U.S. Department of Agriculture's Economic Research Service, of the 3,333 miles of stream channels below Wappapello, only 118 are in a natural state.

Today, only a remnant of the great Mississippi River lowland forest remains. Over 20 million of the original 25 million acres are now in intensively managed croplands. According to USDA figures, Missouri has 98,000 acres left of its original 2.4 million acres of delta wetlands, and Arkansas 1.4 million of its original 10 million. Other states show the same relative decline.

Of equal importance to waterfowl, winter rains no longer stand on harvested croplands as they once did. More efficient

drainage has effectively moved this invaluable component of waterfowl habitat down into the Gulf of Mexico. Waterfowl use of this vast wintering ground is lessening in duration. Conditions required by wintering waterfowl occur less and less frequently and for shorter periods. If this trend continues, where will the birds be in 1990?

But the picture is not entirely bleak, and there is still time. We must simply make it economically feasible for landowners to protect, manage, and enhance both wetlands and croplands for waterfowl. For remaining wetlands, tax incentives similar to the Water Bank Program should be expanded. Substantial tax breaks to landowners who retain, manage, and enhance wetlands would be a major step in assuring they are maintained in a productive state.

Hunting clubs and hunting leases provided protection for much of our remaining wetlands in private ownership. In the mid-1960s, approximately 2.3 million acres of waterfowl habitat in the Mississippi Flyway were controlled by private clubs. Hunters must recognize that, for it to be economically feasible for landowners to retain these wetlands, hunting rentals must be equal to their potential crop value. In many areas, private leases protect the last productive wetlands remaining.

Hunters and other conservationists must become increasingly active in shaping federal and state wetland projects. They should ensure that losses are not simply mitigated, but that these projects actually enhance waterfowl habitat.

Where acquisition of critical wetlands is possible from willing sellers, state and federal wildlife agencies must be encouraged to purchase and enhance them for waterfowl habitat. Environmental easements are also an attractive tool to protect wetlands and still allow private ownership and such use as is compatible with good waterfowl habitat management.

Many prime areas have already been cleared and put into crop production. In most instances these are not a total loss and, when properly managed, can provide high-quality wintering habitat as well as recreational use. But the conservationist/hunter must make it economically beneficial for the landowner/farmer to manage these lands for a crop of waterfowl.

The time and money required to double-crop for waterfowl are usually not great. Many times a simple structure to retain rainwater will turn a harvested field into prime waterfowling wintering habitat that also provides excellent hunting. Similarly, cost-sharing opportunities between federal and nonfederal entities should be aggressively explored and expanded to provide additional economic incentives for the landowner to implement waterfowl habitat enhancement practices on his land.

State and federal wildlife agencies should be strongly encouraged to direct practical research toward the development of better techniques that will assist the farmer in meeting his objectives, and at the same time be a direct benefit to waterfowl. An example of this type of applied practical research occurred in Arkansas. Here a joint study between the University of Arkansas Agricultural Experiment Station and the Arkansas Game and Fish Com-

mission revealed that waterfowl feeding on harvested, rolled, and reflooded ricefields removed over 97 percent of the undesirable red rice seed. The beneficial offshoot of this for waterfowl is that while the farmer saves fuel and labor and receives noxious vegetation control, waterfowl are assured another flooded ricefield that provides both food and water.

Man has almost totally changed the face of the lowland hardwood forest and wetlands of this nation in the last 150 years. To a degree waterfowl have adapted and survived this massive landscaping job. Not all land use changes outlined have been detrimental to waterfowl. However, we are at a point where we must ensure that both waterfowl and human needs are served. Land use changes to meet human needs must continue. But at the same time we must seek out and actively pursue every opportunity to ensure that future growth integrates waterfowl and wildlife requirements with progress.

This may seem like an impossible undertaking. But imagine how impossible taming, controlling, and finally conquering the Mississippi lowland forests and wetlands seemed to the pioneers of only 100 years ago. If we apply the same pioneer spirit and determination to solving our current waterfowl habitat problems that our forefathers and fathers applied to taming the Mississippi wilderness, then we can and will succeed.

37

Green-Timber Duck Habitat

C. R. Hopkins

In the lower Mississippi Flyway, water once frequently spilled over the banks of winding rivers during periods of heavy rainfall. The flooded bottomland hardwoods were heaven to millions of migrating ducks. This particular heaven was an array of acorn-producing oaks, which provided not only an energy-rich food source but also protection from the unfriendly elements of the environment.

Man's effort to carve a preconceived improved environment for himself and future generations has created a less favorable environment for waterfowl. Many of the habitat changes are irreversible. Fortunately for those of us who receive life-sustaining benefits from the sight and sound of migrating waterfowl, many species have adapted to these changes. They have what Aldo Leopold called high "environmental tolerance." In other words,

ducks utilizing the river overflow have not declined at the same rate as the bottomland hardwoods.

Mallard and wood duck are the major species that find flooded bottomland hardwoods desirable habitat. In most areas, these two species are more than 90 percent of duck use. Occasionally, pintail, hooded merganser, green-winged teal, and gadwall are found in flooded timber. But the vast majority of the time they are using the openings within the timber.

As early as the late 1930s, man became frustrated with relying on Mother Nature for sufficient rainfall to flood duck habitat. It was near Stuttgart, Arkansas, that the first timberland was artificially flooded to attract ducks on schedule. Such bottomland hardwood areas were called "greentree reservoirs."

Greentree reservoirs come in various

shapes and sizes. The major characteristic is a levee system to maintain water in live timber on a scheduled basis. Levee systems vary from a short dike to close a natural levee, to an extensive levee system complete with pumps.

The reduction in timberland areas that flood seasonally, and the unreliable nature of these areas, have resulted in the construction of greentree reservoirs throughout the eastern half of the United States. A 1982 survey revealed they now extend west into eastern Texas and Oklahoma, as far north as New York, and south into Georgia. The majority are in private ownership. The estimated total in the United States is 397,927 acres, 95 percent in Arkansas.

How important flooded green timber is now to wintering ducks in the lower Mississippi Flyway is not known with certainty. We know that seasonally flooded hardwoods once had an essential role in providing wintering habitat for mallard and wood duck. Acorns, and the waterfowl foods found in association with bottomland hardwoods, were important winter food items.

However, the expansion of grain crops into areas that frequently flood during heavy rainfall has created a new dimension in wintering habitat. When available, flooded green timber is still utilized in conjunction with cropland. Such areas are used mainly for resting when flooded grain crops are available for feeding. Flooded timber does provide more protection from environmental hazards than grainfields, and generally, flooded timber has the potential to provide more man-hours of recreational hunting than fields.

Documented population changes as the result of greentree reservoir construction are scarce. But on Noxubee National Wildlife Refuge near Starkville, Mississippi, the construction of 740 acres of greentree areas was believed the major contributor to a threefold increase in ducks.

Components of a successful greentree reservoir are mast-producing trees, water, suitable terrain, and soils. These ingredients, brought together under careful management where ducks pass during migration, can result in many hours of waterfowl enjoyment.

The trees in a greentree reservoir should include at least 50 percent oaks large enough to produce a substantial mast crop. The smaller acorns of pin oak, willow oak, and cherrybark oak are preferred over the larger acorns of Nuttall oak, overcup oak, and chestnut oak. Density of the stand should be between sixty and ninety square feet of basal area per acre. A study of pin oak indicated that large trees at a stocking of ninety square feet per acre would maximize acorn production.

A reliable water source is critical to the success of a greentree reservoir. Possibilities include diversion of stream flow, release from a holding pond, and pumping from a river or deep well. Relying on rainfall, whether by impounding stream overflow with dikes or runoff from a watershed, is not advisable. There will be seasons when ducks arriving at the reservoir will find it suitable only for terrestrial wildlife!

The topography should be relatively flat. This permits maximum flooding for the least expense and effort. Most bottomland hardwood sites have suitable terrain. The soil should have low permeability; those with a high clay content are best.

Levee construction varies from a simple rice dike to a small earth dam with a six-foot top. Terrain, size of area to be flooded, and permanence of levee desired will dictate specifications. All levees need periodic maintenance to ensure their water-holding capacity. Trees growing on a levee will lead to rapid deterioration.

The size of the reservoir will depend on terrain, water supply, and financial resources. An effective reservoir for hunting should be at least fifty acres. However, in duck country, smaller reservoirs may hold sufficient birds, if hunting is carefully managed.

Water management is an important aspect of a successful greentree reservoir. It should be flooded when the trees are dormant to prevent damaging them. In the south, this is normally October through January. If the area is not dewatered prior to the growing season, damage to some species occurs. However, properly managed, inundating some timber stands results in increased tree growth.

Water depth is important to feeding ducks. Mallard and wood duck, the principal users of greentree reservoirs, cannot feed effectively in water deeper than fifteen inches. Since the majority of food is on the bottom, water depth should be between six and fifteen inches.

The hunting schedule for a green-timber reservoir is important to hunter success. Common sense tells us that hunting every day, all day by a host of waterfowlers will force the birds to seek refuge elsewhere. There are numerous hunting schemes.

Greentree reservoir in Mississippi. *Curtis Hopkins photo.*

Acorn production in a greentree reservoir, a prime duck food in fall and winter. *Curtis Hopkins photo.*

Each reservoir should be reviewed in light of its particular characteristics and the desires of the users.

Beaver usually find greentree reservoirs an attractive place to set up housekeeping. Their greatest detriment is their attempt to retard dewatering. This skillful engineer must be carefully watched to ensure that a greentree reservoir is not converted into a permanent beaver pond. Some levee damage may result from increased beaver activity. Periodic control may be necessary.

One effect of greentree reservoirs on the plant community is the delayed development of herbaceous cover. Over an extended period of time, tree composition will also shift toward more water-tolerant forms and plant diversity will decrease.

The small mammal population (mice, shrews, and others) will also be reduced. The size and total acreage of islands within the reservoir will determine the impact on rabbits, raccoons, and squirrels. The availability of winter forage and mast for deer will be reduced, but the overall effect will depend on population density and surrounding support habitat. Islands within reservoirs will serve as deer escape areas.

Greentree reservoirs are man's substitute for thousands of acres of bottomland timber that were once seasonally flooded. They will not replace the loss, but they do have the potential to mitigate it.

Properly managed greentree reservoirs have the advantage of dependability. Waiting for Mother Nature to provide sufficient rainfall for stream overflow can be frustrating to management, hunters, and probably to waterfowl too!

38

Gulf Coast Marsh Management

W. J. Lorio

The Gulf Coast Marshes extend from the lower tip of Texas into Florida. Narrow at first, they widen near the mouth of the Brazos River in Texas to the Pearl River in Louisiana, and then narrow to Florida, where they again widen.

There are two basic marsh types, saline and fresh, and an intermediate brackish condition. They are generally influenced by tidal action. Fresh to brackish marshes vary in salt concentration because they are inundated periodically by saltier water initiated by hurricanes and abnormally high tides.

These marshes lie in high rainfall areas and are among the most productive habitats known. They support a wide range of both plant and animal life. Unfortunately, many of the more inland marshes have been reclaimed for agriculture, mainly for rice and pasture. Much of the saline marsh has been altered by petrochemical industries, shipping, and recreational developments. Alteration has come mainly from the navigational canals that traverse the marshes. Both fresh and saline types are being lost at an alarming rate.

Prerequisite to managing a complex environment, such as a marsh, is understanding that a productive marsh is constantly undergoing change. Natural cycles of succession, evolving around the hydrological cycle of drought and extremely high water associated with hurricanes, periodically change these marshes significantly. Such extreme changes tend to have a rejuvenating effect by redistributing nutrients and starting the pattern of plant succession all over.

A marsh that remains stable for an extended period of time becomes stagnant and less productive. No matter what ex-

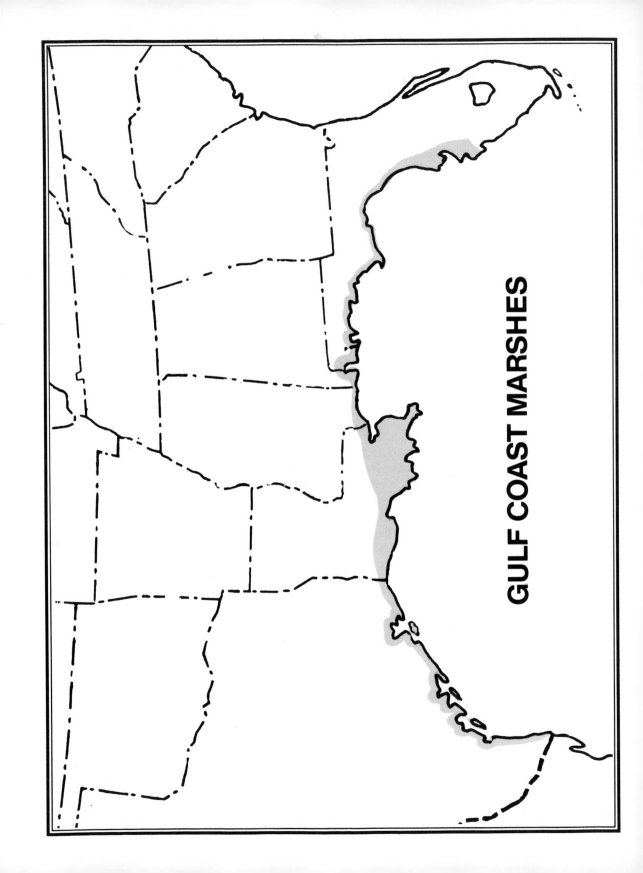

GULF COAST MARSHES

treme conditions exist, some life forms will benefit and become more prolific.

Each individual area in the coastal marsh zone is different. Management should thus be directed to individual situations and objectives. Costs, short-term and long-term effects, legal permits, and many other components must be considered before management practices are implemented.

Controlling water levels is a major component of marsh management. In many ways it is the most difficult to achieve, both physically and financially, of all management techniques. Simple levees, stopgates, and other mechanical devices are commonly used to maintain water at a desired level during specific periods of the year.

Water levels affect plant composition, so the objective will determine the water management plan. As a rule, dewatering a freshwater marsh during midsummer has a desirable effect. It gives many plants a chance to germinate, especially food-producing plants such as millet. Water levels should be increased during the fall and maintained through the winter period.

Mother Nature will prevail during some years and undermine the best of management schemes, so periodic failures are to be expected. In addition, a summer drawdown is often in direct conflict with fishermen. If freshwater fishing and waterfowl demands are made of the same marsh, be prepared for conflicts.

Water control structures in marshes are generally not recommended if multiple use is intended, because they have a tendency to reduce the salt content by retaining more rainwater. This may adversely affect the marsh's productivity as a nursery ground for many important species of fish and shellfish. Management priorities must be determined when multiple-use marshes are manipulated by waterfowl managers.

Burning is a management tool used by trappers, cattle ranchers, and waterfowl managers. Trappers use fall burning to remove dead annual vegetation for easier access to trap furbearers. Fall burning also stimulates plant growth for cattle during the winter grazing period. Waterfowl managers prescribe fall burnings to attract geese, which graze on the exposed tubers and tender new sprouts. Pintail and other puddle ducks also respond readily to burning, utilizing the shallow flats opened up by removal of the dense vegetative canopy.

Burning should be done with caution. A very hot fire may kill the root stocks, or actually burn the top layer of peat (decayed vegetation), which may take several years to recover. Fall burning can be done from mid-September through November. The best time is following a cold front, which generally means lower humidity and a predictable wind pattern. Two or three days after a rain is optimum for "cool" fire results.

It is best to burn when the marsh floor is either covered by water or amply wet. Never burn under extremely dry conditions. Some areas are burned every year, others only once every three years. If an area is unburned longer than three years, the debris becomes thick and the risk of having a "hot" fire is increased.

Burning is generally directed to thick stands of cordgrass or three-corner grass. However, fire can be used to remove most any vegetation that may become too dense: marsh cane, cattail, *Baccharis,* and so on. Removal of all tall vegetation, such as cane, is not desirable, because these provide windbreaks sought out by mallard, mottled duck, and others.

Marsh burning to create better feeding conditions for ducks and geese. *Dave Hall photo.*

Very few marsh fires are ever in control. Some have lasted for over a week before running out of fuel. When humidity is low, a single match will literally explode a dark clump of cordgrass into flame. Check with local authorities regarding regulations on burning.

Selling plants for managed waterfowl areas is a profitable business. Some of these plantings may be beneficial, but as a rule, if marsh conditions are right, many will occur naturally. Good water management without plantings often gives the best results. If plantings are necessary, one of several species of millet should be considered first.

Waterfowl are dependent on grit for the grinding process their gizzards perform in digesting seeds. Grit is sought out almost on the same daily basis as food. Natural outcroppings of sandier soils in the marsh zone or on nearby agricultural lands are the usual sources. Many of the deeper marshes from the upper Texas coast through Louisiana lack sand in their clay soils. Sand placed in these areas along roads, levees, or specially prepared grit pads is a good tool for attracting waterfowl.

The grade of sand used for concrete is best. A sloping mound of dirt scraped out of the marsh (sixty by thirty feet and three feet above water level), when covered with seven to ten cubic yards of sand, will attract waterfowl, especially geese. The grit pad should be near existing goose roosts if possible. It should be accessible by marsh buggy or trucks in order to replenish the sand every year or so. It is amazing how much sand a flock of geese use in a year.

It is best to locate mounds so that the flight line between the roost and the mound can be hunted. But excessive hunting too near the mounds will decrease their effectiveness by causing the birds to relocate. Treat the mounds in the same way as a roost. Hunt the edges but don't run the birds out.

Coastal wetland managers interested in improving wetlands for waterfowl must consider all possible methods and combinations for reaching their management objectives. Some plans may include water control structures such as dams, weirs, and levees. These will require government permission for installation.

The place to start is the U.S. Army Corps of Engineers, which administers Section 404 of the Federal Water Pollution Act. This law requires a permit for any structure or major modification in a wetland. The definition of wetland is broad. If the area proposed for management is in or adjacent to a bay, marsh, river, or stream, it would be wise to check with the Corps before proceeding.

The fact that the site is on private land does not delete the 404 permit requirement. This may seem a case of "big government" interference, but the drastic loss of wetlands in the past calls for determined measures to preserve those remaining. And even though your plan will improve the wetland for waterfowl, it may disrupt other beneficial aspects of the area.

For example, the bays and marshes along the Gulf of Mexico are critical habitat for fish and shellfish supporting valuable sport and commercial fisheries. Installing levees around a brackish marsh to reduce salinity (beneficial to waterfowl) may eliminate access to the area by immature forms of fish and shellfish, thus reducing the habitat available for these species.

If a permit is required, the Corps will provide forms for filing the application. At this time, obtain a list of other governmental agencies that will review the application. This will likely include the U.S. Fish and Wildlife Service, National Marine Fisheries Service, and the various state agencies responsible for fish and wildlife, water quality, water rights, and others.

Contact each agency, giving enough detail of your plan to determine if there will be major objections, and work them out before you formally apply. This can save you much time and money. You may also receive some expert advice from specialists with the fish and wildlife agencies. You may also find that some other management scheme, not requiring permitted structures, would better serve your management objectives, if you receive major objections from the agencies.

Above all, prepare to be patient. The wheels of bureaucracy do turn, but ever so slowly!

Productive waterfowl habitat is lost not only by drainage but also by the infestation of unwanted vegetation such as alligator weed and water hyacinth. These nuisance plants cover valuable waterfowl habitat, smothering emergent and submersed plants that are food for waterfowl and furbearers. Even in winter, when water hyacinth is killed by frost, these areas are unattractive to wintering waterfowl because mats of decaying vegetation remain on the surface.

Wildlife agencies are forced to utilize time, funds, and talent for moderately successful control programs, instead of channeling these efforts toward more direct wildlife management programs. Noxious vegetation poses a serious problem for waterfowl management.

Before implementing any management scheme for a marsh, it is best to consult with a local wildlife biologist. He or she will be able to identify the plants that are indicators of the condition or stage of the marsh, and recommend how to improve conditions, if need be.

Also, keep in tune with what is going on in the entire watershed. A development or drainage project several miles away can alter water quality or other factors, and may adversely affect your area.

Finally, remember that you don't always have to improve an area. Often it is better to maintain it as it is!

39

Wetland Habitat Management by the Private Sector: The Story of Little Pecan

S. Venable

Question: What does a log chain have in common with a delicate gold necklace? Answer: Each is made up of separate, yet vital, links. No one part is stronger than the whole, nor can the whole exist if one link is missing.

Much the same theory applies to fish and wildlife resources, since all the lives in a given ecosystem are linked to each other. Affect one of them and you affect them all. The key to success, then, is knowing how to manage this complex environment to achieve the maximum benefit for all its inhabitants.

Consider the case of southern wetlands, in particular the coastal marshes of Louisiana. The popular image of this area is that of a wintering ground for ducks and geese. And it most certainly lives up to that reputation. Some 3½ to 5 million migratory

fowl spend their winters along the 4 million acres of fresh and salt marsh.

But Louisiana's wetlands provide far more service than temporary housing for transient birds. They are the breadbasket from which springs a vast array of fish and wildlife resources, many with considerable economic importance. Properly maintained and managed, their productivity can be increased, to the benefit of mankind and the resources themselves.

Much of this responsibility falls on the shoulders of the private sector. Even though several state and federal refuges are located in this region, the overwhelming majority of land is owned by private individuals and corporations, neither of which has the acreage or financial resources of the government at their disposal.

What can be done at the grassroots level

to protect and enhance these natural areas? A shining example of stewardship in action can be found at Little Pecan, one of the largest and most intensively managed private wildlife areas in the nation.

Little Pecan Wildlife Management Area is located in southwestern Louisiana near the community of Grand Chenier. It consists of 160-acre Little Pecan Island, surrounded by some 11,000 acres of marsh. Here a team of biologists, guided by a detailed, long-range plan, is proving it is possible to manipulate the environment for the mutual benefit of man and nature. "All it takes is a commitment," says owner Herman Taylor, Jr. "That, and a lot of hard work."

Located on the southern shore of Lake Manitoba, Delta Waterfowl Research Station is the largest private waterfowl educational and research center on the continent. It serves as a proving ground for young wildlife biologists and wetland ecologists. For fifty years, Delta has enabled students to earn credits toward their graduate degrees, at the same time receiving valuable hands-on experience in the fields of waterfowl physiology, propagation of captive birds, habitat assessment and enhancement, food production, and other topics vital to the perpetuation of the species.

Taylor was impressed by this program. He began to envision a similar approach on the wintering grounds, thousands of miles away. The idea for practical, on-site wetlands research and management kept kicking around in the back of his head. The plan finally clicked.

Taylor acquired Little Pecan in the early 1970s. Then he wasted no time transforming his dream into a reality. He hired a team of young, highly trained biologists, each a specialist in various disciplines of marsh management. He challenged them to prove that multiple use is not just a theory but a practical, economically feasible concept.

The goal at Little Pecan is optimum sustained yield of all products from the surface acreage of the marsh. This includes waterfowl, furbearers, alligators, timber, and fisheries, both marine and freshwater. In addition, the management program provides for mineral exploration as long as it remains compatible with the fisheries and wildlife resources.

"In this era of inflation, rising taxes, and increased governmental regulations, we view the multiple-use concept as the best way to manage a wetland," said Ken Guidry, Little Pecan's general manager and chief of operations. "The ideal argument against draining marsh habitat is by proving its financial worth to the owner. As a result, fish and wildlife are the beneficiaries."

The key to management of any marshland habitat is water-level control. Without water, the marsh becomes a scorched desert. But flooding can be just as disastrous. With water control capabilities, however, the level can be raised or lowered to suit any particular need.

"When our ten-year plan was initiated, there were no functioning water control devices at Little Pecan," Guidry continued. "The marsh fluctuated at the whim of tidal action, at times adversely affecting all forms of aquatic life. The first step in countering this problem was the excavation of over twenty-five miles of levees and the construction and installation of sixteen wooden and aluminum structures and two pumping stations. In the process, nine tracts of marsh, ranging in size from twenty-five to several thousand acres, were impounded."

Variable crest control structure to regulate water inflow and outflow. *Little Pecan Properties photo.*

It is a perfect case of man working in harmony with nature. Little Pecan Island is uniquely situated in the transition zone between two ecosystems. Fresh water is provided by a series of canal systems out of the Grand Lake basin to the north. Salt water is available to the south from the Gulf of Mexico via the Mermentau River and Little Pecan Bayou. This option offers the best of both worlds. It permits wildlife managers to draw either type of water into the marsh to fit specific requirements for flora and fauna.

One way this tool can be used is in controlling the spread of water hyacinth, either by draining infested areas or flushing them briefly with salt water. Little Pecan biologists discovered that hyacinth management through water-level control was not only more effective over large acreages than chemicals, but it also required less manpower and had no adverse environmental impact.

But perhaps the most common use of water control is in manipulation of aquatic and annual vegetation utilized by migratory waterfowl. Each fall and winter, the Little Pecan marshes attract a wide variety of species. Among the most common are pintail, green- and blue-winged teal, wigeon, gadwall, mallard, shoveler, wood duck, ring-necked duck, lesser scaup, the native mottled duck, plus blue, snow, and white-fronted geese. Less common, but still present each year are canvasback, redhead, greater scaup, goldeneye, and bufflehead.

No crops are planted at Little Pecan.

Instead, impoundments are dried temporarily to firm up the bottom and stimulate natural reproduction of native plants such as millet, spangletop, and nutgrass. In addition, periodic draining enables several highly desirable aquatic species, like wigeon grass and sago pondweed, to re-establish when the marsh is flooded once again.

"Through this process, we have noted an increased biomass — duck food, in other words," said Guidry. "Our biological staff has proved that both aquatic and annual vegetation can be provided in the same impoundment. This is accomplished by slowly raising the water level as the annual vegetation matures. Areas within the im-poundment where annuals did not grow are soon overtaken by aquatics."

Another tool of marsh management at Little Pecan is the same one utilized in progressive forestry throughout the South — controlled burning. Fire, like water, can be devastating in too large a quantity. But a controlled, "cool" fire, ignited only under specific atmospheric conditions, removes unwanted vegetation and stimulates the growth of new, more desirable species.

"The vegetation program must be monitored at regular intervals," Guidry pointed out. "Each summer, we run transects along set routes. These surveys document plant species, growth stages, production, and

Pump at Little Pecan. *Little Pecan Properties photo.*

overall effect of the management program."

These labors are reflected in the quality and quantity of the waterfowl harvest at Little Pecan. To evaluate the sporting opportunities afforded, Taylor formed a partnership with several close business associates. Guests of these partners assist in supplying statistical data, at the same time enjoying waterfowling experiences that are among the finest in the northern hemisphere. Since 1978, the average bag per hunter at Little Pecan Wildlife Management Area has been a staggering 7.1 birds per day.

"We are able to maintain this high yield by providing ideal wetland habitat, coupled with shooting restrictions stricter than state or federal regulations," Guidry explained. "At Little Pecan, all hunting ceases at 9:00 A.M., and only the guests' limits are filled. The guide does not kill a limit, as is practiced at many private hunting camps."

In addition, each guide at Little Pecan has three or four blinds at his disposal. This system of rotation creates a refuge effect. Finally, the guides all use trained retrievers to help hold cripple losses to a minimum. In combination, these measures ensure a high-quality hunting experience with a minimum of disturbance to the birds.

Detailed daily records are maintained of the species, sex, and age of each duck and goose harvested. These provide a base of data for biologists at the island to evaluate. In addition, this information lends insight to the composition of each year's fall flight. During the 1981–82 season, for example, approximately 55 percent of the birds harvested were young of the year. Since the juvenile/adult ratio in a good breeding year runs about 65:35, the Little

Pecan figures helped substantiate reports of below-average waterfowl production on the Canadian breeding grounds for that particular year.

Furbearers are another beneficiary of sound marshland management practices. Little Pecan supports excellent populations of several income-producing species, including nutria, otter, raccoon, and mink. Manipulation of vegetation and construction of ditches provide a substantial base of food and cover for these animals. In addition, the program of selective, controlled burning sets back vegetative succession and enables the trapper to find sign with less difficulty.

Fur harvests are conducted each winter through contracts with local and staff trappers. The program is supervised by Little Pecan's biological staff. The data gathered through daily inspection of the catch have shown that the fur yield of a controlled wetland can be double that of an area that receives no management.

The alligator also represents a unique, renewable resource that is quite responsive to marsh management. Once again, the key to success is water control.

Without a constant supply of water, alligator reproduction is severely hampered. Hatchling mortality soars in dry years. Food becomes scarce. What few gators remain are crowded into scattered pockets of moisture. Not so in the case of a scientifically managed ecosystem, such as the one offered at Little Pecan. With guaranteed water levels to provide food and cover, alligators have responded beautifully, resulting in a direct economic benefit to the landowner.

Alligator harvests are regulated by the Louisiana Department of Fisheries and Wildlife and the U.S. Fish and Wildlife Service. Harvest tags are issued to landowners based on the quality and quantity of their habitat. Little Pecan's harvest quotas are usually filled within the first few days of the season. As with waterfowl and fur, the gator program is monitored through daily records of age, sex, length, and overall condition of each animal taken.

Fisheries resources also make up an important segment of the operation. Little Pecan Island is bordered on the north by a 427-acre freshwater lake. Prior to the formation of the wildlife management area, this body of water was ravaged by tides and populated mainly with rough fish species. Over a two-year period, structures were installed to maintain the water level. Then a mass renovation of the fish population was carried out, and the lake restocked with bluegill, largemouth bass, and channel catfish. In addition, stabilization of the shoreline, periodic lowering of the water level, and installation of deepwater structures have been carried out to reduce turbidity and create a more suitable habitat for game fish spawning.

Two more fisheries programs, still in the planning stages, involve crawfish and shrimp. Both projects will be operated within existing impoundments on the management area and should provide excellent sources of revenue. Crawfish presently are found in the marsh, but a refined management program will have to be instituted with a one-time introduction of crawfish into the impoundment. The shrimp program can be carried out with little or no additional capital outlay because this species already utilizes the impoundments as a nursery area, where they grow to maturity and a harvestable size.

Timber production in a marsh? You better believe it! The west end of Little Pecan Island is a large cypress swamp. This is second growth of a stand that was heavily logged in the 1920s. In addition, the extremities of the island and many miles of levees have been planted with thousands of seedlings: cypress, sawtooth oak, live oak, water oak, Nuttall oak, and slash pine. As the years go by, these should provide a multitude of benefits, including soil stabilization, wildlife habitat enhancement, storm protection, esthetic values, and timber production.

Oil and natural gas are two more resources being wisely managed at Little Pecan Wildlife Management Area. To permit implementation of the other programs, no exploration was allowed during the first four years. Then in 1978, Taylor's biological staff and oil and gas counsel negotiated agreements that are believed to be a first in the industry. These contracts stipulate procedures whereby exploration and drilling will remain compatible with the overall fisheries and wildlife management programs. This allows mineral operations to take place with a minimum of disturbance to the environment.

Water-level control, vegetation manipulation, sound management programs for fish, wildlife, and forestry, plus an environmentally conscious approach to mineral exploration: all are important at Little Pecan Wildlife Management Area. And they illustrate how wise use of natural resources by the private landowner produces not only esthetic rewards but financial ones as well. Best of all, this is a concept that can be adapted and incorporated into almost any wetland in the country, large or small. In so doing, tracts considered by some as mere "wasteland" can be developed into viable income-producers.

It's like having your cake and eating it too.

40

Food Crops for Waterfowl

D. C. Denton

For centuries wild ducks and geese have been attracted to grain. Archeologists tell us that over 5,000 years ago Indians cleared creek and river bottoms and planted them to corn, beans, and other crops. When the fields and river bottoms flooded, the crops and the ducks that moved up and down the river system were brought together.

The more important crops of early settlers—tobacco, indigo, and cotton—had little waterfowl value. However, rice plantings, which began on the South Carolina and Georgia coasts late in the 1600s, were of considerable importance. *Rice and Rice Plantings in the South Carolina Low Country*, by David Doar, contains an interesting account from an earlier source.

> After the harvest, birds were left to gleen the fields, and no one on the plantation dared molest them. After they had gotten through and the ducks came down, every field was plowed for them and though there were thousands of them in each field, they were as sacred as the white elephant, and neither the negroes on the place or the sons of the planter were bold enough to take a shot.

The explanation is that the ducks cleaned up waste rice and weed seed, reducing volunteer and red rice the following year. Even today, with all our modern technology, rice farmers of Louisiana and Mississippi realize the valuable service waterfowl provide in cleaning up weed and grass seeds from harvested fields.

Land use has changed drastically since the days of the Indians and colonial rice planters. Rapidly expanding agriculture and industry have encroached on waterfowl habitat, seriously reducing once-abundant natural foods. Expanding human populations have required ever-increasing acreages of grain crops, and waterfowl have turned more and more from natural foods to these. To the waterfowl manager, agricultural crops provide the means to offset the loss of natural foods by producing quantities of highly nutritious food on relatively small areas.

Food crops grown for waterfowl are essentially of two types: those that produce seed, and those that produce green forage. Seed-producing annuals, maturing in late summer and early fall, provide "hard food," the "hot food" so necessary for both ducks and geese during cold weather.

Green forage crops include perennial grasses or legumes that are green in the winter, and furnish grazing for geese and some species of ducks. Occasionally, the same crop may supply both seed and green forage. Wheat and barley are eaten in the seed stage in the northwestern states and western Canada. Farther south they mature in June and July, usually sprout or rot before waterfowl arrive, and are useful only as green forage.

Those interested in farming for waterfowl may wonder what to plant. Because of the many species of ducks and geese, food preferences vary. Preferred seeds are corn, rice, and grain sorghum. Millet, barley, and wheat are almost as good. Soybeans and other legume seeds are generally less acceptable. As a forage crop, green wheat is preferred. However, legumes, especially alfalfa and ladino clover, are more nutritious than grain forages. Understandably, when the competition for food is keen, preferences are less well defined.

It is important to remember that farm crops have many strains and varieties, and should be carefully selected for a specific locality. A quick check with the Extension Service county agent or the Soil Conserva-

tion Service district conservationist is well worth the effort.

Perhaps the most valuable of all cultivated waterfowl food crops is corn. High in yield and preference, it is heavily used by both ducks and geese, but has the drawback of being low in protein. While waterfowl are surprisingly adept at extracting the kernels from ears of standing corn, if it is knocked down or flooded, it is more easily available to them.

Manipulation of standing crops, other than by flooding, constitutes baiting under federal regulations. It is illegal to take birds attracted to such feed. Know the federal regulations on handling domestic crops if hunting is planned.

Ducks are heavy eaters. A mallard eats at least one to two pounds of grain each week. In Kansas, a 100-acre field, estimated to contain twenty-five bushels an acre, was mowed and the corn was consumed in a week by 85,000 ducks and 15,000 geese. Average consumption was calculated to be three or four ounces a bird per day.

Hard-seeded strains of corn are best to plant for waterfowl, since the ears can lie on the ground for long periods without excessive rotting or sprouting. The length of growing season varies widely with varieties, but generally ranges from 75 to 120 days.

Rice is one of the best of all waterfowl food crops. Over three million acres are planted annually across the United States. It is a traditional waterfowl food of high preference, but is adapted only to certain specialized soil and water conditions and requires special techniques for planting, growing, and harvesting. Production is high, but the crop is subject to heavy predation from the blackbird group. No waterfowl preference has been noted be-

Most grains, including corn as shown here, attract ducks. *Dan Denton photo.*

tween varieties, and one should select from those recommended locally. The growing season is usually 120 to 130 days.

Rice is particularly attractive to mallard and pintail. Geese feed on the seed and graze the green stubble; white-fronted and snow geese may even eat the straw. Ducks maintain themselves on three or four ounces of rice daily, but may take eight ounces or more a day. Rice for waterfowl is used mainly in Arkansas, Louisiana, Mississippi, Texas, and California.

Ricefields are ready-made duck ponds when certain simple procedures are followed. On an existing rice farm, a 150-acre duck field can be created at a cost for the

season of approximately $3,000. This $20 per acre figure breaks down into a reflood cost of about $12.50 per acre on wet fields and $15 per acre on dry fields. The remainder goes into maintenance of the flooded condition at $4 per acre, incidental labor costs, periodic levee checks, and pump repair and maintenance.

The grain sorghums, such as milo maize, kafir corn, hegari, feterita, and other varieties, are eaten readily by ducks and geese. They grow well over a wide range of soil types and moisture conditions. The grain sorghums are more drought-resistant than corn and have a shorter growing season. They also produce well in broadcast stands. However, they are susceptible to considerable damage by small birds, insects, and disease. Also the grain softens and deteriorates quickly in contact with wet soils. Low-growing varieties are most easily utilized by waterfowl. Growing seasons range from 95 to 130 days, depending on the variety.

Buckwheat is a valuable crop for waterfowl. It has a short growing season of 65 to 75 days, produces good yields from broadcast stands, and is readily accepted by waterfowl. Normally considered a northern crop, buckwheat can be grown as far south as southern Florida. It does best, however, in moist soil and a cool growing season.

Peanuts are another preferred food for both ducks and geese. This crop is best adapted to the sandy coastal plain soils. Running peanuts are better for waterfowl use than the bunch variety. They remain longer without sprouting or rotting when left unharvested. Gumbo and calencia varieties should be avoided, because of light production. Although they rate high in waterfowl preference, peanuts must be row-cropped and clean-cultivated. This makes them expensive to produce. Bunch peanuts require from 100 to 120 days to mature and running peanuts from 120 to 140 days.

The term "millet" is loosely applied to a number of annual grasses, including at least five genera, several species, and many varieties. Although their preference rating is usually below corn, rice, peanuts, and the grain sorghums, they are well used by ducks, especially when flooded. The millets are cheaply produced in broadcast stands and mature in a short season. Compared with the grain sorghums, they are much less subject to disease, insects, and small-bird damage.

Brown top millet grows on soil dry enough to cultivate and plant in midsummer. It must be protected from standing water during its growing season and matures about sixty days after planting. When fertilized as needed, top yields are approximately 1,500 pounds of seed per acre. Brown top millet must be planted each year.

The land is prepared by discing or plowing in early July. This midsummer preparation sets back competing weeds and grasses, and the millet still has enough growing season to produce a full yield of seed. Plant 20 pounds of brown top millet seed per acre and apply at least 500 pounds of 5-10-10 fertilizer or its equivalent. Drill the seed one-half inch deep, or broadcast and cover with a drag.

Japanese millet is an improved variety of barnyard grass and is widely adapted to wet soils from California to the Atlantic Coast. It grows on soils wetter than brown top millet and corn would tolerate, and even in shallow water. Japanese millet volunteers and grows as a weed in ricefields. The name "wild millet" or "duck millet" is often used to include all species of *Echinochola*—barnyard grass, the cockspurs, Japanese millet, and jungle rice. All are eaten by ducks.

Japanese millet seems to be one of the better food plants (if not the best) to use in shallow-water field development. This annual attains a height of three to five feet, is extremely tolerant of flooding, can germinate in four days (under warm, moist conditions), and will mature in approximately sixty days. Seeding rate is twenty pounds per acre, either drilled in a prepared seed bed or broadcast on a moist mudflat where the area is too wet to work. The ability to withstand acid conditions (pH 4.8) and to often reseed itself after a good crop makes

Japanese millet reflooded for the ducks. *Mississippi State University, Department of Wildlife and Fisheries photo.*

it a very versatile plant for waterfowl management areas.

With the recent comeback of the beaver in many parts of the country, Japanese millet has become a very important waterfowl management plant. A beaver pond can be drained in midsummer and the bottom planted to Japanese millet. No fertilizer is required and the total cost of developing a fine waterfowl feeding area is approximately $8 per acre. Many sportsmen throughout the country are utilizing this technique to develop inexpensive but productive waterfowl hunting areas.

Two legumes, soybeans and field peas, are seed foods of some importance, although neither is preferred above cultivated grains and grasses. Soybeans and field peas produce fairly well in broadcast stands, but soybeans should be row-cropped, well-fertilized, and clean-cultivated for maximum production. The large-seeded oil varieties are superior for waterfowl plantings. Field peas are best adapted to light sandy soil. Ducks and geese usually favor them over soybeans. However, field peas decompose quickly after contact with the soil.

Sometimes when geese feed on soybeans their crops become distended and im-

Japanese millet seeds ready for consumption. *Mississippi State University, Department of Wildlife and Fisheries photo.*

pacted. Mortality can range from a few birds to several hundred. The condition is triggered by a combination of factors, especially parasitic infection and lead poisoning.

Wheat and barley are used for both forage and grain. In the early growth stage, whether planted or by volunteer, they provide green forage favored by geese. Wheat and barley sown in the spring in the western and northwestern states and Western Canada mature in early fall. The grain is eagerly taken by geese, mallard, and pintail.

Geese also like young oats for forage. Oats are well adapted to certain soil and climatic conditions, particularly in the Southeast.

In many localities geese show a decided preference for alfalfa, and it is used more extensively than any other forage by ducks.

Annual or Italian rye grass also provides good forage for waterfowl. Its tolerance of silting and flooding makes it particularly useful to wildlife managers.

Crimson, white Dutch, red, and ladino are the clovers most frequently used by waterfowl managers. Mixed with perennial grasses, ladino and white Dutch clovers form fine goose pastures that do not require annual planting. They should be mowed or grazed low for waterfowl use; this keeps the growth succulent.

Succulence seems all-important, particularly for geese, usually determining the use given individual fields. Succulence may depend not only on the kind of crop, but also on the planting date, weather, soil, and moisture conditions.

Recovery rate—the ability of a crop to regenerate after close grazing and the rapidity with which it does so—is another important consideration. This factor determines the weight of green forage produced during the winter months.

Waterfowl may fly ten to twenty miles or more for food. But fields near water are more desirable, especially those on islands, peninsulas, and shores. Locations most accessible to waterfowl should be farmed in the early stages of management. As numbers and competition for food increase, the birds usually become less sensitive to the size and location of the fields, to the nearness of cover, and to disturbance.

Farming programs for waterfowl are conducted by many individuals and private groups. Some hunting clubs make heavy investments in crops, and collectively make a great deal of food available for waterfowl. Those who make a living from agriculture may limit farming for waterfowl to a few unpicked rows of corn near a farm pond. In both instances, the aim is to attract birds and improve hunting.

If you plan to use a particular tract of farm land to attract ducks and improve your hunting, spend a little time to develop a plan that will be effective. Take advantage of the numerous sources of free technical assistance for development of duck ponds, duck fields, and goose pastures. These include:

1. The district conservationists with the U.S. Soil Conservation Service, available in almost every county. The conservationist may call in the wildlife biologist or other specialists from the area office to assist with recommendations. If your place can be developed for waterfowl, the Soil Conservation Service can also make free engineering services available from the area office.
2. Game and fish commissions in most states have a program of assistance

from the district biologist for private landowners and sportsmen. The name of the wildlife biologist serving your particular area can be obtained from the state office. As their workload permits, they give free on-site inspections and technical advice.

3. Free technical assistance and general information are obtainable from the area and regional offices of the U.S. Fish and Wildlife Service. Pamphlets and other material are available from these offices.

4. State extension wildlife specialists working directly with the county extension agents. Their offices are generally located on university campuses. Free technical advice and pamphlets are available to interested sportsmen and landowners.

5. Wildlife specialists of the U.S. Forest Service are on staff in each of their regional offices. Free publications and technical advice on various subjects relating to forestry and wildlife are provided.

The *Conservation Directory*, which lists contact information for organizations, agencies, and officials concerned with natural resource use and management, is available at nominal cost from the National Wildlife Federation, 1412 Sixteenth Street, N.W., Washington, DC 20036 (202-797-6800). This will be of considerable assistance in locating the individuals who can best supply the information required for any proposed waterfowl development.

Finally, it is worthwhile to mention the Agricultural Conservation Program. This cost-sharing and technical assistance program is available to landowners for waterfowl habitat creation, retention, or development. The level of activity varies county by county and state by state, depending on fund availability and priorities set by county committees. The conservation practice is wildlife wetland habitat. It applies to wetlands or other areas where water can be impounded or regulated by diking, ditching, or flooding. For more information on this program, contact your local Soil Conservation Service office.

41

Down Mexico Way: Waterfowl Habitat and Populations

J. R. Singleton

Any discussion of the continental migratory waterfowl population and associated problems would be incomplete without the wintering grounds south of the U.S. border. Although both Mexico and Central America provide wintering habitat, Mexico is the more important, and winters significant numbers of all species of North American ducks and geese, other than mallard.

In the following discussion, waterfowl population data given for the period 1948–1962 are from *Waterfowl and Their Wintering Grounds in Mexico, 1937–64*, U.S. Dept. of Interior, Fish and Wildlife Service Resource Publication No. 138, by George B. Saunders and Dorothy C. Saunders (1981), and recent data from the U.S. Fish and Wildlife Service.

What has been the fate of wintering habitat down Mexico way over the past four decades? Has it been altered? If so, how, when and where? And what of the numbers of ducks and geese?

Mexico provides very diverse wintering habitat, which can be classified into three zones or broad regions—Gulf and Caribbean coast, interior highlands, and west coast—and includes everything from flat coastal bays and marshes to high mountain wetlands at elevations in excess of 8,000 feet.

The extensive bays and marshes adjacent to the Gulf of Mexico are used primarily by ducks and geese from the central and Mississippi flyways. These broad flatlands receive more rainfall and runoff than other Mexican wetlands, and range from inshore Gulf waters to tidal bays, lagoons, and brackish and freshwater marshes, providing a variety of plant and animal food for waterfowl. Agricultural croplands are

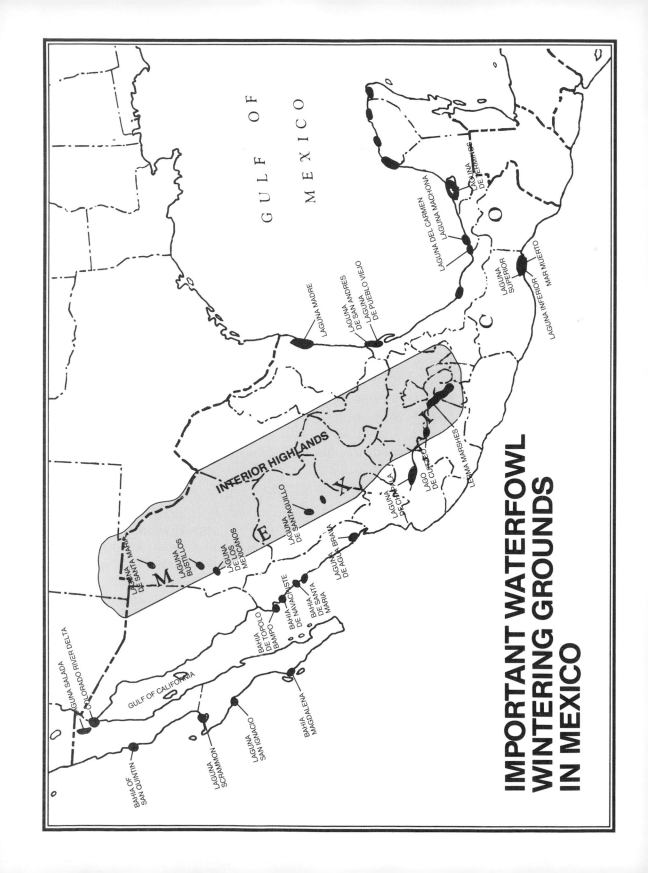

IMPORTANT WATERFOWL
WINTERING GROUNDS
IN MEXICO

GULF OF MEXICO

GULF OF CALIFORNIA

INTERIOR HIGHLANDS

M E X I C O

LAGUNA MADRE

LAGUNA SAN ANDRES

LAGUNA DE PUEBLO VIEJO

LAGUNA DEL CARMEN
LAGUNA MACHONA

LAGUNA DE TERMINOS

LAGUNA SUPERIOR
LAGUNA INFERIOR
MAR MUERTO

LERMA MARSHES

LAGO DE CUITZEO

LAGUNA DE CHAPALA

LAGUNA BRAVA DE AGUA BRAVA

LAGUNA DE SANTAGUILLO

LAGUNA BUSTILLOS

LAGUNA DE LOS MEXICANOS

LAGUNA DE SANTA MARIA

BAHIA DE TOPOLO BAMPO

BAHIA DE NAVACHISTE

BAHIA DE SANTA MARIA

LAGUNA SALADA
COLORADO RIVER DELTA

BAHIA OF SAN QUINTIN

LAGUNA SCRAMMON

LAGUNA SAN IGNACIO

BAHIA MAGDALENA

One of Mexico's wintering wetlands. *J. R. Singleton photo.*

also used by wintering ducks and geese. Farther south are the extensive marshes and mangrove lagoons on the Yucatan coastline, which are also important nesting and feeding sites for flamingos.

January 1948–1962 waterfowl numbers observed in this zone ranged from a 1948 high of 5,771,000 to a 1951 low of 742,000. More recent counts put the 1981 number at 2,550,700 and 1982 at 1,140,900. Lesser scaup, pintail, blue-winged teal, and wigeon accounted for 70 percent of the ducks.

A continuing decline in the carrying capacity of the extensive lagoons and marshes is reported; this is the result of reduced river flows from upstream impoundments, agricultural clearing, and drainage. More recently, oil developments

have become an additional threat.

Habitat conditions along the Yucatan peninsula are either very good or very poor. Much of the mangrove lagoon in the vicinity of Progresso has been drained; the mangrove are dead, and the lagoons are subject to saltwater inundation during periods of high tide. An effort is underway to control tidal flooding and retain fresh water in a portion of this marsh. Excessive drainage and roadfills across the lagoon, which prevent natural water exchange, also contribute to loss of habitat.

In the interior highlands, westward and inland from the Gulf and Caribbean toward the mountainous terrain of the interior of Mexico, there are many diverse wetlands. While most are relatively free from pollution, many have suffered from deforestation, on-stream impoundments, and, in some instance, overgrazing and agricultural encroachment. Dabbling ducks, geese, and occasionally diving ducks winter on these wetlands.

Duck and goose population counts in the interior highlands fluctuated from a low of 255,000 in 1962 to a high of 1,519,500 in 1982. In 1985, surveyors observed 498,000 ducks and geese in this area. There were 187,200 coot counted there in 1981, 162,100 in 1982, and 50,200 in 1985.

Significant populations also frequent the intensively farmed croplands of northern Mexico, south of Texas, New Mexico, and Arizona.

Lake Chapala, south of Guadalajara, Jalisco, formerly wintered more than 100,000 ducks, including canvasbacks. This population has declined severely in recent years from increased farming, siltation, and other factors. Lake Chapala is fed primarily by the Rio Lerma, which rises in the mountains near Toluca, west and southwest of Mexico City.

The Rio Lerma marsh complex is situated in the valley near Toluca at an elevation slightly more than 8,300 feet. Three separate and rather distinctive marshes occur in the valley, and obviously were outstanding in earlier times. Drainage, water diversion, and intensive farming of the rich marsh basin soils have resulted in many changes and a decline in carrying capacity.

Two sites in the interior highlands typify present conditions and problems. The Lerma River marsh near Toluca, west of Mexico City, is at approximately 8,300 feet. Diversion of the river flow at Mexico City has resulted in a smaller marsh acreage and the extension of farming operations into what was once the lake bed. Carrying capacity has been reduced, and

efforts to reverse this trend have met with questionable success. Wintering counts on the area plunged from a high of 95,150 in 1958 to a low of only 665 in 1982. The marsh is reported to be nearing total destruction.

The Laguna de Santaguillo is located north of Durango, state of Durango. It is a closed basin, with drainage in but no outflow. While conditions are good in some years, the laguna suffers from deforestation, small reservoir impoundments for cropland irrigation, and severe overgrazing. Soils are slightly alkaline, and surface water fluctuates significantly. In 1951–1953 conditions were poor; in 1955 water levels were good and 92,000 ducks and 5,450 geese were observed. However, population counts varied from 400 birds in 1953 to 93,000 in 1959. Conditions were favorable in 1982, and 54,300 ducks and 25,750 geese were using the wetland.

Compared to the Gulf and Caribbean coast, some of the Pacific Coast wintering areas are narrow and crowded by mountains. Also, Tampico, on the Gulf side, receives forty-nine inches of precipitation, compared to twenty-three inches in Culiacan on the Pacific Coast.

Examples of Pacific Coast marshes vary from the large marsh on the Rio Colorado south of Mexicali, to tidal bays and freshwater marshes.

The Rio Colorado marsh complex, located at the northernmost end of the Gulf of California, comprises possibly 75,000 acres, but has limited carrying capacity for waterfowl. At one time it was subject to tidal inundation. But in the early 1970s the river flow was diverted to the Laguna Salada, and the mouth of the Rio Colorado became blocked by sand and silt deposits. The marsh is slowly becoming fresh, but with an infestation of noxious plants in the upper freshwater reaches. Carrying capacity is reported to have declined between 1937 and 1964 as a result of these upstream reservoirs and other uses of the river flow. Average annual population figures for the period 1952–1964 were about 2,000 geese, 25,000 ducks, and 300,000 coot. Many were in flooded fields and farmlands.

But high-water levels and abundant surface water have characterized the marsh for the past several years, 1979–1984, and more recent population counts show the following:

	Ducks	Geese	Coot
1979	70,740	4,100	2,000
1984	15,400	15	3,900

Mexican wintering habitat has not been as intensively studied, mapped, or managed as that of the United States. Yet everything indicates that the factors that have resulted in degradation or loss of wetland habitat in Mexico are little different from those north of the border, and remain much the same today.

However, the total numbers of both ducks and geese also indicate a rather stable population level. Total waterfowl observed in winter counts in Mexico, as reported by the U.S. Fish and Wildlife Service for the years 1978–1982, were as follows:

Winter Counts
(Expressed in thousands)

	1978	1979	1980	1981	1982
Total ducks	3,798	3,502	3,164	3,329	3,659
Total geese	276	266	285	311	298

It is important to realize that the numbers presented here, and throughout this chapter, are merely an index to the population and not an actual population estimate.

Obviously, species composition varied somewhat each year, as did distribution of these species on the wintering grounds. On the average, divers made up approximately 20 percent of the total ducks. Redheads and scaup were the two principal diving species. Among the dabblers, pintail accounted for 25 to 40 percent of the wintering population on the Mexican wetlands. Green-winged, blue-winged, and cinnamon teal, in total, approximately equaled the pintail population. Other dabblers represented in significant numbers included gadwall, wigeon, and shovelers. Brant and snows accounted for most of the goose population.

While there has been great concern for

conservation of wildlife and wildlife habitat in Mexico by several organizations in the United States, progress is slow. Conditions in Mexico, and the concern of a majority of its citizens for better living conditions and other rewards of a better life, do not necessarily translate into a high priority for wildlife conservation.

We in the United States, who participate in the harvest of waterfowl or simply enjoy the spectacular fall flights, should be concerned with wintering conditions in Mexico. Migratory waterfowl are an international resource, and international effort and cooperation are necessary to ensure the future of that resource. Thus we are concerned that ducks and geese wintering in Mexico return to their northern breeding grounds in healthy and reproductive condition.

Part VI
Managing an International Resource

Man has been aware of the hard reality of his dependence on wildlife as long as he has been aware of anything. It is still true. Modern animal husbandry is merely management of wildlife in captivity.

But the first recorded reference to that dependence, and the first attempt to manage wildlife, is probably that recorded in the Book of Deuteronomy 22:6. "You may take the young, but be sure to let the mother go, so that it may go well with you and you may have a long life." And in Exodus 23:11. "But during the seventh year let the land lie unplowed and unused. Then the poor among your people may get food from it, and the wild animals may eat what they leave."

Thus man, for a very long time, has been aware of the need to manage wildlife for his needs or comfort. He has not always been successful. There have been many examples of gross exploitation and habitat destruction, sometimes resulting in extermination of entire species. But even in these instances, usually associated with commercialism, there were always voices raised in protest. And even some participants questioned the morality of their activities.

Sportsmen may not be more concerned about the wildlife they hunt than other wildlife groups, but they seem more inclined toward positive action. Modern waterfowl management and the acquisition, management, and preservation of waterfowl habitat by both government and private agencies — stimulated and usually paid for by sportsmen themselves in special taxes or donations — demonstrates this pragmatism.

Those who decry hunting should consider how very different the situation would be without the sportsman's defensive attitude toward wildlife — and his dollars.

42

Breeding Ground Surveys

D. D. Kennedy

The months of May, June, and July are critical periods in the waterfowl calendar. This is the time of nesting, hatching, and brood rearing. The drakes and hens have done their thing; the abundance and quality of water are now critical. It is up to the hen to incubate her clutch of eggs, get them hatched, and successfully lead the brood to water. If water conditions hold up; if invertebrate population peaks coincide with brood demands for food; if there is a good crop of emergent and submergent vegetation; and if no drastic weather occurs—maybe, just maybe, mother mallard may be able to get a respectable number of young to the flight stage and on the way south.

That's a lot of "ifs," you say? It sure is. Beginning with the most critical element in the waterfowl reproduction formula—wetland habitat—and moving through nest

destruction, egg infertility, duckling mortality, disease, predation, and just plain bad luck, it's difficult at best to get ducks on the wing.

A logical question arises. How does anyone make any sense out of all the "ifs" and imponderables of this situation, and predict the magnitude of the fall flight? Well, the U.S. Fish and Wildlife Service does just that—with much cooperation in time and manpower by the Canadian Wildlife Service.

As you might expect, it's not easy. In fact, to forecast the fall flight, the U.S. Fish and Wildlife Service mobilizes the world's most extensive wildlife survey. It comes in two steps, one in May to assess water conditions and breeding populations, and a second in July for water conditions and duck production. Experienced aerial crews of pilot/biologists log over

66,000 miles each year to come up with these estimates. Additionally, various state agencies have developed annual waterfowl surveys and provide important information on duck breeding populations inside the major survey area.

The Migratory Bird Treaty Act requires the Secretary of the Interior to protect migratory birds and carefully regulate use of the surplus if hunted. With this mandate, the waterfowl breeding ground population and habitat surveys were instituted in 1947.

Previously a number of organizations were involved in various kinds of waterfowl surveys. The old U.S. Biological Survey and the Canadian authorities recognized the need, and made some early effort; but in 1935, the parent organization of Ducks Unlimited, More Game Birds in America, Inc., made the first major breeding ground survey. Their pioneer work was followed by today's intensive annual undertaking by the U.S. Fish and Wildlife Service, whose May and July surveys became standardized and fully operational in 1955 and 1966, respectively. Along the way there have been additions and refinements to procedures and considerable evolution in how the data are interpreted and presented to the regulatory bodies.

To the average duck hunter, a waterfowl biologist is a man up to his knees in marsh; surveying the topography, vegetation and waterfowl, or doing a nesting study. Or he is someone involved in low level inventories of waterfowl across the continent. Unfortunately, only a few waterfowl biologists get to spend much time in this latter pursuit, but those few are admired and envied within the profession.

There are normally nine U.S. Fish and Wildlife Service aerial crews. Those working in Alaska, the Yukon Territory, the Northwest Territories, and the northern parts of Alberta, Saskatchewan, Manitoba, and Ontario, are "bush" crews. The "prairie" crews fly southern Alberta, Saskatchewan, and Manitoba along with Montana and the Dakotas. The May survey covers 38,000 miles of transects and the July survey 28,000 miles of the same transects. Because of the time constraint relating to regulations, Alaska, the Yukon, and the Northwest Territories are not surveyed in July. The area monitored constitutes 1.3 million square miles but only about 1 percent of this area is sampled annually.

The technique is basically the same for the two surveys. Aircraft ground speed is 90 knots and altitude between 100 and 200 feet. The pilot records data 220 yards to the left and the observer 220 yards to the right during the May surveys. Transect width is reduced by one half during the July flights because of reduced visibility from over-water cover.

In May, the objective is to record breeding waterfowl and pond conditions. Birds encountered fall into the following categories: pairs, lone drakes, lone females, and flocks of various sizes. A lone drake, for most species, indicates a breeding pair and a hen in some stage of nesting, laying, or incubation. Groups of up to four drakes are considered to be paired birds whose hens are in advanced stages of incubation or rearing broods. They might also represent a reservoir of bachelor drakes. Pairs in close association indicate the early stages of mating and nesting. Groups of mixed sexes that cannot be separated into singles or pairs are in uncertain breeding status, or may not be involved in production at all.

While the pilot is keeping the plane on the transect line and counting ducks, the observer is recording ducks and also tabulating and categorizing water bodies.

Water, the vital component of the prairie duck factory, is an all-important aspect of these surveys. Water conditions, in the final analysis, may be the best predictor of fall flights.

Prairie crews record any water body capable of serving as breeding territory or brood habitat. These may be rivers, lakes, or large marshes, but most are small potholes and marshes. Stock ponds are included when they are considered capable of supporting breeding ducks or geese. In fact, any depression with water that appears it will last for at least three weeks from the survey date and is considered to have value for waterfowl is included.

The number of prairie water bodies from year to year is variable in the extreme. The survey data show that, in wet years on the southern prairies, there may be as many as seven million ponds; in dry years, less than two million. The contrast between the good years and the dry years is dramatic indeed.

Aerial crews are busy! Keeping the plane on the transect, at proper speed and altitude, is topped off by counting ducks and water. Recording equipment is used to simplify the data-keeping chores. There is little time for elaborate notes, with marshes flying by the window at several per minute.

Crews are expected to have all their morning rituals and preparation done and be airborne and on the transect line by no later than one hour after sunrise. Weather conditions that would affect the operation of the aircraft, the ability to observe, or the normal activities of waterfowl cancel these daily flights.

The prairie transects are flown from May 1 through May 25, bush transects from May 12 through June 12. These dates are not absolute. The crews must use bio-

logical indicators to know when to begin the surveys. If they are started too early, there will be a lot of transient ducks to fuzz up the data. Transient ducks, such as scaup and the northern breeding components of other species, loaf around on the southern prairies waiting for weather or other conditions to dictate a move farther north. Also, late migrating species such as blue-winged teal must arrive before the surveys can begin. Proper timing of the surveys requires some preliminary reconnaissance, and a lot of experience and savvy by the pilot/biologists and ground crew leaders.

North of the prairie and parklands, ducks have less time to decide when to begin the nesting processes. Weather chronology offers less flexibility. In Alaska and the northern bush, spring breakup is immediately followed by nest initiation. Because water conditions are more dependable farther north, the bush crews do not record water or pond conditions.

The survey design has become standardized. There are fifty strata defined by their geographical or biological similarities. In each stratum the transects, mostly east and west, are centered on section lines in the prairies and along latitudinal lines in the northern bush. Transect spacing is based on waterfowl densities. In high-density areas, such as the southern prairies, they will be closer together. Each transect is divided into a series of segments, about eighteen miles long, each with a well-defined start and end point.

So much for the May surveys. Come July, the crews go out and resurvey most of the area. This time, pond counts are strong indicators of the water loss that has taken place during the critical nesting and initial brood rearing periods. How successful the breeding ducks from the May counts have been can also be determined. The crews are

Surveying waterfowl to determine what's ahead for the fall flight. *Robert J. Long photo.*

looking for broods and the age class and the number of ducklings in each. These data can be analyzed for the success of early nesting attempts, the peaks of nest initiation and hatching, and duckling mortality during the brooding period.

A logical concern at this point is, if these data are to be used to determine the waterfowl regulations for the coming season, and if these crews are flying day in and day out at low levels and relatively high speeds, just how good are the data?

Fair question, and one that is addressed every year. Built into the survey design is a ground/air comparison. A ground crew,

composed of Canadian Wildlife Service personnel, covers several segments of the transect on the same day or the day following the aerial counts. Ground crews try to count every single duck on each wetland in the ground sample. Their data are compared with those of the aerial crew. This input is essential to the accuracy of the entire survey, for adjustments can then be made for vegetation and poor visibility, and other errors inherent in the quick flyover.

As it turns out, the aerial crews are reasonably consistent. It's a good thing. The vastness and inaccessibility of much of the breeding grounds preclude the use of ground crews alone. Even after several weeks of flying, all the crews combined are able to cover only 1 percent. There is some real hope in the future that satellite imagery may be able to handle the water data portions of the survey; thus in the next few years the potential for increased precision is tremendous.

Now to the bottom line. What happens to all this good survey information? It appears in a very impressive report in late July, and is put in the hands of the administrators and biologists of the various wildlife agencies: the U.S. Fish and Wildlife Service, the Canadian Wildlife Service, all the state and provincial agencies, and the private conservation groups around the continent. With this document, "Status of Waterfowl and Fall Flight Forecast," as a base, the regulation process begins. The report includes specifics of May and July pond data and compares current and long-term trends. It gives a species by species report on the status of breeding populations, and compares them to the historical data. Finally, it gives general forecasts, by flyway, on the anticipated volume of the fall flight.

The immediate interest of the "Status Report" for hunters is the waterfowl forecast for the coming season. Far more important to biologists are the comparative data over the years and the trends that are being established. Here the problem areas can be seen that suggest changes in regulations or management, and also the bright spots demonstrating the wisdom of earlier decisions and management successes.

The most extensive wildlife survey in the world is also the most critical to the future of the continental waterfowl resource. It provides the first warning signs of serious problems, and it indicates the warm rewards of good management.

43

Ducks Unlimited Canada Waterfowl and Wetland Surveys

P. J. Caldwell

Ducks Unlimited Canada has a long history of waterfowl and habitat surveys extending back to its progenitor, the More Game Birds in America Foundation. This organization carried out, in 1935, the first comprehensive North American waterfowl breeding-ground population survey; this also marked the first use of aircraft to inventory waterfowl and wetland habitat in the roadless and inaccessible north.

When Ducks Unlimited Canada became operational in 1938, these ground and aerial surveys became an annual activity. An aerial survey was continued until 1967, though it was somewhat curtailed during the war years because of shortages of aviation fuel.

Ground surveys are still being run, although techniques have been greatly modified over the years. The 1935 survey, and those from 1938 to 1952, depended heavily on reports of waterfowl and water conditions from local observers, called Keemen, across the prairies and parklands. They reported three times a year, spring, summer, and freezeup, on waterfowl numbers, habitat conditions, brood production, and migration. The summer report involved an actual count of ducks and broods in the Keeman's area. These reports were compiled to estimate a total waterfowl population for the area surveyed.

In November 1938, there were 3,200 Keemen. The corps remained near this number until 1952, when an expanding Ducks Unlimited Canada was able to field sufficient personnel to carry out more sophisticated surveys. The number of Keemen was then permitted to decline to the present 250 well-distributed reporters with whom much closer contact is now maintained. Their reports are presently used to augment surveys carried out by company biologists.

A typical survey year actually begins the previous fall when conditions at freezeup are reported. High soil moisture, and a subsequent good frost seal, mean meltwater the following spring will flow overland to wetland basins instead of percolating directly into the dry earth. This early predictor of the upcoming year's production is followed by bimonthly reports on snow accumulation and existing snowpack conditions.

Each of the thirty-four area offices of Ducks Unlimited across Canada report regularly on conditions in their respective areas. With the arrival of warmer weather, reports begin to focus on the progress and quantity of the runoff, and resulting water levels of wetlands in general and Ducks Unlimited projects in particular. The quality of the habitat available to returning waterfowl is now essentially fixed, and, in broad terms, the year's production can now be predicted.

The spring survey season begins with a general survey by the chief biologist of the prairies and parklands, where conditions are highly variable but key to a successful production year. The survey is carried out in early May by car along an established route. By also talking to Keemen and area staff along the way and assessing various key habitats for water conditions, the chief biologist determines the current spring production potential. In most years this predicted potential forms part of the chief biologist's report to the Ducks Unlimited, Inc., annual convention.

In mid-May, Ducks Unlimited staff carry out actual counts of water bodies and breeding pairs of waterfowl. These counts take place on long-established tran-

sects and traditional DU projects across Canada. A single transect, following roads "usually" passable in the spring, is four miles long and a quarter mile wide (one-eighth mile on each side of the road) and thus covers one square mile of habitat.

Transects are distributed along the route to sample the different habitat types through which the route passes. On the transect, water bodies are counted and their current condition (water levels, emergent vegetation, and shoreline condition) recorded. The number of breeding pairs, lone drakes, and flocked birds is recorded by species.

Breeding season chronology is considered in survey timing, and counts take place only during morning peaks of waterfowl activity. Consideration of daily weather conditions is also important. These surveys have been designed to establish trends in waterfowl numbers with no attempt to establish total waterfowl populations. The assessment of habitat conditions is the critical component of the surveys.

Thirty years of comparative data exist for many transects. Some have been run by the same observer for over twenty years. They are rerun in early July to determine midseason water conditions and to assess the potential of these conditions to sustain the broods through the fledging period.

While the prairies and parklands, with visibility mostly unlimited by trees and one-square-mile road grids, lend themselves to the transect technique, this is not true of the forested regions of the prairie provinces or British Columbia, Ontario, Quebec, and the Maritimes. Poor visibility or lack of access requires other techniques.

In British Columbia and Ontario, waterfowl counts and habitat evaluations of specific wetlands and Ducks Unlimited projects are done annually from the ground. Some of these wetlands have been surveyed for over fifteen years. In the forested regions of the Saskatchewan River Delta, which spans the Saskatchewan-Manitoba border, in Quebec along the St. Lawrence and Ottawa Rivers, and in the Maritimes, traditional aerial surveys of the same wetland basins are carried out each year.

Utilizing helicopters, total counts are attempted on small basins, while on large basins, a system of transects or shoreline surveys is used. While fewer wetlands are involved than on the prairies, and sometimes their size is greater, these surveys tend to be more intensive and in more stable habitats.

Many other sources provide background for Ducks Unlimited's news releases and production reports during the waterfowl breeding season. These include data from intensive studies carried out to determine the productive rates of various DU projects. These studies, done by DU's research and evaluation arm, are completed on a biweekly basis over the breeding period, and at the same locations for three succes-

sive years. They represent the best estimates of production coming from individual DU wetlands.

Monthly reports and periodic updates are also received from each of DU's 34 area offices, which are widely distributed across Canada but concentrated in the prairies, the heart of the North American waterfowl production region. Ducks Unlimited also cooperates with other agencies, such as the Canadian Wildlife Service and the U.S. Fish and Wildlife Service, by sharing information with them. All these sources are finally distilled down into the news releases, in DU magazines and elsewhere, that report on the success of the production year in Canada.

A final summary report is prepared in mid-July. All the above reports and information are used in this final forecast. It is used by Ducks Unlimited, Inc., as background information at flyway council meetings on the success of the current breeding season. These deliberations produce final recommendations for harvest regulations.

44

The Canadian Wildlife Service and Waterfowl Management

C. Hyslop and F. G. Cooch

The Canadian federal government has responsibility for conserving migratory birds and their habitats, including waterfowl, under the Migratory Birds Convention of 1916 with the United States and the Canada Wildlife Act of 1973.

Waterfowl management in Canada is a complex cooperative venture, involving the Canadian Wildlife Service (CWS), provincial agencies, nongovernmental organizations, and private foundations such as the recently chartered Wildlife Habitat Canada Foundation. Close cooperation is also required with the U.S. Fish and Wildlife Service (USFWS) and state agencies. Canada and the United States recently negotiated a North American waterfowl management plan, in concert with the provinces and the U.S. flyway councils. An essential element of this plan is even closer integration of effort by all levels of government and the private sector. Successful implementation of the plan will carry waterfowl management into the twenty-first century.

CWS activities in waterfowl conservation and management in Canada are extremely diverse. They include surveying and monitoring population levels and trends, setting and enforcing hunting regulations, estimating hunting kill, conserving and managing habitat, preventing damage by waterfowl to agricultural crops, assessing the impacts of toxic chemicals and avian diseases on waterfowl, negotiating questions of hunting rights in aboriginal land claims, and research to understand the basic relationships between waterfowl and the natural (and man-made) environment.

In the early 1950s, the CWS and USFWS began a series of exploratory aerial and ground surveys throughout most of Canada, to determine the distribution and numbers of breeding waterfowl. These surveys were gradually reduced geographically to focus on the main production areas. The present Cooperative Waterfowl Breeding Ground Survey is now limited in Canada to the prairie provinces and the Mackenzie district, with Old Crow Flats in the Yukon Territory surveyed as part of the Alaskan effort.

The survey has two parts: a May air/ground survey of breeding waterfowl, and a July aerial survey that counts broods and water areas. These surveys allow waterfowl managers to determine how successful the breeding season has been and to predict the number of young that will fledge and be recruited to the population in the fall.

In recent years, drought on the Canadian prairies has resulted in poor breeding success and a concomitant reduction in waterfowl populations in this region. The potential breeding success of geese in the Arctic and sub-Arctic is assessed from satellite images of the breeding areas, weather reports and forecasts, and on-site reports from a network of local observers.

Closely tied to surveys of population size and recruitment are those to estimate numbers and species of waterfowl killed by sport hunters.

Since 1966, all Canadian sport hunters have had to purchase a federal Migratory Game Bird Hunting Permit. This was introduced to provide the basis for the National Harvest Survey and Species Composition Survey.

The national harvest survey is a mail survey of selected permit purchasers. It has been run annually in Canada since 1967. Information is gathered on the number of ducks, geese, and other migratory game birds reported killed and retrieved, the date and location of the hunt, and the

number of days spent hunting. Results are extrapolated to estimate the total number of waterfowl killed by sport hunters in each province or territory.

The Species Composition Survey is also a mail survey sent to a different set of purchasers of migratory game bird hunting permits. Respondents are asked to return one wing from each duck they kill, or the tail feathers from each goose. Waterfowl biologists can then tell the species, age, and sex of the birds from feather coloration and wear. The results of this survey are used in combination with those from the National Harvest Survey to estimate numbers of each species killed, by age and sex, and the spatial and temporal distribution of the kill of each species.

These data are useful to waterfowl managers in setting hunting regulations; they also provide an index over time of trends in hunter activity and success and waterfowl distribution. They also provide an independent guide to waterfowl population trends, for comparison with the results of the May and July surveys in the west and north. At present they are the chief index to population changes in eastern Canada, where extensive breeding surveys have been too expensive to run regularly.

The CWS protects key migratory bird habitat through its system of National Wildlife Areas and Migratory Bird Sanctuaries. Many of these areas are wetlands that are critical nesting, feeding, and staging grounds for waterfowl.

In 1887 by Order-in-Council, the Canadian government set aside the islands and shores of the north end of Last Mountain Lake in Saskatchewan as a breeding ground for migratory birds. This is believed to be the first area so designated in North America.

In a further Order-in-Council of March

1925, which set aside several other areas for the same purpose, the following appears:

> That the Great Plains region of Canada contains probably the most valuable breeding grounds in North America for the wildfowl of the continent and that it is important that measures should be taken to set apart permanently certain areas for the propagation of bird life, a resource of economic value in providing sport and food.
>
> That the advance of settlement, following cultivation of the land, the drainage of lakes and marsh areas for development purposes has seriously restricted the areas suitable for the propagation of wild waterfowl and under present conditions it is necessary that proper means should be taken to check the decrease in the number of these birds and to guard against the danger of extermination.

The most important thing here is the intent, at such an early date. These areas were not sanctuaries in the modern sense, for shooting was permitted on most of them, but were meant to preserve the means of reproduction.

Following the tabling of the National Wildlife Policy and Program in the House of Commons in 1966, a system of Wildlife Areas was initiated throughout southern Canada. There are currently forty-two Wildlife Areas, totaling about fifty square kilometers, throughout the provinces: six in Nova Scotia, four in New Brunswick, six in Quebec, ten in Ontario, two in Manitoba, six in Saskatchewan, three in Alberta, and five in British Columbia. Land has been acquired through purchase, lease, donation, or transfer from other federal or provincial government agencies. Lands acquired and managed by the CWS are called National Wildlife Areas; those managed jointly with the provinces are called Cooperative Wildlife Areas.

National Wildlife Areas are managed to preserve or increase the value of the habitat to wildlife. This may include restricting hunting or fishing, or minimizing the disturbance to wildlife of other human activities, such as hiking or picnicking. The habitat may also be managed to increase the benefit to wildlife. At Last Mountain Lake Cooperative Wildlife Area in Saskatchewan, for example, controlled burning increases the amount of upland grass cover for nesting ducks and their broods. Cap-Tourmente National Wildlife Area in Quebec provides feeding and resting areas for more than half of the world population of greater snow geese, which pass through it on migration.

Migratory Bird Sanctuaries are established to protect migratory birds and their habitat, both north and south of latitude 60° in Canada. The land may be federal or provincial or it may be privately owned. Hunting and other disturbance of the birds or their habitat during the breeding season are prohibited. North of 60°, thirteen sanctuaries have been established, totaling 106,422 square kilometers, many for the protection of colonially nesting white geese (lesser and greater snow and Ross geese). The Dewey Soper Sanctuary on southwestern Baffin Island protects the world's largest colony of lesser snow geese. South of 60°, sixty-six sanctuaries have been established, totaling 7,492 square kilometers.

The CWS has a continuing program to identify and evaluate important migratory bird habitat, especially wetlands, throughout Canada. Priority areas are mapped and rated according to nationally established criteria. This information is useful to further protection and management initiatives by the CWS and other agencies.

Canada became party, in 1981, to the Convention on the Conservation of Wetlands of International Importance, which originated at Ramsar, Iran, in 1971. The convention calls for the contracting parties to identify important wetlands within their boundaries, especially those valuable as waterfowl habitat. The process has no base in legislation, but increases the profile of an identified wetland internationally.

So far, Canada has identified seventeen sites through the cooperation of federal and provincial agencies. They comprise about 107,000 square kilometers, most of which already lie within National Wildlife Areas, Migratory Bird Sanctuaries, or national parks. This international labeling of key areas has proved a very useful device in other countries for helping to ensure that sites are not damaged or destroyed by unsuitable development proposals.

Understanding the fundamental relationships between waterfowl and their environment is necessary for making sensible decisions on their conservation and management. The CWS undertakes studies to address diverse problems in waterfowl management.

In eastern Canada, concern has been expressed at the apparent decline in black duck populations, especially in Ontario and western Quebec. The causes are not accurately known, but may include habitat alteration, hunting, and competition from and hybridization with the mallard, which has expanded its range eastward in recent years. Black duck population decreases have been reported in the eastern United States as well, and both countries recently imposed additional hunting restrictions for the species. The CWS will monitor the effect of these regulation changes on breeding populations, and has plans to expand recent studies of the effects of large-scale habitat changes in the boreal forest on duck numbers and breeding success.

Additional studies are proposed, in conjunction with university researchers, to determine the effects and extent of black duck–mallard interactions, including hybridization and competition for resources during the breeding season.

There is concern that acid rain may pose a threat to waterfowl breeding on unbuffered lakes on the Canadian Shield, where they rely on aquatic food resources including fish, invertebrates, and plants.

The CWS has carried out studies in southern Quebec and northern Ontario to determine the effects on waterfowl of increasing acidification of lakes. One major finding is that when fish disappear from acidified lakes, populations of invertebrates tend to increase, because of the lack of predation. This could prove beneficial in the short term for generalized feeders such as the hooded merganser, ring-necked duck, black duck and mallard, but detrimental to piscivorous species such as common mergansers. Highly acidified lakes will not even support invertebrates, and become useless to waterfowl except as resting areas.

Waterfowl on the prairies are troubled by drought and loss of habitat, not by acid rain. Low precipitation and wetland drainage for agriculture and urban development in recent years have contributed to considerable declines in prairie duck populations.

Over the last five years, in cooperation with a similar program in the United States, the CWS has implemented a period of stabilized waterfowl hunting regulations, to investigate the roles of hunting and other factors in regulating duck populations. Waterfowl populations and harvests on the prairies have been intensively monitored during this time, to answer questions on the effects of regulations on hunter numbers and levels of kill, the interactions between hunters and birds and how these factors influence kill, and levels of crippling loss and within-season illegal kill.

On the west coast, the CWS is undertaking studies to enhance the understanding and management of the trumpeter swan, a species listed as rare by the Committee on the Status of Endangered Wildlife in Canada (COSEWIC). A significant proportion of the world population of trumpeter swan winter in British Columbia, either on coastal estuaries or inland water bodies that remain at least partly ice-free. It had been assumed that they migrate down the coast from breeding grounds in Alaska, but recent banding and neck-collaring studies indicate that some may use an inland migration path instead. This makes protection of inland resting and staging areas, as well as coastal ones, important in the management of this species.

The CWS also contributes funds to studies by university researchers, such as that of lesser snow geese at La Perouse Bay on the Hudson Bay coast in Manitoba. Researchers from Queen's University in Kingston have studied the colony for fifteen years, covering diverse aspects of their biology and ecology. A greater understanding has been gained of the requirements of the geese on the breeding grounds, as well as on migratory and wintering areas.

In times of increasing government restraint, both federal and provincial, much must be accomplished in wildlife management with dwindling resources. The problems facing waterfowl, and wildlife in general, continue to grow and become more complex. The CWS must focus its attention and resources on issues of high priority, and continue to ensure the maximum benefit for wildlife through cooperation with other agencies.

45

U.S. Waterfowl Habitat Protection Programs

G. K. Brakhage

The U.S. government, mainly through the Fish and Wildlife Service and its predecessor agencies, has long engaged in programs to protect wildlife habitat. As early as 1864, wildlife considerations were noted by Congress and included in acts setting aside land in the public domain. But it was 1903 before President Theodore Roosevelt, a great sportsman-conservationist, proclaimed the three-acre Pelican Island in Florida a federal bird reservation and thus triggered establishment of a national system to protect land specifically for its wildlife values.

From that modest beginning, the National Wildlife Refuge System has increased greatly in both size and diversity. In January 1985 the system consisted of 428 refuges totaling almost 90 million acres in forty-nine of the fifty states. (West Virginia has no national wildlife refuge.) Part of this acreage consists of habitat especially valuable to waterfowl for breeding, resting, and wintering purposes.

Achieving a national system to preserve wildlife habitat, particularly waterfowl habitat, has been a challenging task. The rapid disappearance of wetlands was noted by conservation-minded sportsmen early in the 1900s. They were concerned that the loss of marshes and sloughs, vital to perpetuation of waterfowl and many other forms of wildlife, would lead to diminished numbers of the birds and other animals they sought for sport. The need to stem the loss of wetland habitat was obvious, but the means of achieving that end seemed beyond reach.

Through the 1920s, small groups of influential men attempted to stimulate interest in the protection of wildlife habitat. On October 1, 1930, the More Game Birds in America Foundation was formed specifically to determine the cause and extent of wetland losses and to provide a factual basis for action programs to protect them. The severe drought in the 1930s accentuated the problem. More citizens became aware that waterfowl numbers were much reduced and that the loss of wetlands was the principal reason.

In 1934, Congress passed the Migratory Bird Hunting Stamp Act. For the first time, federal funds became available specifically to preserve waterfowl habitat through acquisition. In the next fifty years, $285 million was raised from the sale of duck stamps required of persons wishing to hunt ducks and geese. This direct tax on sportsmen has resulted in the acquisition of 3.5 million acres of habitat specifically of benefit to waterfowl.

The studies funded by the More Game Birds in America Foundation also documented the tremendous importance of wetlands in prairie Canada as breeding habitat for ducks. The U.S. government was then and remains today either unable or unwilling to act in Canada to preserve these habitats. This led to formation in 1937 of a private conservation organization—Ducks Unlimited, Inc.—that eventually would become a powerful force to do a wetland development job that was beyond the ability of the U.S. government.

The federal government's initial approach toward wetland protection focused on acquisition of large units of habitat. These were the marshes that hosted spectacular numbers of birds during migration and wintering periods. Many were in pristine condition but some, such as Horicon Marsh in Wisconsin and Mingo Swamp in Missouri, had been destroyed as habitat for ducks. Ill-advised attempts had been made to drain these wetlands and convert them to farmland. After federal acquisition placed them in public ownership, restoration and management programs were conducted to make them valued waterfowl habitat once again.

The pressure to drain wetlands increased enormously after World War II, largely as a result of federal programs to increase production of food and fiber. Even with the infusion of duck-stamp dollars, wetland protection through federal acquisition was far outpaced by wetland destruction. The states were keenly aware of this situation and more of their conservation dollars were directed toward wetland protection programs. Much of their funding was a result of the 1937 Federal Aid in Wildlife Restoration Act. Under that act, funds from an 11 percent federal excise tax on sporting arms and ammunition were made available to the states on a 3:1 matching basis. Many states used these funds to acquire and develop waterfowl habitat. Again, sportsmen provided the funds to fill an important conservation need.

In 1950, the federal government and state conservation agencies, under the aegis of the International Association of Fish and Wildlife Agencies, determined that 12.5 million acres of habitat were needed in the Lower 48 to maintain waterfowl populations at then desired levels. The responsibility to preserve these habitats was divided: 8 million acres were to be protected by the federal government and 4.5 million acres by the states collectively. Thirty-five years have passed and these acquisition goals are yet to be reached. The reasons are many, and include accelerated land costs and resistance by agencies that fear loss of tax revenues when land is placed in public ownership.

In 1958, the Migratory Bird Hunting

Stamp Act was amended. Among other things, authority was provided for acquiring less than fee title interest in lands. Thus, the Waterfowl Production Area (WPA) program got underway. This was a clear shift in federal policy from acquisition of large units of habitat to protection of numerous small units. The program involved both fee title and easement acquisitions. Fee title acquisition protected both wetland and adjacent upland nesting habitat. The easements were perpetual, but they assured only the prevention of draining, filling, or burning of wetlands without regard to adjacent uplands essential as nesting habitat for most species.

The WPA program received major stimulation in 1961 with passage of the Wetland Loan Act. An interest-free loan of $105 million was made available to the Fish and Wildlife Service to accelerate acquisition of migratory bird habitats. The act was amended on several occasions to extend the life of the program and increase the funding authority to $200 million. When appropriated by Congress, loan funds are merged with duck stamp receipts for the purchase of migratory bird refuges and WPAs.

The WPA program has, as of January 1985, resulted in the protection of nearly 1.7 million acres of habitat. Much of this habitat (71 percent) has been protected through easements, and the rest through fee title purchases.

In summary, federal and state acquisition programs have contributed importantly toward stemming the loss of waterfowl habitat. These units of public land provide valuable habitat, and in some areas the only habitat, for ducks, geese, and other aquatic wildlife. But the job of protecting wetland values is far from over. The 215 million acres of wetlands that once provided habitat for myriads of water birds and other wildlife in the Lower 48 have dwindled to less than 92 million acres. Losses in the United States averaged almost one-half million acres per year from the mid-1950s to the mid-1970s, and this rate continues today.

Much of the remaining habitat is degraded to the point that waterfowl use is marginal, or in some cases even dangerous to the birds that do use it because of poisoning, pollution, or predation. Some habitats produce foods that are nutritionally inadequate.

Federal and state agencies have contributed significantly to protection of Lower 48 wetland habitats through their acquisition programs. When the stated goals are reached, about one wetland acre in seven will be protected by public agencies. Obviously, the future of waterfowl depends heavily upon what happens to the remaining 86 percent of wetland acres not now in public ownership.

46

The Winter Inventory

D. D. Kennedy

In late January the duck seasons have passed and man's thoughts are lodged somewhere between the Super Bowl and the spring turkey season. But never far from the surface of his thought processes are his dreams for the coming fall. For it is during the frigid winds of winter that the hopes and aspirations for a new season are born and nurtured. The disappointments of the previous season are behind us — the dry prairies, the poor production, the sloppy shooting, or the missed days afield. Now we look forward to the promise of the coming year as the annual cycle is renewed for both man and waterfowl.

Waterfowlers and biologists alike are beginning to gear their thinking and activities to the upcoming breeding and hunting seasons. The hunter keeps his eyes peeled for winter sales on decoys and is mentally rebuilding or relocating his blind. The late-night TV weather forecast takes on a new meaning. The hunter will brace for an impending storm, knowing that while the blizzard will force his heating bill skyward, it will also dump snow into the shallow depressions of Saskatchewan, Alberta, and the other Canadian provinces.

Waterfowl biologists are busy, too. This is the time when they reflect on the past season and are up to their eyeballs in harvest estimates, migration reports, and band returns. Hopefully, age and sex ratios, derived from the bag, will tie in nicely to confirm guesses from last year's production data, and add precision to future predictions of production and harvest. But these biologists are also gearing up for the winter surveys.

By January the continental waterfowl population has pushed deep into the milder climate of their wintering habitats.

Concentrated into federal and state refuges and private habitat, they will ride out the remainder of the hunting seasons and the harshest, most difficult time of their annual cycle. These concentrations in traditional areas offer an annual opportunity for waterfowl management organizations to census this mass of waterfowl and to review the status of the winter habitat. This opportunity has been seized each of the last fifty years, and is known as The Winter Waterfowl Survey.

To understand the important biological role of this survey, one must first recall the migratory travels of North America's wild ducks and geese. There is, of course, the southern push of birds reverently referred to as the "fall flight"—the result of the previous spring's breeding season. It is from this peak number of waterfowl that man draws his recreation. Those that arrive on the wintering ground will have gone through the rigors of the hunting season, and, after sustaining the natural mortality that befalls them during the winter, are referred to in the spring as the "breeding population."

During January and February, the birds beef up with layers of fat in the ricefields and cornfields of the South. Here some hens will choose an early mate before returning to the spring breeding grounds, after the drakes go through the courtship procedure necessary to win them. It is also during this time, on these critical wintering habitats, that the annual winter survey is made. The responsibility for monitoring these wintering populations, and recording the status of the habitat they utilize, falls to federal and state biologists.

The survey began in the mid-1930s. It is the oldest continuous survey of its kind in North America. It, in fact, had the same dramatic beginnings as Ducks Unlimited,

springing from the relentless droughts that focused critical attention on the future of the continental waterfowl population and its habitat.

Data from the winter survey, and the condition of the breeding habitat, provide the first critical indicators of what can be expected for the coming fall. Where breeding habitat is concerned, we can be little more than spectators, cheering for heavy snow and saturated soils. The winter waterfowl counts, on the other hand, require active participation in terms of manpower.

Counting the wintering population of ducks and geese is truly a monumental task for men and machines. Coordination and timing alone are not unlike that needed for a major invasion. For example, in 1981, when state and federal personnel conducted the winter survey from January 5 to January 9, participating were 1,002 wildlife professionals with binoculars, calculators, counters, and all the other paraphernalia necessary to identify, count, and tabulate millions of waterfowl. Merely transporting these trained observers to the appropriate locations required 148 aircraft, 63 watercraft, and 478 cars and trucks. Total mileage covered by this conglomerate of metal and muscle was 152,990 miles!

Biologists and sportsmen alike have always had the fond hope that this survey would prove the ultimate tool for determining wintering population estimates. Such may be the case with a few species, but for the vast majority of waterfowl these counts don't hold such magical powers. Their real value lies in their role as general indicators of the population overall and, more importantly, as monitors of the condition of the wintering habitat.

Because of the variables and the inher-

Census airplane on a transect counting geese. *Doug Benning photo.*

ent errors in the survey system, the counts are indicators rather than total population estimates. To demonstrate just how difficult it is to relate these figures to accurate continental waterfowl population projections, let's go through an exercise.

In 1981, the total inventory for all waterfowl in the areas censused was 26,270,513 birds. If we use the frequently referenced figure of 100 million birds in the fall flight, does this mean that some 74 million birds have fallen to natural mortality or the gun?

Hardly. What it does mean is that we are not surveying all the wintering habitat. It would be utterly unrealistic to do so. Many areas that hold vast numbers of waterfowl are simply not included in the surveys.

Counts are not made, for instance, in offshore areas, or in Central and South America. Even Mexico is not counted completely. The areas included are the traditional and easily accessible wintering habitats.

These counts, then, are samples, which

have meaning only when compared to those previously made over the same area.

The most interesting relate to individual species by flyway. For example, total waterfowl in the Pacific Flyway were down 20 percent from 1980 to 1981. The Central Flyway was down 13 percent; the Mississippi Flyway up by 8 percent; and the Atlantic Flyway up by 4 percent. Some figures totaled as expected. Others brought surprises. But bear in mind these figures relate to all waterfowl, so the total represents a mixed bag. Some species increased; others decreased.

By a more specific look at the Pacific Flyway, we can see how certain species groups and individual species affected the total percentage.

Dabbling ducks were down 26 percent, but divers, as a group, were down only 5 percent. Within the dabblers, the pintail (bread-and-butter duck of the Pacific Flyway) was down 38 percent. Balancing this, however, were increases in wood duck of 38 percent and gadwall of 70 percent. Diving duck data were even stranger. Canvasback were down 48 percent; ring-necked up 21 percent. Geese showed similar inconsistencies. Overall they were up by 8 percent, but within this percentage, lesser Canadas were down 90 percent and the common Canada goose up 28 percent.

The point, put simply, is that there are many variables to be considered other than the actual numbers of birds that may or may not have been counted. They include consistency of observers from year to year, weather conditions, and any number of local conditions on the ground unknown to counters in the sky.

As an example, consider this. National Guard helicopter pilots thought it would be neat to fly over a refuge area where there was a heavy concentration of Canada geese. Since the geese didn't cotton to the thump of the rotors, 50,000 of them took off for a wheatfield some ten miles from the refuge. All this happened within minutes of the winter survey aircraft arrival. Result? A "miss" of about 20 percent of this goose population. Variables do exist!

By now you're probably wondering, if these counts are so unreliable, why continue to use them? Valid question. The answer lies in the fact that trained biologist/statisticians review these data in great detail. They are able to account for many of the variables and detect gross changes in populations and species from year to year. They also are able to relate the data to many years of census figures. Very often it is these long-term trends that have the greatest value.

The winter survey has great value for certain species and particular populations. Breeding ground surveys are quite reliable for making fall flight predictions, but for several species, the winter counts are the only data from which to establish regulations. Canada geese are a prime example. Since very few of the populations across the continent are sampled by breeding ground surveys, the fall population forecast and hunting regulations are based on the previous winter's aerial census. Winter counts also provide the best data available for canvasback, black duck, and the Atlantic and Pacific brant. Ditto for other species of geese.

But perhaps the greatest value of the winter count lies in the annual evaluation of winter habitat conditions. Though a respectable chunk of this habitat is in the competent hands—and under the watchful eye—of federal and state refuge managers, the vast percentage remains in private ownership. Much of it is thus susceptible to loss from drainage, permanent flooding, clearing, or changing land use patterns.

Conservation agencies can sometimes be relied upon to detect major transitions in the quality of this habitat, but too often subtle deterioration can be spotted only by trained professionals with an aerial perspective. Since a mass exodus of waterfowl from an area may indicate pollution or a drastically changing ecological pattern, wintering waterfowl become our most reliable monitor of the status and condition of wintering habitat.

The annual winter waterfowl survey will remain one of the most valuable tools U.S. biologists have for evaluating the status of waterfowl populations and their respective wintering habitats. Assuming this year's count turns up some reasonable numbers to work with, and given a decent snowpack for runoff across the northern prairies, you can begin to patch the duck boat and tune up the old retriever.

Your favorite season is once more coming round the bend.

47

Waterfowl Harvest and Conservation in Mexico

E. W. Gustafson

Mexico shares a 2,000-mile border with the United States and, together with Canada, completes the triad of North American countries most concerned with the waterfowl resource.

The topography is strikingly diverse, ranging from swamps to snow-capped mountain peaks and from arid desert to rain forest. Diversity is also characteristic of the flora and fauna. In birds alone, nearly 1,000 full species (not counting many subspecies) have been authentically recorded. This is nearly 50 percent more than have been found in the rest of North America, which is much larger and has been investigated more thoroughly. The challenge now is to preserve this beauty and diversity so generously given by nature.

Mexico is also an important wintering ground for most species of North Ameri-

can migratory ducks and geese, primarily from the Mississippi, Central and Pacific Flyways. The Atlantic Flyway contribution is small. Most originate in the Pacific. The Central is second, with two main migration routes, one over the interior highlands and the other following the Gulf Coast. The Gulf Coast is also fed by the Mississippi Flyway. There is some crossing over by flyway populations, but these are the most important routes.

Six species of ducks also nest consistently in Mexico: the wild muscovy duck, black-bellied whistling duck, masked duck, Mexican duck, fulvous whistling duck, and the mottled duck.

Like the United States and Canada, Mexico has clearly defined rules for harvesting ducks and geese. Hunting seasons for each state are published by the Direccion de Flora y Fauna Silvestre (Department of Wildlife) each year. Dates, daily bag limit, and possession limit are clearly established. Hunting licenses, gun registration, and transport permits are required.

The legal structure is in place to control the harvest, but there are too few enforcement officers, and abuses of individual bag limits result. However, the overall harvest is still small, much less than in the United States and Canada. Mexico takes less than a twelfth of the total North American harvest.

Relative to the population, there are few sport hunters. Most hunting is for food; and deer, peccary, turkey, and other species offer more meat than waterfowl. Guns and shells are also more expensive in Mexico than in the United States, relative to disposable personal income.

Some organized hunting clubs allow individual guests to shoot more than their limit; however, they try to balance the total daily take of the club so the number of hunters multiplied by the individual bag limits is not exceeded. This practice has been confirmed, though not sanctioned, by top government officials. They reason that foreign duck and white-winged dove hunters pay healthy sums to hunt in Mexico, and thus should be allowed to take home their lawful limit. If some hunters shoot less than their limit, the difference is made up by others who go over.

Saunders in *South of the Border* (1964) states:

> Some misunderstanding has arisen regarding hunting in Mexico. It stems partly from a failure to appreciate the size of the Latin American wintering grounds and the lack of hunting pressure on most of them. Allegations that great numbers of waterfowl are slaughtered in Mexico are baseless or exaggerated.

The fact is that a few hunters shoot too many birds, but the total kill is a relatively small percentage of the waterfowl present. . . . One must keep in mind that the number of resident duck hunters in Mexico is very small, and the total bag taken is light compared to those taken by hunters in the United States. In addition, much of the small harvest of waterfowl is made by or for visiting Americans.

Leopold corroborates these points of view in *Mexico and Migratory Waterfowl Conservation* (1964):

> Mexico contributes substantially to continental waterfowl through its great wealth of wintering habitat. Hunting of waterfowl in Mexico is on a very small scale compared to that in the U.S. and Canada. . . .

It is important to realize that the waterfowl taken by Mexican residents is mostly for food, especially by people in small localities. When you recognize the economic need of these locals, their small harvest is justified.

The sportsmen in the U.S. and Canada often misunderstand the progress Mexico has made in the illegal kill of waterfowl. In general, their legislative authority is satisfactory, but present financing for enforcement and research is insufficient.

A determining factor in promoting the protection of some forms of wildlife has been their value to sportsmen, strangely enough. An intrinsic value, greater than that of its worth as meat or hide, is important in preserving a species.

For example, hunting of white-winged dove, migratory waterfowl, bighorn sheep, mule deer, and white-tailed deer are specially controlled because of their economic value as sports game. An *ejidatario* (commune dweller) can be convinced to conserve rather than consume because there is a greater economic benefit in allowing a sportsman the hunt. The benefit to the community is greater because the hunter pays for the right to hunt the animal (aside from the permit) and pays guides or bird-boys. The total money transferred to the community by sportsmen is significantly greater than the value of the game for direct community consumption.

Mexico urgently needs a multifaceted program of habitat conservation. Many programs are already underway. The new Secretariat of Urban Development and Ecology (SEDUE) and its Department of Wildlife are making a good beginning. Special parks and preserves have been designated and receive federal protection. Individuals and organizations are working intensely.

Hunting in Mexico. *Jack Samson photo.*

But the intention here is not to catalog all the good work being done, but to emphasize that the surface has been barely scratched in Mexico. A general awareness and understanding of habitat conservation by the Mexican people is necessary to preserve specific wildlife species and to maintain a biological diversity.

Wildlife protection through law enforcement is unsatisfactory. It is virtually impossible to police the entire country with the number of officers available. In 1980, there were ninety-seven wildlife inspectors. If these were distributed homogeneously, each would be responsible for 20,000 square kilometers!

In the same year, 70,000 hunting permits were issued for nationals and 12,000 for foreigners. But it is estimated that over a million nationals hunted to some degree, without regard for official hunting seasons or federal hunting laws.

Ironically, programs normally associated with conservation sometimes work against it. Designating an area as habitat reserved for a specific species, and asking people to stay out, can actually attract poachers. They assume that if an effort is being made to keep people out, surely game must be plentiful.

Because many Mexicans have had to undergo economic hardships and many are undernourished, wildlife is considered a free source of food. In essence, conservation is a luxury for Mexico at this time.

To put this concept into perspective, one must realize that Mexico today views wildlife conservation as Americans did a hundred years ago. The livelihood of the average country-dweller in Mexico comes through subsistence agriculture and ranching. It is difficult for these people to understand the need to conserve natural habitats when the primary concern is the family's stomach. Because the people cannot understand or afford conservation, they do not demand that the government act to bring it about.

What then can be done to conserve habitat? In the long run, we must await the acquisition of knowledge and the development of sufficient cultural affluence that would allow the luxury of conservation.

Even though it may be true that conservation is a luxury in Mexico, and law enforcement cannot be too heavy-handed when wildlife is being taken for human subsistence, we cannot just sit around and wait for understanding and awareness to take place. We must act, each in our own small way.

Ducks Unlimited of Mexico (DUMAC) is working hard to conserve habitat and to rehabilitate deteriorated wetlands. Even though singleness of purpose has been a determining factor in Ducks Unlimited's success in Canada, the United States, and Mexico, habitat projects benefit not only ducks and geese. Those that include water and food, island refuges, and nesting boxes also benefit many other wildlife species.

Man, too, is benefited in several ways. Often projects provide jobs, water management, irrigation water, and fish and other food sources.

The main thrust of DUMAC's philosophy of habitat development is to provide the best possible wintering habitat for migratory waterfowl, so they can return north in good breeding condition in the spring. This is carried out in harmony and cooperation with Ducks Unlimited of the United States and Canada. DUMAC's philosophy is also to provide food, water, and nesting areas for resident waterfowl and to make these available for other species of wildlife as well. DUMAC has secured the active support and cooperation of various agencies of the federal government of Mexico, and increased consideration of the importance of natural resources has resulted.

Wetlands in the states of Nuevo Leon, Colima, Mexico, Durango, Baja California Norte, Tamaulipas, Yucatan, Morelos, Puebla, San Luis Potosi, Quintana Roo, Coahuila, and Chihuahua have been targeted for reconnaissance. Development has already been completed on some of these wetlands, and will be scheduled for many others in the future.

48

The Law

J. E. Nagel

Game laws became a part of contemporary society about the time Robin Hood and his Merry Men began poaching the king's deer and generally making life unbearable for the Sheriff of Nottingham. Since then regulations in both Europe and North America have become an integral part of modern wildlife management.

The basic difference between European and North American game management lies in the concept of who owns or controls the wildlife in question. Both systems recognize the need for regulations to protect wildlife, regulate individuals who directly use the resource, and try to assure some type of equitable harvest.

European management places the control of fish and game with the landowner; in effect, he who controls the land owns the wildlife on it. Hunting seasons and bag limits are set by the owner for his exclusive use and enjoyment. In North America, ownership of wildlife rests with the people. As a result, regulations are developed and implemented by governmental agencies charged by law with the protection and propagation of wildlife within their particular sphere of responsibility.

Wildlife regulations were initially adopted in America by Massachusetts in the 1700s, when deer were protected for the first time. Game remained relatively plentiful in the rest of the United States until the late 1800s and early 1900s. Habitat destruction, overharvest, and a general change from primitive farming and the emergence of an industrial society then brought about widespread declines.

The idea that wildlife populations were inexhaustible was proved wrong, and individual states began to adopt protective regulations through closed seasons, bag limits, and enforcement. As the decline continued, regulations began to proliferate, in hopes of reversing the general downward trend.

Waterfowl were no exception. Significant declines in ducks and geese were noted in the early 1900s. States began to impose more stringent regulations to preserve the birds that were left. Bag limits were cut and seasons drastically shortened. Steps were also taken to eliminate spring shooting and market hunting. All these were effective to a degree, but lacked conformity because of the inherent differences, both geographical and political, between the individual states.

Because waterfowl are an international resource (70 percent are raised north of the U.S.–Canadian border), it became readily apparent that sound waterfowl management involved both Canada and the United States. Agreements between countries require formal ratification by treaty. After several false starts, such an agreement was reached between the United States and Canada in 1916 — the Migratory Bird Treaty Act. Similar treaties included Mexico in 1936, Japan in 1972, and the USSR in 1976.

Under the U.S. Constitution, treaty-making powers are reserved for the federal government. Adoption of the Migratory Bird Treaty Act and subsequent legislation placed primary enforcement and regulatory authority with the federal government. This added a degree of conformity to regulations nationwide. But many states felt such federal involvement was an infringement on their authority to manage wildlife. Two court cases, *Cochrane* v. *United States* and *Missouri* v. *Holland*, dealt with the question of states' rights in waterfowl regulations, and reaffirmed the position of the federal government.

Once the Migratory Bird Treaty Act was in place, basic regulations for waterfowl hunting were adopted. These form the basis of today's more complex and diverse laws. Initial federal regulations were prohibition of waterfowl hunting from March 16 through August 15, banning of market hunting and the use of market hunting paraphernalia (punt guns, sinkboxes, and so on), eliminating the use of live decoys, and closed seasons on swans and shorebirds.

As time passed and new problems became apparent, additional federal regulations were adopted to restrict the use of bait, unplugged shotguns, hunting at night, motorized craft, waterfowl, and elimination of shotguns larger than 10 gauge for hunting.

An interesting concept in the relationship between individual states and the federal government is that if a state feels waterfowl need protection beyond that offered federally, that state can further restrict by implementing its own regulations. However, the reverse is not true. States can only restrict; they cannot adopt more liberal regulations than set forth by the federal government.

Naturally, the incursion of the federal government into an area previously left to individual states caused problems. Many states attempted to circumvent portions of the Migratory Bird Treaty Act through noncompliance in their individual regulations, nonenforcement of sections they took exception to, or by simply ignoring the whole problem. Jurisdictional disputes over who controlled waterfowl and associated hunting seasons thus continued. It culminated in the case of *Missouri* v. *Holland*, where the decision sustained the provisions of the Migratory Bird Treaty Act, holding that waterfowl were only transitory in individual states.

Since then, relations between states and

the federal government in managing waterfowl have generally improved. Today's system of individual input by states and other
interested groups, through flyway technical committees and councils, avoids past
procedural problems. Conflicts and differences of opinions are usually settled within
the system, rather than in court. Current
regulations work fairly well in meeting the
needs of individual states, and at the same
time provide adequate protection to waterfowl as they move up and down the flyways.

How well any law works is determined
in two areas, enforcement in the field and
in court. To be effective it must hold up
in both areas. Field enforcement requires
practicality; the court requires that both
the enforcement procedures and the regulation meet the test of the Constitution.

Ask any group its opinion of today's
waterfowl regulations and enforcement
procedures, and the response will be as
varied as the group. Hunters will say regulations are unnecessarily complicated and
restrictive; antihunters that both enforcement and the enabling legislation are weak
and ineffectual; attorneys that many stat-
utes violate basic individual rights. Courts
are often irritated by cases they consider
trivial and insignificant; wildlife administrators see both enforcement procedures
and regulations as problem areas. Budget
analysts look on enforcement programs as
costly; enforcement officers see their work
as an essential activity. Obviously, the correct analysis lies somewhere within the
extremes of each position.

By necessity today's regulations are
complicated. The days of simply having a
season of a certain number of days and
shooting until the daily bag limit is attained, are gone, and will not return. Contemporary management of waterfowl re-

quires regulations be tailored to meet the
needs of individual species and, in some
instances, management of local populations or flocks of birds. Detailed regulations put a burden on both hunters and
enforcement personnel. Hunters must be
aware of the law and willing to accept its
provisions when they go afield. Wildlife
officers have to be sure enforcement procedures are applied equitably, and are not so
detailed as to become petty when enforced
in the field.

Future regulations will undoubtedly become more detailed as management techniques become more refined. This will require increased awareness on the part of
hunters, and careful interpretation and application of regulations by officers when
contacting hunters.

There are two basic types of violations—those that are *mala in se*, or wrong
in and of themselves, and those that are
mala prohibita, or wrong merely because
they are prohibited by law. Originally these
terms distinguished major crimes, such as
murder, from lesser crimes or misdemean-
ors, such as traffic violations. A similar
analogy can be applied to wildlife regulations today.

Violations that could be construed to be
mala in se impact wildlife directly and are
potentially damaging. These would include spring shooting, taking overlimits,
killing protected species, and market hunting. Such items as license requirements,
trespass, firearm regulations, shot size restrictions, and special clothing requirements do not directly impact wildlife, and
belong in the *mala prohibita* category.

When they were first adopted, wildlife
laws in general and those specifically dealing with waterfowl were considered mis-
demeanors. Because of this, and because
wildlife violations were given little consid-

eration by local courts, no one took them very seriously. This meant there was little deterent value to the regulations, and many violations remained unchecked even though violators were being apprehended in the field.

Since that time, legislators, courts, hunters, and the general public have realized that waterfowl violations are not simply fun and games, but rather they do have significant impact on the resource and hunting opportunities. Sections of both state and federal wildlife codes consider certain violations to be felonies, with high fines and jail sentences regularly imposed. However, there is still room for improvement. The seriousness of deliberate waterfowl violations should be stressed to all courts.

In far too many areas of the country, outwitting the local game warden is considered good clean fun, and waterfowl still do not receive the consideration they need and deserve. This is not only harmful to the resource, but plays into the hands of antihunters, who typically characterize hunters as a group who routinely ignore all regulations.

Many hunters, particularly those with limited experience, don't realize that violations and other forms of unethical conduct in the marsh do have a negative effect on the waterfowl resource. A pair of mallards killed in the spring doesn't simply eliminate two birds from next fall's flight; it removes a potential six to nine birds. Shooting at birds beyond range results in four or five unrecovered dead birds for every one killed and retrieved. Wasted birds don't contribute to future fall flights, and smaller fall flights mean less hunting opportunity.

Regulations and enforcement allow the U.S. Fish and Wildlife Service and state fish and game departments a degree of control over individuals who utilize the resource. Thus regulations can be tailored to meet the needs of individual areas or species that require them. These are usually more changeable than basic long-term regulations. Although waterfowl regulations are the primary concern of the federal government, most of the routine enforcement is carried out by state personnel.

Violations encountered in the field result almost exclusively from two situations: deliberate decisions to ignore regulations, and carelessness. This often results in a problem for enforcement personnel.

Obviously, the area with the greatest potential for damage to the waterfowl resource lies with deliberate violations. This would seem to be the area in which enforcement activities should be concentrated. Yet the violations most often encountered in the field, and those most easily detected, result from carelessness. This means significant violations often go undetected, because officers are tied up with petty routine violations, which are usually less damaging than those of a deliberate nature. Eliminating or reducing careless violations would allow enforcement officers and courts to devote more time to cases with the greatest impact on waterfowl.

Eighty percent of the unwitting violations would be eliminated if hunters did one thing—read the waterfowl regulations before going afield. Admittedly, regulations today are complicated, but most states publish summaries of the most pertinent rules that are easily reviewed. These are small enough to fit into a hunting coat and be carried in the field. Contrary to popular belief, fish and game agencies don't purposely design regulations to ensnare hunters, but they do become more complicated as management techniques are refined. Shooting hours, open areas, license requirements, shot size restrictions, special rules for specific hunting areas, and other routine regulations are covered in the summary. Familiarization with them will eliminate the chance of a careless violation.

The other 20 percent of violations could be taken care of by a pre-hunt check. Do you have your license and duck stamp? Is the stamp signed? Is your gun plugged? Do you have the correct shells? All these questions seem basic. But each year thousands of hunts are ruined by officers finding an infraction in one of these areas. Since most of us don't hunt as often as we would like, why take a chance on an infraction that would spoil an enjoyable outing?

Deliberate violations of waterfowl laws are another matter. Since they are deliberate, no amount of public relations, pre-hunt checks, or regulation review will solve the problem. The solution lies in a vigorous enforcement program and in courts that take a dim view of individuals who

Hunter bag check at Lake Hood, Alaska. *Alaska Fish and Game photo.*

hunt out of season, exceed bag limits, or shoot over bait.

Good wildlife law enforcement is not cheap. It requires well-trained officers who understand wildlife, the laws they are enforcing, and the people they are trying to apprehend. It requires a competitive pay scale. It requires equipment at least as sophisticated as that of the violator. Nothing is more frustrating to an officer than to see a violation and, because of lack of equipment or an equipment failure, be unable to make an arrest. All of which causes wildlife administrators problems at budget time!

Because of limited manpower and resulting large work areas, apprehension rates on serious violations are extremely low. In most states, it runs about 2 percent. Most hard-core violators will take a chance under these circumstances, believing (and rightly so) that the odds are in their favor. All of us have talked to people who have hunted or fished for twenty years and never been checked in the field. This may reflect a poor enforcement program. But in all likelihood, it simply results from relatively few officers working large individual areas.

Elimination of deliberate violations ultimately rests with the courts. The best enforcement effort in the world can be nullified by courts that treat waterfowl violations as unimportant or look upon violators sympathetically.

It is in the regulatory area that most hunters encounter modern-day wildlife management in the field. Those who hunt for enjoyment and don't deliberately set out to ignore game laws can eliminate potential conflicts with the law through some pre-hunt planning and research. Deliberate and flagrant violations can be controlled through judicious enforcement and severe penalties from the courts.

However, these goals will be achieved only with adequate funding of enforcement programs and continued pressure on courts to recognize the seriousness of deliberate waterfowl violations and the damage such violations do to the resource.

49

The Point System

J. R. Grieb

"Let me look at the book, Howard, so I can tell what duck I shot." That conversation remains in my memory of the first experimental point system season held in the San Luis Valley of Colorado in 1968.

The experimental season was developed to evaluate the response of hunters to this new approach to harvest regulations. We did this by going hunting with them, dressed as hunters, and recording what they did. Those of us involved in that first season were pleased at what happened. We had never seen so many identification books in hunters' pockets in other seasons, and it was obvious from their actions they were doing their best to follow the new regulations.

The pleasing aspect was not only that they "did good," but that the regulations, which seemed complicated on the surface, were not that difficult to follow. That was

the beginning, but let me tell you how and why it came about.

In the early 1960s, there were some tough times for ducks in their prime prairie pothole breeding area in the northcentral United States and southcentral Canada. Duck stocks, particularly mallard, were down, and the result was some of the most restrictive harvest regulations on record, including a one-mallard limit in 1962 and 1965. Even after the water and the ducks came back, regulations remained tight.

As a result, many state biologists were looking at ways to provide the best harvest opportunity. This was particularly true in the Mississippi and Central Flyways, which seemed hardest hit by the regulation crunch. Agendas at the annual flyway technical committee meetings dealt with alternatives. What could be done?

One of the suggestions contained in a

list of alternatives prepared by the Mississippi Flyway Technical Committee in the mid-1960s was that of assigning points to ducks. This would permit different species to be assigned point values on the basis of their ability to contribute to the harvest. This approach had been suggested to one of the state representatives by a sportsman interested in improving regulations from a species management approach.

There was something about the idea that seemed to catch hold in the Central Flyway. If we were ever going to crack the regulation logjam, we had to demonstrate we were doing it on the basis of species or sexes that could take it. The idea fit the mallard picture perfectly, and this was the approach biologists of the Central Flyway used as we began to explore the possibility of a system that used points, instead of ducks, to determine the bag limit.

In our particular case, we were looking at wintering mallard populations composed of many more drakes than hens. Banding data compiled by the states indicated that survival was significantly higher for drakes — probably because they left for safe quarters soon after the honeymoon was over each year, while hens were stuck with nesting and protecting the young until they were on the wing. This made hens more vulnerable to predators and all the other hazards associated with the nesting season.

Here was a real opportunity. If a regulation could be devised that would take more drakes and fewer hens, we could provide more hunting opportunity and the resource could sustain more harvest. Of course it wasn't that simple.

We were simultaneously conducting a "late mallard drake" experimental season in eastern Colorado in 1968. The bag limit was four mallard drakes — period. No other species or sexes were legal. The idea was great but there was one problem. What happened if you shot a duck other than a drake mallard even though you didn't intend to? Simple — you were in violation of the law. You could either stomp the duck in the mud, or go looking for the nearest game warden.

Analysis of that experiment revealed it was easy to make those kinds of mistakes, and we had to look for an approach that would get around this serious flaw. Data from the point system experiment indicated we had the answer.

Obtaining agreement of the Fish and Wildlife Service to conduct an experimental point system season in the San Luis Valley was not simple, nor should it have been. Vast quantities of data were analyzed and numerous proposals written before agreement was reached. One of the factors in favor of the original experiment was the location. The San Luis Valley is an isolated mountain valley about 50 miles wide and 100 miles long at considerable distances from large cities. It was an area ideally suited for gathering information to evaluate the experiment.

One other aspect should also be mentioned, the establishment of the regulation that implemented the point system approach. Devising the regulation was not an easy task. It seems simple to assign points to duck species on the basis of harvest and survival rates, so that low point values are assigned for those that can sustain increased harvest, such as teal and shoveler; and those that should be protected — redhead, canvasback, and mallard hens — are assigned high point values; and that the bread-and-butter species, such as mallard drakes, are assigned medium point values. That part is easy; but how does one describe such a regulation so the hunter will know when he has reached his bag limit?

We looked at many approaches, including a fixed point bag of 70 or 100 points, where the hunter would have to stop hunting when he reached the numerical limit. We even thought of listing the combinations of species and sexes of ducks that could be legally taken, but there were so many that they would have filled pages of regulations. Besides, none of this fulfilled the one important requirement that made us dislike the mallard drake-only season — that hunters would not be forced to violate if they did not intend to do so.

The idea came down to a flexible approach, which would let the hunter identify the bird taken in the hand and add its point value to the sum of points from birds previously taken. That concept is still used today: "The daily bag limit shall have been reached when the point total of birds taken equals or exceeds 100 points with the last bird taken."

The rest is history. In the 1969–70 season the experiment was expanded to the Central Flyway portions of Montana, Wyoming, New Mexico, Colorado, and portions of western South Dakota and Nebraska. It was set up as a late drake mallard season of forty points, with drakes at ten points and all other species and sexes forty points. The next year it spread to other states in other flyways.

The Pacific Flyway, where duck supplies were more stable so that season lengths and bag limits remained liberal, chose not to select the point system approach. This was also true for several of the northern states, where seasons are held early in the fall before birds have attained their full plumage, making them difficult to identify.

What is the point system and what does it accomplish? Not everyone likes it because, unless you actually watch the order

in which birds are taken, the most liberal bag limit interpretation applies. This encourages reordering, the most serious flaw in the regulation.

Reordering occurs when a high-point bird, such as a mallard hen (seventy points), is taken as an early bird in the bag limit. Even though this is close to the limit, the hunter can continue to shoot low-point birds, claiming the mallard hen as the last bird taken. I do not condone reordering, do not practice it, nor will I. That is up to the individual hunter. It is an individual moral judgment, just like that associated with any bag limit regulations. The good points of the system, however, far outweigh the bad.

Testing of the point system by a number of states revealed some interesting information.

1. Harvest was redistributed among species and sexes. Hunters avoided high-point birds and concentrated on those with lower points.

2. The point system was not necessarily more liberal with regard to daily bag and total harvest. Contrary to popular belief, harvest of ten-point birds did not increase overall to a great degree, even though the regulation seemed liberal on the surface.

3. There was no evidence that the overall magnitude of the unretrieved kill was any greater than under conventional species or sex-oriented regulations.

4. Violation rates were similar for point system regulations and conventional regulations.

In summary, the point system was no better or no worse than conventional species or sex-oriented regulations as far as violation rates were concerned, but it had the benefit of preparing hunters to shoot under increasingly specific species-

The point system permits the hunter to identify the bird in hand and add its point value to the sum of birds already taken. *Ed Bry photo.*

oriented regulations, by giving them incentives to recognize species and sexes of ducks.

I have heard it said that waterfowl managers should not expect hunters to identify ducks in the air before they shoot them. But isn't that exactly what we expect with the current crop of so-called conventional regulations? The old fixed bag limit of four, five, or more ducks of any species is a thing of the past. Now regulations include restrictions on such species as redhead, canvasback, and mallard hens. And once you shoot a redhead when the bag limit is one, you had better be able to recognize that the next duck you shoot isn't a redhead or you will be in trouble. Species management is here to stay. And it's an important opportunity for the future of wildfowling.

This is where the point system works best. If you pick up each bird as you shoot it, identify it, and add the points to the birds previously taken, you will never violate. It's a system that accommodates a hunting public possessing a variety of hunting skills, from the beginner right on to the seasoned veteran. It provides the incentive to learn to identify species and sexes, so that managers can establish hunting seasons that will take advantage of surpluses within the resource.

In my judgment, the point system approach has been a valuable addition to harvest regulation options in the United States.

50

Flyway Management and Custodial Services

O. E. Frye, Jr.

In the beginning God created the U.S. Bureau of Biological Survey. The general opinion—especially among the "Feds"—was that state conservation agencies were strictly exploiters, and that only the dedication of the "Feds" prevented decimation of the waterfowl resource.

There was, perhaps, some basis for this attitude, particularly when we consider the prevalent belief that regulations were a major factor in determining populations of small game, especially waterfowl. In addition, to a large extent, the Biological Survey was way ahead of the states in the area of waterfowl biology—most had no, or very few, biologically trained personnel, especially in waterfowl management. Also, to some extent, the more politically oriented state game departments seemed to believe that their primary responsibility was to their hunting constituency, rather than the waterfowl resource.

But in the 1930s and 1940s the science, or art, of wildlife management began to blossom under the influence of such pioneers as Drs. Aldo Leopold and Herbert Stoddard. More and more states began to employ trained biologists. This trend accelerated tremendously after the 1940 passage of the Pittman-Robertson Act, which placed an excise tax on sporting arms and ammunition and provided that funds resulting from the tax would be distributed to the states on a basis of three federal dollars to one state dollar.

The combined fund was to be spent, under strict guidelines, for wildlife land acquisition and research, or for habitat improvement, under the administration of the U.S. Biological Survey—now the U.S. Fish and Wildlife Service. This Act was probably the most important single factor in bringing about today's well-staffed and scientifically informed state game departments. As a part of this development, while devoting most of their attention to resident wildlife, most states began to get involved in waterfowl management and research.

It was with this background that state and federal agencies, encouraged and stimulated by private groups, notably Ducks Unlimited and the Wildlife Management Institute, began searching for a system or vehicle that would allow more effective communication between the various groups interested in waterfowl. Ideally, it would also provide geographical subdivisions that would allow waterfowl managers to address specific geographic areas and waterfowl populations, or species of special interest to particular parts of North America.

The vehicle that seemed to offer the most promise was based on the delineation by Dr. Frederick C. Lincoln in the mid-1930s of four major waterfowl migration routes: the Atlantic, Mississippi, Central, and Pacific Flyways. Since each flyway encompassed most of its waterfowl populations throughout the geographical extent of their life cycle—breeding, migration and wintering—close monitoring seemed possible and management by flyway the logical route to take. Time has confirmed the wisdom of this approach.

Additional banding and other studies have refined and expanded our knowledge of waterfowl biology, including migration, and confirmed the accuracy of Lincoln's basic concept. They have also shown that flyway boundaries are not inviolate, and that variables such as species behavior, weather, and habitat conditions contribute to deviations from the major accepted migration patterns, including exchanges of birds between flyways. Nevertheless, the flyway concept is a practical and useful

basis for continental waterfowl management.

With the geographical subdivision accomplished, the next step was the establishment of an organizational framework that would facilitate communication between the various waterfowl interests. In the late 1940s efforts were being made in all four flyways to create an organization to deal with the management, especially the harvest regulations, of the flyway waterfowl resource.

Establishment of each of the four flyway organizations was motivated by basically the same desire—the development of a management system that would address the area of each flyway's principal interest, allow for more active participation by the states, and retain the necessary federal responsibility over migratory waterfowl.

Although the four flyway organizations appeared about the same time and for the same fundamental reasons, they originated independently. Today they retain their independence, individual by-laws, and modes of operation.

The following is a brief summary of organizational efforts and accomplishments in the four flyways leading up to the formal councils as they exist today.

Pacific Flyway: The Pacific Flyway Study Committee was organized at a "Waterfowl Conference" held on February 17 and 19, 1948, in Portland, Oregon. James F. Ashley of the California Division of Fish and Game was the first chairman. Representatives of the U.S. Fish and Wildlife Service and the game departments of California, Oregon, Washington, and British Columbia attended. One of the items agreed upon at the initial meeting was the urgent need for information in four basic categories:

1. A complete inventory of resident and migratory waterfowl populations.
2. A complete kill analysis to determine the annual harvest.
3. Waterfowl production by states, provinces, or regions.
4. An extensive banding program to determine movements and area relationships.

Discussed in detail were problems associated with these needs. In June 1949, Leo K. Couch was appointed by the U.S. Fish and Wildlife Service as coordinator for the cooperative waterfowl studies in the flyway. The Committee established guidelines for and began to prepare and distribute the Pacific Flyway Waterfowl Report. Eighty-four reports were compiled between 1948 and 1980. The Committee met at least once each year until it became the Pacific Flyway Council at Pendleton, Oregon, on January 16, 1952. Ben Glading of the California Division of Fish and Game was the first chairman. John E. Chattin was the first Flyway Representative.

Central Flyway: The Central Flyway Council was organized at Glenwood Springs, Colorado, on August 12 and 13, 1948. C. N. Feast, Director of the Colorado Game and Fish Department, was the first chairman. A detailed document, *Aims and Purposes of the Central Flyway Council,* was prepared. Representatives of nine states, the U.S. Fish and Wildlife Service, and the Wildlife Management Institute attended.

Unlike the other three flyways, the preceding organization in the Central Flyway had been named "Council" when it was formed in 1948. The record indicates that

the most significant meeting since its inception occurred on May 8, 1953, in Oklahoma City when the Council reaffirmed its organizational structure and accepted the appointment by the U.S. Fish and Wildlife Service of Cecil E. Williams as the first Central Flyway Representative.

Mississippi Flyway: The Mississippi Flyway Waterfowl Committee was informally organized as a data collecting technical body in 1947. On March 1, 1948, it issued its first newsletter. Organizers were J. D. Smith of the Minnesota Conservation Department, Tom Evans of the Wildlife Management Institute, Frank Bellrose of the Illinois Natural History Survey, and Frosty Anderson of Winous Point Club. Two university professors, Bill Marshall of the University of Minnesota and Joe Hickey of the University of Wisconsin, and four Fish and Wildlife Service biologists, Bob Smith, Art Hawkins, John Lynch, and George Saunders, and Bill Leitch of Ducks Unlimited Canada, were enthusiastic supporters and contributors.

There is no record that the group was ever officially organized with officers, minutes, and such. It was held together by interest in a common goal—to gather as much information as possible about waterfowl. The group was aware of the need for gathering data cooperatively, and it established procedures for estimating breeding, migration, and wintering populations, and determining vital statistics, numbers, age, sex, species, and so on, of waterfowl harvests.

With this background the organization of the Mississippi Flyway Council in St. Louis on January 24, 1952, was a simple process. Arthur S. Hawkins was named Flyway Representative by the U.S. Fish and Wildlife Service. The technical section was formed on July 14, 1952. It was clear from the beginning that the Council needed a management plan to help guide its efforts. On August 3, 1952, the Council named a management plan committee, which produced a first draft for the Council's consideration at its July 1954 meeting.

Atlantic Flyway: The first successful organized effort in the Atlantic Flyway was the Black Duck Committee appointed by the Ducks Unlimited Board of Trustees at its meeting in Milwaukee, April 5, 1946. Robert Leasen of Boston was named temporary chairman. The first meeting was held on December 13, 1946, in New York City, at which time the full committee was elected. The name was changed to Joint Black Duck Committee, and Philip C. Barney of Ducks Unlimited and the Commissioner of the Connecticut Board of Fisheries and Game, was elected chairman.

No effective effort to organize the southern end of the flyway existed until the formation of the South Atlantic Flyway Waterfowl Committee in December 1949 at Nags Head, North Carolina. E. B. Chamberlain, Jr., Waterfowl Biologist of the Florida Game and Fresh Water Fish Commission, was elected chairman. On October 24, 1951, at a meeting at Edgewater Park, Mississippi, the northern and southern organizations agreed to combine as the Joint Waterfowl Council of the Atlantic Flyway. Clyde Patton, Director, North Carolina Department of Wildlife Resources, was elected to serve as chairman until formal organization of the Atlantic Flyway Council. This occurred at a meeting held in Washington, D.C., on January 28 and 29, 1952. Charles B. Belt of New York was elected chairman.

The preceding organizational efforts were crystallized in 1952 by the formation of the four Flyway Councils, which was prompted and guided by a resolution of the International Association of Fish, Wildlife and Conservation Commissioners adopted in September 1951. This resolution, among other things, pointed out that the U.S. Fish and Wildlife Service had adopted the four flyways as the basis for migratory waterfowl regulations; that the states bear a major share of the burden for enforcing migratory bird regulations; that a flyway council composed of representatives of state conservation agencies be established in each flyway; that two representatives from each flyway serve as members of a National Flyway Council; and that the Fish and Wildlife Service appoint a coordinator to be assigned to each flyway to act as liaison for the coordination of research and management of the various states and the federal government.

This resolution was well thought out and comprehensive. It provided a simple, concise blueprint for the organization of the councils and their functions and objectives. That the councils exist today basically as they were formed in 1952 is a tribute to the quality of the International resolution. Probably the principal reason it has served so well is that it reflected several years of planning by the preliminary organizations of biologists and administrators that preceded it.

Thus a system of cooperation between state, federal, and private conservation groups, unparalleled in the history of wildlife management, was established across the continent. It should not be assumed that the sailing was always smooth. Council meetings were often the scenes of spectacular conflicts between practically every existing waterfowl interest—particularly between representatives of the states and their opposite numbers in the federal establishment — but also between northern and southern elements of the flyways. This was inevitable when we consider how our knowledge and understanding of the waterfowl resource, its management and the diversity of objectives, and waterfowl populations and habitats were increasing.

Fortunately, as knowledge about waterfowl grew and all sides became better informed, conflicts that raged in the early years had given way to an almost tranquil agreement on the way to go. This was demonstrated when anti-hunting organizations, such as Friends of Animals, unsuccessfully brought suit in Federal Court to prohibit representatives of the Councils from attending non-public regulations meetings of the U.S. Fish and Wildlife Service. These organizations alleged that the Councils had no more right than other non-governmental conservation groups to participate in such meetings. This ignored the fact that Council representatives were representing the states, which have regulatory authority and management responsibility for waterfowl. It's believed that this was simply a harassment tactic by the "antis," stimulated principally by their frustration at the united front generally presented by federal and state wildlife agencies on most hunting questions.

Probably one of the most important reasons for the early conflicts between state and federal agencies was that, as previously mentioned, most of the first trained and experienced waterfowl biologists were part of the U.S. Fish & Wildlife Service. Few game departments had trained waterfowl people and, if they did, they were relatively inexperienced.

Many state administrators viewed these "federal experts" and their graphs, figures, and statistics with suspicion, but they were unable to argue effectively with the data

presented. In addition, the basic philosophy held by the "Feds," and many other conservationists, was protectionist. Wildlife was just beginning to recover from overharvest by our pioneer ancestors, and the philosophy was, in case of doubt, restrict. In the early days, about all a state director could do was make an impassioned plea for the benefit of the folks back home. So he hired some biologists.

In the late fifties and early sixties, things began to happen. On the federal side the numbers game flourished, and to a great extent the thinking of the Fish and Wildlife Service on regulations was dominated by statisticians. The argument went like this: "Our breeding ground surveys — within the confidence limits — show a 10 percent decline in numbers of ducks predicted for the fall flight. Therefore, we must modify the regulations so the kill will be reduced by 10 percent." This is obviously an oversimplification, but it accurately reflects the prevailing attitude during the late sixties.

The "numbers" game reached its peak of absurdity when the U.S. Fish and Wildlife Service recommended that, since the dove coo count (a survey based on the number of doves heard calling within a given time over an established route) was down, the daily bag limit should be reduced from 12 to 10 birds. The states, particularly in the Southeast, raised such a fuss over this recommendation that it was never adopted. Later the southeastern states conducted a research project, in cooperation with the Fish and Wildlife Service, that demonstrated no significant effect on the dove population, or kill, from an increase in the bag limit from 12 to 18!

On the state side, the young biologists were maturing. And with their knowledge and experience, they were moving up in the state game department hierarchies — many to the director's chair—to the extent where the states were competitive with the "Feds." Research was demonstrating that with many game birds, quail and dove for example, the effect of the gun on the population was minimal at most.

On both sides came the realization that surveys and statistics are great as long as they are interpreted in the light of other biological and sociological facts. These include:

1. The effect of weather patterns on waterfowl movement and hunter success.
2. Hunter behavior. When waterfowl populations are low, the law of diminishing returns affects his effort and he doesn't hunt as much.
3. The likelihood that breeding habitat conditions, including weather, is of much greater importance in determining fall population levels than the number of breeding birds.
4. "Nature abhors a vacuum," and consequently, depressed populations are likely to produce more young per pair in underpopulated habitat.
5. Finally, but most important, to a presently unknown degree, waterfowl populations resemble other small game populations in that hunter mortality is largely offset by decreased natural mortality. In other words, this concept— which has been well documented with bobwhite quail and mourning doves— holds that hunter kill is unimportant to a game bird population, since most of the birds killed by hunters would have succumbed to natural causes.

In the beginning, the belief—advanced primarily by the states—was that perhaps the gun's effect on waterfowl populations resembled its effect on dove and quail. This is understandable because the states had been much more closely involved in the quail and dove research, which led to these conclusions. This was especially true in the Southeast where these birds are so important.

Contributing to the controversy was the previously mentioned concept that the Fish and Wildlife Service was the protector of the waterfowl resource, standing staunchly between the states and their supposed desire to over-exploit waterfowl. Added to this was the traditional belief that regulation of hunting was the most important element in waterfowl management and, to compound the situation even further, the regulation controversy was not limited to the state-federal battle. Within the Service, many biologists, especially younger ones with state experience, were beginning to question the traditional dogma of protection and regulation. Little wonder then that during the sixties waterfowl council meetings were, to a great extent, battlegrounds about regulations, not only between the states and the federal establishment, but also between individuals in both camps.

As the forum for this controversy the councils again prove their worth. Fortunately, the arguments were not in vain. In 1969 the Fish and Wildlife Service addressed the question by initiating a comprehensive study that resulted in a series of reports titled *Population Ecology of the Mallard*. The sixth report of the series, "The Effect of Exploitation on Survival," explored the effect of hunting on the mallard population. The researchers were unable to demonstrate that survival rates increased in years when kill rates were low because of restrictive hunting regulations.

The results also implied that mallards cannot be stockpiled, and they supported the hypothesis that hunting mortality is largely compensated for by decreased natural mortality *when hunting mortality is below some threshold point*. They further implied that restrictive hunting regulations are unlikely to save birds and increase the number available for breeding. Finally, the results emphasized the need for careful and detailed field testing of these implications.

An important step in this direction was the *Regulation Freeze,* a closely monitored five-year period with no change in basic hunting regulations regardless of waterfowl population fluctuations. The objective was to test the need for, and effectiveness of, the traditional practice of annual regulation adjustment in response to current changes in waterfowl numbers.

This program was initiated in the Pacific Flyway in 1979. At the end of five years of stabilized regulations, no changes in duck populations were apparent that could be related to either hunting regulations or harvests. Similar five-year stabilization periods were implemented in the other three flyways. An excellent presentation of the philosophical factors and findings of the regulation stabilization studies was presented in the November/December 1982 *Ducks Unlimited* magazine by John P. Rogers.

It is important to make a distinction here between *regulation* and *over-regulation*. The type and degree of regulation is the issue. While the studies discussed above do indicate that annual regulation changes based on annual population figures, at the levels historically applied, generally have had little or no effect upon waterfowl populations, they do not indicate that regulations are unnecessary or unimportant, but only that they should be put in proper perspective with other management tools. Regulations should be used to protect the resource and to improve the quality of its use.

We are just beginning to learn enough about regulations and waterfowl population dynamics to apply this management tool in a positive rather than a negative manner. But, at least some of the traditional sacred cows that have plagued and divided waterfowl enthusiasts through so many years have been dissipated.

51

Management Successes and Failures for Critical Species

A. E. Barnard

In most resource fields, management implies change. In managing North America's waterfowl resource, the ability to impose changes has often been limited by the resource's mobility and geographical distribution. Not surprisingly, these constraints have created both management successes and failures.

Waterfowl management techniques are still being perfected. The first attempts, primarily regulatory, began in the late 1800s, prompted by a noticeable decline in many species. In the ensuing years, a number of significant events unfolded, each of which heralded another step forward in waterfowl resource management.

A prime example was the institution of management-oriented legislation prompted by the precariously low numbers of trumpeter swan and wood duck.

The trumpeter swan once nested through north, west, and central North America, but was reduced to a known population of sixty-nine birds at Red Rock Lakes in Montana by 1932. Until the discovery of breeding trumpeters in Alaska in 1952, this population of U.S. birds, together with a small breeding flock near Grande Prairie, Alberta, was believed to be the entire North American population.

Establishment of the Red Rock Lakes National Wildlife Refuge in 1935 was a key step in the long-term success of trumpeter swan management. That population increased rapidly, and now provides surplus stock for restoration programs elsewhere in the United States and Canada. The Montana initiative was repeated elsewhere over the next five decades. The continental population has now reached between 7,000

The majestic trumpeter swam. *Ducks Unlimited Canada photo.*

and 8,000 birds, and the trumpeter swan is no longer an endangered species in North America.

Wood duck populations reached very low levels at the turn of the century, primarily from overhunting. The Migratory Bird Treaty Convention of 1916 made it possible to give them complete protection, and their response justified a limited season with restrictive bag limits in 1941. The population again declined during the early 1950s. The season was closed throughout the Mississippi Flyway in 1956 but was opened in 1957 and 1958 in several states. By the early 1960s, the population recovered to the point where 165,000 wood duck were harvested in 1963.

To date, no single reason has been identified for the resurgence of the wood duck. Increased nesting sites, provided by thousands of artificial nest boxes, and harvest regulations have played major roles. The explosion of the beaver population throughout much of the wood ducks' range, coupled with construction of numerous farm ponds, have also contributed heavily to the species' return from the brink.

Perhaps the most notable waterfowl management success in North America involves Canada geese. Examples of successful management exist in all the flyways. These undoubtedly contributed to the Canada goose assuming from the lesser snow goose, in the fall of 1978, the role of the world's most numerous goose, with an estimated population of 4.8 million.

The successes realized with Canada geese are, in part, the result of taking advantage of their inherent traits, including a strong attachment to migration, breeding, wintering and staging traditions, and aggressive and prolific breeding behavior.

Specific examples of all the documented management successes with Canada geese constitute a book in themselves. However, some examples will serve to demonstrate the importance and magnitude of the efforts involved.

The giant Canada goose, the largest race of wild geese in the world and a distinct subspecies, was virtually written into extinction twenty-five years ago throughout the Great Plains where it once thrived.

Following the realization that there were pockets of this subspecies scattered throughout its native range, restocking and protection programs have rebuilt the populations of this giant bird to a healthy level in the plains states as well as the Midwest.

In terms of sheer numbers, the Mississippi Valley Population (MVP) and the Eastern Prairie Population (EPP) of Canada geese also provide classic examples.

The MVP, which now winters primarily in Illinois and Wisconsin, by 1946 had been reduced to less than 30,000 geese, which prompted a complete hunting closure at that time. Much of the reduction was attributed to excessive kill, which reflected the extreme crowding of the birds into the Horseshoe Lake Refuge in Illinois.

Many techniques were employed to reduce the kill. These included additional refuges, dispersal by hazing with aircraft and other forms of disturbance, and stringent harvest regulations. The dynamics and demography of the population were determined by banding and surveys. The geese themselves aided by modifying their feeding behavior, turning to standing corn as a food source. The result was a steady increase in population, which now stands at over 400,000.

The EPP recovery was similar. The flock of 114,700 birds in 1939 plummeted to 11,300 by 1947, a decrease of 90 percent. The drastic decline was probably caused by excessive harvest, coupled with significant destruction of migration and wintering habitat in the Missouri, Arkansas, and Mississippi River systems.

To counteract the decline, the entire Mississippi Flyway was closed to Canada goose hunting for the 1946 season. Data were gathered on nesting sites, nesting areas, migration routes, major harvest areas, mortality rates, and overall population trends. Data on productivity rates, differential vulnerability of age classes to harvest, and physical needs such as space, sanctuary, and food were also obtained.

In 1969, based on this information, a target to increase the 1968 population of 135,000 to 200,000 was established. Techniques to be used included regulating harvest by season length, bag limit, and area quotas. Success was evidenced by a flock numbering 210,000 geese in 1975 and 180,000 in 1982.

Although the response of the Canada goose to management is undoubtedly the best known for North American geese, several others have also reacted positively to management on a regional basis.

In eastern Canada and the Atlantic states, the dramatic increase in greater snow geese has been welcomed by hunter and birdwatcher alike. Yet, in the early 1900s, there were only a few thousand. Hunting was closed in the United States in 1932 and resumed in 1975. The combined

Greater snow geese at Goose Island, St. Lawrence River estuary. *Y. Bedard photo.*

U.S.–Canada harvest presently balances the recent average recruitment rate. Today the greater snow goose population numbers over 200,000, with some expansion of range and adoption of new habitats.

While the initial problem of abundance has now been solved, there are new potential threats. Perhaps the most worrisome are a possible oil spill or outbreak of disease when the population is massed at staging sites in the St. Lawrence River estuary or Delaware Bay. Several means for dispersing these large concentrations have been proposed. These include first establishing sanctuaries, and then increasing hunting pressure within the present areas of concentration to encourage dispersal to the new sanctuaries and adjacent unused habitats.

Across the continent in the Pacific Flyway, Ross' goose, tiny cousin of the other snow geese, has also received considerable attention. By the 1900s, it was considered rare. In 1931, this prompted protective legislation to prevent overhunting.

Over the years, Ross' geese have been managed by various regulatory restrictions such as area closures, restricted bag limits, and timing of hunting seasons throughout its migration routes and wintering areas. Management has also been directed at refining census techniques and establishing a more accurate delineation of distribution and movement on the wintering grounds.

The present population is now estimated to be in excess of 100,000 geese. This indicates an annual growth rate of 7 percent since 1964, part of which is real growth and part the result of better census techniques. New initiatives for the Ross' goose may now be considered, particularly as they pertain to regulatory options.

Despite obvious management successes, some species of geese continue to challenge the ingenuity and resolve of waterfowl managers. One of these is the tule goose, a larger subspecies of the white-fronted goose, and distinct from the white-fronts wintering in Texas and California. Even today, the total number of tule geese is not positively known; recent estimates approximate 3,000 birds.

Discovery of the tule goose breeding grounds at Redoubt Bay, Alaska, in 1979 should greatly assist in developing new programs encompassing most of the major aspects of their life cycle. In the interim, wintering ground management has the primary objective of maximizing the number returning to the breeding grounds.

Two other species, the Atlantic brant and the black brant, pose problems that have not so far been entirely addressed by management. The Atlantic brant population fluctuates widely, for example going from 151,000 birds in 1971 to 42,000 in 1973. The decline was attributed to a very high harvest in 1971–1972 and an almost total production failure in 1972. Hunting was immediately restricted, and the population bounced back to 87,600 in 1974, and averaged 83,400 from 1975 to 1982. In that ten-year period, hunting seasons for Atlantic brant in the United States were closed during eight years.

It is now realized that, for the Atlantic brant, hunting mortality seldom acts alone. Vagaries of weather, on both breeding and wintering grounds, can overwhelm any potential benefits from manipulation of hunting regulations. This was clearly demonstrated during the period 1976–1978 when, despite a closed season, 87,000 wintering brant starved to death when ice prevented them from feeding.

Waterfowl management problems are not limited to geese. Indeed, the bird most synonymous with concern over the status of waterfowl is the canvasback. Never very abundant, the canvasback's rather rigid habitat requirements and behavioral traits have resulted in severe population fluctuations. It continues to be the subject of numerous field studies and research projects.

A variety of investigative techniques have been used. These include aerial photography to census molting, staging, and wintering concentrations; banding to determine mortality and migration routes; marking, including plumage dyes and radio telemetry, for tracing migratory movements; and delineation of important migrational and wintering habitats. Key areas are thus identified for application of harvest controls and eventual habitat acquisition.

It seems increasingly apparent that only through active and ongoing research will there someday be the tools to better manage canvasback. In the interim, today's tools will have to suffice to maintain a viable population.

While there is justifiably much concern for one of the least abundant of North American ducks, it is ironic and alarming that there is increasing concern over the status of a species considered to be the most abundant—the mallard. Although not yet in deep trouble, there are disquieting signs that all is not well. This ubiquitous bird ranges from coast to coast in North America, but nowhere is it more

Flightless black brant rounded up for banding; Anderson River delta, on Canada's western Arctic coast. *Canadian Wildlife Service photo.*

abundant than on the Great Central Plain. Mallard are the number one game duck in North America, both in abundance and harvest.

Numerous data-collecting techniques have evolved to optimize management opportunities. A study published in 1976 produced substantial evidence that mallard hunting mortality can be either "compensatory" or "additive" to natural mortality. When the mallard population is above some low threshold level, the total mortality rate is relatively constant. Mortality from hunting is then said to be compensatory, because it "replaces" losses from other causes, which would otherwise ac-

count for a similar proportion of total mortality.

The study also suggested that mallard populations have been above this threshold level, at least on a continental basis. Only in years when the population falls below the threshold would hunting mortality be additive to natural mortality. In this case, hunting mortality could be said to contribute to population decline.

The management significance of these findings becomes apparent when recent mallard population trends are considered. From 1955 to 1974, the twenty-year average May population was 8.7 million. Today it is between 6 and 7 million, a decline of as much as 20 percent. If the study is correct in postulating that hunting mortality, on a general basis, is not reducing the population but the population is in a downward turn, then some other environmental factors must be limiting it. Complicating the picture is the possibility that the critical threshold population level varies from year to year in response to variations in habitat.

Several major avenues of research were identified. The first was that the study results should be field tested to determine if a compensatory mortality mechanism is indeed operating.

A five-year period of stabilized regulations has now been completed in much of Canada and the United States. The impact of the subsequent hunting mortality will be assessed. Confirmation of a compensating mortality mechanism will then shift the emphasis to the second major avenue of research—identification of the environmental factors limiting the mallard population. Successful conclusion of the investigation would, it is hoped, result in recommendations for better mallard management.

The black duck in eastern Canada and the United States is also cause for concern. Based on current information, the black duck population is declining or, at best, is stable at a level substantially below that of the mid-1950s. It is thus assumed that annual mortality has recently been greater

Black duck—an Atlantic Flyway tradition. *Kit Breen photo.*

than or equal to recruitment. Where, what kind, and how much mortality can be reduced, must be determined.

Only mortality from hunting has been assessed so far. It indicates that harvest may be reducing local black duck populations. Banding data show survival of young of the year is relatively low. It is assumed that, in some localities, black duck breeding populations could be improved, if the immature survival rate was increased.

Another primary factor, which may be affecting black duck populations, is deteriorating habitat. Black duck breeding habitat can be described in two categories: the boreal forest of eastern North America, which is relatively undisturbed; and the hardwood forest fringe of southern Ontario, southern Quebec, the Maritimes and mid-Atlantic U.S. states, all of which have been adversely affected by human activities.

Land clearing has extended the range of the mallard throughout the eastern United States and into the fringes of eastern boreal Canada. Increased hybridization between blacks and mallard has resulted in a subtle but definite dilution of the black duck gene pool.

An encouraging facet of black duck management is the new breeding habitat created by an increased beaver population. This requires intensive beaver management, if the promise of increased black duck production is to be realized.

Waterfowl managers have some strong leads concerning the negative factors affecting the black duck population. But at present only the status quo is being maintained. Considerably more refined information is required if black duck populations are to be returned to their former levels of abundance.

An overview of waterfowl management in North America shows that, although there have been successes, challenges still exist. That it is unlikely we will solve all the problems is apparent from this review. But with continuing support from all those segments of the North American public to whom waterfowl mean so much, we can be optimistic of more successes than failures in the future.

52

Waterfowl Disease in the Past and Future

R. E. Lange

While waterfowl have probably always suffered from a variety of diseases, a strong case can be made that disease losses are increasingly significant, and the magnitude of loss is tremendous. Man, through his influence on habitat and waterfowl populations, bears responsibility for much of the increase. Disease will become a greater negative influence on waterfowl populations unless better management is practiced.

Management, based on our best understanding of nature's interactions, creates the best environmental conditions in a location that we can realistically expect. We can manipulate habitat and the birds in ways less likely to cause disease and, based on our present knowledge, may be able to prevent some diseases. However, our first priority may be to develop the perspective that disease is abnormal, and that some

diseases can be prevented or their impacts lessened. Improved disease management will not be developed without the strength of this perspective.

An estimated 250,000 ducks died of avian botulism during the summer of 1932 at Great Salt Lake in Utah. This disease, caused by a toxin produced by bacterial action in a highly organic medium under conditions of high temperature and low oxygen, killed a minimum of 1.5 million ducks in California between 1934 and 1970.

Botulism outbreaks occur annually during the summer in the Central and San Joaquin valleys and the Tulare Lake Basin of California. Over 100,000 birds died in summer 1982 on Great Salt Lake. While duck losses are often emphasized, many thousand other birds are lost. Furthermore, we read short news clips of only the

Shoveler sick with botulism, Rice Lake, North Dakota. *Ed Bry photo.*

Pickup of birds killed by botulism at Long Lake, North Dakota. *Ed Bry photo.*

Duck plague losses at Lake Andes. *South Dakota Department of Game, Fish and Parks photo.*

largest outbreaks. Hundreds of smaller ones occur, unknown except to diagnosticians and managers.

Avian cholera, a bacterial disease unknown in free-flying wild birds in the United States prior to 1944, killed an estimated 70,000–100,000 waterfowl in March and April 1980 in Nebraska's Rainwater Basin. Some 60,000 birds were lost at Muleshoe National Wildlife Refuge, Texas, in the winter of 1956–57, and an estimated 70,000 in northcentral California in the winter of 1965–66. Thousands of waterfowl as well as other birds are lost annually in hundreds of outbreaks occur-

ring from September through May in the United States and Canada.

Duck plague, a viral disease, was first diagnosed in North America among domestic duck flocks on Long Island, New York, in 1967. Six years later, during January and February 1973, over 40,000 waterfowl died at Lake Andes National Refuge in South Dakota, the only major outbreak of duck plague among free-flying wild birds in North America to date. But over forty incidences have now been diagnosed in the United States and Canada, generally involving semidomesticated ducks in city parks.

There are estimates that fall flights of waterfowl in early America may have approached 200 million, that they may have fallen as low as 40 million during the 1930s, and may be as high as 80 million in the 1980s. What happened? Habitat changes provide a large part of the answer, and disease can be linked to habitat.

Continuing development of the country is inevitable, and with that fact goes the threat to waterfowl habitat. A significant factor contributing to waterfowl disease has been massive loss of wetlands and decline in quality of others. Over 90 percent of the historic wetlands in Nebraska's Rainwater Basin are gone. Over 80 percent are gone in the Central Valley of California. Nationally, 75 percent are gone, and the trend continues.

Conservationists have been aware of this trend for over fifty years, and have a proud history of habitat preservation and restoration, resulting in many hundreds of refuges administered by federal and state governments or by private organizations. Recovery of waterfowl populations since the 1930s may in large part be due to these efforts. Still, loss of many wetlands and degradation of others continue.

The effect of wetland losses has been to concentrate waterfowl. Perhaps it is true that in Nebraska historic fall and spring flights were two to three times their present size, but wetlands are only one-tenth their

Burning of geese that succumbed to DVE (duck viral enteritis) and pneumonia in North Dakota. *John Violett photo.*

former number! Thus, in March, near Kearney, Nebraska, it is possible to see 125,000 ducks and geese on a 100-acre sheet of water no more than twelve inches deep. Estimates of 1.5 to 2 million waterfowl at a time during spring staging in the area are not unrealistic. When bad spring weather occurs, as is often the case, and northward migration is blocked, much larger concentrations build.

Similar concentrations can be seen in the Central Valley through which as many as 18 million waterfowl pass; at the Playa Lakes in the Texas Panhandle; at Bear River, Utah, on the northern end of the Great Salt Lake; and at many other locations. Certainly waterfowl have always concentrated at some locations at some times of the year, but those concentrations were distributed through far more habitat.

Dense waterfowl concentrations are susceptible to infectious disease, particularly where little alternate habitat exists. Avian cholera, duck plague, and other diseases are transmitted from bird to bird through fecal contamination. With restricted habitat, succeeding flocks of migrating waterfowl use the same water; bad weather increases density and fecal contamination because migration is blocked.

Waterfowl utilizing the same wetlands over a period are repeatedly exposed to any pathogens that might be present. Those carrying disease pathogens may be constantly shedding them. Transmission is facilitated by crowding, and increased stress may also result. Water quality can be adversely affected by the large amount of fecal matter, and survival of pathogenic agents may actually be increased. Even landing and taking off may increase transmission by aerosol formation as thousands of wings create a fog of water droplets.

Habitat quality is another significant problem. Despite the best of intentions we have often created refuges incapable of handling the waterfowl populations dependent on them. Many wetlands are simply low spots, which, when filled seasonally by melting snow or rain, form shallow sheet water with little circulation. Nebraska's Rainwater Basins and the Texas Panhandle are good locations to see these wetlands, some hundreds of acres in size but only a few inches deep.

Some have been developed with pumped water, but wells are expensive to operate, and pumping for waterfowl instead of agriculture often becomes controversial, particularly in basins whose aquifers are being depleted. These wetlands may have large outbreaks of avian cholera in the late winter and early spring.

Some of the worst are simple impoundments with no capability for prompt filling, draining, or regulating levels. Some are a long string of wetland units along a watercourse where an impoundment can't be drained when an outbreak occurs, or another unit filled to draw birds to a better location. When one of a string of wetland units has an outbreak, the manager often must drain them all, thus denying all the habitat to waterfowl rather than just the problem area. More recent wetland developments usually have greater flexibility built in, including an adequate water supply that can be diverted to individual units, which can then be regulated to the desired level or drained promptly if necessary.

Habitat degradation is increased by activities often distant from the wetland itself. Agricultural, residential, industrial, commercial, or transportation infrastructure areas drain into most wetlands. Agricultural runoff includes fertilizers, pesticides, and soil. Many of the same agents are received from residential areas, and chemical wastes and salt from the other sources.

It is the norm rather than the exception for wetlands to be surrounded by these influences. Logic suggests that many of these agents are harmful to waterfowl. Large-scale waterfowl mortality from pesticides or metals such as selenium has been traced to water contamination in many states.

Tile drain systems, used by agriculture in alkaline soils of the West, collect irrigation water that has been percolated through soils to remove salts, and all too often finds its way to a wetland being used by ducks. These drain waters adversely affect many invertebrates and plants that provide food and cover for ducks, and may directly harm waterfowl as well.

There are other types of habitat degradation, some occurring on and others off wetlands. Lead shot deposited by hunting is one type. Surely we are past the point where the fact of lead poisoning is in dispute. However, there is less agreement on the significance of lead poisoning—how many birds die, and in how many locations. As a wildlife veterinarian who has worked in many states and had the opportunity to diagnose many cases, first by gross pathology and later by laboratory analysis, I can say that this disease is common.

Modern agriculture, with its high yields and mechanized harvests, has been a mixed blessing. Harvest waste and unharvested crops provide a major food source for waterfowl. But they also constitute part of the disease problem. Sometimes the problem is poisoning by pesticides applied to unharvested crops, such as malathion to alfalfa in Texas or endrin to winter wheat in Montana.

Other times the problem develops after harvesting or after spreading moldy silage as fertilizer. Waste peanuts, exposed on the soil surface under suitable conditions of moisture and temperature, develop a mold toxin called aflatoxin, and moldy silage causes aspergillosis, both fatal to large numbers of waterfowl.

Waterfowl are concentrated by crops and harvest wastage. In many areas waterfowl populations are much larger now than those known earlier in the century. Canada geese in southern Illinois and elsewhere are good examples. Many thousand waterfowl may concentrate in a single field, significantly increasing their vulnerability.

Man may actually have introduced some diseases such as duck plague, unknown in North America prior to 1967 and since diagnosed over forty times in the United States and Canada. Avian cholera, unknown in the United States before 1944 except as a disease of domestic poultry, is now essentially continental in distribution, and diagnosed hundreds if not thousands of times annually.

No one can say for certain whether duck plague will become a major mortality factor, but avian cholera already is. It is seen in nesting eiders off the Maine coast in May, in snow geese in June in northern Canada, in ducks in the California's Central Valley in September, and in sandhill cranes in southern Colorado in January. We cannot prove that man introduced avian cholera to migratory birds, but these outbreaks were unheard of fifty years ago.

Waterfowl diseases will become of greater significance because of loss and degradation of habitat, and because of direct introduction by man. We will hear more about waterfowl diseases as our awareness of their significance increases and as they increase in frequency. We will learn how to manage some waterfowl diseases well enough to prevent them, and others well enough to reduce their impact.

Management will consist of manipulating habitat and waterfowl populations, based on our best understanding of the interactions between them at a given time and location. Some management techniques usually produce similar results at different locations, while others, because we don't yet understand the diseases, don't produce these consistent results. We haven't the research to prove that a specific action will always stop a disease outbreak. In lieu of those answers, disease managers and habitat managers often operate on the premise that good habitat management is good disease management.

Consider the disease problems created by large waterfowl concentrations. Basic management strategies are to decrease densities and improve habitat. Density can be reduced by dissemination of food or habitat, or dispersal by hunting or propane exploders. Food distribution, and incidentally content, can be affected by cooperative farm programs both on and off refuges.

The size and distribution of fields will affect waterfowl concentrations. A field can be specifically prepared to affect waterfowl distribution. For example, corn knocked down in smaller strips or blocks will attract fewer geese. Water can also be distributed to several widely separated wetlands rather than a single large area or a cluster.

Active dispersal of waterfowl must be carefully considered. Botulism and lead poisoning are toxic diseases, so dispersal is designed to move birds away from the source of toxin. But avian cholera and duck plague are infectious diseases, and dispersal may spread the disease. And the stress associated with harassment techniques to achieve dispersal may increase losses. Certainly waterfowl concentrated by inclement weather or faced with an adverse weather system should not be dispersed.

Dispersal is very difficult once birds are using an area. Wetlands that cause disease problems for a short period annually can be denied fairly easily by placing propane exploders before birds arrive in the spring.

Management to counteract habitat degradation is another vital need. Key components are a source of good-quality water, free of chemicals and organic effluents, the ability to regulate water levels, and the ability to add or remove water rapidly on a unit-by-unit basis. Water management starts with wetland design or rehabilitation, and it is never completed.

The water source must be adequate and reliable. Adequate may mean sufficient to provide depths exceeding eighteen inches at one stabilized level, while maintaining some circulation in the case of botulism prevention and management. Thus units that are flooded, sealed, and gradually subjected to lowering water levels by evaporation and seepage lack the manipulatory potential to prevent botulism.

Shallow units where sheet water may flood adjacent flats, as a result of small fluctuation in water levels such as wind tides, are very conducive to botulism. Some refuges where botulism is anticipated now maintain one unit at the upper end at a relatively greater depth as a source of flushing water for the disease area during an outbreak. This technique has been associated with a great decline in botulism losses at Benton Lake National Wildlife Refuge in Montana.

Individual unit water management capability is important to prevent and manage disease. If the water source is inadequate, the number of wetland units can be reduced. Some earlier wetland units were designed as an interconnected chain. If a disease broke out or water supply was inadequate, the problem units could not be eliminated. Newer systems not only solve this problem but often allow dispersal of waterfowl to more widely distributed units.

Degradation of wetlands caused by influx of chemicals and organic effluents can be alleviated by proper management. By working cooperatively with point sources, managers may reduce influx. Seasonal diversion of water away from waterfowl wetlands during peak effluent influx may also be of value.

Public education offers the best opportunity to prevent some disease problems. Aflatoxicosis occurs because mechanized harvesting techniques leave exposed waste that develops mold, with subsequent toxin formation. Moldy silage and hay spread on fields for mulching and fertilizing also cause aspergillosis in birds in some cases. Managers and disease specialists must work with agricultural interests to find alternatives to farming practices that can potentially cause disease in waterfowl.

Agriculture is not alone in causing problems for waterfowl. Lead poisoning is a good example of another. If lead poisoning was a simple biological problem, resolution might be easier. But, like agricultural effluents, industrial and residential by-products, and other trouble areas, lead in the environment is complicated by other complex socioeconomic problems. Realistically, all these issues have to be dealt with on a site-specific basis.

Introduction of diseases such as duck plague can be prevented only by coordination and cooperation between governments and industry. Resource agencies must develop functional relationships with diverse segments of the economy, recognizing that waterfowl and waterfowl habitat are affected by many other activities.

Part VII
The Future

Man holds the future of waterfowl and waterfowling in his hands. Without him there would be no waterfowl crisis, and without him there will be no salvation.

Waterfowl populations over eons of time have fluctuated with the habitat, abundant in wet years, reduced in droughts, and rebounding quickly to predrought levels with the return of water. Through drainage and intensive agriculture, man is eliminating the ability of waterfowl to rebound from temporary adverse habitat conditions.

Waterfowl managers must learn to accept and plan for the natural fluctuations in waterfowl population that are beyond their control. But most important, they must preserve and manage the habitat upon which the waterfowl population depends for resurgence. To do otherwise is to condemn waterfowl populations to drought levels — permanently.

53

Duckonomics

D. E. Wesley

The onslaught moves on! Wetlands that our waterfowl depend on for food, rest, and reproduction are obviously disappearing at an alarming and accelerating pace. Within North Dakota, South Dakota, and Minnesota, an area that encompasses the major waterfowl breeding habitat of the United States, 335,000 acres of prime wetlands were lost in the ten-year period from 1964 to 1974. This is 10 percent of the original acreage of this habitat. Virtually all Iowa wetlands have been drained since the early 1900s. The same growing demand for agricultural land exists in Canada, which produces over 70 percent of North America's waterfowl.

The squeeze on waterfowl wintering habitat is tantamount to what has happened in the nesting areas. A high percentage of our inland wetlands, so important to waterfowl, can be converted easily to productive croplands. Of the original twenty-five million acres of bottomland hardwood wetlands along the Mississippi River system, only 30 percent remained in 1969. The loss approached 200,000 acres per year.

The coastal marshlands of the United States are also rapidly changing, to the detriment of waterfowl. A recent mapping survey by the U.S. Fish and Wildlife service showed a loss of fresh marsh in the Louisiana portion of the Mississippi River deltaic plain of nearly 500,000 acres between 1956 and 1978. Unfortunately, fresh marsh is the most valuable type of coastal marsh for ducks.

Prompted by the recognition of wetland values, the various wildland habitat agencies of state and federal governments are making every effort to stay the tide of habitat destruction, but with success that must be kept in perspective with our incessant losses.

Perhaps a stronghold of overlooked potential for averting inevitable and permanent drought for ducks lies within the private sector and the capitalist system. Herein lies the point of this chapter.

For the private sector to affect positively the waterfowl habitat, nesting or wintering, it must understand the philosophy that Bill Leitch, retired chief biologist for Ducks Unlimited Canada, referred to in describing the inevitable confrontation between agriculture and ducks. "In such a confrontation, where there are values on both sides, reconciliation and cooperation are essential to each. Society itself must also be convinced that waterfowl, as a recreational resource, are a public good and must assume, with special interest groups, the cost of their perpetuation."

Speaking of habitat preservation, he wrote, "It must be in the farmer's economic interest to manage his land to benefit waterfowl. Waterfowl and agriculture can cooperate for their mutual benefit in many situations. Purists who cannot condone multiple use of such areas should realize that this is the only way waterfowl can survive in acceptable numbers. It is impossible to set aside sufficient land for waterfowl use alone."

Although the preceding quotations specifically referred to breeding habitat, the same principles apply to wintering habitat. The key to a landowner's involvement with waterfowl in a democratic society is monetary incentive. By paying for our recreation, we may well provide the farmer with more reason to leave his wetlands intact than to clear and drain them.

Most drainage today is privately financed because the landowner's economics seem to dictate it. With cognizance of the basic laws of supply and demand, we must place a price tag on a duck, and on the time we spend in his pursuit, that will stimulate a demand to keep him flying.

An integrated approach for preservation and management of prime waterfowl habitat through generating stronger demands for its recreational use, and tax reforms that provide incentives for a farmer to leave his wetlands, are necessary if waterfowl are to be maintained in sufficient numbers for future generations to use and enjoy.

There must be something special about the four teal occupying a miniscule portion of the bottom of an $8,000 mudboat zooming through the frigid marsh at midmorning, following four hours of intensive hide and seek. Typically, the boat is shared by four or more hunters, who have spent $200 to $300 each for a two-day hunt, hosted by a fellow sportsman. He, in addition, has spent $150 to $300 per guest per day in dogs, lodging, gasoline, equipment, food and drink, just to give them an opportunity to pursue these peregrinating wildfowl.

Understanding "duckonomics" requires some insight into the psychology of the hunter, the habits of the hunted, and the value of the places where the two meet. Understanding and evaluating this total recreational experience, epitomized by the four teal, leads us to the abstract realm called esthetics—a difficult commodity to evaluate.

Numerous economists have tried to evaluate recreational experiences by measuring various direct and indirect factors associated with it. Direct methods usually measure actual expenses such as travel and equipment costs. Indirect methods involve a hypothetical valuation designed to determine a willingness to pay or willingness to accept compensation for giving up a recreational experience. Most past and current economic surveys involving waterfowl include elements of both. The economic data presented were accumulated for a variety of purposes, but are used here with the single objective of illustrating the massive expenditures of waterfowlers in pursuit of their favorite pastime.

Using the direct cost approach, a survey of 1,882 randomly selected Ducks Unlimited members was made to determine how much money they spent waterfowling. Extrapolated to the full membership, a conservative personal investment in equipment and supplies alone approached $1 billion. Of this, over $100 million is an annual expense.

The survey revealed that 56 percent of the Ducks Unlimited members hunted waterfowl ten days or more per year, and that 43 percent traveled over 100 miles to hunt. No attempt was made to estimate travel, food, lodging, ammunition, and other incidental costs.

Data gathered by the U.S. Fish and Wildlife Service in a 1980 survey showed 33,774,000 days were spent by 4.1 million sportsmen (with some overlap) hunting ducks and geese. And they spent nearly $500 million in that pursuit.

Waterfowling is a montage of beauty of sunrise, cupped wings, frosted decoys, attentive retrievers, warm laughter, and hot buttered rum. The value of such abstract experiences can't be easily expressed by a price tag. Some insight into these values was, however, obtained by studying the value placed on early season goose hunting permits for the horicon zone of eastcentral Wisconsin.

These permits entitled a hunter to take one goose during the first two weeks of October 1978. Cash offers accepted for a predetermined number of permits averaged $63 per permit. Adjusting this figure by using the Consumer Price Index shows a permit today to be worth $102. Twelve percent of the hunters would not have sold their permit for $200, which was the maximum offer made. In today's dollars, this would equate to $325.

The "Economic Survey of Wildlife Recreation in the Southeastern United States" by the Environmental Research Group at Georgia State University set the dollar value required in 1974 to get a waterfowler to give up one day of duck hunting at $67. If these values have increased with the Consumer Price Index, that same day of duck hunting would currently be worth $144. Considering inflation and the reduced availability of prime habitat and hunting, this figure would be quite reasonable. Using these figures, it can be easily calculated that the total recreational value of a season of waterfowling in the United States could approach $4 billion!

A random sampling of commercial fees charged for duck and goose hunting agrees well with these real and hypothetical values. The fee for one well-known and respected commercial hunt in Louisiana is $135 per day per hunter, excluding food, travel, lodging, and other personal items. The price for a day's hunting with lodging, food, and drinks included is $260 per person; shells, game cleaning, and gratuities are not included.

In one four-county area of southern Illinois, which winters approximately 400,000 Canada geese, fees for a day's hunting were substantially less than most of the other clubs surveyed. Here they usually run $50 or so per day per hunter, excluding meals and lodging. Additional costs to the hunter for meals, lodging, and guide services would be $50 as a minimum. It is signifi-

Expenditures aplenty. *Glenn Chambers photo.*

cant that this four-county area supports 40,000 to 70,000 hunter-days for geese each year, which adds $4 to $5 million to the area's economy. None of these figures include other expenses such as shells, personal gear, hunting licenses, etc.

Another method of controlling and using hunting lands is by lease. This sets a price for exclusive hunting rights on land owned by someone else. Obviously, this varies immensely among areas. Supply and demand establish the cost figures.

In northeast Louisiana, ricefields and greentree reservoirs are the most valuable locations for duck hunting. Blinds currently cost from $3,500 to $7,500 each. This usually includes about ten acres of water on a forty-acre site. In southwest Louisiana, similar arrangements in ricefield locations usually cost $2,500 to $3,000 per year, and are typically not flooded; these areas are primarily for goose hunting. If a pit blind is added or pumping necessary, additional costs are added.

The coastal marshes of south Louisiana leased for duck and goose hunting vary from $2 to $18 per acre. One particular school board section in Cameron Parish has been leased for $12,000 (640 acres) with four blinds on the property. Another school board section in north Cameron Parish in the rice country leased for over $20,000 with four blinds, but also had a camp on the property.

Louisiana has approximately 4,000,000 acres of marsh, and over 500,000 acres of rice were planted in 1984. Most of it is leased for duck hunting, thus creating enormous revenues for Louisiana.

It has been reported that the current supply of waterfowl hunting, in one sizable area of Louisiana, could accommodate only 78 percent of the demand. By the year 2000, this supply and demand ratio would be 49 percent and by 2020, 31 percent. Demand estimates were based on use by Louisiana residents only; total demand would be considerably greater. At the upper end of these lease figures, waterfowling is competing quite well on a per-acre basis with what a farmer could expect from using his land for soybeans.

Where bottomlands have already been converted to soybeans and rice, double-cropping, with ducks as a second crop, is a natural. Such lands have excellent marketability, and the process of preparing them for waterfowling is usually simple and relatively inexpensive. With a shrinking supply and a swelling demand, the concept of managing lands for waterfowl becomes more feasible.

In some cases, progressive-thinking hunters have found that purchasing, rather than leasing, makes for excellent hunting—and sound investment. This is particularly true when a group of hunter-investors form a corporation to purchase lands with both income and recreational potential.

Can waterfowlers afford to play a role in the marketplace where wetlands are bought, sold, and leased? The real question is, Can those who love ducks afford not to, since their involvement, or lack of it, may ultimately determine the fate of the wintering habitat?

Perhaps more than any other single group of sportsmen, duck hunters have the financial capacity for preserving wetlands. In the 1980 National Survey of Fishing and Hunting, over 35 percent of the respondents made $25,000 or more per year, and 11 percent reported incomes over $40,000. In Ducks Unlimited's 1984 survey of its own membership, over 53 percent had incomes of over $35,000 per year and over 32 percent topped $50,000 annually. From these figures, it appears that waterfowlers have the financial resources to create a demand for wetlands.

If we want to save our wetlands, and the ducks that frequent them each fall, we must develop a strong willingness to pay for the commodity, and let the landowner know it! To some extent, this approach has been successful. In the mid-1960s, about 2.3 million acres of waterfowl habitat in the Mississippi Flyway were maintained by private hunting clubs. During the same period, the Wildlife Management Institute estimated that waterfowl clubs had preserved a minimum of 33 million acres in the United States. This figure did not include acreage from Louisiana, Mississippi, and several other states.

The land ethic that Aldo Leopold spoke of more than forty years ago is alive and well, at least with those who place high priority on being good stewards of the land. It is a noble philosophy for all who have a sense of accountability for our natural resources. But for the farmer, who must face the loan officer of his local bank or production credit association each fall, nobility is secondary to paying his debts. In a capitalist system, dollars are the universal language!

Waterfowl can speak this language if we recognize their tremendous value to man's spirit, and place them prominently in the marketplace. Let's recognize the value of whistling wings.

Waterfowl can best be served by forming a hunting group and encouraging the farmer, by putting dollars in his pocket, to leave bottomland wetlands intact. Some lost waterfowl habitat can also be salvaged by providing financial incentives for landowners to flood their stubble for waterfowl following harvest. Assistance for this is available in every state through the Soil Conservation Service, Cooperative Extension Service, or through private wildlife consultants.

Perhaps an infusion of conservation spirit into certain federal agencies could be stimulated, particularly in areas where massive losses of bottomland habitat seems imminent. The federal policy to mitigate such losses is to acquire similar bottomland in fee title. While this provides future protection for wetlands that would someday succumb to our society's rapacious appetite for developing "worthless" lands to croplands, parking lots, and subdivisions, it does little for the habitat already a victim of the shearing blade and smoking windrow.

The Corps of Engineers and private landowners should be encouraged, on solid "duckonomics," to take a positive position in improving and enhancing the habitat remaining. Modifications of water control structures and pump operations, to maintain a diversity of waterfowl feeding and resting areas during the winter migration, would enhance the future of the resource.

Cost-sharing incentives between federal and nonfederal entities, designed to leave grain or stubble in the fields and to maintain a waterfowl-oriented water regime, would effectively reclaim some of the wintering habitat and recreational opportunities lost to the plow. The Fish and Wildlife Coordination Act of 1958, the National Environmental Policy Act of 1969, the Food Security Act of 1985, and the North American Waterfowl Management Plan provide excellent opportunities for such habitat-enhancing action. We need only to move in a positive way — and work with the landowner by putting dollars in his jeans!

The first step in positive action to save

A sight worth paying for. *Glenn Chambers photo.*

our waterfowl resources is to identify the remaining wetlands with prime nesting or wintering potential and their owners. If they are still wooded or otherwise undisturbed, a group of investors or lessees should be formed quickly for purchase or lease. Current technology in remote sensing by satellite imagery provides an excellent tool for such monitoring.

For those interested in the investment potential, a group may consider an entire farm with crops and wetlands. If a wetland has already been converted to crops, some real tenacity should be practiced, and the landowner approached with a management plan that would enable him to benefit financially from his flooded stubble fields. Help him double-crop waterfowl!

To keep our flyways alive across the face of America each fall, we might have to sacrifice some of our idealism to the more pragmatic approach of working with what resources and habitat a demanding world has left us. This does not mean that we should acquiesce to the habitat onslaught, but we must recognize the pressures of an overpopulated world and carve out the best existence possible for waterfowl.

54

New Agricultural Techniques: The Hope of the Future

A. J. Macaulay et al.

In Western Canada, agriculture has a status akin to motherhood. It's regarded as a good and wholesome way to earn a living in a free-enterprise society. Besides, feeding the hungry masses of the world is as honorable a career as any, so it's easy to understand why criticism of this noble and meaningful pursuit is regarded in some quarters as sacrilege.

But along came wildlife biologists who established that declining North American wildlife populations were primarily a result of habitat loss. They identified agricultural development as the primary cause and, in doing so, became critics of agriculture by laying at the farmer's doorstep a large portion of blame for habitat destruction.

A farmer's belief in the quintessential goodness of what he does for a living, his respect for tradition, and his struggle

against production costs rising faster than his returns, all set the stage for conflict. Farmers want to increase yields and profits by producing more crop on more land, regardless of habitat consequences.

The battle lines between farmers and wildlife managers have been drawn in a war of words over a variety of environmental issues including herbicides, drainage, excessive tillage, overgrazing, and crop damage by wildlife.

The inevitable result is an "either-or" philosophy that holds that healthy wildlife populations and agriculture cannot coexist on the same parcel of land. With present-day approaches to food production, this is certainly true.

However, changing attitudes on both sides may resolve the conflict. There is concern that traditional agricultural practices are seriously affecting more than wildlife habitat. There's evidence they may be affecting the land's long-term ability to sustain even a viable agricultural industry.

It's an important revelation, which may eventually encourage what wildlife interests see as badly needed changes in agricultural practices, new ideas that would offer striking spinoffs for waterfowl and other wildlife.

Historically, the single most important threat to prairie waterfowl has been drainage. Since the turn of the century, 40 to 70 percent of our wetlands in various regions of Canada have been lost, with the greatest impact on waterfowl taking place in the three prairie provinces — Alberta, Saskatchewan, and Manitoba.

In the past, drainage has been funded or subsidized by government to increase arable land, eliminating many temporary wetlands. As the quest for more farmland continues, drainage attention is now being focused on semipermanent wetlands. The result has been development of marginal agricultural land that too often has severe cropping limitations, because of saline soils, low fertility, or spring flooding. The costs, both immediate and long term, for these questionable drainage undertakings are coming under more careful scrutiny.

The immediate costs are readily identified; the long-term costs are less easily defined, since they are cumulative and spread over a wider sector of society. They involve increased soil erosion and siltation of river systems, increasing frequency and severity of downstream flooding, and elimination of important sources of replacement water for underground aquifers.

The attitude of society and governments toward drainage is changing. At one time, drainage was undertaken without regard for the side effects; now proposals must be reviewed to evaluate possible long-term consequences. Governments in each of the three prairie provinces have established review committees, and Ducks Unlimited Canada participates actively wherever significant amounts of waterfowl habitat are concerned.

This is not to imply that wetland drainage has been halted. But the rate at which it is happening is decreasing, giving evidence of a change in attitude brought about by greater public environmental concern, the cumulative experience of several decades of drainage, and more accurate cost-benefit analyses of drainage schemes.

Also, the public is beginning to realize that the costs of protecting residents from floodwaters and compensating flood victims are mounting. And they will continue to increase, if increasing volumes of runoff are dumped into river systems through drainage ditch networks.

It is ironic that in the Great Plains of Western Canada, where the lack of water is the major detriment to agricultural crop production, farmers should be looking for ways to dispose of excess water. Fortunately, the public is beginning to question the validity of current drainage schemes and seek alternative answers.

The severity of the situation is illustrated by increasing flood problems along the Red River running through the Dakotas and Minnesota into Canada. The city of Grand Forks, North Dakota, has had eight floods in the last ten years, at an estimated cost of $93 million. Paradoxically, four of those ten years have been classified by climatologists as drought years.

"Improved drainage" of agricultural lands has resulted in greater volumes of water reaching the rivers in a shorter runoff period. One Manitoba researcher has calculated that the 1979 flood, the most severe in recent times, could have been avoided if farmers had retained an average of two inches of additional moisture on the land and allowed it to soak into the soil. For the most part, he pointed out, these soils are considered to be water-deficient for agricultural crops and prime targets for costly irrigation schemes.

Such bizarre imbalances in water distribution—upstream drought and downstream flooding in the same watershed—are attributed only in part to drainage. They are also the result of other agricultural practices, specifically excessive tillage and summer fallowing practices.

In Western Canada, the tradition has been to crop a piece of land roughly twice in a three-year rotation, leaving it fallow the third year to conserve moisture and nutrients and control weeds. Thus only approximately 65 percent of the land is productive each year. The fallow land, which requires frequent tillage to maintain a weed-free and pulverized surface, lies not only unproductive but costly in terms of machinery and fuel to maintain it.

Soil scientists are now beginning to question the practice of summer fallowing. They believe it is at least partly responsible for the growing problems of soil salinity, reduction of organic matter, and topsoil erosion.

There is a documented increase in the amount of agricultural soils with impaired cropping potential from increased salt content. In some regions, the increase in saline land is estimated to have doubled in a twenty-year period.

Under pristine conditions, grassland soils of the northern Great Plains contained 6 to 8 percent humus, a major organic element in the highly fertile, easily worked prairie soils that were so prized by early settlers.

In less than a century, the organic content has been reduced by 50 percent through excessive tillage and summer fallow. The result has been increased wind and water erosion. In addition, modern agricultural operations often do not return straw and chaff to the soil, and fertility and ability to absorb and hold moisture are thereby diminished. These results bode poorly for the long-term future of agriculture if the trend continues.

These same factors have also resulted in annual soil nitrogen losses which, if averaged over the last sixty years, are two and a half times the present annual world consumption of nitrogen fertilizer. This marked reduction in soil nitrogen is now being made up by large fertilizer applications, a major cause of increased crop production costs.

Present multiple-tillage agricultural practices, which use summer fallow for moisture conservation or weed control, wreak havoc on ground-dwelling animals. Upland nesting waterfowl species have their initial nesting efforts destroyed by spring tillage operations, which also eliminates the stubble and trash used as nesting cover. Ducks are forced to renest in remnant patches of undisturbed vegetation, where their nests are easily located by predators.

Fortunately, excessive tillage is now being identified as undesirable, even from an agricultural viewpoint. To reduce costs, farmers are exploring alternative techniques while maintaining, or even improving, soil tilth and yields.

One such technique is zero tillage, a concept successfully applied in much of the United States and Europe and now rapidly gaining support in Western Canada. In zero tillage, summer fallow is eliminated. Seeding is done directly into the previous

Seeding winter wheat into stubble. *Ducks Unlimited Canada photo.*

year's standing stubble. In the long term, weed control is expected to be less of a problem under this system, but initially chemical control measures are necessary.·

The implications of this technique for waterfowl and other ground-nesting birds are profound. Based on field studies by Ducks Unlimited staff, waterfowl production in pothole farmlands such as Minnedosa, Manitoba, could be expected to increase three- to fivefold in zero-tilled fields.

Widespread adoption of zero tillage in Western Canada will be encouraged because of the reduced tillage costs and yield increases inherent in the technique. Rather than relying on yields from half to two-thirds of his farmland for his income, while one-third lies fallow, the farmer can bring all his land into production on a continuous cropping basis.

A more recent zero-tillage spinoff involves winter wheat production. With conventional tillage, seed bed preparation involves several operations that incorporate the trash into the soil, leaving it black and unprotected. Winter wheat planted into this situation is subject to frost damage during the winter because the plants lack the insulation provided by snow.

If the seed is "zero tilled" into standing stubble, an insulating snow blanket is retained, which reduces winter damage. Because winter wheat is harvested earlier than spring-seeded crops, it spreads out the farmer's work load and reduces harvest losses from uncertain fall weather, which often adversely affects spring-seeded cereal crops.

Benefits to wildlife, particularly waterfowl, are even more significant than first meets the eye. Since the only field operations during the nesting season are herbicide applications of chemicals with negligible effects on waterfowl nests, few are lost. And because winter wheat ripens earlier than its spring-seeded cousins, earlier harvests make it virtually immune to damage by feeding waterfowl.

Although the conflict between agriculture and wildlife interests remains a volatile land-use issue, there are grounds for optimism that attitudes are changing. Development of more conservation-oriented farming practices, and recognition of a common dependence on the quality of the environment, are bridging the differences between agricultural and wildlife interests as each recognizes a joint concern for the health of the land.

55

A North American Waterfowl Management Plan

D. S. Morrison

Waterfowl management in North America is the most complex wildlife management and administration program in the world. It's the result of trying to manage a resource consisting of about fifty species whose habitat requirements vary dramatically, change seasonally to include at least two continents and more than a dozen sovereign countries, and involve a host of subnational governments, including the fifty state governments of the United States and ten provincial and two territorial governments in Canada.

Complexity is further increased because waterfowl are prized gamebirds, subject to high annual hunting mortality from more than 2.5 million hunters. And if these considerations don't have you shaking your head, throw into the mixture the huge manufacturing and distribution industries related to waterfowling that have developed in North America and the vast array of nongovernment organizations that also play a role in waterfowl conservation. The result is a bewilderingly complex situation.

Consider now, for a moment, the problems of keeping all this organized. Who does it? How is it done?

The answer to the first question is relatively straightforward. Federal governments of nations harboring the waterfowl resource play the major international coordinating role. On a national scene, this is shared between the federal governments and state or provincial agencies, at least in North America. To their efforts are added the resources of private organizations, including sportsmen and naturalist groups, and management and research organizations at the state or provincial and national levels.

To the second question — How is it

done? — the answer is less straightforward. It relies mainly on a seventy-year-old treaty between the United States and Canada — the Migratory Birds Convention, which was also signed by Mexico in 1936. Since 1916, this agreement has been the basis for all cooperation between the United States and Canada in managing the migratory waterfowl resource.

Considering the complexity of this resource and the problems to be dealt with, the convention has served amazingly well. But, not unexpectedly, it has its limitations. It was designed primarily to *protect* migratory birds, not *manage* them. The convention, enacted in national legislation in both the United States and Canada, assigned this responsibility to the federal governments and established a regulatory framework for waterfowl hunting to control the kill. However, there are numerous aspects of waterfowl management, not dealt with by the convention, that are vitally important to maintaining this resource in the face of ever-increasing pressures.

For instance, the convention did not specify how many waterfowl should be maintained on the North American continent, nor suggest how many could be safely killed continentally without endangering breeding stocks. It didn't foresee some of the massive management problems that would confront the resource in the years after ratification.

Problems for which the convention gives no guidance include: substantial losses of habitat in both the United States and Canada; potential for increased mortality from factors other than hunting, lead shot poisoning, contagious diseases, pollution, etc.; and the fundamental difficulty of an increasing demand for access to the resource by a burgeoning population.

The seemingly simple problem of inventory, which in reality is a monumental task, was never addressed in the convention. And while joint responsibility of the two nations for maintaining the resource was identified, there was no suggestion of how the responsibility would be apportioned.

These are some of the fundamental problems waterfowl administrators grapple with today. Potentially, they could threaten the maintenance of waterfowl populations at the levels we have come to expect.

In order to improve our system, new initiatives are required, and there are basically only two options. The first is to scrap the old convention, building into a new treaty those management components required today. The other is to enter into a subsidiary agreement to the existing convention, developing a protocol between the two countries to provide the direction presently lacking.

The first option, to start anew, would be a long and difficult road. Waterfowl administrators foresee numerous "chuckholes" and perhaps impassable stretches. They view the Migratory Birds Convention as a unique achievement that has generally served us well. In the words of one grizzled sage, "If the wheel ain't broke, don't fix it!"

Migratory bird officials don't view this situation as a broken wheel, but merely one that squeaks badly. But they warn of serious difficulty if some grease isn't applied. They have thus opted for the second approach: to develop an international management plan to which both countries are party, and which identifies the problems facing waterfowl managers today and provides solutions.

Furthermore, they don't see this a static one-time achievement, but an ongoing process of continual review and revision, as changing situations dictate. They see a

North American waterfowl management plan as a means to coordinate international efforts to perpetuate the waterfowl resource and the benefits North Americans derive from it.

To be effective, certain fundamentals must be contained in such a management plan. It must, first of all, provide for an agreed population level that North Americans wish to see maintained. These population goals must be defined in such a way that all management agencies use the same numbers. Furthermore, they must be expressed so they relate in a straightforward manner to an ongoing process of inventory; the plan must ensure that we always know where we are relative to where we want to go!

Goals must be developed in such a way that the welfare of all species of waterfowl is assured, particularly those subject to mortality by hunting. If these population goals, which are the basis for all subsequent management, are to receive public support, it must be possible to state them simply, so that the layman can understand what management agencies are attempting to accomplish.

Having established the number of waterfowl we want, the plan must then identify how we wish to use them. The major use, of biological significance, is the annual hunter kill. We must determine whether we want to kill more, less, or the same number as we do now. In making this decision, we must take into account current social trends such as the changes in the demand for waterfowl harvest by sport hunters and in the native subsistence harvest.

Our management system must also ensure an equitable distribution of the harvest, taking into account historical practices and the political considerations necessary to ensure that all governments with a stake in this resource feel the needs of their constituents are being dealt with fairly.

The plan must deal with the needs of nonconsumptive users, the millions of North Americans who don't hunt but enjoy watching or photographing waterfowl. Generally speaking, from a management standpoint, the needs of this group are less demanding than those of the consumptive user, because hunters require a much higher population to enjoy their recreation without endangering the resource.

The street-wise wildlife administrator knows, however, that for waterfowl conservation programs to be progressive and well funded, he must have public support. To achieve this, there must be opportunities to see, learn, and develop an appreciation for the waterfowl resource. So even though nonconsumptive use poses relatively little demand on waterfowl populations, it still requires programs to provide access and facilities for public education.

Having determined the "inventory" of waterfowl we wish to maintain on this continent, our plan must then identify the obstacles to attaining those objectives. The problems that waterfowl managers face, and with which they must successfully contend if we are to maintain waterfowl populations, are numerous and ever-changing.

Foremost is the problem of maintaining adequate habitat. It is illogical to expect that we can simply identify the amount of habitat required and then "set it aside" for exclusive use of waterfowl and perhaps other wildlife. With increasing populations and expanding economies, our two countries can ill afford the luxury of setting aside the vast acreages required by waterfowl and excluding all other uses.

Rather, we must develop a philosophy, and ensuing programs, to ensure that the most critical habitat is, in fact, set aside, managed primarily for waterfowl. But the remainder of the land base should be managed, at least in part, for the benefit of waterfowl and other wildlife. Exclusive use of any land base is socially unacceptable today.

Another problem that waterfowl administrators must contend with is the massive task of monitoring the parameters of waterfowl populations to ensure a relative stability. Waterfowl managers must have at their disposal mechanisms for measuring annual recruitment and mortality. A management plan must clearly spell out the objectives of such a program, ideally heading toward a "balance sheet" approach. This need not be a massively complicated process, but simply one that accounts for major sources of input and output from the population.

Existing surveys are generally thought to do a pretty good job here; probably all that is required is some fine tuning. The plan would simply make this fine tuning possible, and explain the system clearly for all to understand.

Fundamental to maintaining a population balance sheet is knowledge of the habitat base that supports it. Recent technological advances in remote sensing should make it relatively simple to establish a system whereby we are able, periodically at least, to determine the gains or losses in waterfowl habitat on the continent. This is fundamental to developing effective habitat maintenance programs.

In its absence, waterfowl managers will continue in the unenviable situation of opposing loss of *any* habitat, because current and future requirements of the waterfowl resource are unknown. The plan must establish the need for an ongoing method of monitoring the quality and quantity of waterfowl habitat on the continent.

To be a truly useful document, a plan must anticipate the future. It is characteristic of waterfowl populations and their management that the situation is never static; there is always a crisis of some sort. If populations are not plummeting because of drought or some other factor, a component of the population is becoming too abundant, with the attendant conflicts with human interests. Waterfowl managers will always have these problems—and others: the arrival of new contagious waterfowl diseases, the precipitous decline of an individual species, and progressive changes in distribution of waterfowl populations.

It is impossible to foresee all the problems that will arise in the future, but an effective plan must lay out the strategy by which managers can effectively deal with them when they do. This is particularly critical when deciding on international responsibilities. The time to determine which country will take action is *not* in the midst of a crisis; the principles must be agreed to before the crisis arrives.

History has judged the Migratory Birds Convention a major achievement in the field of wildlife management. For all its strengths, we now recognize, seventy years later, that the situation requires something more. Discussions presently underway by the governments of Canada and the United States relative to the newly developed North American Waterfowl Management Plan under the umbrella of the Migratory Birds Convention of 1916 will similarly be judged by history.

We are poised for a major step forward. Let us hope that history will judge our current efforts as favorably as it does those of our predecessors.

56

The Future

D. E. Whitesell

Users with a vested interest will determine the future of waterfowl conservation in North America, and they will do it with dollars and deeds.

It doesn't matter whether those users hunt waterfowl or just watch them, they will need to assess what waterfowl are worth to them, and act accordingly. It is such a simple premise that it sometimes gets lost in the rhetoric and rubric of waterfowl resource management. But without it all such programs are destined to fail.

Better than anyone, users understand the need for habitat in any successful wildlife conservation program. Man has been unsuccessful at exterminating pests, except on a very short-term basis, largely because he has failed to eradicate their habitat. On the other hand, he has been fantastically successful at exterminating species by al-

tering or destroying habitat—witness the passenger pigeon. Market hunting helped the process of extinction, but it was not critical; it merely helped aggravate the effect of lost habitat. Dinosaurs, saber-toothed tigers, and hairy mastadons would be around today if there were places for them to live.

Unfortunately, hunters, who are the largest segment of users, have allowed themselves to be duped into believing that they have a more significant impact on waterfowl than is the case. Thus when populations are down, it is the hunters, acting in what they believe to be in the best interests of the resource, who often call for reduced bag limits and seasons. The danger is that such action obfuscates the need for habitat. It reinforces in the minds of hunters and nonhunters alike that hunting is bad for waterfowl populations. It takes

The past, present, and future of waterfowling. *Glenn Chambers photo.*

no great leap in logic to then conclude that if hunting waterfowl is bad, not hunting waterfowl is good. That's where the problem begins.

The scene unfolds something like this: Hunters, who in July believe waterfowl need a dose of reduced bags and seasons, discover in October that short seasons and small bags hardly justify the time and expense to bother hunting waterfowl at all. Never mind that the hunter rarely takes his bag or hunts more than a few days in the most liberal seasons, any reduction in opportunity has a psychological effect that discourages hunters.

The normal press of business and family life make it that much easier to "postpone" this year's hunting season. Why bother

buying a duck-hunting stamp? Certainly there is no need for shells. That means less money for the Fish and Wildlife Service's habitat acquisition program and less money for federal and state waterfowl programs partially funded through excise taxes on arms and ammunition. (Since 1934, the duck-stamp program alone has raised more than $300 million and helped conserve more than 4 million acres of wetlands. Ducks Unlimited, which is largely composed of hunters, has raised nearly $400 million and conserved some 3.8 million acres of wetland in Canada, where U.S. federal dollars cannot go. In addition, Ducks Unlimited has projects and programs in Mexico and throughout the United States.)

So instead of doing waterfowl conservation a favor by not hunting, the nonactive hunter may well be doing it a disservice.

The answer lies not in providing glowing and untrue reports of waterfowl populations. The answer lies in setting realistic population goals tied to habitat. Which takes us right back to the habitat issue.

If there is to be any promise for waterfowl and waterfowlers, it is going to lie with setting goals, first for habitat and second for population. There needs to be a continentwide approach to the problem, beginning with an accurate inventory of the remaining wetlands (see color pages on inventorying by satellite, preceding book's title page). Within that inventory, we need to determine the amount of critical breeding, staging, and wintering habitat remaining. We need to determine which habitat is marginal. Then we need to begin setting population goals, allowing for drought years and normal years. Only after that has been accomplished need we bring the hunter into the picture. Only then does the setting of regulations make any sense.

Unfortunately, such things take time, and the bureaucracy is geared toward the "quick-fix" approach. Administrations come and go, leaving their mark on conservation. But the marks are generally no more lasting than footprints in shifting sand. Such programs provide little good for the resource, but potentially significant harm.

Since the drought in the 1960s, when waterfowl populations were at their lowest ebb since the 1930s, wildlife managers have depended on hunting regulations to manage waterfowl. They've set no goals, they've offered no long-term plan. The only significant effort dealt with the five-year plan of stabilized hunting regulations, and even that was fraught with controversy and philosophical changes.

Agencies are able to mismanage only so long as their publics let them. Ineffective waterfowl programs are as much the fault of the users as they are the fault of the managers, because the users stand for it. While some users, like the preservationists, are busy filing lawsuits and making noise, others, like the hunters, are content to sit by and let government decide what's best for everybody.

It should not be. But nothing will change until the largest group of the most knowledgeable users — the hunters — decide that they need to take an active role in conserving habitat and a watchdog role in conservation programs. Until that time, hunting, not habitat, will continue to receive a disproportionate share of the responsibility for maintaining waterfowl populations.

About the Authors

C. Edward Addy ("The Atlantic Coastal Area: How It Was") worked as a state game biologist in West Virginia and Massachusetts before joining the U.S. Fish and Wildlife Service in 1945. He was the Atlantic Flyway Representative for the service from 1953 until he retired in 1973. His M.S. degree was from Virginia Polytechnic Institute. (*Editor's note:* Mr. Addy died in September, 1985.)

A. E. Barnard ("Management Successes and Failures for Critical Species") received an M.S. in wildlife management from the University of British Columbia. After spending several years as a waterfowl biologist with the province of British Columbia, he joined Ducks Unlimited Canada as Alberta provincial biologist in 1977, a position he held until September 1983.

C. J. (Cal) Barstow ("Hunting Management") was supervisor of waterfowl management for the Tennessee Game and Fish Commission from 1958 until he joined Ducks Unlimited, Inc., in 1971. He is presently regional director and regional supervisor for Wisconsin and Iowa. He has an M.S. in wildlife ecology from Oklahoma State University.

Frank C. Bellrose ("Up from the South" and "Flight South") has spent forty-seven years researching waterfowl for the Illinois Natural History Survey. He has written almost 100 technical articles and the award-winning book, *Ducks, Geese and Swans of North America*. He graduated from the University of Illinois with a B.S. degree and was honored with an Sc.D. degree by Western Illinois University in 1974. His two particular research interests have been nest biology and populations of the wood duck, and migration and navigation of waterfowl.

George K. Brakhage ("U.S. Waterfowl Habitat Protection Programs") received his B.S. and M.S. degrees from the University of Missouri. He has served as an area wildlife manager and waterfowl research biologist for the Missouri Department of Conservation. In 1967, he became the assistant regional supervisor for management, Division of Management and Enforcement for the U.S. Fish and Wildlife Service in Minneapolis. From 1972 through 1984, he was assistant chief, Office of Migratory Bird Management, Washington, D.C. In 1985, he became regional director for Ducks Unlimited in northern Missouri.

Bernard F. Brown ("Freezeout Swans") has been an instructor in forestry and wildlife at the community college level and worked as a reforestation forester for the Confederated Salish and Kontenai Tribes in Montana before joining Ducks Unlimited in 1983 as regional director for eastern Washington. He has B.S. and M.S. degrees in forestry from the University of Southern Illinois.

Patrick J. Caldwell ("Ducks Unlimited Canada Waterfowl and Wetland Surveys") joined Ducks Unlimited Canada in 1976 as Manitoba provincial biologist. He is presently manager of biological services for the organization in Winnipeg. He holds a B.S. degree from Colorado State, an M.S. from the University of Florida, and a Ph.D. from Kansas State. During his graduate degree programs, he was associated with the Delta Waterfowl Research Station in Manitoba.

Robert H. Chabreck ("Wintering Grounds in Perspective") is professor of wildlife at Louisiana State University. He was formerly employed by the Louisiana Department of Wildlife and Fisheries (1957–1967) at Rockefeller Refuge, the U.S. Fish and Wildlife Service with the Louisiana Cooperative Wildlife Research Unit (1967–1972), and the National Coastal Ecosystem Team (1975–1976). Dr. Chabreck's research interests are waterfowl and wetland ecology, and he has written more than 100 scientific publications on these subjects.

Ron W. Coley ("Of Ducks and Dikes") has been chief engineer of Ducks Unlimited Canada for the past eleven years. He has worked in water resources for twenty years, with experience in construction, design, and management in the energy and environmental areas. He has a B.Sc. in civil engineering from the University of Manitoba and an M.Sc. in Water Resources from the University of Strathclyde in Scotland on an Athlone Fellowship.

F. Graham Cooch ("The Canadian Wildlife Service and Waterfowl Management") is senior research scientist with the CWS in Ottawa, with which he has been associated since 1947. He has held a number of positions, including Arctic ornithologist, staff specialist migratory birds, chief of the toxic chemicals division, and chief of the populations and surveys division. He played a major role in the development of national waterfowl surveys and creation of the Canadian bird banding office, and in conjunction with T. W. Barry, directed the establishment of thirteen migratory bird sanctuaries north of 60°, totaling 106,000 square kilometers. He received a B.A. from Queen's at Kingston, Ontario, and an M.S. and Ph.D. from Cornell University. He is a fellow of several learned societies and has published approximately 125 scientific papers.

Wayne F. Cowan ("Agriculture and Waterfowl") is the agricultural extension biologist with Ducks Unlimited Canada in Winnipeg, promoting conservation-minded farming techniques and agricultural policy developments through on-farm demonstration and education techniques. He is chairman of the land use committee of the Manitoba Environmental Council and adjunct professor to the Natural Resources Institute, University of Manitoba. He received his Ph.D. from the University of North Dakota. He served as river basins and habitat biologist with the Canadian Wildlife Service before coming to Ducks Unlimited in 1976.

L. M. Cowardin ("Problems and Potentials for Prairie Ducks") received his B.A. degree from Harvard University, his M.S. from the University of Massachusetts, and Ph.D. from Cornell University. He has conducted studies of the breeding biology of ducks and ecology of wetland habitats in New York, Minnesota, and North Dakota. His current research includes studies of the breeding biology and population dynamics of the mallard, development of simulation models, and remote sensing and classification of wetland habitats.

Dan C. Denton ("Food Crops for Waterfowl") lives in Atlanta and serves as regional supervisor with Ducks Unlimited for Georgia and Florida. In 1965 and 1967 he completed a B.S. degree and M.S. degree in fish and wildlife studies at Mississippi State University. Following that he served five years as an Air Force pilot, including one year as a bush pilot in Vietnam. After military service he worked a short time as field biologist with the Soil Conservation Service in Hattiesburg, Mississippi. In 1971 he joined Ducks Unlimited as a regional director.

H. F. Duebbert ("Problems and Potentials for Prairie Ducks") has a twenty-five-year career with the U.S. Fish and Wildlife Service, including waterfowl management and research in the prairie pothole region at the Northern Prairie Wildlife Research Center. His research has focused on ecological factors affecting duck nesting success in upland habitats and on islands. During his entire career, he has been keenly interested in the development of sound management strategies to improve waterfowl production for the perpetuation of wildfowling. He holds an M.A. degree from the University of Missouri.

Leslie F. Edgerton ("California Duck Hunting" and "West Coast Wetlands") was with the California Department of Fish and Game from 1942 to 1979 (except for 1943–1946 service in the U.S. Army Air Force), the last eight years as executive secretary. He joined Ducks Unlimited in 1979 and is now flyway MARSH coordinator for the Pacific Flyway. He holds a degree from the Eastern College of Education.

C. B. (Bernie) Forbes ("Canadian Waterfowling Traditions") spent his boyhood on the Saskatchewan prairies and developed an early appreciation for the outdoors. His background in farming and ranching later provided a valuable insight into land-use conflicts affecting Saskatchewan wildlife habitat. He maintained active involvement with the Saskatchewan Wildlife Federation and was appointed director of wildlife in the Saskatchewan Department of Natural Resources in 1967. In 1970 he joined Ducks Unlimited Canada as provincial manager in British Columbia, later returning to Saskatchewan as provincial manager. He is currently the regional manager for Manitoba and Saskatchewan.

Ozro E. (Earl) Frye, Jr. ("Hunting the Atlantic Flyway" and "Flyway Management and Custodial Services") served with the Florida Game

and Freshwater Fish Commission from 1937 to 1977 and as its director from 1965 to 1977. He then joined Ducks Unlimited as Florida regional director. He holds a Ph.D. degree from the University of Florida.

William Fuchs ("In the Old Days") started his career as an Iowa State conservation officer, then worked with the U.S. Fish and Wildlife Service for twenty-two years, becoming supervisor of the central California district before joining Ducks Unlimited as regional director for Wisconsin in 1979. He has extensive experience in waterfowl surveys and banding in Canada and received a Superior Performance Award from the government for his management and law enforcement work.

John D. Giles ("Of Ducks and Dikes") has been manager of public relations for Ducks Unlimited Canada since April 1984. He has had long experience in communications, particularly in the agricultural field. He holds a B.S. degree in agriculture from the University of Manitoba, a B. Journalism from Carleton University Ottawa, and an M.A. in communications from the University of Kentucky.

John R. Grieb ("The Point System") served thirty-two years with the Colorado Division of Wildlife, the last eleven as director. After retirement, he worked as a consultant with the U.S. Fish and Wildlife Service as the U.S. coordinator of the North American Waterfowl Management Plan. His B.S. and M.S. degrees in wildlife management were from Colorado State University. (*Editor's note:* Mr. Grieb died in October, 1986.)

E. W. Gustafson ("Waterfowl Harvest and Conservation in Mexico") holds a B.A. degree from Duke University in economics and business, an M.S. degree in business from Monterrey (Mexico) Institute of Technology, and a Ph.D. from the University of Massachusetts. He serves as international director of the VISA Group, third largest private enterprise group in Mexico, and national vice-president of Ducks Unlimited of Mexico.

Van Campen Heilner ("Canvasbacks from North to South") was a household name to sportsmen of the 1930s and 1940s. He also wrote *Our American Game Birds, Salt Water Fishing, Beneath the Southern Cross* and *Adventures in Angling.*

Edward G. Hennan ("Nesting, Renesting, Hatching, Brooding") is provincial biologist for Ducks Unlimited in British Columbia. Other than a two-year stint with the Canadian Wildlife Service, working on migratory birds in the Alberta Oil Sands, he has served Ducks Unlimited since 1970 as special projects biologist working in the four western provinces and as habitat biologist in British Columbia, prior to assuming his present position in 1983. He received his B.Sc. and M.Sc. from the University of Guelph, Ontario.

Curtis R. Hopkins ("Green-Timber Duck Habitat") was employed five years as a wildlife biologist with the U.S. Forest Service before joining Ducks Unlimited in 1981 as regional director for the northern Mississippi region. He holds B.S. and M.S. degrees in wildlife ecology from Mississippi State University and a Ph.D. in wildlife science from Texas A&M.

Joseph M. Hyland ("Production in the Tri-State and Nebraska" and "A New Look at U.S. Duck Production") was formerly Nebraska state waterfowl biologist prior to joining Ducks Unlimited in 1983 as regional director for western Nebraska. A lifelong waterfowler, he has served on numerous flyway committees and written several technical and popular articles on waterfowl. He has a B.S. degree from the University of Nebraska.

Colleen Hyslop ("The Canadian Wildlife Service and Waterfowl Management") is a biologist with the Canadian Wildlife Service in Ottawa. She joined as a research biologist in 1980 and was in charge of the Canadian bird banding office until 1983. She is currently coordinator of CWS's Latin American program. Ms. Hyslop studied biology at the University of Calgary and earned an M.Sc. degree in 1978, specializing in population biology.

Richard M. Kaminski ("Essential Ingredients of Breeding Habitat" and "More Ducks per Acre Through Habitat Management") has been assistant professor of wildlife in the Department of Wildlife and Fisheries, Mississippi State University, since 1983. Previously, he was a research biologist in the biological services group of Ducks Unlimited Canada. He has conducted and directed waterfowl and wetland research in Michigan, in eastern and western Canada, and in the southeastern United States. He holds a B.S. degree from the University of Wisconsin (Stevens Point) and M.S. and Ph.D. degrees from Michigan State University.

David D. Kennedy ("Breeding Ground Surveys" and "The Winter Inventory") is completing his twenty-fifth year as a waterfowl biologist. Before joining Ducks Unlimited in 1976, he worked for the Indiana Department of Natural Resources and the Illinois Department of Conservation. He has written or co-authored three books and numerous articles both technical and popular. At present he is the field operations supervisor for the southern Mississippi region. He has a B.A. in zoology and an M.S. in wildlife management from the University of Southern Illinois.

Greg Koeln joined Ducks Unlimited, Inc. at the National Headquarters in 1984. He directs DU's new Habitat Inventory and Evaluation Program, which utilizes state-of-the-art computers, satellites, and space-age technologies. Prior to joining Ducks Unlimited, Greg was an assistant professor at the University of Missouri, where he taught courses in computer mapping, remote sensing, and computer techniques. He also worked with various state and federal agencies in developing computer systems to aid in resource management and research. All Greg's degrees are in wildlife management, with his B.S. from Colorado State University, his M.S. from Mississippi State University, and his Ph.D. from Virginia Polytechnic Institute and State University.

Thomas L. Kuck ("Dakota Waterfowling" and "Production in the Tri-State and Nebraska") was employed by South Dakota Game, Fish and Parks from 1967 to 1983, the last sixteen years as migratory bird specialist, prior to joining Ducks Unlimited as regional director for eastern South Dakota. He has written several publications, the most noteworthy being *Waterfowl Identification in the Central Flyway* with over 500,000 copies in circulation. He holds B.S. and M.S. degrees from South Dakota University.

Robert E. Lange ("Waterfowl Disease in the Past and Future") is employed by the Fish and Wildlife Service's wildlife resources program in Washington, D.C. He was field diagnostician for the National Wildlife Health Laboratory in Madison, Wisconsin, from 1980 to 1984. His role was field diagnosis and initiation of management efforts during outbreaks of waterfowl disease in the National Wildlife Refuge System. Dr. Lange was state wildlife veterinarian for the New Mexico Department of Game and Fish from 1974 to 1980 and worked for the Colorado Wild Animal Disease Center at Colorado State University and with the Colorado Division of Wildlife from 1971 to 1974. He has a D.V.M., an M.S. in Pathology, a B.S. in wildlife biology, and a B.S. in veterinary science from Colorado State University.

William G. Leitch ("Major Canadian Production Areas," "Drought-Proofing the Prairies," and "Spring, Fall, and Migration Staging") joined Ducks Unlimited in 1939 and was chief biologist when he retired in 1977. He holds an M.Sc. from the University of Manitoba and authored *Ducks and Men*, the history of the first forty years of Ducks Unlimited Canada.

Wendell J. Lorio ("Duck Hunting, Louisiana Style" and "Gulf Coast Marsh Management") was formerly regional director for Ducks Unlimited, serving the southern portion of Louisiana. He has also held positions as assistant professor, associate professor, and professor of wildlife and fisheries at Mississippi State University. Immediately prior to joining Ducks Unlimited, he was director of the Mississippi State University Research Center at the National Space Technology Laboratories in Bay St. Louis, Mississippi. He holds a B.S. in wildlife management and conservation from Louisiana Polytechnic Institute, an M.S. in fishery biology from Louisiana State University, and a Ph.D. from the University of Georgia.

A. J. (Sandy) Macaulay ("New Agricultural Techniques: The Hope of the Future") is the chief biologist of Ducks Unlimited Canada. Before joining Ducks Unlimited in 1973, he taught biology at Concordia College, Edmonton, Alberta. From March 1983 until September 1984, he was on loan to the Canadian Wildlife Service, acting as Canadian coordinator for the North American Waterfowl Management Plan. He obtained his M.Sc. in zoology from the University of Alberta and a Ph.D. in botany from the University of Manitoba.

D. Stewart Morrison ("A North American Waterfowl Management Plan") is executive vice president of Ducks Unlimited Canada. After brief employment with Canadian Industries Limited and the Manitoba government, he joined Ducks Unlimited in 1969 and assumed his present position in 1970. He was elected the first chairman of Wildlife Habitat Canada and is a member of the advisory board of the Natural Resources Institute at the University of Manitoba. He is a graduate in commerce from St. Francis Xavier University in Nova Scotia. An avid hunter, he is also well known in local skeet and trap circles.

Elmer E. (Sonny) Mowbray ("Rehabilitating Northern Marshes") has worked both north and south ends of the flyways and lots of area in between. He served with the U.S. Fish and Wildlife Service's refuge division and taught wildlife management at the University of Maryland before joining Ducks Unlimited Canada in 1977. He has an M.S. degree from Louisiana Polytechnical University.

John E. Nagel ("Interior Western Wetlands" and "The Law") was with the Utah Division of Wildlife Resources in a variety of positions, including waterfowl management area superintendent, waterfowl biologist, waterfowl supervisor, law enforcement chief, and operations director, before joining Ducks Unlimited in 1979 as regional director in southern and eastern Oregon. He has a B.S. from Utah State University and an M.S. from the University of Utah and is a graduate of the FBI National Academy.

Jeffrey W. Nelson ("Interspersed Breeding Marshes: Generators of High-Protein Food") is a waterfowl research biologist for Ducks Unlimited Canada stationed in Winnipeg, Manitoba. In addition to conducting research programs for Ducks Unlimited, he is an active member of the scientific team for the marsh ecology research program at the Delta Waterfowl and Wetlands Research Station. He is a graduate of the University of Minnesota and holds an M.S. from Utah State University.

Terrence G. Neraasen ("Droughts, Floods, Predation") is Manitoba provincial manager for Ducks Unlimited Canada. Prior to joining DU, initially as provincial biologist, he taught zoology at Brandon University after completing M.Sc. and Ph.D. degrees at the University of Alberta and the University of Manitoba respectively. Work in the Arctic and at the Delta Waterfowl Research Station provided a broad spectrum of experience related to waterfowl and wetland ecology.

John M. Parrish ("West Coast Wetlands") served briefly with the U.S. Fish and Wildlife Service and Oregon State Game Commission, then spent thirty-two years with the California Fish and Game Department as a waterfowl area manager and administrator before taking a position with Ducks Unlimited in 1982. He is currently regional habitat supervisor for DU's West Coast region. After serving as a Marine in the South Pacific in World War II, he matriculated with a wildlife degree from Washington State University.

Carl A. Radimer ("Crop Depredation: The Problem and the Politics") is a Winnipeg-based journalist and public relations consultant specializing in agricultural communications. He served as managing editor of Canada's largest farm magazine, *Country Guide*, has contributed to a number of North American farm magazines, and was public relations manager of Ducks Unlimited Canada from 1979 to 1983. Carl is a member of the Canadian Public Relations Society, the Canadian Farm Writers' Federation, and the American Association of Agricultural Editors. He is a graduate of the Southern Alberta Institute of Technology.

Mitchell J. Rogers ("Vanishing Hardwoods") worked with the Arkansas Game and Fish Commission for thirteen years, the last years as chief of game management, prior to joining Ducks Unlimited in 1981 as regional director for southern Missouri and northern Arkansas. He holds a B.S. degree in wildlife management/

zoology from Arkansas Polytechnic University.

A. B. Sargeant ("Problems and Potentials for Prairie Ducks") is a research biologist at the U.S. Fish and Wildlife Service Northern Prairie Wildlife Research Center, where for the past eighteen years he has studied mammalian predator ecology and behavior as it relates to predation on prairie nesting ducks. His current research includes evaluating effects of different predator communities on waterfowl nesting success, developing guidelines for identifying duck nest predators, and assessing coyote–red fox impacts on nesting ducks. Alan received a B.S. at the University of Minnesota.

J. R. (Bob) Singleton ("Down Mexico Way: Waterfowl Habitat and Populations") spent many years with the Texas Parks and Wildlife Department and its predecessors as a waterfowl biologist and in supervisory and administrative positions including several years as executive director. He holds B.S. and M.S. degrees in wildlife management from Texas A&M University. He joined Ducks Unlimited, Inc., in 1971 and retired in 1985.

R. Thomas Sterling ("Fall Migration: Moving Out") has been employed in waterfowl management with Ducks Unlimited Canada since 1949, working mainly in Saskatchewan and British Columbia with some surveys in the northern territories. He is a graduate in biology from the University of British Columbia with a M.Sc. from the University of Saskatchewan.

Hugh L. Thomas ("Hunting the Black Brant") worked for the California Department of Fish and Game for twenty-six years prior to joining Ducks Unlimited in 1982 as regional director for central California. He is currently a regional supervisor in central and southern California. He lived on Morro Bay for fourteen years and became very familiar with the black brant, their habits and related problems, both biological and consumptive. He attended UCLA, with a major in ichthyology.

Daniel E. Timm ("Alaska") spent his younger years in eastern Iowa and received a degree in wildlife ecology from Iowa State University in 1966. He was a waterfowl biologist for the Nebraska Game and Parks Commission until

1971, when he moved to Alaska. From 1971 to 1982, he was in charge of the waterfowl program for the Alaska Department of Fish and Game, and since 1982 has been responsible for game management programs in southcentral Alaska. Although he has been mostly out of waterfowl management since 1982, his "true love" is ducks and geese, whether studying them with binoculars, shotgun, or pencil.

Sam Venable ("Wetland Habitat Management by the Private Sector: The Story of Little Pecan") is staff writer for Little Pecan Wildlife Management Area, Grand Chenier, Louisiana.

David E. Wesley ("Duckonomics") currently serves as director of MARSH operations for Ducks Unlimited, Inc. Prior to this appointment he served as director of field operations, regional director for Louisiana (1977–1981) and regional director for the south Atlantic region (1971–1972). From 1972 to 1977, he held the rank of associate professor in the department of wildlife and fisheries at Mississippi State University. He is a graduate of Mississippi State University (B.A. 1962; M.S. 1967) and Colorado State University (Ph.D. 1971).

Dale E. Whitesell ("The Future") received his B.S. in agriculture in 1950 and his M.S. in wildlife management in 1951 from Ohio State University. After serving as a wildlife district game

management supervisor for the Ohio Division of Wildlife, he was appointed chief of that division in 1963. He joined Ducks Unlimited, Inc. as executive vice president in 1965. Under his leadership, the organization's annual income increased from $867,000 in 1965 to over $50,000,000 in 1986.

Gary B. Will ("Hunting the Atlantic Flyway") was employed by the New York State Department of Environmental Conservation as a wildlife biologist for twelve years prior to joining Ducks Unlimited in 1982 as regional director for northeastern New York. His wildlife research and management expertise involved big game, fur-bearers, endangered species, wetland acquisition, and conservation education. He holds a B.S. degree from the College of Forestry at Syracuse.

Richard A. Wishart ("Up from the South," "The Pairing Process and Social Behavior of Waterfowl in Spring" and "Habitat Conditions and Waterfowl Overflights") is Manitoba provincial biologist for Ducks Unlimited Canada, stationed in Winnipeg. He has written a number of research papers on waterfowl, woodcock, and other shorebirds and received part of his training through the Delta Waterfowl Research Station. He has a B.S. and M.S. degree from McGill University and obtained his Ph.D. from the University of Manitoba.

Index